ISAIAH

TRANSLATED AND EXPLAINED

BY

JOSEPH ADDISON ALEXANDER.

AN ABRIDGMENT OF THE AUTHOR'S CRITICAL COMMENTARY ON ISAIAH.

VOLUME I.

NEW YORK:
WILEY & HALSTED,
351 BROADWAY,
1856.

PREFACE.

THIS abridgment of the author's larger work upon Isaiah* has been prepared in deference rather to the wishes of others than to his own judgment. He has always desired and hitherto intended to defer reprinting it in any form, until he should have had the opportunity of thoroughly reviewing the whole subject, with the valuable aid to be derived from later expositions, criticisms, and discussions. But as this laborious process, which might possibly result in the re-writing of the whole work, is precluded for the present and perhaps forever by engrossing occupations of another kind, he no longer feels himself at liberty to disregard the double call which has long been made upon him, for a new impression of the commentary, and for such a reduction of its size as may render it accessible and useful to a larger class of readers. As these demands, although distinct in themselves, have been made to coincide by the unexpected sale of the first edition which is now exhausted, he is willing to believe that both may, to some extent, be satis-

* The Earlier Prophecies of Isaiah. New York, 1846. 8vo. The Later Prophecies of Isaiah. New York, 1847. 8vo.

fied by the abridgment here presented to the public. He is only solicitous that it should not be misconceived as an intended or professed advance upon his former publication, but indulgently received as an attempt to place it within the reach of those who, for any reason, have been hitherto unable to make use of it. To this course he has been the more easily reconciled, because his views have undergone no material change, and because he has the satisfaction of knowing that his book has proved acceptable, at least as a version and a verbal explanation, even to some who do not fully concur in his exegetical conclusions. If the work in its new form should meet with even a small share of the favour and success which have attended the kindred publication on the Psalms,* the authors expectations will be far exceeded.

To those who are familiar with the larger work, a slight comparison will show that it has not been rewritten but merely contracted, and that for the most part by simple omission. The rule of abridgment which has been adopted, although not perhaps applied with perfect uniformity, has been to retain only what was necessary to convey the author's view of the essential meaning, and to exclude what belonged merely to the history of the interpretation or the discussion of conflicting opinions. Of the meagerness and awkwardness too frequently resulting from this process, none can be more fully aware than the author and abridger; but the hope is entertained that by a large proportion even of those readers who become

* The Psalms Translated and Explained by J. A. Alexander. New York, 1850. 3 vols. 12mo.

acquainted with the work for the first time under its present disadvantages of form, these literary blemishes will be reckoned but a small price to be paid for wider circulation and a further contribution, however humble in degree and kind, to the just appreciation and correct interpretation of a difficult but eminently interesting and important part of Scripture.

PRINCETON, New Jersey, April 15, 1851.

Theological Seminary,

INTRODUCTION.

The gift of prophecy included that of foresight and prediction, but it included more. The prophet was inspired to reveal the will of God, to act as an organ of communication between God and man. The subject of the revelations thus conveyed was not and could not be restricted to the future. It embraced the past and present, and extended to those absolute and universal truths which have no relation to time. This is what we should naturally expect in a divine revelation, and it is what we actually find it to contain. That the prophets of the old dispensation were not mere foretellers of things future, is apparent from their history as well as from their writings. It has been well said, that Daniel proved himself a prophet by telling Nebuchadnezzar what he had dreamed, as much as by interpreting the dream itself; that it was only by prophetic inspiration that Elijah knew what Gehazi had been doing; and that the woman of Samaria very properly called Christ a prophet, because he told her all things that ever she did. In all these cases, and in multitudes of others, the essential idea is that of inspiration, its frequent reference to things still future being accidental, that is to say, not included in the uniform and necessary import of the terms.

The restriction of these terms in modern parlance to the prediction of events still future has arisen from the fact that a large proportion of the revelations made in Scripture, and precisely those which are the most surprising and impressive, are of this description. The frequency of such revelations, and the prominence given to them, not in this modern usage merely, but in the word of God itself, admit of easy explanation. It is partly owing to the fact that revelations of the future would be naturally sought with more avidity, and treated with more deference, than any other by mankind in general. It is further owing to the fact that of all the kinds of revelation, this is the one which affords the most direct and convincing proof of the prophet's inspiration. The knowledge of the present or the past or of general truths might be imparted by special inspiration, but it might also be acquired in other ways; and this possibility of course makes the evidence of inspiration thus afforded more complete and irresistible than any other. Hence the function of foretelling what was future, although but a part of the prophetic office, was peculiarly conspicuous and prominent in public view, and apt to be more intimately associated with the office itself in the memory of man. But there is still another reason, more important than either of these, afforded by the fact, that the old dispensation, with all its peculiar institutions, was prospective in its character, a preparation for better things to come. It is not surprising, therefore, that a part of this economy so marked and prominent, should have exhibited a special leaning towards futurity.

This naturally leads us from the theoretical idea of a prophet as a person speaking by divine authority and inspiration, to the practical consideration of the end or purpose aimed at in the whole prophetic institution. This was not merely the relief of private doubts, much less the gratification of private curiosity. The gift of prophecy was closely connected with the general design of the old economy. The foundation of the system was the Law, as recorded in the five books of Moses. In that, as an epitome, the rest of the Old Testament is contained, at least as to its seminal principles. The single book of Deuteronomy exhibits specimens of almost every style employed by the sacred writers elsewhere. Still more remarkably is this true of the whole Pentateuch, in reference not merely to its manner but its matter, as comprising virtually all that is developed and applied in the revelations of the later books. To make this development and application was the business of the prophets. The necessity for such an institution was no after-thought. The law itself provides for it. The promise of a prophet like unto Moses, in the eighteenth chapter of Deuteronomy, comprehends the promise of a constant succession of inspired men, so far as this should be required by the circumstances of the people, which succession was to terminate in Christ.

This promise was abundantly fulfilled. In every emergency requiring such an interposition, we find prophets present and active, and in some important periods of the history of Israel they existed in great numbers. These, though not all inspired writers, were all inspired men, raised up and directed by a special divine influence, to signify and sometimes to execute the will of God, in the administration of the theocracy. Joshua is expressly represented as enjoying such an influence, and is reckoned in the Jewish tradition as a prophet. The Judges who succeeded him were all raised up in special emergencies, and were directed and controlled by a special divine influence or inspiration. Samuel was one of the most eminent prophets. After the institution of the monarchy we read constantly of prophets distinct from the civil rulers. After the schism between Judah and Ephraim, there continued to be prophets, even in the kingdom of the ten tribes. They were peculiarly necessary there indeed, because the people of that kingdom were cut off from the sanctuary and its services, as bonds of union with Jehovah. The prophetic ministry continued through the Babylonish exile, and ceased some years after the restoration, in the person of Malachi, whom the Jews unanimously represent as the last of their prophets.

With respect to the nature of the inspiration under which these prophets spoke and acted, there can be no doubt that the Bible itself represents it as plenary, or fully adequate to the attainment of its end. (2 Tim. 3 : 16. 2 Pet. 1 : 21.) Where this end was external action, it was sufficiently secured by the gift of courage, strength, or practical wisdom. Where the instruction of God's people was the object, whether in reference to the past, the present, or the future; whether in word, in writing, or in both; whether for temporary ends, or with a view to perpetual preservation; the prophets are clearly represented as infallible, that is, incapable of erring or deceiving, with respect to the matter of their revelation. How far this object was secured by direct suggestion, by negative control, or by an elevating influence upon the native powers, is a question of no practical importance to those who hold the essential doctrine that the inspiration was in all cases such as to render those who were inspired infallible. Between this supposition and the opposite extreme, which denies inspiration altogether, or resolves it into mere excitement of the imagination and the sensibilities, like the afflatus of a poet or an orator, there seems to be no definite and safe position. Either the prophets were not inspired at all in any proper sense, or they were so inspired as to be infallible.

As to the mode in which the required impression was made, it seems both vain and needless to attempt any definite description of it. The ultimate effect would be the same in any case, if not upon the prophet, upon those who heard or read his prophecies. So far as anything can be inferred from incidental or explicit statements of the Scripture, the most usual method of communication would appear to have been that of immediate vision, that is, the presentation of the thing to be revealed as if it were an object of sight. Thus Micaiah *saw* Israel scattered on the hills like sheep without a shepherd (1 Kings 22 : 17), and Isaiah *saw* Jehovah sitting on a lofty throne (Isai. 6 : 1). That this was the most usual mode of presentation, is probable not only from occasional expressions such as those just quoted, but from the fact, that a very large proportion of the prophetic revelations are precisely such as might be painted and subjected to the sense of sight. The same conclusion is confirmed by the use of the words *seer* and *vision* as essentially equivalent to *prophet* and *prophecy*. There is no need, however, of supposing that this method of communication, even if it were the common one, was used invariably. Some things in the prophecies require us to suppose that they were made known to the prophet just as he made them known to others, to wit, by the simple suggestion of appropriate words. But this whole question is rather one of curiosity than use.

It has been disputed whether the prophets of the old dispensation had any training for their work, at all analogous to what we call a professional education. Some have supposed the *sons of the prophets*, frequently mentioned in the books of Kings, to have been young men in a course of preparation for the prophetic ministry. To this it has been objected, that their ministry depended on the gift of inspiration, for which no human training could compensate or prepare them. But although they could not act as prophets without inspiration, they might be prepared for those parts of the work which depended upon culture, such as a correct mode of expression, just as men may now be trained by education for the work of the ministry, although convinced that its success depends entirely on the divine blessing. It is not to be forgotten that the inspiration under which the prophets acted left them in full possession of their faculties, native and acquired, and with all their peculiarities of thought and feeling unimpaired. The whole subject of prophetic education is, however, one of surmise and conjecture, rather than of definite knowledge or of practical utility.

To the government the prophets do not seem to have sustained any definite or fixed relation, as component parts of a political system. The extent and manner of their influence, in this respect, depended on the character of the rulers, the state of affairs, and the nature of the messages which they were commissioned to deliver. As a class, the prophets influenced the government, not by official formal action, but as special messengers from God, by whom he was represented in particular emergencies, and whose authority could neither be disputed nor resisted by any magistrate without abjuring the fundamental principles of the theocracy. Even the apostate kings of Israel acknowledged the divine legation of the prophets of Jehovah.

With respect to the promulgation and preservation of the prophecies, there have been various opinions and many fanciful conjectures. Some suppose the prophets to have been a kind of demagogues or popular orators, whose speeches, if not previously prepared, were afterwards recorded by themselves or others. Another supposition is that the prophets were inspired writers, and that their prophecies were published only as written compositions. A distinction as to this point has by some been drawn between the earlier and the later prophets. From the death of Moses to the accession of Uzziah, a period of nearly seven hundred years, a large proportion of the prophets are supposed to have performed their functions orally and without leaving anything on record; whereas after that period they were led to act not only for the present but the future. We have no cause to doubt, however, that we now have in possession all that was "written aforetime for our learning." And in the case of any prophecy, the question whether it was orally delivered before it was written is comparatively unimportant, as our only concern with it is in its written form. The idea that the prophecies now extant are mere summaries of long discourses is ingenious and plausible in certain cases, but admits of no historical or certain demonstration.

A question of more moment is that with respect to the way

in which the writings were preserved, whether by private circulation as detached compositions, or by solemn enrolment and deposit in the sanctuary. The modern critics who dispute the integrity and genuineness of many passages lean to the former supposition ; but the latter is unquestionably favoured by the whole drift of Scripture and the current of ancient usage, sacred and profane, with respect to writings which were looked upon as sacred. It may well be doubted whether among the ancient Hebrews there was any extensive circulation of books at all, and it seems to me to be as hard to disprove as to prove the position, that the only literature of the nation was THE BOOK or SCRIPTURE (הַסֵּפֶר), which from the time of Moses was kept open, and in which the writings of the prophets may have been recorded as they were produced. At all events, it seems unreasonable and at variance with the tenor of Scripture to suppose, that writings held to be inspired were left to circulate at random and to share the fate of other compositions, without any effort to attest their genuineness or to secure their preservation.

The uniform tradition of the Jews is, that the sacred books were finally collected and arranged by Ezra under the guidance of divine inspiration, and that among them a prominent place, and for the most part the first place, has been always held, by a book bearing the name of Isaiah.

The name Isaiah is a compound word denoting the *Salvation of Jehovah*, to which some imagine that the Prophet himself alludes in ch. 8 : 18. The abbreviated form (יְשַׁעְיָה) is never applied in Scripture to the Prophet, though the rabbins employ it in titles and inscriptions. Both forms of the name are applied in the Old Testament to other persons, in all which cases the English Version employs a different orthography, viz. *Jeshaiah* or *Jesaiah*. In the New Testament our Version writes the name *Esaias*, after the example of the Vulgate, varying slightly from the Greek *Ἡσαΐας*, used both in the Septuagint and the New Testament. To the name of the Prophet we find several times added that of his father Amoz. Of his domestic circumstances we know merely, that his wife and two of his sons are mentioned by himself (ch. 7 : 3; 8 : 3, 4) to which some add a third, as we shall see below.

The only historical account of this Prophet is contained in the book which bears his name, and in the parallel passages of Second Kings, which exhibit unequivocal signs of being from the hand of the same writer. The first sentence of Isaiah's own book, assigns as the period of his ministry the four successive reigns of Uzziah, Jotham, Ahaz, and Hezekiah, one of the most eventful periods in the history of Judah. The two first reigns here mentioned were exceedingly prosperous, although a change for the worse appears to have commenced before the death of Jotham, and continued through the reign of Ahaz, bringing the state to the very verge of ruin, from which it was not restored to a prosperous condition until long after the accession of Hezekiah. During this period the kingdom of the ten tribes, which had flourished greatly under Jeroboam II, for many years contemporary with Uzziah, passed through the hands of a succession of usurpers, and was at length overthrown by the Assyrians, in the sixth year of Hezekiah's reign over Judah.

Among the neighbouring powers, with whom Israel was more or less engaged in conflict during these four reigns, the most important were Damascene Syria, Moab, Edom, and the Philistines, who although resident within the allotted bounds of Judah, still endeavoured to maintain their position as an independent and a hostile nation. But the foreign powers which chiefly influenced the condition of south-western Asia during this period, were the two great empires of Assyria in the east, and Egypt in the south-west. By a rapid succession of important conquests, the former had suddenly acquired a magnitude and strength which it had not possessed for ages, if at all.

Egypt had been subdued, at least in part, by Ethiopia; but this very event, by combining the forces of two great nations, had given unexampled strength to the Ethiopian dynasty in Upper Egypt. The mutual jealousy and emulation between this state and Assyria, naturally tended to make Palestine, which lay between them, a theatre of war, at least at intervals, for many years. It also led the kings of Israel and Judah to take part in the contentions of these two great powers, and to secure themselves by uniting, sometimes with Egypt against Assyria, sometimes with Assyria against Egypt. It was this inconstant policy that hastened the destruction of the kingdom of the ten tribes, and exposed that of Judah to imminent peril. Against this policy the prophets, and especially Isaiah, were commissioned to remonstrate, no only as unworthy in itself, but as implying a distrust of God's protection, and indifference to the fundamental law of the theocracy. The Babylonian monarchy began to gather strength before the end of this period, but was less conspicuous, because not yet permanently independent of Assyria.

The two most remarkable conjunctures in the history of Judah during Isaiah's ministry are the invasion of the combined force of Syria and Israel in the reign of Ahaz, followed by the destruction of the kingdom of the ten tribes, and the Assyrian invasion in the fourteenth year of Hezekiah, ending in the miraculous destruction of Sennacherib's army and his own ignominious flight. The historical interest of this important period is further heightened by the fact, that two of the most noted eras in chronology fall within it, to wit, the era of Nabonassar, and that computed from the building of Rome.

The length of Isaiah's public ministry is doubtful. The aggregate duration of the four reigns mentioned in the title is above one hunded and twelve years; but it is not said that he prophesied throughout the whole reign either of Uzziah or Hezekiah. Some, it is true, have inferred that his ministry was co-extensive with the whole reign of Uzziah, because he is said to have written the history of that prince (2 Chron. 26 : 22), which he surely might have done without being strictly his contemporary, just as he may have written that of Hezekiah to a certain date (2 Chron. 32 : 32), and yet have died before him. Neither of these incidental statements can be understood as throwing any light upon the question of chronology. Most writers, both among the Jews and Christians, understood the first verse of the sixth chapter as determining the year of king Uzziah's death to be the first of Isaiah's public ministry. Some of the Jewish writers, who adopt this supposition, at the same time understand Uzziah's death to mean his civil death, occasioned by the leprosy with which he was smitten in the twenty-fifth year of his reign, for his sacrilegious invasion of the house of God, so that he dwelt in a separate house until his death. There seems to be no sufficient ground for this explanation of the language, or for the alleged coincidence of the event with the twenty-fifth year of Uzziah's reign, any more than for the notion of the oriental Christians, that Uzziah was deprived of the prophetic office for his sin in not withstanding Uzziah, and after twenty-eight years of silence was restored in the year of that king's death, a fanciful interpretation of the facts recorded in chap. vi. The modern writers are agreed in understanding the expression literally, and in connecting the last year of Uzziah's life with the first year of Isaiah's ministry. It is by no means certain, as we shall see below, that the sixth chapter is descriptive of Isaiah's inauguration into office, still less that it was written before any of the others. But it cannot be denied that the chronological hypothesis just stated is strongly recommended by the fact of its removing all objections to the truth of the inscription (chap. 1 : 1) founded on the extreme longevity which it would otherwise ascribe to the prophet, by enabling us at once to deduct half a century. If we reckon from the last year of Uzziah to the fourteenth of Hezekiah, the last in which we find any certain historical traces of Isaiah, we obtain as the minimum of his prophetic ministry a period of forty-seven years, and this, supposing that he entered on it even at the age of thirty, would leave him at his death less than eighty years old. And even if it be assumed that he survived Hezekiah, and continued some years under his successor, the length of his life will after all be far less than that of Jehoiada, the high-priest, who died in the reign of Joash at the age of 130 years. (2 Chron. 24 : 15.)

The Jews have a positive tradition that he did die in the reign of Manasseh, and as victim of the bloody persecutions by which that king is said to have filled Jerusalem with innocent blood from one end to the other. (2 Kings 21 : 16.) This tradition is received as true by several of the Fathers, who suppose it to be clearly alluded to in Heb. 11 : 37.

From the references, which have been already quoted, to the historical writings of Isaiah, some have inferred that he was an official historiographer, in which capacity the older prophets seem to have acted, as appears from the canonical insertion of such books as those of Joshua, Judges, Samuel, and Kings, among the Prophets. We have no reason to suppose, however, that Isaiah held any secular office of the kind, distinct from his prophetic ministry. Nor is it clear in what sense the citation of Isaiah by the Chronicles as an historical authority should be understood. The reference may be simply to the historical portions of his book, or to the corresponding passages of Second Kings, of which, in strict discharge of his official functions, he may well have been the author. That the books referred to were more copious histories or annals, of which only summaries or fragments are now extant, is a supposition which, however credible or even plausible it may be in itself, is not susceptible of demonstration.

This book not only forms a part of the Old Testament Canon as far as we can trace it back, but has held its place there without any change of form, size, or contents, of which the least external evidence can be adduced. The allusions to this Prophet, and the imitations of him, in the later books of the Old Testament, are not confined to any one part of the book or any single class of passages. The apocryphal writers who make mention of it, use no expressions which imply that it was not already long complete in its present form and size. The same thing seems to be implied in the numerous citations of this book in the New Testament. Without going here into minute details, a correct idea of the general fact may be conveyed by simply stating, that of the sixty-six chapters of Isaiah, as divided in our modern Bibles, forty-seven are commonly supposed to be directly quoted or distinctly alluded to, and some of them repeatedly. The same thing may be illustrated clearly on a smaller scale by stating, that in the twenty-one cases where Isaiah is expressly named in the New Testament, the quotations are drawn from the first, sixth, eighth, tenth, eleventh, twenty-ninth, forty-second, sixty-first, and sixty-fifth chapters of the book before us. These facts, together with the absence of all countervailing evidence, show clearly that the *Book of the Prophet Isaiah* (Luke 4 : 17) known and quoted by our Lord and his apostles was, as a whole, identical with that which we have under the same name. We find accordingly a long unbroken series of interpreters, Jewish and Christian, through a course of ages, not only acquiescing in this general statement, but regarding all the passages and parts, of which the book consists, as clearly and unquestionably genuine.

Isaiah himself, even leaving out of view the large part of his book which a capricious criticism has called in question, may be said to express everywhere his own belief that he was writing under an extraordinary influence, not merely human but divine. This is at least the *prima facie* view which any unsophisticated reader would derive from a simple perusal of his undisputed writings. However mistaken he might think the prophet, in asserting or assuming his own inspiration, such a reader could scarcely hesitate to grant that he believed it and expected it to be believed by others. In one of the oldest and best of the Jewish Apocrypha (Sirach 24 : 25), Isaiah is called the great and faithful prophet who foresaw what was to happen till the end of time. Josephus and Philo incidentally bear witness to his universal recognition by their countrymen as one inspired of God.

We have seen already that our Lord and his Apostles cite the whole book of Isaiah with more frequency than any other part of the Old Testament. It now becomes a question of historical interest at least, in what capacity and character Isaiah is thus quoted, and with what authority he seems to be invested in the New Testament. The simple fact that he is there so often quoted, when connected with another undisputed fact, to wit, that his writings, even at that early date, held a conspicuous place among the *Sacred Scriptures* (ἱερὰ γράμματα, γραφαὶ ἅγιαι) of the Jews, would of itself create a strong presumption that our Lord and his apostles recognized his inspiration and divine authority. We are not left, however, to infer this incidentally; for it is proved directly by the frequent combination of the title Prophet with the name Isaiah (Matt. 3 : 3; 4 : 14; 8 : 17; 12 : 17. Luke 3 : 4; 4 : 17. John 1 : 23. Acts 8 : 28–30; 28 : 25); by the repeated statement that he prophesied or spoke by inspiration (Mark 7 : 6. Rom. 9 : 29); by the express declaration that some of his predictions were fulfilled in the history of Christ and his contemporaries (Matt. 3 : 3; 4 : 14; 8 : 17. Acts 28 : 25); and by the still more remarkable statement that Isaiah saw Christ and spoke of his glory (John 12 : 41). These expressions place it beyond all possibility of doubt that the New Testament describes Isaiah as a Prophet in the strictest and the highest sense inspired of God.

With respect to the prophetic parts of Scripture, and to the writings of Isaiah in particular, a few exegetical maxims may be stated. These, for the most part, will be negative in form, as being intended to preclude certain fallacies and practical errors, which have greatly hindered the correct interpretation of the book before us. The generic formulas here used will be abundantly exemplified hereafter by specific instances arising in the course of the interpretation.

1. All prophecies are not predictions, i. e. all the writings of the Prophets, and of this one in particular, are not to be regarded as descriptive of future events. The contrary error, which has arisen chiefly from the modern and restricted usage of the word prophet and its cognate terms, has generated some of the most crude extravagancies of prophetic exegesis. It has been shown already, by an historical and philological induction, that the scriptural idea of prophecy is far more extensive, that the prophets were inspired to reveal the truth and will of God, in reference to the past and present, no less than the future. In Isaiah, for example, we find many statements of a general nature, and particularly exhibitions of the general principles which govern the divine administration, especially in reference to the chosen people and their enemies or persecutors.

2. All predictions, or prophecies in the restricted sense, are not specific and exclusive, i. e. limited to one occasion or emergency, but many are descriptive of a sequence of events which has been often realized. The vagueness and indefiniteness which might seem to attach to such predictions, and by making their fulfilment more uncertain to detract from their impressiveness and value, are precluded by the fact that, while the whole prediction frequently admits of this extensive application, it includes allusions to particular events, which can hardly be mistaken. Thus in some parts of Isaiah, there are prophetic pictures of the sieges of Jerusalem, which cannot be exclusively applied to any one event of that kind, but the terms and images of which are borrowed partly from one and partly

from another through a course of ages. This kind of prophecy, so far from being vague and unimpressive, is the clearest proof of real inspiration, because more than any other beyond the reach of ordinary human foresight. Thus the threatening against Babylon, contained in the thirteenth and fourteenth chapters of Isaiah, if explained as a specific and exclusive prophecy of the Medo-Persian conquest, seems to represent the downfall of the city as more sudden and complete than it appears in history, and on the other hand affords a pretext, though a very insufficient one, for the assertion that it may have been composed so near the time of the events foretold as to bring them within the reach of uninspired but sagacious foresight. No such hypothesis, however, will account for the extraordinary truth of the prediction when regarded as a panorama of the fall of Babylon, and not in its first inception merely, but through all its stages till its consummation.

3. All the predictions of Isaiah, whether general or specific, are not to be literally understood. The ground of this position is the fact, universally admitted, that the prophecies abound in metaphorical expressions. To assert that this figurative character is limited to words and clauses, or at most to single sentences, is wholly arbitrary, and at variance with the acknowledged use of parables, both in the Old and New Testament, in which important doctrines and events are presented under a tropical costume, throughout a passage sometimes of considerable length. These facts are sufficient to sustain the negative position, that the prophecies are not invariably clothed in literal expressions, or in other words are not to be always literally understood.

4. The prophecies of this book are not to be always understood in a figurative or spiritual sense. The contrary assumption has engendered a vast motley multitude of mystical and anagogical interpretations, sometimes superadded to the obvious sense, and sometimes substituted for it, but in either case

obscuring the true import and defeating the design of the prediction. The same application of the laws of common sense and of general analogy, which shows that some predictions must be metaphorical, shows that others must be literal. To assert, without express authority, that prophecy must always and exclusively be one or the other, is as foolish as it would be to assert the same thing of the whole conversation of an individual throughout his lifetime, or of human speech in general. No valid reason can be given for applying this exclusive canon of interpretation to the prophecies, which would not justify its application to the Iliad, the Æneid, the Divina Commedia, or the Paradise Lost, an application fruitful only in absurdities. Isaiah's prophecies are therefore not to be expounded on the general principle, that either a literal or a figurative sense must be assumed wherever it is possible. We have already seen the fallacies resulting from the assumption, that whatever is possible is probable or certain. To set aside the obvious and strict sense, wherever it may be done without absurdity, is forbidden by the very nature of the difference between literal and figurative language. That which is regular and normal must at times assert its rights or it becomes anomalous. On the other hand, to claim precedence for the strict and proper sense in every case, is inconsistent with the fact that symbols, emblems, images, and tropes, are characteristic of prophetic language. In a word, the question between literal and tropical interpretation is not to be determined by the application of invariable formulas. The same remark may be applied to the vexed question with respect to types and double senses. The old extreme of constantly assuming these wherever it is possible, and the later extreme of denying their existence, may be both considered as exploded errors.

The question, under which of these descriptions any prophecy must be arranged, i. e. the question whether it is strictly a prediction, and if so, whether it is general or particular, literal or figurative, can only be determined by a thorough independent scrutiny of each case by itself, in reference to form and substance, text and context, without regard to arbitrary and exclusive theories, but with a due regard to the analogy of Scripture in general, and of other prophecies in particular, especially of such as belong to the same writer, or at least to the same period, and apparently relate to the same subject. This is far from being so attractive or so easy as the sweeping application of a comprehensive canon to all cases, like and unlike; but it seems to be the only process likely to afford a satisfactory result, and one main purpose of the following exposition is to prove its efficacy by a laborious and fair experiment.

In executing this design, it is essential that regard should be paid to the exterior form as well as to the substance of a passage, that rhetorical embellishments should be distinguished from didactic propositions, that prosaic and poetical peculiarities should be distinctly and correctly estimated at their real value. This discriminating process necessarily involves a scrupulous avoidance of two opposite extremes, which have, at different periods, and in some cases simultaneously, done much to pervert and hinder the interpretation of the book before us. The first extreme, particularly prevalent in earlier times, is that of understanding the most highly wrought descriptions, the most vivid imagery, the boldest personifications, as mere prose. This is especially exemplified in the irrational and tasteless manner of expounding apologues and parables by many of the older writers, who insist on giving a specific sense to circumstances which are significant only as parts of one harmonious whole. The other extreme, is that of turning elevated prose diversified by bursts of poetry, into a regular poem or series of poems, technically so considered, and subjecting them as such to all the tests and rules of classical poetry, and even to the canons of its versification. The golden mean between these hurtful and irrational extremes appears to lie in the assiduous observance of the true poetical ingredients of Isaiah's style, both in themselves and in their various combinations, with a rigid abstinence from all scholastic and pedantic theories of Hebrew poetry, and all peculiar forms and methods which have sprung from them or tend to their promotion.

No attempt has here been made to give a new translation of the book, complete in itself, and suited for continuous perusal. The translation is part and parcel of the commentary, closely incorporated with it, and in some degree inseparable from it. After the study of a passage with the aid here furnished, it may no doubt be again read with advantage in this version, for the sake of which it has been not only printed in a different type, but generally placed at the beginning of the paragraph. This explanation seems to be required, as the whole form and manner of the version have been modified by this design. If meant for separate continuous perusal, it must of course have been so constructed as to be easily intelligible by itself; whereas a version introduced as a text or basis of immediate exposition, admitted of a closer approximation to the idiomatic form of the original, with all its occasional obscurity and harshness, than would probably have been endured by readers of refined taste in an independent version.

The arrangement of the Prophecies is assumed to be chronological. The apparent exceptions will be pointed out as we proceed. The usual division into chapters (although no older than the thirteenth century) is here retained, as universally familiar and in general convenient, but in no case suffered to determine any question of interpretation.

CHAPTER I.

The design of this chapter is to show the connection between the sins and sufferings of God's people, and the necessity of further judgments, as means of purification and deliverance.

The popular corruption is first exhibited as the effect of alienation from God, and as the cause of national calamities, vs. 2–9. It is then exhibited as coexisting with punctilious exactness in religious duties, and as rendering them worthless, vs. 10–20. It is finally exhibited in twofold contrast, first with a former state of things, and then with one still future, to be brought about by the destruction of the wicked, and especially of wicked rulers, vs. 21–31.

The first part of the chapter describes the sin and then the suffering of the people. The former is characterized as filial ingratitude, stupid inconsideration, habitual transgression, contempt of God, and alienation from him, vs. 2–4. The suffering is first represented by the figure of disease and wounds, and then in literal terms as the effect of an invasion, by which the nation was left desolate, and only saved by God's regard for his elect from the total destruction of Sodom and Gomorrah, vs. 5–9.

The second part is connected with the first by the double allusion to Sodom and Gomorrah, with which one closes and the other opens. In this part the Prophet shows the utter inefficacy of religious rites to counteract the natural effect of their iniquities, and then exhorts them to the use of the true remedy.

Under the former head, addressing them as similar in character to Sodom and Gomorrah, he describes their sacrifices as abundant and exact, but not acceptable; their attendance at the temple as punctual, and yet insulting; their bloodless offerings as abhorrent, and their holy days as wearisome and hateful on account of their iniquities; their very prayers as useless, because their hands were stained with blood, vs. 10–15. As a necessary means of restoration to God's favor, he exhorts them to forsake their evil courses and to exercise benevolence and justice, assuring them that God was willing to forgive them and restore the advantages which they had forfeited by sin, but at the same time resolved to punish the impenitent transgressor, vs. 16–20.

The transition from the second to the third part is abrupt, and introduced by a pathetic exclamation. In this part the Prophet compares Israel as it is with what it has been and with what it shall be. In the former comparison, he employs two metaphors, each followed by a literal explanation of its meaning; that of a faithful wife become a harlot, and that of adulterated wine and silver, both expressive of a moral deterioration, with special reference to magistrates and rulers, vs. 21–23. In the other comparison, the coming judgments are presented in the twofold aspect of purification and deliverance to the church, and of destruction to its wicked members. The Prophet sees the leading men of Israel destroyed, first as oppressors, to make room for righteous rulers and thus save the state, then as idolaters consumed by that in which they trusted for protection, vs. 24–31.

It is probable, that this prophecy belongs to the class already mentioned (in the Introduction) as exhibiting a sequence of events, or providential scheme, which might be realized in more than one emergency; not so much a prediction as a prophetic lesson with respect to the effects which certain causes must infallibly produce. Such a discourse would be peculiarly appropriate as an introduction to the prophecies which follow; and its seeming inconsistencies are all accounted for, by simply supposing that it was written for this purpose about the time of Sennacherib's invasion in the fourteenth year of Hezekiah's reign, and that in it the Prophet takes a general survey of the changes which the church had undergone since the beginning of his public ministry.

1. This is a general title of the whole book or one of its larger divisions, (ch. i.–xxxix. or i.–xii.) defining its character, author, subject, and date. *The Vision* (supernatural perception, inspiration, revelation, prophecy, here put collectively for *Prophecies*) *of Isaiah the son of Amoz, which he saw* (perceived, received by inspiration) *concerning Judah* (the kingdom of the two tribes which adhered to the theocracy after the revolt of Jeroboam) *and Jerusalem* (its capital, the chosen seat of the true religion), *in the days of Uzziah, Jotham, Ahaz, Hezekiah, kings of Judah.* The prophecies relating to the ten tribes and to foreign powers owe their place in this collection to their bearing, more or less direct, upon the interests of Judah. With respect to the names *Isaiah* and *Amoz*, and the chronology of this verse, see the Introduction.

2. The Prophet first describes the moral state of Judah, vs. 2–4, and then the miseries arising from it, vs. 5–9. To the former he invites attention by summoning the universe to hear the Lord's complaint against his people, who are first charged with filial ingratitude. *Hear, O heavens, and give ear, O earth,* as witnesses and judges, and as being less insensible yourselves than men, *for Jehovah speaks,* not man. *Sons I have reared and brought up,* literally made great and made high, *and they,* with emphasis on the pronoun which is otherwise superfluous, *even they have revolted from me,* or rebelled against me, not merely in a general sense by sinning, but in a special sense by violating that peculiar covenant which bound God to his people. It is

in reference to this bond and to the conjugal relation which the Scriptures represent God as sustaining to his church or people, that its constituent members are here called his *children.* The English Bible and many other versions read *Jehovah has spoken*, which seems to refer to a previous revelation, or to indicate a mere repetition of his words, whereas he is himself introduced as speaking. The preterite may be here used to express the present for the purpose of suggesting that he did not thus speak for the first time. Compare Heb. 1 : 1.

3. Having tacitly compared the insensible Jews with the inanimate creation, he now explicitly compares them with the brutes, selecting for that purpose two which were especially familiar as domesticated animals, subjected to man's power and dependent on him for subsistence, and at the same time as proverbially stupid, inferiority to which must therefore be peculiarly disgraceful. *The ox knoweth his owner and the ass his master's crib* or feeding place. *Israel*, the chosen people, as a whole, without regard to those who had seceded from it, *doth not know, my people doth not consider*, pay attention or take notice. Like the ox and the ass, Israel had a master, upon whom he was dependent, and to whom he owed obedience ; but, unlike them, he did not recognize and would not serve his rightful sovereign and the author of his mercies.

4. As the foregoing verses render prominent the false position of Israel with respect to God, considered first as a father and then as a master (comp. Mal. 1 : 6), so this brings into view their moral state in general, resulting from that alienation, and still represented as inseparable from it. The Prophet speaks again in his own person, and expresses wonder, pity, and indignation at the state to which his people had reduced themselves. *Ah, sinful nation*, literally *nation sinning*, i. e. habitually, which is the force here of the active participle, *people heavy with iniquity*,

weighed down by guilt as an oppressive burden, *a seed of evil-doers*, i. e. the offspring of wicked parents, *sons corrupting themselves*, i. e. doing worse than their fathers, in which sense the same verb isused, Judges. 2 : 19. The *evil-doers* are of course not the Patriarchs or Fathers of the nation, but the intervening wicked generations. As the first clause tells us what they were, so the second tells us what they did, by what acts they had merited the character just given. *They have forsaken Jehovah*, a phrase descriptive of iniquity in general, but peculiarly expressive of the breach of covenant obligations. *They have treated with contempt the Holy One of Israel*, a title almost peculiar to Isaiah, and expressing a twofold aggravation of their sin; first that he was infinitely excellent; and then, that he was theirs, their own peculiar God. *They are alienated back again.* The verb denotes estrangement from God, the adverb retrocession or backsliding into a former state.

5. To the description of their moral state, beginning and ending with apostasy from God, the Prophet now adds a description of the consequences, vs. 5–9. This he introduces by an expostulation on their mad perseverance in transgression, notwithstanding the extremities to which it had reduced them. *Whereupon*, i. e. on what part of the body, *can ye be stricken*, smitten, punished, *any more*, that *ye add revolt*, departure or apostasy from God, i. e. revolt more and more? Already *the whole head is sick and the whole heart faint.*—The same sense is attained, but in a less striking form, by reading *why*, to what purpose, *will ye be smitten any more? why continue to revolt?* If their object was to make themselves miserable, it was already accomplished.—Calvin, followed by the English version and others, gives a different turn to the interrogation: *Why should ye be smitten any more?* of what use is it? *ye will revolt more and more.* But the reason thus assigned for their ceasing to be smitten is wholly different from that given in the last clause

and amplified in the following verse, viz. that they were already faint and covered with wounds. The head and heart are mentioned as well-known and important parts of the body, to which the church or nation had been likened.

6. The idea suggested at the beginning of v. 5, that there was no more room for further strokes, is now carried out with great particularity. *From the sole of the foot and* (i. e. even) *to the head* (a common scriptural expression for the body in its whole extent) *there is not in it* (the people, or in him, i. e. Judah, considered as a body) *a sound place ; (it is) wound and bruise* (vibex, the tumor produced by stripes) *and fresh stroke.* The wounds are then described as not only grievous but neglected. *They have not been pressed, and they have not been bound* or bandaged, *and it has not been mollified with ointment*, all familiar processes of ancient surgery.

7. Thus far the sufferings of the people have been represented by strong figures, giving no intimation of their actual form, or of the outward causes which produced them. But now the Prophet brings distinctly into view foreign invasion as the instrument of vengeance, and describes the country as already desolated by it. The absence of verbs in the first clause gives great rapidity and life to the description. *Your land* (including town and country, which are afterwards distinctly mentioned) *a waste! Your towns* (including cities and villages of every size) *burnt with fire! Your ground* (including its produce), i. e. as to your ground, *before you* (in your presence, but beyond your reach) *strangers (are) devouring* it, *and a waste* (it is a waste) *like the overthrow of strangers*, i. e. as foreign foes are wont to waste a country, in which they have no interest, and for which they have no pity.

8. The extent of the desolation is expressed by comparing

the church or nation to a watch-shed in a field or vineyard, far from other habitations, and forsaken after the ingathering. *And the daughter of Zion*, i. e. the people of Zion or Jerusalem, considered as the capital of Judah, and therefore representing the whole nation, *is left*, not forsaken, but left over or behind as a survivor, *like a booth*, a temporary covert of leaves and branches, *in a vineyard, like a lodge in a melon-field, like a watched city*, i. e. watched by friends and foes, besieged and garrisoned, and therefore insulated, cut off from all communication with the country. That Jerusalem is not called the *daughter of Zion* from its local situation on that mountain, is clear from the analogous phrases *daughter of Tyre*, *daughter of Babylon*, where no such explanation is admissible.

9. The idea of a desolation almost total is expressed in other words, and with an intimation that the narrow escape was owing to God's favor for the remnant according to the election of grace, who still existed in the Jewish church. *Except Jehovah of Hosts had left unto us* (or caused to remain over, to survive, for us) *a very small remnant, we should have been like Sodom, we should have resembled Gomorrah*, i. e. we should have been totally and justly destroyed. That the verse has reference to quality as well as quantity, is evident from Rom. 9 : 29, where Paul makes use of it, not as an illustration, but as an argument to show that mere connection with the church could not save men from the wrath of God. The citation would have been irrelevant if this phrase denoted merely a small number of survivors, and not a minority of true believers in the midst of the prevailing unbelief. Jehovah of Hosts means the Sovereign Ruler of "heaven and earth and all the hosts of them," i. e. all their inhabitants (Gen. 2 : 1).

10. Having assigned the corruption of the people as the cause of their calamities, the Prophet now guards against the

error of supposing that the sin thus visited was that of neglecting the external duties of religion, which were in fact punctiliously performed, but unavailing because joined with the practice of iniquity, vs. 10–15. This part of the chapter is connected with what goes before by repeating the allusion to Sodom and Gomorrah. Having just said that God's sparing mercy had alone prevented their resembling Sodom and Gomorrah in condition, he now reminds them that they do resemble Sodom and Gomorrah in iniquity. The reference is not to particular vices, but to general character, as Jerusalem, when reproached for her iniquities, 'is spiritually called Sodom' (Rev. 11 : 8). The comparison is here made by the form of address. *Hear the word of Jehovah, ye judges* (or rulers) *of Sodom, give ear to the law of our God, ye people of Gomorrah.* Word and law both denote the revelation of God's will as a rule of faith and duty. The particular exhibition of it meant, is that which follows, and to which this verse invites attention like that frequent exhortation of our Saviour, *He that hath ears to hear, let him hear.*

11. Resuming the form of interrogation and expostulation, he teaches them that God had no need of sacrifices on his own account, and that even those sacrifices which he had required might become offensive to him. *For what* (for what purpose, to what end, of what use) *is the multitude of your sacrifices to me?* (i. e. offered *to me*, or of what use *to me*) *saith Jehovah. I am full* (i. e. sated, I have had enough, I desire no more) *of burnt-offerings of rams and the fat of fed beasts* (fattened for the altar), *and the blood of bullocks and lambs and he-goats I desire not* (or delight not in). Male animals are mentioned, as the only ones admitted in the burnt-offering; the fat and blood, as the parts in which the sacrifice essentially consisted, the one being always burnt upon the altar, and the other sprinkled or poured out around it.

12. What had just been said of the offerings themselves, is now said of attendance at the temple to present them. *When you come to appear before me, who hath required this at your hand to tread my courts*, not merely to frequent them, but to trample on them, as a gesture of contempt? The courts here meant are the enclosures around Solomon's temple, for the priests, worshippers, and victims. The interrogative form implies negation. Such appearance, such attendance, God had not required, although it was their duty to frequent his courts. The word tread appears to be applied to the worshippers themselves in a twofold sense, which cannot be expressed by any single word in English. They were bound to *tread* his courts, but not to *trample* them.

13. What he said before of animal sacrifices and of attendance at the temple to present them, is now extended to bloodless offerings, such as incense and the meal-offering, as well as to the observance of sacred times, and followed by a brief intimation of the sense in which they were all unacceptable to God, viz. when combined with the practice of iniquity. The interrogative form is here exchanged for that of direct prohibition. *Ye shall not add* (i. e. continue) *to bring a vain offering* (that is, a useless one, because hypocritical and impious). *Incense is an abomination to me: (so are) new moon and sabbath, the calling of the convocation* (at those times, or at the annual feasts, which are then distinctly mentioned with the weekly and monthly ones): *I cannot bear iniquity and holy day* (abstinence from labor, religious observance), meaning of course, I cannot bear them together. This last clause is a key to the preceding verses. It was not religious observance in itself, but its combination with iniquity, that God abhorred.

14. The very rights ordained by God himself, and once acceptable to him, had, through the sin of those who used them,

become irksome and disgusting. *Your new moons* (an emphatic repetition, as if he had said, Yes, your new moons) *and your convocations* (sabbaths and yearly feasts) *my soul hateth* (not a mere periphrasis for *I hate*, but an emphatic phrase denoting cordial hatred, *they have become a burden on me* (implying that they were not so at first). *I am weary of bearing* (or have wearied myself bearing them). The common version of the second clause (*they are a trouble unto me*) is too vague. The noun should have its specific sense of *burden*, *load*, and the preposition its proper local sense of *on*.

15. Not only ceremonial observances but even prayer was rendered useless by the sins of those who offered it. *And in your spreading* (when you spread) *your hands* (or stretch them out towards heaven as a gesture of entreaty) *I will hide mine eyes from you* (avert my face, refuse to see or hear, not only in ordinary but) *also when ye multiply prayer* (by fervent importunity in time of danger) *I am not hearing* (or about to hear, the participle bringing the act nearer to the present than the future would do). *Your hands are full of blood* (literally *bloods*, the form commonly used when the reference is to bloodshed or the guilt of murder). Thus the Prophet comes back to the point from which he set out, the iniquity of Israel as the cause of his calamities, but with this difference, that at first he viewed sin in its higher aspect, as committed against God, whereas in this place its injurious effects on men are rendered prominent. It is a strange opinion mentioned by Fabricius that the blood here meant is the blood of the victims hypocritically offered.

16. Having shown the insufficiency of ceremonial rites and even of more spiritual duties to avert or cure the evils which the people had brought upon themselves by their iniquities, he exhorts them to abandon these and urges reformation. *Wash you* (the word translated *wash you* is appropriated to ablution

of the body, as distinguished from all other washings), *purify yourselves* (in a moral or figurative sense, as appears from what follows). *Remove the evil of your doings from before mine eyes* (out of my sight, which could only be done by putting an end to them, an idea literally expressed in the last clause), *cease to do evil.*

17. The negative exhortation is now followed by a positive one. Ceasing to do evil was not enough, or rather was not possible, without beginning to do good. *Learn to do good*, implying that they never yet had known what it was. This general expression is explained by several specifications, showing how they were to do good. *Seek judgment*, i. e. justice ; not in the abstract, but in act ; not for yourselves, but for others ; be not content with abstinence from wrong, but seek opportunities of doing justice, especially to those who cannot right themselves. *Redress wrong*, *judge the fatherless*, i. e. act as a judge for his benefit, or more specifically, do him justice ; *befriend the widow*, take her part, espouse her cause. Orphans and widows are continually spoken of in Scripture as special objects of divine compassion, and as representing the whole class of helpless innocents.

18. Having shown that the cause of their ill success in seeking God was in themselves, and pointed out the only means by which the evil could be remedied, he now invites them to determine by experiment on which side the fault of their destruction lay, promising pardon and deliverance to the penitent and threatening total ruin to the disobedient, vs. 18–20.—This verse contains an invitation to discuss the question whether God was willing or unwilling to show mercy, implying that reason as well as justice was on his side, and asserting his power and his willingness to pardon the most aggravated sins. *Come now* (a common formula of exhortation) *and let us reason* (argue or discuss the case) *together* (the form of the verb denoting a

reciprocal action), *saith Jehovah. Though your sins be as scarlet they shall be white as snow, though they be red as crimson they shall be as wool*, i. e. clean white wool. Guilt being regarded as a stain, its removal denotes restoration to purity. The implied conclusion of the *reasoning* is that God's willingness to pardon threw the blame of their destruction on themselves.—The words translated *crimson and scarlet* are commonly combined to denote one color, and are here separated only as poetical equivalents.

19. The unconditional promise is now qualified and yet enlarged. If obedient, they should not only escape punishment but be highly favored. *If ye consent* to my terms, *and hear* my commands, implying obedience, *the good of the land*, its choicest products, *ye shall eat*, instead of seeing them devoured by strangers.

20. This is the converse of the nineteenth verse, a threat corresponding to the promise. *And if ye refuse* to comply with my conditions, *and rebel*, continue to resist my authority, *by the sword* of the enemy *shall ye be eaten.* This is no human menace but a sure prediction, *for the mouth of Jehovah speaks*, not man's.

21. Here the Prophet seems to pause for a reply, and on receiving no response to the promises and invitations of the foregoing context, bursts forth into a sudden exclamation at the change which Israel has undergone, which he then describes both in figurative and literal expressions, vs. 21–23. In the verse before us he contrasts her former state, as the chaste bride of Jehovah, with her present pollution, the ancient home of justice with the present haunt of cruelty and violence. *How has she become an harlot* (faithless to her covenant with Jehovah), *the faithful city* (including the ideas of a city and a state, *urbs et civitas*, the body politic, the church of which Jerusalem was the

centre and metropolis), *full of justice* (i. e. once full), *righteousness lodged* (i. e. habitually, had its home, resided) *in it, and now murderers*, as the worst class of violent wrong-doers, whose name suggests though it does not properly include all others. The particle at the beginning of the verse is properly interrogative, but like the English *how* is also used to express surprise. 'How has she become?' i. e. how could she possibly become? how strange that she should become!

22. The change, which had just been represented under the figure of adultery, is now expressed by that of adulteration, first of silver, then of wine. *Thy silver* (addressing the unfaithful church or city) *is become dross* (alloy, base metal), *thy wine weakened* (literally *cut, mutilated*) *with water*. The essential idea seems to be that of impairing strength. The Septuagint applies this text in a literal sense to dishonest arts in the sale of wines and the exchange of money. But this interpretation, besides its unworthiness and incongruity, is set aside by the Prophet's own explanation of his figures, in the next verse.

23. The same idea is now expressed in literal terms, and with special application to magistrates and rulers. They who were bound officially to suppress disorder and protect the helpless, were themselves greedy of gain, rebellious against God, and tyrannical towards man. *Thy rulers are rebels and fellows of thieves* (not merely like them or belonging to the same class, but accomplices, partakers of their sin), *every one of them loving a bribe* (the participle denoting present and habitual action) *and pursuing rewards. The fatherless* (as being unable to reward them, or as an object of cupidity to others) *they judge not, and the cause of the widow cometh not unto them*, or before them; they will not hear it; they will not act as judges for their benefit. They are not simply unjust judges, they are no judges at all, they will not act as such, except when they can profit by it.

24. To this description of the general corruption the Prophet now adds a promise of purgation, which is at the same time a threatening of sorer judgments, as the appointed means by which the church was to be restored to her original condition, vs. 24–31.—In this verse the destruction of God's enemies is represented as a necessary satisfaction to his justice. *Therefore*, because the very fountains of justice have thus become corrupt, *saith the Lord*, the word properly so rendered, *Jehovah of Hosts*, the eternal Sovereign, *the mighty one of Israel*, the almighty God who is the God of Israel, *Ah*, an interjection expressing both displeasure and concern, *I will comfort myself*, ease or relieve myself, *of my adversaries*, literally, *from them*, i. e. by ridding myself of them, *and I will avenge myself of mine enemies*, not foreign foes, of whom there is no mention in the context, but the enemies of God among the Jews themselves.

25. The mingled promise and threatening is repeated under one of the figures used in v. 22. The adulterated silver must be purified by the separation of its impure particles. *And I will turn my hand upon thee*, i. e. take thee in hand, address myself to thy case, *and will purge out thy dross like purity* itself, i. e. most purely, thoroughly, *and will take away all thine alloy*, tin, lead, or other base metal found in combination with the precious ores. Although to *turn the hand* has elsewhere an unfavourable sense (Ps. 81 : 14. Amos 1 : 8), it does not of itself express it, but simply means to take in hand, address one's self to any thing, make it the object of attention.

26. Here again the figurative promise is succeeded by a literal one of restoration to a former state of purity, to be effected not by the conversion of the wicked rulers but by filling their places with better men. *And I will restore*, bring back, cause to return, *thy judges*, rulers, *as at first*, in the earliest and best days of the commonwealth, *and thy counsellors*, ministers of state,

as in the beginning, after which it shall be called to thee, a Hebrew idiom for *thou shalt be called*, i. e. deservedly, with truth, *City of Righteousness, a Faithful State.* There is here a twofold allusion to v. 21. She who from being a faithful wife had become an adulteress or harlot, should again be what she was; and justice which once dwelt in her should return to its old home.

27. Thus far the promise to God's faithful people and the threatening to his enemies among them had been intermingled, or so expressed as to involve each other. Thus the promise of purification to the silver involved a threatening of destruction to the dross. But now the two elements of the prediction are exhibited distinctly, and first the promise to the church. *Zion*, the chosen people, as a whole, here considered as consisting of believers only, *shall be redeemed*, delivered from destruction, *in judgment*, i. e. in the exercise of justice upon God's part, *and her converts*, those of her who *return* to God by true repentance, *in righteousness*, here used as an equivalent to justice. The verse means that the very same events, by which the divine justice was to manifest itself in the destruction of the wicked, should be the occasion and the means of deliverance to Zion or the true people of God.

28. The other element is now brought out, viz. the destruction of the wicked, which was to be simultaneous and coincident with the deliverance promised to God's people in the verse preceding. *And the breaking*, crushing, utter ruin, *of apostates*, revolters, deserters from Jehovah, *and sinners*, is or shall be *together*, i. e. at the same time with Zion's redemption, *and the forsakers of Jehovah*, an equivalent expression to *apostates* in the first clause, *shall cease*, come to an end, be totally destroyed. The terms of this verse are appropriate to all kinds of sin, but seem to be peculiarly descriptive of idolatry, as defection or desertion from the true God to idols, and thus prepare the way

for the remainder of the chapter, in which that class of transgressors are made prominent. The same judgments which destroyed the wicked should redeem the righteous, or in other words, that the purification of the church could be effected only by the excision of her wicked members.

29. From the final destruction of idolaters the Prophet now reverts to their present security and confidence in idols, which he tells them shall be put to shame and disappointment. *For they shall be ashamed of the oaks* or terebinths *which ye have desired, and ye shall be confounded for the gardens which ye have chosen* as places of idolatrous worship. As these are terms constantly employed to express the frustration of religious trust, and as groves and gardens are continually spoken of as chosen scenes of idol-worship (see, for example, ch. 65 : 3. 66 : 17. Ezek. 6 : 13. Hos. 4 : 13), there can be little doubt that both this verse and the one preceding have particular allusion to idolatry.

30. The mention of trees and gardens, as places of idolatrous worship, suggests a beautiful comparison, under which the destruction of the idolaters is again set forth. They who choose trees and gardens, in preference to God's appointed place of worship, shall themselves be like trees and gardens, but in the most alarming sense. *For*, in answer to the tacit question why they should be ashamed and confounded for their oaks and gardens, *ye* yourselves *shall be like an oak* or terebinth, *fading*, decaying, in *its leaf* or as to *its leaf*, *and like a garden which has no water*, a lively emblem, to an oriental reader, of entire desolation.—Some writers understand the Prophet to allude to the terebinth when dead, on the ground that it never sheds its leaves when living; but according to Robinson and Smith (Bib. Res. vol. iii. p. 15), the terebinth or "*butm* is not an ever-

green, as is often represented; its small, feathered, lancet-shaped leaves fall in the autumn and are renewed in the spring."

31. This verse contains a closing threat of sudden, total, instantaneous destruction to the Jewish idolaters, to be occasioned by the very things which they preferred to God, and in which they confided. *And the strong*, the mighty man, alluding no doubt to the unjust rulers of the previous context, *shall become tow*, an exceedingly inflammable substance, *and his work*, his idols, often spoken of in Scripture as the work of men's hands, shall become *a spark*, the means and occasion of destruction to their worshippers, *and they shall burn both of them together*, and there shall *shall be no one quenching* or to quench them. The frequent mention of idols as the work of men's hands, and the prominence given to idolatry in the immediately preceding context, seem to justify us in understanding the whole verse as a prediction that the very gods, in whom the strong men of Jerusalem now trusted, should involve their worshippers and makers with themselves in total, instantaneous, irrecoverable ruin.

CHAPTERS II, III, IV.

These chapters constitute the second prophecy, the two grand themes of which are the reign of the Messiah and intervening judgments on the Jews for their iniquities. The first and greatest of these subjects occupies the smallest space, but stands both at the opening and the close of the whole prophecy. Considered in relation to its subject, it may therefore be conveniently divided into three unequal parts. In the first, the

Prophet foretells the future exaltation of the church and the accession of the gentiles, ch. 2: 1–4. In the second, he sets forth the actual condition of the church and its inevitable consequences, ch. 2 : 5—4 : 1. In the third, he reverts to its pure, safe, and glorious condition under the Messiah, ch. 4 : 2–6. The division of the chapters is peculiarly unfortunate, the last verse of the second and the first of the fourth being both dissevered from their proper context. As the state of things which this chapter describes could scarcely have existed in the prosperous reigns of Uzziah and Jotham or in the pious reign of Hezekiah, it is referred with much probability to the reign of Ahaz, when Judah was dependent on a foreign power and corrupted by its intercourse with heathenism. The particular grounds of this conclusion will appear in the course of the interpretation.

CHAPTER II.

THIS chapter contains an introductory prediction of the reign of the Messiah, and the first part of a threatening against Judah.

After a title similar to that in ch. 1 : 1, the Prophet sees the church, at some distant period, exalted and conspicuous, and the nations resorting to it for instruction in the true religion, as a consequence of which he sees war cease and universal peace prevail, vs. 2–4.

These verses are found, with very little variation, in the fourth chapter of Micah (vs. 1–3), to explain which some suppose, that a motto or quotation has been accidentally transferred from the margin to the text of Isaiah; others, that both Prophets quote from Joel; others, that both quote from an older writer now unknown; others, that Micah quotes from Isaiah; others, that Isaiah quotes from Micah. This diversity of judgment may at least suffice to show how vain conjecture is in such a case. The close connection of the passage with the context, as it stands in Micah, somewhat favors the conclusion that Isaiah took the text or theme of his prediction from the younger though contemporary Prophet. The verbal variations may be best explained, however, by supposing that they both adopted a traditional prediction current among the people in their day, or that both received the words directly from the Holy Spirit. So long as we have reason to regard both places as authentic and inspired, it matters little what is the literary history of either.

At the close of this prediction, whether borrowed or original, the Prophet suddenly reverts to the condition of the church in his own times, so different from that which had been just foretold, and begins a description of the present guilt and future punishment of Judah, which extends not only through this chapter but the next, including the first verse of the fourth. The part contained in the remainder of this chapter may be subdivided into two unequal portions, one containing a description of the sin, the other a prediction of the punishment.

The first begins with an exhortation to the Jews themselves to walk in that light which the gentiles were so eagerly to seek hereafter, v. 5. The Prophet then explains this exhortation by describing three great evils which the foreign alliances of Judah had engendered, namely, superstitious practices and occult arts; unbelieving dependence upon foreign wealth and power; and idolatry itself, vs. 6–8.

The rest of the chapter has respect to the punishment of these great sins. This is first described generally as humiliation, such as they deserved who humbled themselves to idols, and such as tended to the exclusive exaltation of Jehovah, both by contrast and by the display of his natural and moral attributes, vs. 9–11. This general threatening is then amplified in a detailed enumeration of exalted objects which should be brought low, ending again with a prediction of Jehovah's exaltation in the same words as before, so as to form a kind of choral or strophical arrangement, vs. 12–17. The destruction or rather the rejection of idols, as contemptible and useless, is then explicitly foretold, as an accompanying circumstance of men's flight from the avenging presence of Jehovah, vs. 18–21. Here again the strophical arrangement reappears in the precisely similar conclusions of the nineteenth and twenty-first verses, so that the twenty-second is as clearly unconnected with this chapter in form, as it is closely connected with the next in sense.

1. This is the title of the second prophecy, ch. 2–4. *The word*, revelation or divine communication, *which Isaiah the son of Amoz saw*, perceived, received by inspiration, *concerning Judah and Jerusalem.* *Word* is here a synonyme of *vision* in ch. 1 : 1. For the technical use of *word* and *vision* in the sense of prophecy, see 1 Sam. 3 : 1. Jer. 18 : 18.

2. The prophecy begins with an abrupt prediction of the exaltation of the church, the confluence of nations to it, and a general pacification as the consequence, vs. 2–4. In this verse the Prophet sees the church permanently placed in a conspicuous position, so as to be a source of attraction to surrounding nations. To express this idea, he makes use of terms which are strictly applicable only to the local habitation of the church under the old economy. Instead of saying, in modern phraseology, that the church, as a society, shall become conspicuous and attract all nations, he represents the mountain upon which the temple stood as being raised and fixed above the other mountains, so as to be visible in all directions. *And it shall be* (happen, come to pass, a prefatory formula of constant use in prophecy) *in the end* (or latter part) *of the days* (i. e. hereafter) *the mountain of Jehovah's house* (i. e. mount Zion, in the widest

sense, including mount Moriah where the temple stood) *shall be established* (permanently fixed) *in the head of the mountains* (i. e. above them), *and exalted from* (away from and by implication *more than* or *higher than*) *the hills* (a poetical equivalent to mountains), *and the nations shall flow unto it.* It was not to be established *on the top* of the mountains, but either *at the head* or simply *high among* the mountains, which idea is expressed by other words in the parallel clause, and by the same words in 1 Kings 21 : 10, 12. The verb in the last clause is always used to signify a confluence of nations.

3. This confluence of nations is described more fully, and its motive stated in their own words, namely, a desire to be instructed in the true religion, of which Jerusalem or Zion, under the old dispensation, was the sole depository. *And many nations shall go* (set out, put themselves in motion) *and shall say* (to one another), *Go ye* (as a formula of exhortation, where the English idiom requires *come*), *and we will ascend* (or *let us ascend*, for which the Hebrew has no other form) *to the mountain of Jehovah* (where his house is, where he dwells), *to the house of the God of Jacob, and he will teach us of his ways* (the ways in which he requires us to walk), *and we will go in his paths* (a synonymous expression). *For out of Zion shall go forth law* (the true religion, as a rule of duty), *and the word of Jehovah* (the true religion as a revelation) *from Jerusalem.* These last words may be either the words of the gentiles, telling why they looked to Zion as a source of saving knowledge, or the words of the Prophet, telling why the truth must be thus diffused, namely, because it had been given to the church for this very purpose. The common version *many people* conveys to a modern ear the wrong sense *many persons*, and was only used for want of such a plural form as *peoples*, which, though employed by Lowth and others, has never become current, and was certainly not so when the Bible was translated, as appears from

the circumlocution used instead of it in Gen. 25 : 23. The plural form is here essential to the meaning. *Go* is not here used as the opposite of *come*, but as denoting active motion. The word *ascend* is not used in reference to an alleged Jewish notion that the Holy Land was physically higher than all other countries, nor simply to the natural site of Jerusalem, nor even to its moral elevation as the seat of the true religion, but to the new elevation and conspicuous position just ascribed to it. The subjunctive construction *that he may teach* is rather paraphrastical and exegetical than simply expressive of the sense of the original, which implies hope as well as purpose.

4. He who appeared in the preceding verses as the lawgiver and teacher of the nations, is now represented as an arbiter or umpire, ending their disputes by a pacific intervention, as a necessary consequence of which war ceases, the very knowledge of the art is lost, and its implements applied to other uses. This prediction was not fulfilled in the general peace under Augustus, which was only temporary; nor is it now fulfilled. The event is suspended on a previous condition, viz. the confluence of the nations to the church, which has not yet taken place; a strong inducement to diffuse the gospel, which, in the meantime, is peaceful in its spirit, tendency, and actual effect, wherever and so far as it exerts its influence without obstruction. *And he shall judge* (or arbitrate) *between the nations, and decide for* (or respecting) *many peoples. And they shall beat their swords into ploughshares and their spears into pruning-hooks. Nation shall not lift up sword against nation, neither shall they learn war any more.* The whole idea meant to be expressed is the conversion of martial weapons into implements of husbandry. *Hook*, in old English, is a crooked knife, such as a *sickle*, which is not however here meant, but a knife for pruning vines. Not *learning war* is something more than not continuing to practise it, and signifies their ceasing to know how to practise it.

To *judge* is here not to *rule* which is too vague, nor to *punish* which is too specific, but to *arbitrate* or act as umpire, as appears from the effect described, and also from the use of the preposition, meaning not merely *among*, with reference to the sphere of jurisdiction, but *between*, with reference to contending parties.

5. From this distant prospect of the calling of the gentiles, the Prophet now reverts to his own times and countrymen, and calls upon them not to be behind the nations in the use of their distinguishing advantages. If even the heathen were one day to be enlightened, surely they who were already in possession of the light ought to make use of it. *O house of Jacob* (family of Israel the church or chosen people) *come ye* (literally *go ye*, as in v. 3) *and we will go* (or *let us walk*, including himself in the exhortation) *in the light of Jehovah* (in the path of truth and duty upon which the light of revelation shines). The *light* is mentioned as a common designation of the Scriptures and of Christ himself. (Prov. 6 : 23. Ps. 119 : 105. Isai. 51 : 4. Acts 26 : 23. 2 Cor. 4 : 4.)

6. The exhortation in v. 5 implied that the Jews were not actually walking in God's light, but were alienated from him, a fact which is now explicitly asserted and the reason of it given, viz. illicit intercourse with foreign nations, as evinced by the adoption of their superstitious practices, reliance on their martial and pecuniary aid, and last but worst of all, the worship of their idols. In this verse, the first of these effects is ascribed to intercourse with those eastern countries, which are always represented by the ancients as the cradle of the occult arts and sciences. As if he had said, I thus exhort, O Lord, thy chosen people, *because thou hast forsaken thy people, because they are replenished from the East and* (full of) *soothsayers like the Philistines, and with the children of strangers they abound. From the east* denotes not mere influence or imitation, but an actual in-

flux of diviners from that quarter. The Philistines are here mentioned rather by way of comparison than as an actual source of the corruption. That the Jews were familiar with their superstitions may be learned from 1 Sam. 6 : 2. 2 Kings 1 : 2.—The last verb does not mean they please themselves, but *they abound.* By *children of strangers* we are not to understand the fruits, i. e. doctrines and practices of strangers. It rather means strangers themselves, not strange gods or their children, i. e. worshippers, but foreigners considered as descendants of a strange stock, and therefore as aliens from the commonwealth of Israel.

7. The second proof of undue intercourse with heathen nations, which the Prophet mentions, is the influx of foreign money and of foreign troops, with which he represents the land as filled. *And his land* (referring to the singular noun *people* in v. 6) *is filled with silver and gold, and there is no end to his treasures; and his land is filled with horses, and there is no end to his chariots.*—The common interpretation makes this verse descriptive of domestic wealth and luxury. But these would hardly have been placed between the superstitions and the idols, with which Judah had been flooded from abroad. Besides, this interpretation fails to account for gold and silver being here combined with horses and chariots. Some suppose the latter to be mentioned only as articles of luxury; but as such they are never mentioned elsewhere, not even in the case of Absalom and Naaman, both of whom were military chiefs as well as nobles. Even the chariots of the peaceful Solomon were probably designed for martial show. The horses and chariots of the Old Testament are horses and chariots of war. The common riding animals were mules and asses, the latter of which, as contrasted with the horse, are emblematic of peace (Zech. 9 : 9. Matt. 21 : 7). But on the supposition that the verse has reference to undue dependence upon foreign powers,

the money and the armies of the latter would be naturally named together. Thus understood, this verse affords no proof that the prophecy belongs to the prosperous reign of Uzziah or Jotham, since it merely represents the land as flooded with foreign gold and foreign troops, a description rather applicable to the reign of Ahaz. The form of expression, too, suggests the idea of a recent acquisition, as the strict sense of the verb is not *it is full*, nor even *it is filled*, but *it was* or *has been filled.*

8. The third and greatest evil flowing from this intercourse with foreign nations was idolatry itself, which was usually introduced under the cloak of mere political alliances (see e. g. 2 Kings 16:10). Here as elsewhere the terms used to describe it are contemptuous in a high degree. *And his land is filled with idols* (properly *nonentities*, 'gods which yet are no gods,' Jer. 2: 11; 'for we know that an idol is nothing in the world,' 1 Cor. 8: 4), *to the work of their hands they bow down, to that which their fingers have made*, one of the great absurdities charged by the Prophets on idolaters, "as if that could be a god to them which was not only a creature but their own creature" (Matthew Henry).

9. Here the Prophet passes from the sin to its punishment, or rather simultaneously alludes to both, the verbs in the first clause being naturally applicable as well to voluntary humiliation in sin as to compulsory humiliation in punishment, while the verb in the last clause would suggest of course to a Jewish reader the twofold idea of pardoning and lifting up. They who bowed themselves to idols should be bowed down by the mighty hand of God, instead of being raised up from their wilful self-abasement by the pardon of their sins. The relative futures denote not only succession in time but the relation of cause and effect. *And so* (by this means, for this reason) *the mean man* (not in the modern but the old sense of inferior, low in

rank) *is bowed down, and the great man is brought low, and do not thou* (O Lord) *forgive them.* This prayer, for such it is, may be understood as expressing, not so much the Prophet's own desire, as the certainty of the event, arising from the righteousness of God.

10. Instead of simply predicting that their sinful course should be interrupted by a terrible manifestation of God's presence, the Prophet views him as already come or near at hand, and addressing the people as an individual, or singling out one of their number, exhorts him to take refuge under ground or in the rocks, an advice peculiarly significant in Palestine, a country full of caves, often used, if not originally made, for this very purpose (1 Sam. 13 : 6. 14 : 11. Judg. 6 : 2). *Go into the rock and hide thee in the dust, from before the terror of Jehovah and from the glory of his majesty.* The nouns in the last clause differ, according to their derivation, very much as *sublimity* and *beauty* do in English, and express in combination the idea of sublime beauty or beautiful sublimity. The tone of this address is not sarcastic but terrific. By the *terror of Jehovah* seems to be intended not the feeling of fear which he inspires but some terrible manifestation of his presence. The preposition, therefore, should not be taken in the vague sense of *for*, *on account of*, but in its proper local sense of *from*, *before*, or *from before.*

11. As the Prophet, in the preceding verse, views the terror of Jehovah as approaching, so here he views it as already past, and describes the effect which it has wrought. *The eyes of the loftiness of man* (i. e. his haughty looks) *are cast down, and the height* (or pride) *of men is brought low, and Jehovah alone is exalted in that day*, not only in fact, but in the estimation of his creatures, as the passive form here used may intimate.

12. The general threatening of humiliation is now applied

specifically to a variety of lofty objects in which the people might be supposed to delight and trust, vs. 12–16. This enumeration is connected with what goes before, by an explanation of the phrase used at the close of the eleventh verse. I say that day, *for there is a day to Jehovah of Hosts* (i. e. an appointed time for the manifestation of his power) *upon* (or against) *every thing high and lofty, and upon every thing exalted, and it comes* (or shall come) *down.* There is a day to Jehovah, i. e. *he has a day, has it appointed,* has it in reserve. The version *every one,* restricts the phrase too much to persons, which is only a part of the idea conveyed by the expression *every thing.*

13. To convey the idea of lofty and imposing objects, the Prophet makes use, not of symbols but of specimens selected from among the things of this class most familiar to his readers, beginning with the two noblest species of forest-trees. *And on all the cedars of Lebanon* (or the White Mountain, the chain dividing Palestine from Syria), *and on all the oaks of Bashan* (now called El Bethenyeh, a mountainous district, east of Jordan, famous of old for its pastures and oak-forests). Cedars and oaks are supposed by some to be here named, as emblems of *great men* in general, or of the great men of Syria and Israel distinctively; but this is not in keeping with the subsequent context, in which some things are mentioned, which cannot be understood as emblems, but only as samples of their several classes. On the trees and places mentioned in this verse, see Robinson's Palestine, vol. iii. p. 440, and Appendix, p. 158.

14. The mention of Lebanon and Bashan in v. 13 now leads to that of mountains in general, as lofty objects in themselves, and therefore helping to complete the general conception of high things, which the Prophet threatens with humiliation. *And upon all the high mountains and upon all the elevated hills.*

This must be explained as an additional specification of the general statement in v. 12, that *every high thing* should be humbled.

15. To trees and hills he now adds walls and towers, as a third class of objects with which the ideas of loftiness and strength are commonly associated. *And upon every high tower and upon every fenced wall*, literally, *cut off*, i. e. rendered inaccessible by being *fortified.*

16. The Prophet now concludes his catalogue of lofty and conspicuous objects by adding, first, as a specific item, maritime vessels of the largest class, and then a general expression, summing up the whole in one descriptive phrase, as things attractive and imposing to the eye. *And upon all ships of Tarshish* (such as were built to navigate the whole length of the Mediterranean sea) *and upon all images* (i. e. visible objects) *of desire*, or rather admiration and delight. It is a very old opinion that *Tarshish* means the *sea*, and ships of Tarshish sea-faring vessels, as distinguished from mere coast or river craft. From the earliest times, however, it has also been explained as the name of a place, either Tarsus in Cilicia or Cilicia itself, or Carthage, or a port in Ethiopia, or Africa in general, or a port in India, or, which is now the common opinion, *Tartessus*, a Phenician settlement in the south-west of Spain, between the mouths of the Baetis or Guadalquivir, sometimes put for the extreme west (Ps. 72 : 10). As the principal maritime trade, with which the Hebrews were acquainted, was to this region, *ships of Tarshish* would suggest the idea of the largest class of vessels, justly included in this catalogue of lofty and imposing objects. To suppose a direct allusion either to commercial wealth or naval strength, is inconsistent with the context, although these ideas would of course be suggested by association. Most writers understand the last clause, like the first, as a specific addition to

the foregoing catalogue, denoting some particular object or class of objects, such as pictures, statues, lofty images or obelisks, palaces, tapestry, and ships. But this indefinite diversity of explanation, as well as the general form of the expression, makes it probable that this clause, notwithstanding the parallelism, was intended as a general expression for such lofty and imposing objects as had just been enumerated,—'cedars, oaks, mountains, hills, towers, walls, ships, and in short, all attractive and majestic objects.'

17. This verse, by repeating the terms of v. 11, brings us back from details to the general proposition which they were designed to illustrate and enforce, and at the same time has the effect of a strophical arrangement, in which the same burden or chorus recurs at stated intervals. *And* (thus, by this means, or in this way) *shall the loftiness of man be cast down, and the pride of men be brought low, and Jehovah alone be exalted in that day.* Or retaining the form of the first two verbs, which are not passive but neuter, and exchanging the future for the present, the sentence may be thus translated. *So sinks the loftiness of man and bows the pride of men, and Jehovah alone is exalted in that day.*

18. To the humiliation of all lofty things the Prophet now adds the entire disappearance of their idols. *And the idols* (as for the idols) *the whole shall pass away.* The brevity of this verse, consisting of a single clause, has been commonly regarded as highly emphatic and, as some think, sarcastic.

19. This verse differs from the tenth only by substituting a direct prediction for a warning or exhortation, and by adding the design of God's terrible appearance. *And they* (the idolaters, or men indefinitely) *shall enter into the caves of the rocks and into the holes of the earth, from before the terror of Jehovah*

and the glory of his majesty in his arising (i. e. when he arises) *to terrify the earth.* The first word rendered *earth* is the same that was translated *dust* in v. 10, but even there it signifies the solid surface rather than the crumbling particles which we call dust. The most exact translation would perhaps be *ground.* God is said to *arise* when he addresses himself to any thing, especially after a season of apparent inaction.

20. This is an amplification of v. 18, explaining how the idols were to disappear, viz. by being thrown away in haste, terror, shame, and desperate contempt, by those who had worshipped them and trusted in them, as a means of facilitating their escape from the avenging presence of Jehovah. *In that day shall man cast his idols of silver and his idols of gold* (here named as the most splendid and expensive, in order to make the act of throwing them away still more significant) *which they have made* (an indefinite construction, equivalent in meaning to *which have been made*) *for him to worship, to the moles and to the bats* (a proverbial expression for contemptuous rejection.) The idols made for them to worship they shall cast to the moles and bats, not to idolaters still blinder than themselves, but to literal moles and bats, or the spots which they frequent, i. e. dark and filthy places. Moles and bats are put together on account of their defect of sight.

21. Continuing the sentence, he declares the end for which they should throw away their idols, namely, to save themselves, casting them off as worthless incumbrances in order the more quickly to take refuge in the rocks. *To go into the clefts of the rocks, and into the fissures of the cliffs* (or crags) *from before the terror of Jehovah, and from the glory of his majesty in his arising to terrify the earth,* or as Lowth more poetically renders it, *to strike the earth with terror.*—The final recurrence of the same *refrain* which closed the eleventh and seventeenth verses, marks

the conclusion of the choral or strophical arrangement at this verse, the next beginning a new context.

22. Having predicted that the people would soon lose their confidence in idols, he now shows the folly of transferring that confidence to human patrons, by a general statement of man's weakness and mortality, explained and amplified in the following chapter. *Cease ye from man* (i. e. cease to trust him or depend upon him) *whose breath is in his nostrils* (i. e. whose life is transient and precarious, with obvious allusion to Gen. 2: 7) *for wherein is he to be accounted of* (or at what rate is he to be valued)? The interrogation forcibly implies that man's protection cannot be relied upon.—In the Septuagint this verse is wholly wanting, and some suppose the translators to have left it out, as being an unwelcome truth to kings and princes; but such a motive must have led to much more extensive expurgation of unpalatable scriptures. It is found in the other ancient versions and its genuineness has not been disputed.—To *cease from* is to *let alone;* in what specific sense must be determined by the context (compare 2 Chron. 35 : 21 with Prov. 23 : 4).

CHAPTER III.

THIS chapter continues the threatenings against Judah on account of the prevailing iniquities, with special reference to female pride and luxury.

The Prophet first explains his exhortation at the close of the last chapter, by showing that God was about to take away the leading men of Judah and to let it fall into a state of anarchy, vs. 1–7. He then shows that this was the effect of sin, particularly that of wicked rulers, vs. 8–15. He then exposes in detail the pride and luxury of the Jewish women, and threatens them not only with the loss of that in which they now delighted, but with widowhood, captivity, and degradation, v. 16—4 : 1.

The first part opens with a general prediction of the loss of what they trusted in, beginning with the necessary means of subsistence, v. 1. We have then an enumeration of the public men who were about to be removed, including civil, military, and religious functionaries, with the practitioners of certain arts, vs. 2, 3. As the effect of this removal, the government falls into incompetent hands, v. 4. This is followed by insubordination and confusion, v. 5. At length, no one is willing to accept public office, the people are wretched, and the commonwealth a ruin, vs. 6, 7.

This ruin is declared to be the consequence of sin, and the people represented as their own destroyers, vs. 8, 9. God's judgments, it is true, are not indiscriminate. The innocent shall not perish with the guilty, but the guilty must suffer, vs. 10, 11. Incompetent and faithless rulers must especially be punished, who instead of being the guardians are spoilers of the vineyard, instead of protectors the oppressors of the poor, vs. 12–15.

As a principal cause of these prevailing evils, the Prophet now denounces female luxury and threatens it with condign punishment, privation and disgrace, vs. 16, 17. This general denunciation is then amplified at great length, in a detailed enumeration of the ornaments which were about to be taken from them and succeeded by the badges of captivity and mourning, vs. 18–24. The agency to be employed in this retribution is a disastrous war, by which the men are to be swept off and the country left desolate, vs. 25, 26. The extent of this calamity is represented by a lively exhibition of the disproportion between the male survivors and the other sex, suggesting at the same time the forlorn condition of the widows of the slain, chap. 4 : 1.

1. This verse assigns as a reason for the exhortation in the one preceding, that God was about to take away from the people every ground of reliance, natural and moral. Cease ye from man, i. e. cease to trust in any human protection, *for behold* (implying a proximate futurity) *the Lord* (God considered as a sovereign) *Jehovah of Hosts* (as self-existent and eternal, and at the same time as the God of revelation and the God of his people) *is taking away* (or about to take away) *from Jerusalem and from Judah* (not only from the capital but from the whole kingdom) *the stay and the staff* (i. e. all kinds of support, and first of all) *the whole stay of bread and the whole stay of water* (the natural and necessary means of subsistence). The terms are applicable either to a general famine produced by natural causes, or to a scarcity arising from invasion or blockade, such as actually took place when Judah was overrun by Nebuchadnezzar) 2 Kings 25 : 4. Jer. 52 : 6. 38 : 9. Lam. 4 : 4).—Instead of *the whole stay*, prose usage would require *every stay.* But the other construction is sustained by the analogy of *the whole head* and *the whole heart*, ch. 1 : 5, and by the impossibility of expressing this idea otherwise without circumlocution.—The old version *stay and staff* is an approximation to the form of the original, in which a masculine and feminine form of the same noun are combined, by an idiom common in Arabic and not unknown in Hebrew, to denote universality, or rather *all kinds* of the object named.

2. Next to the necessary means of subsistence, the Prophet enumerates the great men of the commonwealth, vs. 2, 3. The first clause has reference to military strength, the second to civil and religious dignities. In the second clause there is an inverse parallelism, the first and fourth terms denoting civil officers, the second and third religious ones. The omission of the article before the nouns, though not uncommon in poetry, adds much to the rapidity and life of the description. *Hero and*

warrior, judge and prophet, and divine and elder. That the first is not a generic term including all that follow (the great men, viz. the warriors, etc.) is clear from the parallelism, the terms being arranged in pairs as often elsewhere, (ch. 11 : 2. 19 : 3, 6–9. 22 : 12, 13. 42 : 19). The idea here expressed is not simply that of personal strength and prowess but the higher one of military eminence or heroism.—The literal version of the next phrase, *man of war*, has acquired a different sense in modern English. It may here denote either a warrior of high rank, as synonymous with mighty man, or one of ordinary rank, as distinguished from it. *Judge* may either be taken in its restricted modern sense or in the wider one of magistrate or ruler. The people are threatened with the loss of all their *stays*, good or bad, true or false. The last word in the verse is not to be taken in its primary and proper sense of *old man*, much less in the factitious one of *sage*, or *wise man*, since all the foregoing terms are *titles* denoting rank and office, but in its secondary sense of *elder* or hereditary chief, and as such a magistrate under the patriarchal system. It is here equivalent or parallel to *judge*, the one term denoting the functions of the office, the other the right by which it was held.

3. To persons of official rank and influence, the Prophet adds, in order to complete his catalogue, practitioners of those arts upon which the people set most value. As the prophet and diviner stand together in v. 2, so mechanical and magical arts are put together here. The first clause simply finishes the list of public functionaries which had been begun in the preceding verse. *The chief of fifty, and the favourite, and the counsellor, and the skilful artificer, and the expert enchanter.*—The first title is derived from the decimal arrangement of the people in the wilderness for judicial purposes (Exod. 18 : 25, 26), but is afterwards used only as a military title. The next phrase literally signifies *lifted up in countenance*, which is commonly understood

as a description of an eminent or honourable person. But as the same words are employed to signify respect of persons or judicial partiality, the phrase may here denote one highly favoured by a sovereign, a royal favourite (2 Kings 5 : 1. Lev. 19 : 15, Deut. 10 : 17. Job 13 : 10. Mal. 2 : 9), or respected, reverenced by the people (Lam. 4 : 16. Deut. 28 : 50).—The *counsellor* here meant is not a private or professional adviser, but a public counsellor or minister of state. The last word in the verse is taken strictly, as denoting a 'whisper' or the act of whispering, by some; but in its secondary sense of incantation, with allusion to the mutterings and whisperings which formed a part of magical ceremonies, by most modern writers.

4. The natural consequence of the removal of the leading men must be the rise of incompetent successors, persons without capacity, experience, or principle, a change which is here ascribed to God's retributive justice. *And I will give children to be their rulers, and childish things shall govern them.* Some apply this, in a strict sense, to the weak and wicked reign of Ahaz; others in a wider sense to the series of weak kings after Isaiah. But there is no need of restricting it to kings at all. The most probable opinion is that the incompetent rulers are called boys or children not in respect to age but character.

5. As the preceding verse describes bad government, so this describes anarchy, the suspension of all government, and a consequent disorder in the relations of society, betraying itself in mutual violence, and in the disregard of natural and artificial claims to deference. *And the people shall act tyrannically, man against man, and man against his fellow. They shall be insolent, the youth to the old man, and the mean man to the noble.* On contempt of old age, as a sign of barbarism, see Lam. 4 : 16, Deut. 28 : 50.

6. Having predicted the removal of those qualified to govern, the rise of incompetent successors, and a consequent insubordination and confusion, the Prophet now describes this last as having reached such a height that no one is willing to hold office, or, as Matthew Henry says, "the government goes a begging." This verse, notwithstanding its length, seems to contain only the protasis or conditional clause of the sentence, in which the commonwealth is represented as a ruin, and the task of managing it pressed upon one living in retirement, on the ground that he still possesses decent raiment, a lively picture both of general anarchy and general wretchedness. *When a man shall take hold of his brother* (i. e. one man of another) *in his father's house* (at home in a private station, saying) *thou hast raiment, a ruler shalt thou be to us, and this ruin* (shall be) *under thy hand* (i. e. under thy power, control, and management). It is equally consistent with the syntax and the usage of the words to understand the man as addressing his brother, in the proper sense, or in that of a near kinsman, of or belonging to the house of his (the speaker's) father, i. e. one of the same family. But the offer would then seem to be simply that of headship or chieftainship over a family or house, whereas a wider meaning is required by the connection. Some explain the phrase as meaning *thou art rich*, because clothing forms a large part of oriental wealth. But others understand the words more probably as meaning 'thou hast still a garment,' whereas we have none, implying general distress as well as anarchy.

7. This verse contains the refusal of the invitation given in the one preceding. *In that day he shall lift up* (his voice in reply) *saying* I will *not be a healer, and in my house there is no bread, and there is no clothing; ye shall not make me a ruler of people.* In that day may either mean at once, without deliberation, or continue the narrative without special emphasis. Some

supply *hand* after *lift up*, as a gesture of swearing, or the name of God as in the third commandment, and understand the phrase to mean that *he shall swear*. But the great majority of writers supply *voice*, some in the specific sense of *answering*, or in the simple sense of *uttering*, but others with more probability in that of speaking with a loud voice, or distinctly and with emphasis, *he shall protest*, or *openly declare*. The whole connexion seems to show that this is a profession of great poverty, which, if true, shows more clearly the condition of the people, and if false, the general aversion to office. The last clause does not simply mean *do not make me*, but *you must not*, or *you shall not make me* a ruler.

8. The Prophet here explains his use of the word *ruin* in reference to the commonwealth of Israel, by declaring that it had in fact destroyed itself by the offence which its iniquities had given to the holiness of God, here compared to the sensitiveness of the human eye. Do not wonder at its being called a ruin, *for Jerusalem totters and Judah falls* (or Jerusalem is tottering, and Judah falling), because their *tongue and their doings* (words and deeds being put for the whole conduct) *are against Jehovah* (strictly *to* or *towards*, but in this connection necessarily implying opposition and hostility), *to resist* (i. e. so as to resist, implying both the purpose and effect) *his holy eyes* (and thereby to offend them). Jerusalem and Judah, though peculiarly the Lord's, were nevertheless to fall and be destroyed for their iniquities.

9. As they make no secret of their depravity, and as sin and suffering are inseparably connected, they must bear the blame of their own destruction. *The expression of their countenances testifies against them, and their sin, like Sodom, they hide it not. Woe unto their soul, for they have done evil to themselves.* The context seems to show that the Prophet has reference to gen-

eral character and not to a specific sin, while the parallel expressions in this verse make it almost certain that the phrase relates to the expression of the countenance. The sense is not that their looks betray them, but that they make no effort at concealment, as appears from the reference to Sodom. The expression of the same idea first in a positive and then in a negative form is not uncommon in Scripture, and is a natural if not an English idiom. Madame d'Arblay, in her memoirs of Dr. Burney, speaks of Omiah, the Tahitian brought home by Capt. Cook, as "uttering first affirmatively and then negatively all the little sentences that he attempted to pronounce."

10. The righteous are encouraged by the assurance that the judgments of God shall not be indiscriminate. *Say ye of the righteous that it shall be well, for the fruits of their doings they shall eat.* The object of address seems to be not the prophets or ministers of God, but the people at large or men indefinitely. The concise and elliptical first clause may be variously construed. 'Say, it is right (or righteous) that (they should eat) good, that they should eat the fruit of their doings.' 'Say, it is right, (or God is righteous), for it is good that they should eat,' etc. 'Say (what is) right,' i. e. pronounce just judgment.

11. This is the converse of the foregoing proposition, a threatening corresponding to the promise. *Woe unto the wicked,* (it shall be) *ill* (with him), *for the thing done by his hand shall be done to him.*

12. The Prophet now recurs to the evil of unworthy and implacable rulers, and expresses, by an exclamation, wonder and concern at the result. *My people! their oppressors are childish and women rule over them. My people! thy leaders are seducers, and the way of thy paths* (the way where thy path lies) *they swallow up* (cause to disappear, destroy).

13. Though human governments might be overthrown, God still remained a sovereign and a judge, and is here represented as appearing, coming forward, or assuming his position, not only as a judge but as an advocate, or rather an accuser, in both which characters he acts at once, implying that he who brings this charge against his people has at the same time power to condemn. *Jehovah standeth up to plead, and is standing to judge the nations.* The first verb properly denotes a reflexive act, viz. that of placing or presenting himself. *Nations* here as often elsewhere means the tribes of Israel. See Gen. 49 : 10. Deut. 32 : 8. 33 : 3, 19. 1 Kings 22 : 28. Mich. 1 : 2.

14. This verse describes the parties more distinctly and begins the accusation. *Jehovah will enter into judgment* (engage in litigation, both as a party and a judge) *with the elders of his people* (the heads of houses, families and tribes) *and the chiefs thereof* (the hereditary chiefs of Israel, here and elsewhere treated as responsible representatives of the people). *And ye* (even ye) *have consumed the vineyard* (of Jehovah, his church or chosen people), *the spoil of the poor* (that which is taken from him by violence) *is in your houses.* Some regard the last clause as the language of the Prophet, giving a reason why God would enter into judgment with them; but it is commonly regarded as the commencement of the judge's own address, which is continued through the following verse.

15. The Lord's address to the elders of Israel is continued in a tone of indignant expostulation. *What mean ye* (literally *what* is *to you*, equivalent in English to what have you, i. e. what right, what reason, what motive, what advantage) *that ye crush my people* (a common figure for severe oppression, Job 5 : 4. Prov. 22 : 22) *and grind the faces of the poor* (upon the ground, by trampling on their bodies, another strong figure for contemptuous and oppressive violence), *saith the Lord Jehovah of*

Hosts (which is added to remind the accused of the sovereign authority, omniscience, and omnipotence of Him by whom the charge is brought against them). The first verb does not mean merely to weaken, bruise, or break, but to break in pieces, to break utterly, to *crush.* By the *faces* of the poor some understand their *persons* or the poor themselves, and by *grinding* them, reducing, attenuating, by exaction and oppression. Others refer the phrase to literal injuries of the face by blows or wounds. But the simplest and most natural interpretation is that which applies it to the act of grinding the face upon the ground by trampling on the body, thus giving both the noun and verb their proper meaning, and making the parallelism more exact. The phrase at the beginning of the verse, *what mean ye?* merely serves to introduce the question.

16, 17. The Prophet here resumes the thread which had been dropped or broken at the close of v. 12, and recurs to the undue predominance of female influence, but particularly to the prevalent excess of female luxury, not only as sinful in itself, but as a chief cause of the violence and social disorder previously mentioned, and therefore to be punished by disease, widowhood, and shameful exposure. These two verses, like the sixth and seventh, form one continued sentence. *And Jehovah said* (in addition to what goes before, as if beginning a new section of the prophecy), *because the daughters of Zion* (the women of Jerusalem, with special reference to those connected with the leading men) *are lofty* (in their mien and carriage) *and walk with outstretched neck* (literally *stretched of neck*, so as to seem taller), *and gazing* (ogling, leering, looking wantonly) *with their eyes, and with a tripping walk they walk, and with their feet they make a tinkling* (i. e. with the metallic rings or bands worn around the ankles), *therefore the Lord will make bald the crown of the daughters of Zion, and their nakedness Jehovah will uncover* (i. e. he will reduce them to a state the very opposite of their present pride and finery). They are described as stretching out the neck, not by bending forwards, nor by tossing the head backwards, but by holding it high, so that the phrase corresponds to *lofty* in the clause preceding. The baldness mentioned in the last clause is variously explained as an allusion to the shaving of the heads of prisoners or captives, or as a sign of mourning, or as the effect of disease, and particularly of the disease which bears a name (Lev. 13 : 2) derived from the verb here used. Neither of these ideas is expressed, though all may be implied, in the terms of the original.

18. Although the prediction in v. 17 implies the loss of all ornaments whatever, we have now a minute specification of the things to be taken away. This specification had a double use; it made the judgment threatened more explicit and significant to those whom it concerned, while to others it gave some idea of the length to which extravagance in dress was carried. There is no need of supposing that all these articles were ever worn at once, or that the passage was designed to be descriptive of a complete dress. It is rather an enumeration of detached particulars which might or might not be combined in any individual case. As in other cases where a variety of detached particulars are enumerated simply by their names, it is now very difficult to identify some of them. This is the less to be regretted, as the main design of the enumeration was to show the prevalent extravagance in dress, an effect not wholly dependent on an exact interpretation of the several items. The interest of the passage, in its details, is not exegetical but archaeological. Nothing more will be here attempted than to give what is now most commonly regarded as the true meaning of the terms, with a few of the more important variations in the doubtful cases. *In that day* (the time appointed for the judgments just denounced) *the Lord will take away* (literally, cause to depart, from the daughters of Zion) *the bravery* (in the old

English sense of finery) *of the ankle bands* (the noun from which the last verb in v. 16 is derived) *and the cauls* (or caps of net-work) *and the crescents* (or little moons, metallic ornaments of that shape).

19. *The pendants* (literally, drops, i. e. ear-rings) *and the bracelets* (for the arm, or collars for the neck) *and the veils* (the word here used denoting the peculiar oriental veil, composed of two pieces hooked together below the eyes, one of which pieces is thrown back over the head, while the other hides the face).

20. *The caps* (or other ornamental head-dresses) and *the ankle chains* (connecting the ankle bands, so as to regulate the length of the step) *and the girdles, and the houses* (i. e. places or receptacles) *of breath* (meaning probably the perfume boxes or smelling-bottles worn by the oriental women at their girdles), *and the amulets* (the same word used above in v. 3, in the sense of *incantations*, but which seems to have also signified the antidote). The first word of this verse is now commonly explained to mean *turbans*, but as these are distinctly mentioned afterwards, this term may denote an ornamental cap, or perhaps a diadem or circlet of gold or silver. The next word is explained to mean *bracelets* by the Septuagint, but by the English Version more correctly, though perhaps too vaguely, *ornaments of the leg*. For *girdles, smelling bottles and amulets*, the English Version has *head-bands, tablets* (but in the margin, *houses of the soul*), *and ear-rings*, perhaps on account of the superstitious use which was sometimes made of these (Gen. 35 : 4).

21. *The rings*, strictly signet-rings, but here put for finger-rings or rings in general, *and the nose jewels*, a common and very ancient ornament in eastern countries, so that the version, *jewels of the face*, is unnecessary, as well as inconsistent with the derivation from a word meaning to perforate.

22. *The holiday-dresses and the mantles and the robes and the purses.* The first word is almost universally explained to mean clothes that are taken off and laid aside, i. e. the best suit, holiday or gala dresses, although this general expression seems misplaced in an enumeration of minute details. The common version, *changeable suits of apparel*, though ambiguous, seems intended to express the same idea. The next two words, according to their etymology, denote wide and flowing upper garments. The common version of the last word, *crisping-pins*, supposes it to relate to the dressing of the hair. The word is now commonly explained, from the Arabic analogy, to signify bags or purses.

23. *The mirrors and the tunics* (inner garments made of linen), *and the turbans* (the common oriental head-dress) *and the veils.* The first word is explained by the Septuagint to mean thin transparent dresses; but most writers understand it to denote the small metallic mirrors carried about by oriental women.

24. The threatening is still continued, but with a change of form, the things to be taken away being now contrasted with those which should succeed them. *And it shall be* or *happen* that *instead of perfume* (aromatic odour or the spices which afford it) *there shall be stench, and instead of a girdle a rope, and instead of braided work baldness* (or loss of hair by disease or shaving, as a sign of captivity or mourning), *and instead of a full robe a girdling of sackcloth, burning instead of beauty.* The inversion of the terms in this last clause, and its brevity, add greatly to the strength of the expression. The *burning* mentioned is supposed by some to be that of the skin from long exposure; most interpreters understand by it a *brand*, here mentioned either as a stigma of captivity, or as a self-inflicted sign of mourning. Sackcloth is mentioned

as the coarsest kind of cloth, and also as that usually worn by mourners.

25. The Prophet now assigns as a reason for the grief predicted in v. 24, a general slaughter of the male population, the effect of which is again described in v. 26, and its extent in chap. 4 : 1, which belongs more directly to this chapter than the next. In the verse before us, he first addresses Zion or Jerusalem directly, but again, as it were, turns away, and in the next verse speaks of her in the third person. *Thy men by the sword shall fall and thy strength in war.*

26. The effect of this slaughter on the community is here described, first by representing the places of chief concourse as vocal with distress, and then by personifying the state or nation as a desolate widow seated on the ground, a sign both of mourning and of degradation. *And her gates* (those of Zion or Jerusalem) *shall lament and mourn* (and), *being emptied* (or exhausted) *she shall sit upon the ground.* The gates are said to mourn, by a rhetorical substitution of the place of action for the agent, or because a place filled with cries seems itself to utter them. She is described not as lying but as sitting on the ground. So on one of Vespasian's coins a woman is represented in a sitting posture, leaning against a palm-tree, with the legend *Judaea Capta.*

Ch. 4 : 1. The paucity of males in the community, resulting from this general slaughter, is now expressed by a lively figure, representing seven women as earnestly soliciting one man in marriage, and that on the most disadvantageous terms, renouncing the support to which they were by law entitled. *And in that day* (then, after the judgment just predicted), *seven women* (i. e. several, this number being often used indefinitely) *shall lay hold of one man* (earnestly accost him), *saying, we will eat our own bread and wear our own apparel, only let thy name be called upon us* (an idiomatic phrase meaning let us be called by thy name, let us be recognized as thine), *take thou away our reproach*, the 'reproach of widowhood' (Isai. 54 : 4) or celibacy, or rather that of childlessness which they imply, and which was regarded with particular aversion by the Jews before the time of Christ. The Prophet simply meant to set forth by a lively figure the disproportion between the sexes introduced by a destructive war.

CHAPTER IV.

Besides the first verse, which has been explained already, this chapter contains a prophecy of Christ and of the future condition of the Church. The Prophet here recurs to the theme with which the prophecy opened (ch. 2 : 1–4), but with this distinction, that instead of dwelling on the influence exerted by the church upon the world, he here exhibits its internal condition under the reign of the Messiah. He first presents to view the person by whose agency the church is to be brought into a glorious and happy state, and who is here described as a partaker both of the divine and human nature, v. 2. He then describes the character of those who are predestined to share in the promised exaltation, v. 3. He then shows the necessity, implied in these promises, of previous purgation from the defilement described in the foregoing chapters, v. 4. When this purgation is effected, God will manifest his presence gloriously throughout his church, v. 5. To these promises of purity and honour he now adds one of protection and security, with which the prophecy concludes, v. 6.

It is commonly agreed that this prediction has been only

partially fulfilled, and that its complete fulfilment is to be expected, not in the literal Mount Zion or Jerusalem, but in those various assemblies or societies of true believers, which now possess in common the privileges once exclusively enjoyed by the Holy City and the chosen race of which it was the centre and metropolis.

2. *In that day* (after this destruction) *shall the Branch* (or Offspring) *of Jehovah be for honour and for glory, and the Fruit of the Earth for sublimity and beauty, to the escaped of Israel,* literally, the *escape* or deliverance of Israel, the abstract being used for the collective concrete, meaning those who should survive these judgments. At this point the Prophet passes from the tone of threatening to that of promise. Having foretold a general destruction, he now intimates that some should escape it, and be rendered glorious and happy by the presence and favour of the Son of God, who is at the same time the Son of Man. The usage of the word Branch in application to an individual will be clear from the following examples. "Behold the days come, saith the Lord, that I will raise unto David a righteous BRANCH, and a king shall reign and prosper" (Jer. 23 : 5). "In those days and at that time will I cause the BRANCH of righteousness to grow up unto David, and he shall execute judgment" (Jer. 33 : 15). "Behold I will bring forth my servant the BRANCH" (Zech. 3 : 8). "Behold the MAN whose name is the BRANCH" (Zech. 6 : 12). The Branch is here represented as a man, a king, a righteous judge, a servant of God. Hence it is reasonable to conclude that the same person, whom Jeremiah calls the *branch* (or son) *of David*, is called by Isaiah in the verse before us *the branch* (or son) *of Jehovah.* The parallel terms correspond exactly to the two parts of Paul's description (Rom. 1 : 3, 4), and to the two titles applied in the New Testament to Christ's two natures, SON OF GOD and SON OF MAN.

3. *And it shall be*, happen, come to pass, *that the left in Zion and the spared in Jerusalem*, singular forms with a collective application, *shall be called holy*, literally, *holy shall be said to him*, i. e. this name shall be used in addressing him, or rather may be used with truth, implying that the persons so called should be what they seemed to be, *every one written*, enrolled, ordained, *to life in Jerusalem* Having foretold the happiness and honour which the Son of God should one day confer upon his people, the Prophet now explains to whom the promise was intended to apply. In the preceding verse they were described by their condition as survivors of God's desolating judgments. In this they are described by their moral character, and by their eternal destination to this character and that which follows it.

4. The construction is continued from the verse preceding. All this shall come to pass, *if* (provided that, on this condition, which idea may be here expressed by *when*) *the Lord shall have washed away* (the Hebrew word denoting specially the washing of the body, and suggesting the idea of the legal ablutions) *the filth* (a very strong term transferred from physical to moral defilement) *of the daughters of Zion* (the women before mentioned), *and the blood* (literally *bloods*, i. e. blood-shed or blood-guiltiness) *of Jerusalem* (i. e. of the people in general), *by a spirit of judgment and spirit of burning*, i. e. by the judgment and burning of the Holy Spirit, with a twofold allusion to the purifying and destroying energy of fire, or rather to its purifying by destroying, purging the whole by the destruction of a part, and thereby manifesting the divine *justice* as an active principle. This verse contains a previous condition of the promise in v. 3, which could not be fulfilled until the church was purged from the pollution brought upon it by the sins of those luxurious women and of the people generally, a work which could be effected only by the convincing and avenging influences of the Holy Spirit. The word *spirit* cannot be regarded as pleonastic

or simply emphatic without affording license to a like interpretation in all other cases. It has been variously explained here as meaning *breath*, *word*, and *power* or *influence*. But since this is the term used in the New Testament to designate that person of the Godhead, whom the Scriptures uniformly represent as the executor of the divine purposes, and since this sense is perfectly appropriate here, the safest and most satisfactory interpretation is that which understands by it a personal spirit.

5. *And Jehovah will create* (implying the exercise of almighty power and the production of a new effect) *over the whole extent* (literally, *place* or *space*) *of Mount Zion* (in its widest and most spiritual sense, as appears from what follows), *and over her assemblies, a cloud by day and smoke* (i. e. a cloud of smoke), *and the brightness of a flaming fire by night; for over all the glory* (previously promised, there shall be) *a covering* (or shelter). The church is not only to be purified by God's judgments, but glorified by his manifested presence, and in that state of glory kept secure by his protection. The presence of God is here denoted by the ancient symbol of a fiery cloud, and is promised to the church in its whole extent and to its several assemblies, as distinguished from the one indivisible congregation, and its one exclusive place of meeting, under the old economy. The two appearances described in this verse are those presented by a fire at different times, a smoke by day and a flame by night. Some regard this as the statement of a general fact, 'over every thing glorious there is protection,' i. e. men are accustomed to protect what they value highly; but the great majority of writers understand it as a prophecy or promise.

6. *And there shall be a shelter* (properly a booth or covert of leaves and branches, to serve) *for a shadow by day* (as a protection) *from heat, and for a covert and for a hiding-place from storm*

and from rain. The promise of refuge and protection is repeated or continued under the figure of a shelter from heat and rain, natural emblems for distress and danger.

CHAPTER V.

This chapter contains a description of the prevalent iniquities of Judah, and of the judgments which, in consequence of these, had been or were to be inflicted on the people. The form of the prophecy is peculiar, consisting of a parable and a commentary on it.

The Prophet first delivers his whole message in a parabolic form, vs. 1–7. He then explains and amplifies it at great length, vs. 8–30.

The parable sets forth the peculiar privileges, obligations, guilt, and doom of Israel, under the figure of a highly favoured vineyard which, instead of good fruit, brings forth only wild grapes, and is therefore given up to desolation, vs. 1–6. The application is expressly made by the Prophet himself, v. 7.

In the remainder of the chapter, he enumerates the sins which were included in the general expressions of v. 7, and describes their punishment. In doing this, he first gives a catalogue of sins with their appropriate punishments annexed, vs. 8–24. He then describes the means used to inflict them, and the final issue, vs. 25–30.

In its general design and subject, this prophecy resembles those which go before it; but it differs remarkably from both in holding up to view exclusively the dark side of the picture, the guilt and doom of the ungodly Jews, without the cheering contrast of purgation and deliverance to be experienced from the same events by the true Israel, the Church of God.

This chapter, like the first, is applicable not to one event exclusively, but to a sequence of events which was repeated more than once, although its terms were never fully realized until the closing period of the Jewish history, after the true Messiah was rejected, when one ray of hope was quenched after another, until all grew dark for ever in the skies of Israel.

1. The parable is given in vs. 1–6, and applied in v. 7. It is introduced in such a manner as to secure a favourable hearing from those whose conduct it condemns, and in some measure to conceal its drift until the application. The Prophet proposes to sing a song, i. e. to utter a rhythmical and figurative narrative, relating to a friend of his, his friend's own song indeed about his vineyard. In the last clause he describes the situation of the vineyard, its favourable exposure and productive soil. I *will sing, if you please* (or let me sing, I pray you), *of my friend* (i. e. concerning him), *my friend's song of his vineyard* (i. e. concerning it). *My friend had a vineyard in a hill of great fertility* (literally, *in a horn, a son of fatness*, according to the oriental idiom which applies the terms of human kindred to relations of every kind). The common version, *now will I sing*, seems to take *now* as an adverb of time, whereas it is a particle of entreaty, used to soften the expression of a purpose, and to give a tone of mildness and courtesy to the address. *Sing* and *song* are used, as with us, in reference to poetry, without implying actual musical performance. The Prophet must be understood as speaking of a human friend, until he explains himself. *Horn* is here used, as in various other languages, for the sharp peak of a mountain, or, as in Arabic, for a detached hill. The preposition does not properly mean *on* but *in*, implying that the vineyard only occupied a part, and that this was not the summit, but the acclivity exposed to the sun, which is the best situation for a vineyard.

2. Not only was the vineyard favourably situated, but assiduously tilled, protected from intrusion, and provided with every thing that seemed to be needed to secure an abundant vintage. *And he digged it up, and gathered out the stones thereof, and planted it with Sorek*, mentioned elsewhere (Jer. 2:21) as the choicest kind of vine, which either gave or owed its name to the valley of Sorek (Judg. 16:4), *and built a tower in the midst of it*, partly for protection from men and beasts, and partly for the pleasure and convenience of the owner, *and also a wine-vat*, to receive the juice from the wine-press immediately above, *he hewed in it*, i. e. in a rock (or *hewed* may be simply used for *excavated* in the ground, a common situation in hot countries for the *lacus*, reservoir, or wine-vat), *and he waited for it*, i. e. he allowed it time, *to make*, (produce, bear, bring forth,) *grapes, and it produced wild grapes.*

3. Having described the advantageous situation, soil, and culture of the vineyard, and its failure to produce good fruit, he submits the case to the decision of his hearers. *And now*, not merely in a temporal but a logical sense, 'this being the case,' *oh inhabitant of Jerusalem and man of Judah*, the singular form adding greatly to the individuality and life of the expression, *judge I pray you*, pray decide or act as arbiters, *between me and my vineyard.* The people are here called upon to judge between a stranger and his vineyard, simply as such, unaware that they are thereby passing judgment on themselves. The meaning and design of the appeal are perfectly illustrated by that which Christ makes (Matt. 21 : 40) in a parable analogous to this and founded on it. There as here the audience are called upon to judge in a case which they regard as foreign to their own, if not fictitious, and it is only after their decision that they are made to see its bearing on themselves. So too in Nathan's parable to David (2 Sam. 12 : 1), it was not till "David's anger was greatly kindled against the man," i. e. the stranger of

whom he understood the Prophet to be speaking, that "Nathan said to David, Thou art the man." A disregard of these analogies impairs both the moral force and the poetical unity and beauty of the apologue. The same thing may be said of the attempt to put a specific figurative sense on each part of the parable, the wall, the tower, the hedge, etc., which is not more reasonable here than it would be in explaining Esop's fables. The parable, as a whole, corresponds to its subject as a whole, but all the particulars included in the one are not separately intended to denote particulars included in the other. A lion may be a striking emblem of a hero, but it does not follow that the mane, claws, etc. of the beast must all be significant of something in the man. Nay, they cannot even be supposed to be so, without sensibly detracting from the force and beauty of the image as a whole.

4. This verse shows that the parable is not yet complete, and that its application would be premature. Having called upon the Jews to act as umpires, he now submits a specific question for their arbitration. *What to do more* (i. e. what more is there to be done) *to my vineyard and I have not* (or in the English idiom, *that I have not*) *done in it* (not only *to* or *for* but *in it*, with reference to the place as well as the object of the action)? *Why did I wait for it to bear grapes and it bore wild grapes?* Some supply *was* instead of *is* in the first clause, *what was there to do more*, i. e. what more was there to be done, or was I bound to do? But this, though grammatically unexceptionable, does not agree so well with the connection between this verse and the next, as a question and answer. Still less exact is the English Version, *what more could have been done?* The question whether God had done all that he could do for the Jews, when the Scriptures were still incomplete and Christ had not yet come, however easy of solution, is a question here irrelevant, because it has relation not to something in the text but to

something supplied by the interpreter, and that not only without necessity but in violation of the context; for the next verse is not an answer to the question what God *could have done* but what he *shall* or *will do.*

5. He now proceeds to answer his own question, in a tone of pungent irony, almost amounting to a sarcasm. The reply which might naturally have been looked for was a statement of some new care, some neglected precaution, some untried mode of culture; but instead of this he threatens to destroy the vineyard, as the only expedient remaining. The rhetorical effect of this sudden turn in the discourse is heightened by the very form of the last clause, in which the simple future, as the natural expression of a purpose, is exchanged for the infinitive, denoting the bare action without specification of person, time, or number. *And now* (since you cannot tell) *I will let you know if you please* (or let me tell you) *what I am doing to my vineyard* (i. e. according to the idiomatic use of the participle, *what I am about to do*, suggesting the idea of a proximate futurity), *remove its hedge and it shall become a pasture* (literally, *a consuming*, but with special reference to cattle), *break down its wall, and it shall become a trampling-place* (i. e. it shall be overrun and trampled down). *Remove* and *break* are not imperatives but infinitives, equivalent in meaning to *I will remove and break*, but more concise and rapid in expression.

6. To the threatening of exposure he now adds that of desolation arising from neglect of culture, while the last clause contains a beautiful though almost imperceptible transition from the apologue to the reality. By adding to the other threats, which any human vine-dresser might have reasonably uttered, one which only God could execute, the parable at one stroke is brought to a conclusion, and the mind prepared for the ensuing application. *And I place it* (render it) *a desolation. It shall*

not be pruned, and it shall not be dressed, and there shall come up thorns and briers. And I will lay my commands upon the clouds from raining rain upon it, i. e. that they rain no rain upon it. The addition of the noun *rain* is emphatic and equivalent to *any rain at all.* The English Version *lay waste* is perhaps toc strong for the original expression, which rather signifies the letting it run to waste by mere exposure and neglect. *To command from* or *away from* is to deter from any act by a command, in other words to *forbid* or to *command not* to do the thing in question. In this sense only can the preposition *from* be said to have a negative meaning.

7. The startling menace at the close of the sixth verse would naturally prompt the question, Who is this that assumes power over clouds and rain, and what is the vineyard which he thus denounces? To this tacit question we have here the answer. As if he had said, do not wonder that the owner of the vineyard should thus speak, *for the vineyard of Jehovah of Hosts is the House of Israel,* the church, considered as a whole, *and the man of Judah is the plant of his pleasures,* or his favourite plant. *And he waited for judgment,* practical justice, as in ch. 1 : 17, *and behold bloodshed, for righteousness and behold a cry,* either outcry and disturbance, or more specifically the cry of the oppressed, which last is more agreeable to usage, and at the same time more poetical and graphic.

8. Here begins a detailed specification of the sins included in the general expressions of v. 7. We have first two woes pronounced against as many sins, each followed by a threatening of appropriate punishment, and a general threatening which applies to both, vs. 8–17. The first sin thus denounced is that of ambitious and avaricious grasping after property in opposition not merely to the peculiar institutions of the law, but to the fundamental principles of morals, connected as it always is with

a neglect of charitable duties and a willingness to sacrifice the good of others. The verse before us may be understood, however, as descriptive rather of the tendency and aim of this ambitious grasping, than of its actual effects. *Woe to the joiners of house with house*, or those making house touch house, *field to field they bring together*, literally, cause them to approach, *even to a failure* (or *defect*) *of place*, i. e. until there is no room left, *and ye*, by a sudden apostrophe addressing those of whom he had been speaking, *are made* (or *left*) *to dwell by yourselves in the midst of the land*, owning all from the centre to the circumference, or simply *within its bounds*, within it.

9. The inordinate desire of lands and houses shall be punished by the loss of them, vs. 9, 10. And first, he threatens that the valuable houses which they coveted, and gained by fraud or violence, shall one day be left empty, an event implying the death, captivity, or degradation of their owners. *In my ears Jehovah of Hosts* is saying, as if his voice were still ringing in the Prophet's ears, *of a truth* (literally, *if not*, being part of an old formula of swearing, 'may it be so and so if' etc. ; so that the negative form conveys the strongest affirmation, *surely*, *certainly*) *many houses shall become a desolation*, *great and good* (*houses*), *for want of an inhabitant.*

10. As the sin related both to lands and houses, so both are mentioned in denouncing punishment. The desolation of the houses was in fact to arise from the unproductiveness of the lands. Ruinous failure of crops and a near approach to absolute sterility are threatened as a condign punishment of those who added field to field and house to house. The meaning of this verse depends, not on the absolute value of the measures mentioned, but on their proportions. The last clause threatens that the seed sown, instead of being multiplied, should be reduced nine tenths; and a similar idea is no doubt expressed

by the analogous terms of the preceding clause. *For ten acres of vineyard shall make* (produce) *one bath*, a liquid measure here put for a very small quantity of wine to be yielded by so large a quantity of land, *and the seed of a homer*, i. e. seed to the amount of a homer, or in our idiom, *a homer of seed, shall produce an ephah*, a dry measure equal to the liquid *bath*, and constituting one tenth of a *homer*, as we learn from Ezek. 45 : 11–14.

11. The second woe is uttered against drunkenness and heartless dissipation, with its usual accompaniment of inattention to God's providential dealings, and is connected with captivity, hunger, thirst, and general mortality, as its appropriate punishment, vs. 11–14. The description of the sin is contained in vs. 11, 12, and first that of drunkenness, considered not as an occasional excess, but as a daily business, diligently prosecuted with a devotion such as would ensure success in any laudable or lawful occupation. *Woe to those rising early in the morning to pursue strong drink* (literally, *strong drink they pursue*), *delaying in the twilight* (until) *wine inflames them.* The idea of *continuing till night* is rather implied than expressed. The allusion is not so much to the disgracefulness of drinking in the morning as to their spending day and night in drinking, rising early and sitting up late. *Strong drink* differs from *wine* only by including all intoxicating liquors, and is here used simply as a parallel expression.

12. This verse completes the picture begun in v. 11, by adding riotous mirth to drunkenness. To express this idea, music is joined with wine as the source of their social enjoyment; but the last clause shows that it is not mere gaiety, nor even the excess of it, that is here intended to be prominently set forth, but the folly and wickedness of merriment at certain times and under certain circumstances, especially amidst impending

judgments. The general idea of music is expressed by naming several instruments belonging to the three great classes, stringed, wind, and pulsatile. The precise form and use of each cannot be ascertained, and is of no importance to the meaning of the sentence. *And the harp and the viol, the tabret* (tambourine or small drum) *and the pipe* (or flute), *and wine* (compose) *their feasts; and the work of Jehovah they will not look at* (or regard), *and the operation of his hands they have not seen*, and do not see. The *work of Jehovah* here meant is not that of creation but his dealings with the people in the way of judgment. Compare ch. 10: 12. 22: 11. 28 : 21. Hab. 1 : 5. 3 : 2. Ps. 64 : 9, and especially Ps. 28 : 5, from which the expressions there used seem to be taken.

13. Here again the sin is directly followed by its condign punishment, drunkenness and disregard of providential warnings, by captivity, hunger, thirst, and general mortality, vs. 13, 14. But instead of the language of direct prediction (as in vs. 9, 10) the Prophet here employs that of description. *Therefore* (for the reasons given in the two preceding verses) *my people has gone into exile* (or captivity) *for want of knowledge* (a wilful ignorance of God's providential work and operation), *and their glory* (literally *his*, referring to the singular noun people) *are men of hunger* (i. e. famished), *and their multitude dry* (parched) *with thirst.*

14. As the effect of the preceding judgments, the Prophet now describes a general mortality, under the figure of the grave, as a ravenous monster, gaping to devour the thoughtless revellers. Here, as in v. 13, he seems to be speaking of events already past. *Therefore* (because famine and captivity have thus prevailed) *the grave has enlarged herself and opened her mouth without measure, and down goes her pomp and her noise and her crowd and he that rejoices in her.* The sense of the term

grave here corresponds almost exactly to the poetical use of *grave* in English, as denoting one great receptacle, to which the grave of individuals may be conceived as inlets. It is thus that we speak of a voice from the grave, without referring to the burial-place of any individual. The idea of a place of torment, which is included in their present meaning, is derived from the peculiar use of ᾅδης in the book of Revelation, and belongs to the Hebrew word only by implication and in certain connections.

15. To the description of the punishment the Prophet now adds that of its design and ultimate effect, to wit, the humiliation of man and the exaltation of God, vs. 15, 16. The former is here foretold in terms almost identical with those of ch. 2:9. *And man is brought low and man is cast down and the eyes of the lofty* (or haughty) *are cast down.* "Let a man be ever so high, death will bring him low; ever so mean, death will bring him lower." (Matthew Henry.)

16. The same events which humble man exalt God, not by contrast, but by the positive exhibition of his attributes. *And Jehovah of Hosts is exalted in judgment* (in the exercise of justice), *and the Mighty, the Holy One, is sanctified*) shown to be a Holy God) *in righteousness. In judgment* and *in righteousness* are used precisely in the same sense, ch. 1:27.

17. Having paused, as it were, to show the ultimate effect of these judgments, he now completes the description of the judgments themselves, by predicting the conversion of the lands possessed by the ungodly Jews, into a vast pasture-ground, occupied only by the flocks of wandering shepherds from the neighbouring deserts. *And lambs shall feed as* (*in*) *their pasture, and the wastes of the fat ones shall sojourners* (temporary occupants) *devour.*

18. The series of woes is now resumed and continued without any interruption, vs. 18–23. Even the description of the punishment, instead of being added directly to that of the sin, as in vs. 9 and 13, is postponed until the catalogue of sins is closed, and then subjoined in a general form, v. 24. This verse contains the third woe, having reference to presumptuous sinners who defy God's judgments. They are here represented not as drawn away by sin (James 1 : 14), but as laboriously drawing it to them by soliciting temptation, drawing it out by obstinate persistency in evil and contempt of divine threatenings. *Woe to the drawers of iniquity* (those drawing, those who draw it) *with cords of vanity, and sin* (a parallel expression to iniquity) as (or *as with*) *a cart-rope*, i. e. a strong rope, implying difficulty and exertion. *Vanity* may be taken in the sense of falsehood or sophistical reasoning by which men persuade themselves to sin. The true interpretation of the verse supposes the act described to be that of laboriously drawing sin to one's self perhaps with the accessory idea of drawing it out by perseverance.

19. The degree of their presumption and depravity is now evinced by a citation of their language with respect to God's threatened judgments, an ironical expression of impatience to behold them, and an implied refusal to believe without experience. The sentence is continued from the verse preceding, and further describes the sinners there denounced, as *the ones saying* (those who say), *let him speed, let him hasten his work* (his providential work, as in v. 12), *that we may see, and let the counsel* (providential plan or purpose) *of the Holy One of Israel* (which, in the mouth of these blasphemers, seems to be a taunting irony) *draw nigh and come, and we will know* (i. e. according to the Hebrew idiom and the parallel expression) *that we may know* what it is, or that it is a real purpose, and that he is able

to accomplish it. (Compare Jer. 17 : 15. Amos 5 : 18. 6 : 13. Isai. 30 : 10, 11. 28 : 15. 2 Peter 3 : 4.)

20. The fourth woe is against those who subvert moral distinctions and confound good and evil, an idea expressed first in literal terms and then by two obvious and intelligible figures. *Woe unto the* (persons) *saying* (those who say) *to evil good and to good evil* (who address them by these titles or call them so), *putting darkness for light and light for darkness, putting bitter for sweet and sweet for bitter.* These are here combined, not merely as natural opposites, but also as common figures for truth and falsehood, right and wrong. See ch. 2 : 5. Prov. 2 : 13. Ec. 2 : 13. James 3 : 11.

21. Here, as in the foregoing verse, one sin follows another without any intervening description of punishment. This arrangement may imply a very intimate connection between the sins thus brought into juxtaposition. As presumptuous sin, such as vs. 18, 19 describe, implies a perversion of the moral sense, such as v. 20 describes, so the latter may be said to presuppose an undue reliance upon human reason, which is elsewhere contrasted with the fear of God (Prov. 3 : 7), and is indeed incompatible with it. *Woe unto the wise in their eyes* (i. e. their own eyes, which cannot be otherwise expressed in Hebrew) *and before their own faces* (in their own sight or estimation) *prudent*, intelligent, a synonyme of *wise.* The sin reproved, as Calvin well observes, is not mere frivolous self-conceit, but that delusive estimate of human wisdom which may coexist with modesty of manners and a high degree of real intellectual merit, but which must be abjured, not only on account of its effects, but also as involving the worst form of pride.

22. The sixth woe, like the second, is directed against drunk-

ards, but with special reference to drunken judges, vs. 22, 23. The tone of this verse is sarcastic, from its using terms which commonly express not only strength but courage and heroic spirit, in application to exploits of drunkenness. There may indeed be a particular allusion to a species of fool-hardiness and brutal ambition not uncommon in our own times, leading men to show the vigour of their frames by mad excess, and to seek eminence in this way no less eagerly than superior spirits seek true glory. Of such it may indeed be said, their god is their belly and they glory in their shame. *Woe to the mighty men* or *heroes* (who are heroes only) *to drink wine, and men of strength to mingle strong drink*, i. e. according to the usual interpretation, to mix wine with spices, thereby making it more stimulating and exciting, a practice spoken of by Pliny and other ancient writers. Some understand the Prophet as referring to the mixture of wine with water. In either case the mixing is here mentioned only as a customary act in the offering or drinking of liquors, just as *making tea* might be mentioned as a common act of modern hospitality, whatever part of the preparatory process the phrase may properly denote.

23. The absence of the interjection shows that this is a continuation of the woe begun in the preceding verse, and thus explains the Prophet's recurrence to a sin which he had denounced already (vs. 11, 12) as productive of general inconsideration, but which he now describes as leading to injustice, and therefore as a vice peculiarly disgraceful in a magistrate. The effect here ascribed to drunkenness is not merely that of incapacitating judges for the discharge of their official functions, but that of tempting them to make a trade of justice, with a view to the indulgence of this appetite. *Justifying* (i. e. acquitting, clearing, a forensic term) *the guilty* (not simply the wicked in a general sense, but the wrong-doer in a judicial sense) *for the sake* (literally *as the result*) *of a bribe, and the*

righteousness of the righteous (i. e. the *right* of the innocent or injured party, or his *character* as such) *they will take from him* (i. e. they do and will do so still).

24. To the series of sins enumerated in the six preceding verses there is now added a general description of their punishment. In the first clause, the Prophet represents the divine visitation, with its sudden, rapid, irresistible effect, by the familiar figure of chaff and dry grass sinking in the flames. In the second clause he passes from simile to metaphor, and speaks of the people as a tree whose root is rotten and its growth above ground pulverized. In the third, he drops both figures, and in literal expressions summarily states the cause of their destruction. *Therefore* (because of the abounding of these sins) *as a tongue of fire* (i. e. a flame, so called from its shape and motion, Acts 2: 3. 1 Kings 18 : 38) *devours chaff* (or stubble), *and as ignited grass falls away, their roots shall be as rottenness, and their blossom as fine dust shall go up* (i. e. be taken up and scattered by the wind). *For they have rejected the law of Jehovah of Hosts, and the word* (the revealed will) *of the Holy One of Israel they have treated with contempt.*

25. Having declared in the foregoing verse what should be, he recalls to mind what has already been. As if he had said, God will visit you for these things ; nay, he has done so already, but without reclaiming you or satisfying his own justice, for which purpose further strokes are still required. The previous inflictions here referred to are described as a stroke from Jehovah's outstretched hand, so violent as to shake the mountains, and so destructive as to fill the streets with corpses. *Therefore* (referring to the last clause of v. 24) *the anger of Jehovah has burned against his people* (literally *in them*, i. e. in the very midst of them as a consuming fire), *and he stretched forth his hand against them* (literally *him*, referring to the singular noun *people*)

and smote them, and the mountains trembled, and their carcass (put collectively for corpses) *was like sweeping* (refuse, filth) *in the midst of the streets. In all this* (i. e. even after all this, or notwithstanding all this) *his anger has not turned back* (abandoned its object, or regarded it as already gained), *and still his hand is stretched out* (to inflict new judgments). It is not necessary to suppose, although it is most probable, that what is here described had actually taken place before the Prophet wrote. In this, as in some other cases, he may be supposed to take his stand between a nearer and a more remote futurity, the former being then of course described as past.—The trembling of the mountains is referred by some to the earthquake mentioned Amos 1 : 1. Zech. 14 : 5. It is most probable, however, that these strong expressions were intended simply to convey the idea of violent commotion and a general mortality. There is no need of referring what is said exclusively to evils suffered in the days of Joash and Amaziah or in those of Ahaz, since the Prophet evidently means to say that *all preceding judgments* had been insufficient and that more were still required.

26. The former stroke having been insufficient, a more effectual one is now impending, in predicting which the Prophet does not confine himself to figurative language, but presents the approaching judgment in its proper form, as the invasion and ultimate subjection of the country by a formidable enemy, vs. 26–30. In this verse he describes the approach of these invaders as invited by Jehovah, to express which idea he employs two figures not uncommon in prophecy, that of a signal-pole or flag, and that of a hiss or whistle, in obedience to which the last clause represents the enemy as rapidly advancing. *And he raises a signal to the nations from afar, and hisses* (or whistles) *for him from the ends of the earth; and behold in haste, swift, he shall come.* The essential idea is that the previous lighter judg-

ments should be followed by another more severe and efficacious, by invasion and subjection. The terms are most emphatically applicable to the Romans.—The hissing or whistling, probably alludes to the ancient mode of swarming bees, described at length by Cyril. In the last clause a substantive meaning *haste*, and an adjective meaning *light*, are both used adverbially in the sense of *swiftly*.

27. The enemy whose approach was just foretold, is now described as not only prompt and rapid, but complete in his equipments, firm and vigorous, ever wakeful, impeded neither by the accidents of the way nor by defective preparation. *There is no one faint* (or exhausted) *and there is no one stumbling* (or faltering) *among them* (literally *in him*). *He* (the enemy, considered as an individual) *sleeps not, and he slumbers not, and the girdle of his loins is not opened* (or loosed), *and the latchet* (string or band) *of his shoes* (or *sandals*) *is not broken*. It is most probable that this last clause relates to accidental interruptions of the march.

28. The description is continued, but with special reference to their weapons and their means of conveyance. For the former, bows and arrows are here put; and for the latter, horses and chariots (see ch. 2:7). *Whose arrows are sharpened and all his bows bent* (literally trod upon); *the hoofs of his horses like flint* (or adamant) *are reckoned, and his wheels like a whirlwind*, in rapidity and violence of motion. From what is said of the bows immediately afterwards, the prominent idea would seem to be not that the arrows were *sharp*, but that they were already *sharpened*, implying present readiness for use.—The bows being *trod upon* has reference to the ancient mode of stringing, or rather of shooting, the bow being large and made of metal or hard wood. Arrian says expressly, in describing the use of the bow by the Indian infantry, "placing it on the

ground, and stepping on it with the left foot, so they shoot, drawing the string back to a great distance."

29. By a sudden transition, the enemy are here represented as lions, roaring, growling, seizing their prey, and carrying it off without resistance; a lively picture, especially to an oriental reader, of the boldness, fierceness, quickness, and success of the attack here threatened. *He has a roar like the lioness, and he shall roar like the young lions, and shall growl, and seize the prey, and secure it, none delivering* (i. e. and none can rescue it).

30. The roaring of the lion suggests the roaring of the sea, and thus a beautiful transition is effected from the one figure to the other, in describing the catastrophe of all these judgments. Israel is threatened by a raging sea, and looking landward sees it growing dark there, until, after a brief fluctuation, the darkness becomes total. *And he* (the enemy) *shall roar against him* (Israel) *in that day like the roaring of a sea. And he shall look to the land, and behold darkness! Anguish and light! It is dark in the clouds thereof* (i. e. of the land, the skies above it).—The Prophet speaks of the vast multitude that was coming up, as a *sea.* On that side there was no safety. It was natural to speak of the other direction as the *land* or shore, and to say that the people would look there for safety. But, says he, there would be no safety there; all would be darkness."

CHAPTER VI.

This chapter contains a vision and a prophecy of awful import. At an early period of his ministry, the Prophet sees the Lord enthroned in the temple and adored by the Seraphim, at whose voice the house is shaken, and the Prophet, smitten with a sense of his own corruption and unworthiness to speak for God or praise him, is relieved by the application of fire from the altar to his lips, and an assurance of forgiveness, after which, in answer to the voice of God inquiring for a messenger, he offers himself and is accepted, but with an assurance that his labours will tend only to aggravate the guilt and condemnation of the people, who are threatened with judicial blindness, and, as its necessary consequence, removal from the desolated country; and the prophecy closes with a promise and a threatening both in one, to wit, that the remnant which survives the threatened judgments shall experience a repetition of the stroke, but that a remnant after all shall continue to exist and to experience God's mercy.

The chapter naturally falls into two parts, the vision, vs. 1–8, and the message or prediction, vs. 9–13. The precise relation between these two parts has been a subject of dispute. The question is, whether the vision is an introduction to the message, or the message an appendage to the vision. Those who take the former view suppose that in order to prepare the Prophet for a discouraging and painful revelation, he was favoured with a new view of the divine majesty and of his own unworthiness, relieved by an assurance of forgiveness, and encouraged by a special designation to the self-denying work which was before him. Those who assume the other ground proceed upon the supposition, that the chapter contains an account of the Prophet's original induction into office, and that the message at the close was added to prepare him for its disappointments, or perhaps to try his faith.

But the chapter contains nothing which would not have been appropriate at any period of that ministry, and some of its expressions seem to favour, if they do not require, the hypothesis of previous experience in the office. The idea of so solemn an *inauguration* is affecting and impressive, but seems hardly sufficient to outweigh the presumption arising from the order of the prophecies in favour of the other supposition, which requires no facts to be assumed without authority, and although less striking, is at least as safe.

1. *In the year that king Uzziah died* (B. C. 758), *I saw the Lord sitting on a throne high and lifted up, and his skirts* (the train of his royal robe) *filling the palace*, or, taking the last word in its more specific sense, *the temple*, so called as being the palace of the great King. "No man hath seen God at any time" (John 1 : 18), and God himself hath said, "There shall no man see me and live" (Ex. 33 : 20). Yet we read not only that "the pure in heart shall see God" (Matt. 5 : 8), but that Jacob said, "I have seen God face to face" (Gen. 32 : 30). It is therefore plain that the phrase to "see God" is employed in different senses, and that although his essence is and must be invisible, he may be seen in the manifestation of his glory or in human form. It has been a general opinion in all ages of the church, that in every such manifestation it was God the Son who thus revealed himself. In John 12 : 41, it is said to have been Christ's glory that Isaiah saw and spoke of, while Paul cites vs. 9 and 10 (Acts 28 : 25, 26) as the language of the Holy Ghost. It seems needless to inquire whether the Prophet saw this sight with his bodily eyes, or in a dream, or in an ecstasy, since the effect upon his own mind must have been the same in either case. The scene of the vision is evidently taken from the temple at Jerusalem, but not confined to its exact dimensions and arrangements. It has been disputed whether what is here recorded took place before or after the death of Uzziah. Those who regard this as the first of Isaiah's prophecies are forced to assume that it belongs to the reign of Uzziah. It is also urged in favour of this opinion, that the time after his death would have been described as the first year of Jotham. The design, however, may have been to fix, not the

reign in which he saw the vision, but the nearest remarkable event. Besides, *the first year of Jotham* would have been ambiguous, because his reign is reckoned from two different epochs, the natural death of his father, and his civil death, when smitten with the leprosy, after which he resided in a separate house, and the government was administered by Jotham as prince-regent, who was therefore virtually king before he was such formally, and is accordingly described in the very same context as having reigned sixteen and twenty years (2 Kings 15 : 30, 33).

2. He sees the Lord not only enthroned but attended by his ministers. *Seraphim*, burning spirits, *standing above it*, the throne, or *above him* that sat upon it. *Six wings, six wings, to one*, i. e. to each. *With two he covers his face*, as a sign of reverence towards God, *and with two he covers his feet*, for the same purpose, or to conceal himself from mortal view, *and with two he flies*, to execute God's will. The Hebrew word *seraphim* means *angels of fire*, the name being descriptive either of their essence, or of their ardent love, or of God's wrath which they execute. The word occurs elsewhere only as the name of the *fiery serpents* of the wilderness (Num. 21 : 6, 8 : Deut. 8 : 15), described by Isaiah (14 : 29. 30 : 6) as *flying serpents*. The transfer of the name to beings so dissimilar rests on their possession of two common attributes. Both are described as *winged* and both as *burning*.—*Standing* does not imply necessarily that they rested on the earth or any other solid surface, but that they were stationary, even in the air. This will remove all objection to the version *above him*, which may also be explained as describing the relative position of persons in a standing and sitting posture. There is no need therefore of the rendering *above it*, which is given in our Bible. The covering of the feet may, according to oriental usage, be regarded as a reverential act. equivalent in import to the hiding of the face.

3. He now describes the seraphim as praising God in an alternate or responsive doxology. *And this cried to this*, i. e. one to another, *and said*, *Holy*, *Holy*, *Holy* (*is*) *Jehovah of Hosts*, *the fulness of the whole earth*, that which fills the whole earth, *is his glory !*—It was commonly agreed among the Fathers, that only two seraphim are mentioned here. It cannot be proved, however, from the words *this to this*, which are elsewhere used in reference to a greater number. (See Ex. 14 : 20.) The allusion to the trinity in this is the more probable because different parts of the chapter are referred in the New Testament to the three persons of the Godhead. *Holy* is here understood by most interpreters as simply denoting moral purity, which is certainly the prominent idea. Most probably, however, it denotes the whole divine perfection, that which *separates* or distinguishes between God and his creatures. "I am God and not man, the Holy One in the midst of thee." Hos. 11 : 9.

4. *Then stirred*, or shook, *the bases of the thresholds at the voice that cried*, or *at the voice of the one crying*, *and the house is filled with smoke*. The effect of this doxology, and of the whole supernatural appearance, is described. The door may be particularly spoken of, because the Prophet was looking through it from the court without into the interior. The participle *crying* may agree with *voice* directly or with *seraph* understood. By *smoke* some understand a cloud or vapour showing the presence of Jehovah. Most interpreters, however, understand it in its proper sense of *smoke*, as the natural attendant of the fire which blazed about the throne of God, or of that which burned upon the altar, as in Lev. 16 : 13 the mercy-seat is said to be covered with a "cloud of incense." In either case it was intended to produce a solemn awe in the beholder.

5. *And I said*, when I saw and heard these things, then I said, *Woe is me*, woe to me, or alas for me, a phrase expressing

lamentation and alarm, *for I am undone*, or destroyed, *for a man impure of lips*, as to the lips, *am I, and in the midst of a people impure of lips*, of impure lips; *I am dwelling*, and am therefore undone, *for the King, Jehovah of Hosts, my eyes have seen.* The allusion is not merely to the ancient and prevalent belief that no one could see God and live (Gen. 32 : 30. Ex. 4 : 10, 11. 33 : 20. Judg. 6 : 22–24. 13 : 22), but to the aggravation of the danger arising from the moral contrast between God and the beholder. The Prophet describes himself as filled with awe, not only by the presence of Jehovah, but also by a deep impression of his own sinfulness, especially considered as unfitting him to praise God, or to be his messenger, and therefore represented as residing in the organs of speech. The lips are mentioned as the seat of his depravity, because its particular effect, then present to his mind, was incapacity to speak for God or in his praise. That it does not refer to official unfaithfulness in his prophetic office, is apparent from the application of the same words to the people. The preterite form of the verb implies that the deed was already done and the effect already certain.

6. *And there flew* (or then flew) *to me one of the seraphim, and in his hand a live coal* (or a hot stone) *; with tongs he took* (*it*) *from off* (or *from upon*) *the altar.* All that is necessary to the understanding of the vision is, that the scene presented was a temple and included an altar. The precise position of the altar or of the Prophet is not only unimportant, but forms no part of the picture as here set before us. He now proceeds to describe the way in which he was relieved from this distress by a symbolical assurance of forgiveness. The word translated *tongs* is elsewhere used to signify the *snuffers* of the golden candlestick, and tongs are not named among the furniture of the altar; but such an implement seems to be indispensable, and

the Hebrew word may be applied to any thing in the nature of a forceps.

7. *And he caused it to touch* (i. e. laid it on) *my mouth, and said, Lo, this hath touched thy lips, and thy iniquity is gone, and thy sin shall be atoned for* (or forgiven). The mention of the altar and the assurance of forgiveness, or rather of atonement, makes it natural to take the application of fire as a symbol of expiation by sacrifice. The fire is applied to the lips for a two-fold reason: first, to show that the particular impediment of which the Prophet had complained was done away; and secondly, to show that the gift of inspiration is included, though it does not constitute the sole or chief meaning of the symbol. The gift of prophecy could scarcely be described as having taken away sin, although it might naturally accompany the work of expiation. The preterite and future forms are here combined, perhaps to intimate, first, that the pardon was already granted, and then that it should still continue. This, at least, seems better than arbitrarily to confound the two as presents.

8. *And I heard the voice of the Lord saying, Whom shall I send, and who will go for us? And I said, Here am I* (literally, *behold me*, or, *lo I* am), *send me.* The form of expression in the first clause may imply that the speaker was now invisible, perhaps concealed by the smoke which filled the house. The assurance of forgiveness produces its usual effect of readiness to do God's will. A beautiful commentary upon this effect of pardoned sin is afforded in David's penitential prayer, Psalm 51: 12–15.

9. The Prophet now receives his commission, together with a solemn declaration that his labours will be fruitless. This prediction is clothed in the form of an exhortation or command addressed to the people themselves, for the purpose of bringing

it more palpably before them, and of aggravating their insanity and wickedness in ruining themselves after such a warning. *And he said, Go and say to this people, Hear indeed*, or hear on, *but understand not, and see indeed*, or continue to see, *but know not.* Not only is their insensibility described in the strongest terms, implying extreme folly as well as extreme guilt, but, as if to provoke them to an opposite course, they are exhorted, with a sort of solemn irony, to do the very thing which would inevitably ruin them, but with an explicit intimation of that issue in the verse ensuing. This form of speech is by no means foreign from the dialect of common life. It is as if one man should say to another in whose good resolutions and engagements he had no faith, 'Go now and do the very opposite of all that you have said.' A similar expression is employed by Christ himself when he says to the Jews (Matt. 23 : 32), *Fill ye up then the measure of your fathers.* The Septuagint version renders the imperatives as futures, and this version is twice quoted in the New Testament (Matt. 13 : 14. Acts 28 : 26), as giving correctly the essential meaning of the sentence as a prophecy, though stripped of its peculiar form as an ironical command. The idea of hearing and seeing without perceiving may have been proverbial among the Jews, as it was among the Greeks.

10. As the foregoing verse contains a prediction of the people's insensibility, but under the form of a command or exhortation to themselves, so this predicts the same event, as the result of Isaiah's labours, under the form of a command to him. *Make fat*, gross, callous, *the heart of this people*, i. e. their affections or their minds in general, *and its ears make heavy*, dull or hard of hearing, *and its eyes smear*, close or blind, *lest it see with its eyes, and with its ears hear, and its heart understand*, perceive or feel, *and it turn*, i. e. repent and be converted, *and be healed*, or literally, *and one heal it*, the indefinite construction

being equivalent in meaning to a passive. The thing predicted is judicial blindness, as the natural result and righteous retribution of the national depravity. This end would be promoted by the very preaching of the truth, and therefore a command to preach was in effect a command to blind and harden them. The act required of the Prophet is here joined with its ultimate effect, while the intervening circumstances, namely, the people's sin and the withholding of God's grace, are passed by in silence. But although not expressed, they are implied in this command. The essential idea is their insensibility, considered as the fruit of their own depravity, as the execution of God's righteous judgment, and as the only visible result of Isaiah's labours. In giving Isaiah his commission, it was natural to make the last of these ideas prominent, and hence the form of exhortation or command in which the prophecy is here presented. Make them insensible, not by an immediate act of power, nor by any direct influence whatever, but by doing your duty, which their wickedness and God's righteous judgments will allow to have no other effect. In other cases, where his personal agency no longer needed to be set forth or alluded to, the verse is quoted, not as a command, but as a description of the people, or as a declaration of God's agency in making them insensible. Thus in Matt. 13 : 15, and in Acts 28 : 26, the Septuagint version is retained, in which the people's own guilt is the prominent idea : 'for this people's heart is waxed gross, and their ears are dull of hearing, and their eyes they have closed, lest' etc. In John 12 : 40, on the other hand, the sentence takes a new form, in order to bring out distinctly the idea of *judicial* blindness : 'he hath blinded their eyes and hardened their heart, lest,' etc. Both these ideas are in fact included in the meaning of the passage, though its form is different, in order to suit the occasion upon which it was originally uttered.

11. *And I said, How long, Lord? And he said, Until that*

cities are desolate for want of an inhabitant, and houses for want of men, and the land shall be desolated, a waste, or utterly desolate. The spiritual death of the people should be followed by external desolation. The common explanation is no doubt the true one, that the Prophet asks how long the blindness of the people shall continue, and is told until it ruins them and drives them from their country. As the foregoing description is repeatedly applied in the New Testament to the Jews who were contemporary with our Saviour, the threatening must be equally extensive, and equivalent to saying that the land should be completely wasted, not at one time, but repeatedly.

12. This verse continues the answer to the Prophet's question in the verse preceding. *And* (until) *Jehovah shall have put far off* (removed to a distance) *the men* (or people of the country) *and great* (much or abundant) *shall be that which is left* (of unoccupied forsaken ground) *in the midst of the land.* This is little more than a repetition, in other words, of the declaration in the verse preceding. The terms of this verse may be applied to all the successive desolations of the country, not excepting that most extreme and remarkable of all which exists at the present moment.

13. The chapter closes with a repetition and extension of the threatening, but in such a form as to involve a promise of the highest import. While it is threatened that the stroke shall be repeated on the remnant that survives its first infliction, it is promised that there shall be such a remnant after every repetition to the last. *And yet* (even after the entire desolation which had first been mentioned) *in it* (the desolated land) (there shall remain) *a tenth* or *tithe* (here put indefinitely for a small proportion) *and* (even this tenth) *shall return and be for a consuming* (i. e. shall again be consumed, but still not utterly, for) *like the terebinth and like the oak* (the two most

common forest-trees of Palestine) *which in falling* (in their fallen state, when felled) *have substance* (or vitality) *in them* (so) *a holy seed* (shall be or is) *the substance* (vital principle) *of it* (the tenth or remnant which appeared to be destroyed). However frequently the people may seem to be destroyed, there shall still be a surviving remnant, and however frequently that very remnant may appear to perish, there shall still be a remnant of the remnant left, and this indestructible residuum shall be the holy seed, the true church (Rom. 11 : 5). This prediction was fulfilled, not once for all, but again and again; not only in the vine-dressers and husbandmen left by Nebuchadnezzar and afterwards destroyed in Egypt; not only in the remnant that survived the destruction of the city by the Romans, and increased until again destroyed by Adrian; but in the present existence of the Jews as a peculiar people, notwithstanding the temptations to amalgamate with others, notwithstanding persecutions and apparent extirpations; a fact which can only be explained by the prediction that "all Israel shall be saved" (Rom. 11 : 26). As in many former instances, throughout the history of the chosen people, under both dispensations, "even so, at this present time also, there is a remnant according to the election of grace."

CHAPTER VII.

HERE begins a series of connected prophecies (ch. VII–XII) belonging to the reign of Ahaz, and relating in general to the same great subjects, the deliverance of Judah from Syria and Israel, its subsequent subjection to Assyria and other foreign powers, the final destruction of its enemies, the advent of Messiah, and the nature of his kingdom. This series admits of different divisions, but it is commonly agreed that one distinct portion is contained in the seventh chapter.

The chapter begins with a brief historical statement of the invasion of Judah by Rezin and Pekah, and of the fear that it excited, to relieve which Isaiah is commissioned to meet Ahaz in a public place, and to assure him that there is nothing more to fear from the invading powers, that their evil design cannot be accomplished, that one of them is soon to perish, and that in the mean time both are to remain without enlargement, vs. 1–9.

Seeing the king to be incredulous, the Prophet invites him to assure himself by choosing any sign or pledge of the event, which he refuses to do, under the pretext of confidence in God, but is charged with unbelief by the Prophet, who nevertheless renews the promise of deliverance in a symbolical form, and in connection with a prophecy of the miraculous conception and nativity of Christ, both as a pledge of the event, and as a measure of the time in which it is to take place, vs. 10–16.

To this assurance of immediate deliverance, he adds a threatening of ulterior evils, to arise from the Assyrian protection which the king preferred to that of God, to wit, the loss of independence, the successive domination of foreign powers, the harassing and predatory occupation of the land by strangers, the removal of its people, the neglect of tillage, and the transformation of its choicest vineyards, fields, and gardens, into wastes or pastures, vs. 17–25.

1. Rezin, the king of Damascene Syria or Aram, from whom Uriah had taken Elath, a port on the Red Sea, and restored it to Judah (2 Kings 14 : 22), appears to have formed an alliance with Pekah, the murderer and successor of Pekahiah king of Israel (2 Kings 15 : 25), during the reign of Jotham (ib. v. 37), but to have deferred the actual invasion of Judah until that king's death and the accession of his feeble son, in the first year

of whose reign it probably took place, with most encouraging success, as the army of Ahaz was entirely destroyed and two hundred thousand persons taken captive, who were afterwards sent back at the instance of the Prophet Oded (2 Chron. 28 : 5–15). But notwithstanding this success, they were unable to effect their main design, the conquest of Jerusalem, whether repelled by the natural strength and artificial defences of the place itself, or interrupted in the siege by the actual or dreaded invasion of their own dominions by the king of Assyria (2 Kings 16 : 7–9). It seems to be at a point of time between their first successes and their final retreat, that the Prophet's narrative begins. *And it was* (happened, came to pass) *in the days of Ahaz, son of Jotham, son of Uzziah, king of Judah* (that), *Rezin king of Aram* (or Syria) *and Pekah, son of Remaliah, king of Israel, came up to* (or against) *Jerusalem, to war against it; and he was not able to war against it* (i. e. with success). The invaders are said to have *come up* to Jerusalem, not merely as a military phrase, but with allusion, more or less distinct, to all the senses in which the holy city was above all others.

2. *And it was told the house of David* (the court, the royal family, of Judah) *saying, Syria resteth* (or is resting) *upon Ephraim; and his heart* (i. e. the king's, as the chief and representative of the house of David) *and the heart of his people shook, like the shaking of the trees of a wood before a wind.* This is commonly applied to the effect produced by the first news of the coalition between Rezin and Pekah or the junction of their forces. It is equally natural, and more consistent with the history, to understand the words as having reference to a later date, i. e. either the time of the advance upon Jerusalem, or that of the retreat of the invaders, laden with the spoil of Judah, and with two hundred thousand captives. In the one case, *Syria*, i. e. the Syrian army, may be said to *rest upon* (the army of) *Ephraim*, in the modern military sense, with reference to their

relative position on the field of battle; in the other, *Syria* may be described as literally *resting* or reposing in the territory of Ephraim, on its homeward march, and as thereby filling Ahaz with the apprehension of a fresh attack. Although neither of these explanations may seem altogether natural, they are really as much so as any of the others which have been proposed, and in a case where we have at best a choice of difficulties, those may claim the preference as tending to harmonize the prophecy with history as given both in Kings and Chronicles. We read in 2 Kings 16:7–9, that Ahaz applied to Tiglathpileser, king of Assyria, to help him against Syria and Israel, which he did. At what precise period of the war this alliance was formed, it is not easy to determine; but there seems to be no doubt that Ahaz, at the time here mentioned, was relying upon some human aid in preference to God.

3. From this alarm Isaiah is sent to free the king. *And Jehovah said to Isaiah son of Amoz, Go out to meet Ahaz, thou and Shearjashub thy son, to the end of the conduit of the upper pool, to the highway of the fuller's field.* The mention of these now obscure localities, although it detracts nothing from the general clearness of the passage, is an incidental proof of authenticity, which no later writer would or could have forged. The upper pool, which has been placed by different writers upon almost every side of Jerusalem, is identified by Robinson and Smith with a large tank at the head of the Valley of Hinnom, about seven hundred yards west-north-west from the Jaffa gate. It is full in the rainy season, and its waters are then conducted by a small rude aqueduct to the vicinity of the gate just mentioned, and so to the Pool of Hezekiah within the walls. This aqueduct is probably the *conduit* mentioned in the text, and the *end* of this conduit the point where it enters the city, as appears from the fact, that when Rabshakeh afterwards conferred with the ministers of Hezekiah at this same spot, he was heard by

the people on the city wall (ch. 36:2, 12). From the same passage it may be inferred that this was a frequented spot, which some suppose to be the reason that Isaiah was directed to it, while others understand the direction as implying that Ahaz was about to fortify the city, or rather to cut off a supply of water from the invaders, as Hezekiah afterwards did when besieged by Sennacherib (2 Chr. 32:4); an example often followed afterwards, particularly in the sieges of Jerusalem by Pompey, Titus, and Godfrey of Bouillon. The Prophet is therefore commanded to *go out*, not merely from his house, but from the city, *to meet Ahaz*, which does not imply that the king was seeking him, or coming to him, but merely specifies the object which he was to seek himself. The Fuller's Field was of course without the city, and the highway or causeway mentioned may have led either to it or along it, so as to divide it from the aqueduct. The command to take his son with him might be regarded merely as an incidental circumstance, but for the fact that the name *Shear-jashub* is significant, and as we may suppose it to have been already known, and the people were familiar with the practice of conveying instruction in this form, the very sight of the child would perhaps suggest a prophecy, or recall one previously uttered, or at least prepare the mind for one to come; and accordingly we find in ch. 10:21 this very phrase employed, not as a name, but in its proper sense, *a remnant shall return.*

4. The assurance, by which Ahaz is encouraged, is that the danger is over, that the fire is nearly quenched, that the enemies, who lately seemed like flaming firebrands of war, are now mere smoking ends of firebrands; he is therefore exhorted to be quiet and confide in the divine protection. *And thou shalt say to him, Be cautious and be quiet* (or take care to be quiet) *fear not, nor let thy heart be soft, before* (or on account of) *these two smoking tails of firebrands, in the heat of the anger*

of Rezin and Syria and the son of Remaliah. The comparison of Rezin and Pekah to the tails or ends of firebrands, instead of firebrands themselves, is not a mere expression of contempt, but a distinct allusion to the evil which they had already done, and which should never be repeated. If the emphasis were only in the use of the word *tails*, the tail of any thing else would have been equally appropriate. The smoking remnant of a firebrand implies a previous flame, if not a conflagration. This confirms the conclusion before drawn, that Judah had already been ravaged, and that the narratives in Kings and Chronicles are perfectly consistent and relate to the same subject.

5. *Because Syria has devised* (meditated, purposed) *evil against thee, also Ephraim and Remaliah's son, saying.* This verse and the next may be regarded as a link or connecting clause between the exhortation in v. 4 and the promise in v. 7. 'Fear not because Syria and Israel thus threaten, for on that very account the Lord declares etc.' Here again Syria appears as the prime agent and controlling power, although Ephraim is added in the second clause. The suppression of Pekah's proper name in this clause, and of Rezin's altogether in the first, has given rise to various far-fetched explanations, though it seems in fact to show, that the use of names in the whole passage is rather euphonic or rhythmical than significant.

6. The invaders themselves are now introduced as consulting or addressing one another, not at the present moment, but at the time when their plan was first concerted. *We will go up*, or let us go up, *into Judah*, or *against it*, although this is rather implied than expressed, *and vex* (i. e. harass or distress) *it, and make a breach in it* (thereby subduing it) *to ourselves, and let us make a king in the midst of it, to wit, the son of Tabeal* or *Tabeel*, as the name is written, Ezra 4 : 7. The reference to

Jerusalem is required by the history, according to which they did succeed in their attack upon the kingdom, but were foiled in their main design of conquering the royal city. The entrance into Judah was proposed only as a means to this end, and it is the failure of this end that is predicted in the next verse. The creation of tributary kings by conquerors is mentioned elsewhere in the sacred history (e. g. 2 Kings 23 : 34. 24 : 17). This familiar reference *en passant* to the names of persons now forgotten, as if familiar to contemporary readers, is a strong incidental proof of authenticity.

7. *Thus saith the Lord Jehovah, it shall not stand* (or it shall not arise) *and it shall not be* (or come to pass). The general sense is clear, viz. that their design should be defeated. The accumulation of divine names is, as usual, emphatic, and seems here intended to afford a pledge of the event, derived from the supremacy and power of the Being who predicts it.

8, 9. The plans of the enemy cannot be accomplished, because God has decreed that while the kingdoms of Syria and Israel continue to exist, they shall remain without enlargement, or at least without the addition of Jerusalem or Judah to their territories. It shall not stand or come to pass, *because the head* (or capital) *of Aram is Damascus* (and shall be so still), *and the head* (chief or sovereign) *of Damascus is Rezin* (and shall be so still; and as for the other power there is as little cause of fear) *for in yet sixty and five years* (in sixty-five years more) *shall Ephraim be broken from a people* (i. e. from being a people, so as not to be a people; and even in the mean time, it shall not be enlarged by the addition of Judah) *for the head* (or capital) *of Ephraim is Samaria, and the head* (chief or sovereign) *of Samaria is Remaliah's son. If you will not believe* (it is) *because you are not to be established.* Here again Syria is the prominent object, and Ephraim subjoined, as if by an afterthought. The order of ideas is, that Syria shall remain as it is, and as for Ephraim it is soon to be destroyed, but while it does last, it shall remain as it is likewise; Pekah shall never reign in any other capital, nor Samaria be the capital of any other kingdom. To this natural expression of the thought corresponds the rhythmical arrangement of the sentences, the first clause of the eighth verse answering exactly to the first clause of the ninth, while the two last clauses, though dissimilar, complete the measure.

> For the head of Syria is Damascus—
> And the head of Damascus Rezin—
>   And in sixty-five years more etc.
> And the head of Ephraim is Samaria—
> And the head of Samaria Remaliah's son—
>   If ye will not believe etc.

Whether this be poetry or not, its structure is as regular as that of any other period of equal length in the writings of Isaiah. As to the substance of these verses, the similar clauses have already been explained, as a prediction that the two invading powers should remain without enlargement. The first of the uneven clauses, i. e. the last of v. 8, adds to this prediction, that Ephraim, or the kingdom of the ten tribes, shall cease to exist within a prescribed period, which period is so defined as to include the three successive strokes by which that power was annihilated: first, the invasion of Tiglath-pileser, two or three years after the date of this prediction (2 Kings 15:29. 16.9); then, the conquest of Samaria, and the deportation of the ten tribes, by Shalmaneser, about the sixth year of Hezekiah (2 Kings 17:6); and finally, the introduction of another race by Esar-haddon in the reign of Manasseh (2 Kings 17:24. 2 Chron. 33:11. Ezra 4:2). Within sixty-five years all these events were to occur, and Ephraim, in all these senses, was to cease to be a people. It seems then that the language of this clause has been carefully selected, so as to include the three events which might be represented as destructive of Ephraim, while in form it balances the last clause of the next verse, and is therefore essential to the rhythmical completeness of the passage.

10. *And he* (i. e. God, by the mouth of Isaiah) *added to speak unto Ahaz, saying.* This, according to usage, may either mean that *he spoke again*, on a different occasion, or that *he spoke further*, on the same occasion, which last is the meaning here.

11. *Ask for thee* (i. e. for thy own satisfaction) *a sign from Jehovah thy God* (literally *from with him*, i. e. from his presence and his power)*; ask deep or high above* (*make deep thy request or make it high*), i. e. ask it either above or below. A *sign* is not necessarily a miracle, nor necessarily a prophecy, but a sensible pledge of the truth of something else, whether present, past, or future; sometimes consisting in a miracle (Ex. 4 : 8. Judg. 6 : 37. Isai. 38 : 7, 8), but sometimes in a mere prediction (Ex. 3 : 12. 1 Sam. 2 : 34. 2 Kings 19 : 29), and sometimes only in a symbol, especially a symbolical name or action (Isai. 8 : 18. 20 : 3. Ezek. 4 : 3). The sign here offered is a proof of Isaiah's divine legation, which Ahaz seemed to doubt. The offer is a general one, including all the kinds of signs which have been mentioned, though the only one which would have answered the purpose of accrediting the Prophet was a present miracle, as in the case of Moses (Ex. 4 : 30). The phrase *thy God* is emphatic and intended to remind Ahaz of his official relation to Jehovah, and as it were to afford him a last opportunity of profiting by the connection.

12. *And Ahaz said, I will not ask, and I will not tempt Jehovah.* Some regard this as a contemptuous irony, implying a belief that God would not be able to perform his promise or a disbelief in the existence of a personal God. We have no reason

to doubt, however, that Ahaz believed in the existence of Jehovah, at least as one among many gods, as a local and national if not a supreme deity. It is better, therefore, to understand the words as a hypocritical excuse for not obeying the command, with obvious allusion to the prohibition in Deut. 6 : 16, which is of course inapplicable to the case of one who is required to choose by God himself. His refusal probably arose, not from speculative doubts or politic considerations, but from the state of his affections, his aversion to the service of Jehovah and his predilection for that of other gods, perhaps combined with a belief that in this case human aid would be sufficient and a divine interposition superfluous; to which may be added a specific expectation of assistance from Assyria, for which he had perhaps already sued (2 Kings 16: 7–9). To *tempt* God is not to try him in the way of trusting him, nor simply to call in question his power, knowledge, or veracity, but to put him practically to the test. The character of Ahaz is illustrated by a comparison of this refusal with the thankful acceptance of such signs by others, and especially by his own son Hezekiah, to whom, as Jerome observes, signs both in heaven and on earth were granted.

13. At first Ahaz seemed to doubt only the authority and divine legation of the Prophet; but his refusal to accept the offered attestation was an insult to God himself, and is therefore indignantly rebuked by the Prophet. *And he said, hear, I pray you, oh house of David! is it too little for you* (is it not enough for you) *to weary men* (i. e. to try men's patience), *that you* (must) *weary* (or try the patience of) *my God?* The meaning is not merely that it is worse to weary God than man, or that it was not man but God whom they were wearying; but that having first wearied man, i. e. the Prophet by disputing his commission, they were now wearying God, by refusing the offered attestation. The plural form of the address implies

that members of his family and court were, in the Prophet's view, already implicated in his unbelief.

14. The king having refused to ask a sign, the Prophet gives him one, by renewing the promise of deliverance (vs. 8, 9) and connecting it with the birth of a child, whose significant name is made a symbol of the divine interposition, and his progress a measure of the subsequent events. Instead of saying that God would be present to deliver them, he says the child shall be called *Immanuel* (God with us); instead of mentioning a term of years, he says, before the child is able to distinguish good from evil; instead of saying that until that time the land shall lie waste, he represents the child as eating *curds and honey*, spontaneous products, here put in opposition to the fruits of cultivation. At the same time, the form of expression is descriptive. Instead of saying simply that the child shall experience all this, he represents its birth and infancy as actually passing in his sight; he sees the child brought forth and named Immanuel; he sees the child eating curds and honey till a certain age. *Therefore* (because you have refused to choose) *the Lord himself will give you a sign. Behold! the virgin pregnant and bringing forth a son, and she calls his name Immanuel* (God with us); *curds and honey shall he eat* (because the land lies waste) *until he shall know* (*how*) *to reject the evil and to choose the good* (but no longer); *for before the child shall know* (*how*) *to reject the evil and to choose the* good, *the land, of whose two kings thou art afraid* (i. e. Syria and Israel), *shall be forsaken* (i. e. desolate), which of course implies the previous deliverance of Judah. All interpreters appear to be agreed that these three verses contain a threatening of destruction to the enemies of Judah, if not a direct promise of deliverance, and that this event is connected, in some way, with the birth of a child, as the *sign* or pledge of its certain occurrence. But what child is meant, or who is the Immanuel here predicted?

The various answers to this question may be all reduced to three fundamental hypotheses, each of which admits of several minor variations.

I. The first hypothesis is that the only birth and infancy referred to in these verses are the birth and infancy of a child born (or supposed to be born), in the ordinary course of nature, and in the days of Isaiah himself. The unessential variations, of which this hypothesis is susceptible, have reference chiefly to the question what particular child is intended. An objection to all the variations of this first hypothesis is, that although they may afford a *sign*, in one of the senses of that term, to wit, that of an emblem or symbol, they do not afford such a sign as the context would lead us to expect. Ahaz had been offered the privilege of choosing any sign whatever, in heaven or on earth. Had he actually chosen one, it would no doubt have been something out of the ordinary course of nature, as in the case of Gideon (Judges 6: 37–40) and Hezekiah (Isai. 38: 7, 8). On his refusal to choose, a sign is given him unasked, and although it does not necessarily follow that it was precisely such as he would have selected—since the object was no longer simply to remove his doubts, but to verify the promise and to mark the event when it occurred as something which had been predicted—yet it seems very improbable that after such an offer, the sign bestowed would be merely a thing of every-day occurrence, or at most the application of a symbolical name. This presumption is strengthened by the solemnity with which the Prophet speaks of the predicted birth, not as a usual and natural event, but as something which excites his own astonishment, as he beholds it in prophetic vision. This may prove nothing by itself, but is significant when taken in connection with the other reasons. The same thing may be said of the address to Immanuel, in ch. 8: 8, and the allusion to the name in v. 11, which, although they may admit of explanation in consistency with this hypothesis, agree much better with the supposition that the prophecy relates to something more than a natural and ordinary birth. A still stronger reason for the same conclusion is afforded by the parallel passage in ch. 9 : 5, 6, occurring in the same connected series of prophecies. There, as here, the birth of a child is given as a pledge of safety and deliverance, but with the important addition of a full description, which, as we shall see below, is wholly inapplicable to any ordinary human child, however high in rank or full of promise. If led by these remarkable coincidences to examine more attentively the terms of the prophecy itself, we find the mother of the promised child described, not as *a woman* or as any particular woman merely, but by a term which in the six places where it occurs elsewhere, is twice applied to young unmarried females certainly (Gen. 24 : 43. Ex. 2 : 8), and twice most probably (Ps. 68 : 25, Sol. S. 1 : 3), while in the two remaining cases (Sol. S. 1 : 8, Prov. 30 : 19) this application is at least as probable as any other. It would therefore naturally suggest the idea of a virgin, or at least of an unmarried woman. A virgin or unmarried woman is designated here as distinctly as she could be by a single word. Its use in this connection, especially when added to the other reasons previously mentioned, makes it, to say the least, extremely probable that the event foretold is something more than a birth in the ordinary course of nature. So too, the name *Immanuel*, although it might be used to signify God's providential presence merely (Ps 46 : 8, 11. 89 : 25. Josh. 1 : 5. Jer. 1 : 8. Isai. 43 : 2), has a latitude and pregnancy of meaning which can scarcely be fortuitous, and which, combined with all the rest, makes the conclusion almost unavoidable, that it was here intended to express a *personal* as well as a *providential* presence. If to this we add the early promise of salvation through the *seed of the woman* (Gen. 3 : 15), rendered more definite by later revelations, and that remarkable expression of Isaiah's contemporary prophet Micah (5 : 2), *until the time that she which travaileth hath brought forth,* immediately following the promise of a *ruler*, to be born in Bethlehem, but *whose goings forth have been from old, from everlasting*—the balance of probabilities, as furnished by the Old Testament exclusively, preponderates decidedly in favour of the supposition, that Isaiah's words had reference to a miraculous conception and nativity. When we read, therefore, in the gospel of Matthew, that Jesus Christ was actually born of a virgin, and that all the circumstances of his birth came to pass that this very prophecy might be fulfilled, it has less the appearance of an unexpected application, than of a conclusion rendered necessary by a series of antecedent facts and reasons, the last link in a long chain of intimations more or less explicit. The question, however, still arises, how the birth of Christ, if here predicted, is to be connected with the promise made to Ahaz, as a sign of the event, or as a measure of the time of its fulfilment?

II. The second hypothesis removes this difficulty by supposing that the prophecy relates to two distinct births and two different children. Of this general theory there are two important modifications. 1. The first supposes one child to be mentioned in v. 14, and another in v. 16. Nothing but extreme exegetical necessity could justify the reference of vs. 15, 16, to any person not referred to in v. 14. 2. This difficulty is avoided in the second modification of the general hypothesis that the passage (as a whole) refers to two distinct births and to different children, by assuming that both are mentioned in the fourteenth verse itself. This is the supposition of a double sense, though some refuse to recognize it by that name. The essence of the theory is this, that while v. 14, in its obvious and primary sense, relates to the birth of a child in the ordinary course of nature, its terms are so selected as to be descriptive, in a higher sense, of the miraculous nativity of Christ. The minor variations of this general hypothesis have reference chiefly to the particular child intended by the prophecy in its lower sense, whether a son of Isaiah himself, or any child born within a certain time. The objections to it are its complexity, and what seems to be the arbitrary nature of the assumption upon which it rests. It seems to be a feeling common to learned and unlearned readers, that although a double sense is not impossible, and must in certain cases be assumed, it is unreasonable to assume it, when any other explanation is admissible. The improbability in this case is increased by the want of similarity between the two events, supposed to be predicted in the very same words, the one miraculous, the other not only natural but common and of every-day occurrence. That two such occurrences should be described in the same words, simply because they were both *signs* or pledges of a promise, though not impossible, can only be made probable by strong corroborating proofs, especially if any simpler mode of exposition be at all admissible. Another objection, which lies equally against this hypothesis and the one first mentioned is, that in its primary and lower sense it does not afford such a sign as the context and the parallel passages would lead us to expect, unless we suppose that the higher secondary sense was fully understood at the time of the prediction, and in that case, though the birth of the Messiah from a virgin would be doubtless a sufficient sign, it would, for that very reason, seem to make the lower one superfluous. None of these reasons seem however to be decisive against the supposition of a double sense, as commonly understood, unless there be some other way in which its complexity and arbitrary character may be avoided, and at the same time the connection between the birth of the Messiah and the deliverance of Judah satisfactorily explained.

III. The third general hypothesis proposes to effect this by applying all three verses directly and exclusively to the Messiah, as the only child whose birth is there predicted, and his growth made the measure of the subsequent events. The minor variations of this general hypothesis relate to the time when these events were to occur, and to the sense in which the growth of the Messiah is adopted as the measure of them. The simplest form in which this theory has been applied, is that exhibited by those who suppose the prediction to relate to the real time of Christ's appearance, and the thing foretold to be the desolation which should take place before the Saviour reached a certain age. To this it is an obvious objection that it makes the event predicted too remote to answer the conditions of the context, or the purpose of the prophecy itself.

In expounding this difficult and interesting passage, it has been considered more important to present a tolerably full view of the different opinions, arranged according to the principles on which they rest, than to assert the exclusive truth of any one interpretation as to all its parts. In summing up the whole, however, it may be confidently stated, that the first hypothesis is false; that the first modifications of the second and third are untenable; and that the choice lies between the supposition of a double sense and that of a reference to Christ exclusively, but in connection with the promise of immediate deliverance to Ahaz. The two particular interpretations which appear to me most plausible and least beset with difficulties are these. Either the Prophet, while he foretells the birth of Christ, foretells that of another child, during whose infancy the promised deliverance shall be experienced; or else he makes the infancy of Christ himself, whether foreseen as still remote or not, the sign and measure of that same deliverance. While some diversity of judgment ought to be expected and allowed, in relation to this secondary question, there is no ground, grammatical, historical, or logical, for doubt as to the main point, that the church in all ages has been right in regarding this passage as a signal and explicit prediction of the miraculous conception and nativity of Jesus Christ.

15. This verse and the next have already been translated in

connection with the fourteenth, upon which connection their interpretation must depend. It will here be necessary only to explain one or two points more distinctly. *Butter* (or curds) *and honey shall he eat, until he knows* (*how*) *to reject the evil and to choose the good.* The simple sense of the prediction is that the desolation of Judah, caused by the invasion of Rezin and Pekah, should be only temporary. This idea is symbolically expressed by making the new-born child subsist during his infancy on curds and honey, instead of the ordinary food of an agricultural population. This is clearly the meaning of the same expression in v. 22, as we shall see below. The essential idea is that the desolation should not last until a child then born could reach maturity, and probably not longer than his first few years.

16. The desolation shall be temporary, *for before the child shall know* (*how*) *to reject the evil and to choose the good, the land, of whose two kings thou art afraid* (or *by whose two kings thou art distressed*), *shall be forsaken*, i. e. left by its inhabitants and given up to desolation, in which sense the same verb is used elsewhere by Isaiah (ch. 17 : 2. 27 : 10. 62 : 12. Comp. 6 : 12). *The land* here meant is Syria and Israel, spoken of as one because confederate against Judah. The wasting of these kingdoms and the deportation of their people by Tiglath-pileser (2 Kings 15 : 29. 16 : 9) is here predicted, which of course implies the previous deliverance of Judah and the brief duration of its own calamity, so that this verse assigns a reason for the representation in the one preceding. The true connection of these verses has been well explained to be this, that Judah shall lie waste for a short time, and *only* for a short time, *for* before that short time is expired, its invaders shall themselves be invaded and destroyed. *A child* is born—*he* learns to distinguish good and evil—but before *the child* is able to distinguish good and evil, something happens. If these three clauses,

thus succeeding one another, do not speak of the same child, it is impossible for language to be so employed as to identify the subject without actually saying that it is the same.

17. Again addressing Ahaz, he assures him that although he shall escape the present danger, God will inflict worse evils on himself and his successors, by means of those very allies whose assistance he is now seeking. *Jehovah will bring upon thee* (not merely as an individual, but as a king) *and on thy people, and on thy father's house* (or family, the royal line of Judah) *days which have not come since the departure of Ephraim from Judah, to wit, the king of Assyria.* All versions and interpreters understand the verse as declaring the days threatened to be worse than any which had come upon Judah since the revolt of the ten tribes, here called Ephraim, from the largest and most powerful tribe, that to which Jeroboam belonged, and within which the chief towns of the kingdom were situated. This declaration seems at first sight inconsistent with the fact, demonstrable from sacred history, that the injuries sustained by Judah, during the interval here specified, from other foreign powers, as for example from the Egyptians in the reign of Rehoboam (2 Chron. 12 : 2–9), from the Philistines and Arabians in the reign of Jehoram (2 Chron. 21 : 16, 17), from the Syrians in the reign of Joash (2 Chron. 24 : 23, 24), not to mention the less successful attacks of the Ethiopians in the reign of Asa (2 Chron. 14 : 8–15), and of Moab and Ammon in the reign of Jehoshaphat (2 Chron. 20 : 1–30), or the frequent incursions of the ten tribes, must have greatly overbalanced the invasion of Sennacherib, by far the most alarming visitation of Judah by the armies of Assyria. But let it be observed that the days here threatened were to be worse, not simply with respect to individual suffering or temporary difficulties of the state itself, but to the loss of its independence, its transition to a servile state, from which it was never permanently freed, the

domination of Assyria being soon succeeded by that of Egypt, and this by that of Babylon, Persia, Syria, and Rome, the last ending only in the downfall of the state, and that general dispersion of the people which continues to this day. The revolt of Hezekiah and even longer intervals of liberty in later times, are mere interruptions of the customary and prevailing bondage. Of this critical change it surely might be said, even though it were to cost not a single drop of blood, nor the personal freedom of a single captive, that the Lord was about to bring upon Judah days which had not been witnessed from the time of Ephraim's apostasy, or according to another construction of the text, at any time whatever; since none of the evils suffered, from Solomon to Ahaz, had destroyed the independence of Judah, not even the Egyptian domination in the reign of Rehoboam, which only lasted long enough to teach the Jews the difference between God's service and *the service of the kingdoms of the countries* (2 Chron. 12 : 8). This view of the matter is abundantly sufficient to reconcile the prophecy with history, whether Assyria be understood to mean the kingdom properly so called, or to include the empires which succeeded it; and whether the threatening be referred exclusively to Ahaz and his times, or to him and his successors jointly, which appears to be the true sense of *thy people and thy father's house*, as distinguished from himself and his own house; but even on the other supposition, as the change of times, i. e. the transition from an independent to a servile state, took place before the death of Ahaz, the expressions used are perfectly consistent with the facts. It is implied, of course, in this interpretation, that Sennacherib's invasion was not the *beginning* of the days here threatened, which is rather to be sought in the alliance between Ahaz and Tiglath-pileser, *who came unto him, and distressed him, and strengthened him not* (2 Chron. 28 : 19, 20), but exacted repeated contributions from him as a vassal; which degrading and oppressive intercourse continued till his death, as appears from the statement (2 Kings 18 : 7) that *Hezekiah rebelled against the king of Assyria, and served him not*, clearly implying that he did at first, as he offered to do afterwards, on Sennacherib's approach, with confession of his fault, a renewal of his tribute, and a repetition of his father's sacrilege (2 Kings 18 : 13–16). That during the whole term of this foreign ascendency, Judah was infested by Assyrian intruders, and by frequent visitations for the purpose of extorting their unwilling tribute, till at last the revolt of Hezekiah, no longer able to endure the burden, led to a formal occupation of the country, is not only probable in itself, but seems to be implied in the subsequent context (vs. 18–20).

18. The evil times just threatened are here more explicitly described as arising from the presence and oppression of foreigners, especially Assyrians and Egyptians, whose number and vexatious impositions are expressed by comparing them to swarms of noxious and annoying insects, pouring into the country by divine command. *And it shall be* (or come to pass) *in that day* (in the *days* just threatened) *that Jehovah will hiss* (or *whistle*) *to* (or *for*) *the fly which* (*is*) *in the end* (or *edge*) *of the rivers of Egypt, and to* (or *for*) *the bee which is in Assyria.* The fly is peculiarly appropriate to Egypt, where the marshy grounds produce it in abundance, and there may be a reference to the plague of flies in Exodus. The *end of the streams* of Egypt evidently means something belonging to Egypt, viz. the arms of the Delta or the remotest streams, implying that the flies should come from the very extremities, or from the whole land. By rendering it *brink* or *border*, as the common version does in Josh. 3 : 8. Ex. 16 : 35, an equally good sense is obtained, viz. that the flies shall come from the banks of the streams, where they are most abundant. The hiss or whistle, denoting God's control over these enemies of Judah, has the same sense as in ch. 5 : 26. Assyria and Egypt are here named as the two great rival powers who disturbed the peace of West-

ern Asia, and to whom the land of Israel was both a place and subject of contention. The reference is not exclusively to actual invasion, but to the annoying and oppressive occupation of the country by civil and military agents of these foreign powers. It was not merely attacked but infested, by the flies and bees of Egypt and Assyria.

19. Carrying out the figures of the preceding verse, the Prophet, instead of simply saying that the land shall be infested by foreigners, represents it as completely filled with bees and flies, who are described as settling upon all the places commonly frequented by such insects. *And they come and rest* (or settle) *all of them in the desolate* (or precipitous) *valleys, and in the clefts of rocks, and in all thorn-hedges, and in all pastures.* The words seem naturally to express the general notion of a country overrun, infested, filled with foreigners and enemies, not only by military occupation but in other ways.

20. Had the Prophet, as Hendewerk suggests, represented the invaders as *locusts,* he would probably have gone on to describe them as devouring the land; but having chosen bees and flies as the emblem, he proceeds to express the idea of their spoliations by a different figure, that of a body closely shorn or shaven by a razor under the control of God and in his service. *In that day* (the same day mentioned in v. 19) *will the Lord shave, with a razor hired in the parts beyond the river* (Euphrates), (that is to say) *with the king of Assyria, the head and the hair of the feet* (i. e. of both extremities, or of the whole body), *and also the beard will it* (the razor) *take away.* As Ahaz had profaned and robbed God's house to hire a foreign razor, with which Israel and Syria might be shaven, so God would make use of that self-same razor to shave Judah, i. e. to remove its population, or its wealth, or both. The separate mention

of the *beard* may have reference to the oriental fondness for it and associations of dishonour with the loss of it.

21, 22. In consequence of these spoliations, the condition of the country will be wholly changed. The population left shall not be agricultural but pastoral. Instead of living on the fruits of the soil, they shall subsist upon spontaneous products, such as milk and honey, which shall be abundant only because the people will be few and the uncultivated grounds extensive. *And it shall be in that day* (*that*) *a man shall save* (or *keep*) *alive a young cow and two sheep; and it shall be* (*that*) *from the abundance of the making* (yielding or production) *of milk, he shall eat butter* (or *curds* or *cheese* or *cream*)*; for butter and honey shall every one eat that is left in the midst of* (or within) *the land.* The word translated save alive is used to denote the *preservation* of one's life in danger (Ps. 30 : 4); so that unless we depart from its proper meaning here, it must denote not merely the *keeping* or *raising* of the cow and sheep, but their being *saved* from a greater number, and preserved with difficulty, not for want of pasture, which was more than ever plentiful, but from the presence of invaders and enemies. Thus understood, the word throws light upon the state of the country, as described in the context. The abundance is of course to be relatively understood, with respect to the small number of persons to be fed, and is therefore an additional and necessary stroke in the prophetic picture—few cattle left, and yet those few sufficient to afford milk in abundance to the few inhabitants. This abundance is expressed still more strongly by describing them as eating not the milk itself, but that which is produced from it, and which of course must bear a small proportion to the whole; and as this is the essential idea meant to be conveyed it matters little whether it be understood to mean butter, cheese, cream, or curds, though the last seems to agree best with what we know of oriental usages. It is here mentioned neither as a delicacy nor as plain and ordinary food, but as a kind of diet independent of the cultivation of the earth, and therefore implying a neglect of tillage and a pastoral mode of life, as well as an unusual extent of pasturage, which may have reference, not only to the milk but to the honey. Boswell, in the journal of his tour with Dr. Johnson to the Hebrides, observes of the inhabitants of one of the poor islands, that "they lived all the spring *without meal*, upon *milk and curds and whey* alone." This verse, then, is descriptive of abundance only as connected with a paucity of people and a general neglect of tillage. It was designed indeed to be directly expressive neither of abundance nor of poverty, but of a change in the condition of the country and of the remaining people, which is further described in the ensuing context.

23. Having described the desolation of the country indirectly, by saying what the food of the inhabitants should be, the Prophet now describes it more directly, by predicting the growth of thorns and briers, even in spots which had been sedulously cultivated, for example the most valuable vineyards. *And it shall be* (or come to pass) *in that day* (*that*) *every place, where there shall be a thousand vines at* (or *for*) *a thousand silverlings* (pieces or shekels of silver), *shall be for* (or *become*) *thorns and briers*, or *shall be* (given up) *to the thorn and to the brier.* Most writers seem to confine the threatening to the thorns and briers, and to regard the thousand silverlings as a part of the description of a valuable vineyard, though they differ on the question whether this was the price for which the vineyard might be sold, or its annual rent, as in Sol. Song 8: 11, where, however, it is said to be the price of the *fruit*, and the number of vines is not mentioned. Henderson computes that it was nearly one-half more than the price at which the vineyards of Mount Lebanon were sold in 1811, according to Burckhardt, namely a piastre for each vine.

24. So complete shall be the desolation of these once favoured spots that men shall pass through them armed as they would through a wilderness. *With arrows and with bow shall one* (or *shall a man*) *go thither, because thorns and briers shall the whole land be.* The essential idea, as the last clause shows, is that of general desolation; there is no need, therefore, of supposing that the bows and arrows have exclusive reference to protection, as it would be natural to carry weapons into such a region both for protection and the chase. It is no objection to the mention of the latter, that the people had just been represented as subsisting upon milk and honey, since these two methods of subsistence often coexist, as belonging to the same state of society, and both imply a general neglect of tillage. The exact sense of the last clause is not that the land shall *become thorns and briers* (English version), as in v. 24, but that it shall actually *be* thorns and briers.

25. Not only the fields, not only the vineyards, shall be overrun with thorns and briers, but the very hills, now laboriously cultivated with the hand, shall be given up to like desolation. *And all the hills* (i. e. even all the hills) *which are digged with the hoe* (because inaccessible to the plough)—*thou shalt not go* (even) *there, for fear of briers and thorns, and* (being thus uncultivated) *they shall be for a sending-place of cattle and a trampling-place of sheep* (i. e. a place where cattle may be sent to pasture, and which may be trodden down by sheep). The reference is probably to the hills of Judea, anciently cultivated to the very top, by means of terraces that still exist, for an account of which by eye-witnesses, see Keith's Land of Israel, chapter XII., and Robinson's Palestine, vol. II. p. 187. Thus understood, the verse merely strengthens the foregoing description, by declaring that even the most carefully cultivated portions of the land should not escape the threatened desolation. This verse continues and completes the description of

the general desolation, as manifested first by the people's living upon milk and honey, then by the growth of thorns and briers in the choicest vineyards and the terraced hills, and by the conversion of these carefully tilled spots into dangerous solitudes, hunting-grounds, and pastures.

CHAPTER VIII.

THE prediction of the overthrow of Syria and Israel is now renewed in the form of a symbolical name, to be inscribed on a tablet and attested by two witnesses, and afterwards applied to the Prophet's new-born son, whose progress as an infant is made the measure of the event, vs. 1–4. It is then foretold that the judgment denounced upon Syria and Israel should extend to Judah, as a punishment for distrust of God and reliance upon human aid, in consequence of which the kingdom should be imminently threatened with destruction, yet delivered for the sake of Immanuel, by whom the strength and wisdom of all enemies should be alike defeated, vs. 5–10. The Messiah himself is then introduced as speaking, warning the Prophet and the true believers neither to share in the apprehensions nor to fear the reproaches of the people, but to let Jehovah be an object of exclusive fear and reverence to them, as he would be an occasion of destruction to the unbelievers, from whom the true sense of this revelation was to be concealed, and restricted to his followers, who, together with the Prophet and the Son of God himself, should be for signs and wonders to the multitude, while waiting for the manifestation of his presence, and refusing to consult any other oracle except the word of God, an authority despised by none but those doomed to the darkness of despair, which is described as settling down upon them, with a sudden intimation, at the close, of a change for the better, especially in reference to that part of the country which had been most afflicted and despised, vs. 11–23.

The Hebrew and English text differ here in the division of the chapters. A better arrangement than either would have been to continue the eighth without interruption to the close of what is now the sixth (or seventh) verse of the ninth chapter, where a new division of the prophecy begins.

1. The prediction of the overthrow of Syria and Israel, contained in ch. 7:8, 9, is here repeated, and as before in a symbolical form. In order to excite immediate attention, and at the same time to verify the prophecy, Isaiah is required to inscribe an enigmatical name on a large tablet in a legible character, with a view to present exhibition and to subsequent preservation. The name itself includes a prophecy of speedy spoliation. *And Jehovah said to me, take thee* (or *for thyself*) *a great tablet* (i. e. great in proportion to the length of the inscription), *and write upon it with a man's pen* (or *stylus*, i. e. in an ordinary and familiar hand), *To Maher-shalal-hash-baz* (i. e. Haste-spoil-quick-prey). The name may also be read as a sentence—*Hasten spoil! Prey hastens.* These four words are not merely the heading or title of the writing, but the writing itself. Both the kind of writing and the size of the tablet (admitting larger characters), have reference to its being legible, *so that he may run that readeth it* (Hab. 2:2).

2. In order to preclude all suspicion of its having been uttered after the event, the prophecy is not only recorded, but attested by two witnesses. *And I* (Jehovah) *will take to witness for me credible witnesses, to wit, Uriah the priest, and Zechariah, son of Jeberechiah.* Uriah is probably the same who connived at the king's profanation of the temple (2 Kings 16:10–16. The word credible does not relate to their true character or standing in the sight of God, but to their credit

with the people, especially perhaps with the king, in which view, as well as on account of his official rank, Uriah was a very suitable witness. The same consideration makes it not improbable that the Zechariah mentioned here was the father-in-law of Ahaz (2 Kings 18 : 2. 2 Chr. 29 : 1), perhaps the same that is mentioned as a Levite of the family of Asaph (2 Chr. 29 : 13).

3. The significant name, before inscribed upon the tablet, is now applied to the Prophet's new-born son, that the child, as well as the inscription, might remind all who saw them of the prophecy. The execution of the previous command is here, as in many other cases, tacitly included in the record of the command itself. (Vide supra, ch. 7 : 4.) *And I approached unto the Prophetess, and she conceived and bare a son, and Jehovah said to me, Call his name Maher-shalal-hash-baz.* This name, like *Immanuel*, may be understood as simply descriptive or symbolical, but its actual imposition is inferred by most interpreters from verse 18, where the Prophet speaks of himself and his children as signs and wonders in Israel, with reference, as they suppose, to the names *Shear-jashub* and *Maher-shalal-hash-baz.* The *Prophetess* is probably so called because she was a prophet's wife, as *queen* usually means a royal consort, not a queen *suo jure.* A remarkable series of prophetic names, imposed upon three children, is recorded in the first chapter of Hosea.

4. It is not merely by its name that the child is connected with the prophecy. The date of the event is determined by a reference to the infant's growth, as in the case of Immanuel. *For before the child shall know* (*how*) *to cry my father and my mother, one* (or *they* indefinitely) *shall take away the wealth of Damascus and the spoil of Samaria before the king of Assyria,* i. e. into his presence, to deliver it to him or simply *in his presence,* that is by his command and under his direction. The

time fixed is that of the child's capacity not to recognize its parents, or to talk, but to utter the simple labial sounds by which in Hebrew as in many other languages *father* and *mother* are expressed. The time denoted was intended to be somewhat indefinite, equivalent perhaps to our familiar phrase *a year or two*, within which time we have reason to believe that the event occurred. There is no reason to doubt that Samaria was plundered by Tiglath-pileser (2 Kings 15 : 29) although not destroyed, which idea is in fact not conveyed by the terms of the description. The carrying away of its wealth does not necessarily imply any thing more than such a spoiling of the capital as might be expected in the course of a brief but successful invasion.

5. *And Jehovah added to speak to me again* (or *further*) *saying*. Here, as in ch. 7 : 10, an interval of time may be assumed.

6. The Assyrian invasion is now represented as a punishment of Judah for distrusting the divine protection and seeking that of the Assyrians themselves. The immediate relief thus secured was to be followed by a worse calamity produced by those in whom they now confided. *Because this people* (Judah, so called in token of divine displeasure) *hath forsaken* (or rejected with contempt) *the waters of Shiloah* (or Siloam, the only perennial fountain of Jerusalem, here used as a symbol of the divine protection) *that go softly* (or flow gently, unaccompanied by noise or danger), *and* (because there is) *joy with respect to Rezin and the son of Remaliah* (i. e. because the Jews are exulting in the retreat of their invaders, caused by the approach of the Assyrians), *therefore*, etc. the apodosis of the sentence being given in the next verse.

7. *Therefore* (because the people had thus ceased to trust in the divine protection, and rejoiced in the success of their ap-

plication to Assyria), *behold* (as if the event were actually present), *Jehovah* (is) *bringing up upon them the waters of the river* (i. e. the Euphrates, as an emblem of the Assyrian power), *its strong and many* waters (here contrasted with the gently flowing waters of Siloam), *to wit*, the *king of Assyria and all his glory* (with particular reference to military strength and display), *and it* (the river) *shall come up over all its channels and go over all its banks*, which may either mean that it shall transcend its usual limits, or that after submerging Israel, it shall overflow into Judah also. In favour of this last interpretation is the language of the next verse, and the fact that otherwise the punishment of Ephraim or the ten tribes is not expressly mentioned. The figure of an overflowing river is peculiarly appropriate, not only as affording a striking antithesis to the fountain mentioned in the sixth verse, but because it is often used absolutely to denote the Euphrates, the great river of the Assyrian and Babylonian empires. The beauty of the metaphor is rendered still more striking by the frequent allusions, both in ancient and modern writers, to the actual inundations of this river. Here, as in ch. 7 : 17, 18, the figures are explained in literal expressions by the Prophet himself.

8. *And it* (the river) *shall pass over* (from Syria and Israel) *into Judah, overflow and pass through* (so as nearly to submerge it), *to the neck shall it reach* (but not above the head), *and the spreadings of its wings shall be the filling of thy land, O Immanuel!* The English version disturbs the metaphor by using the personal pronoun *he* so as to refer this verse directly to the king, and not to the river which represented him. The expression *the neck* was intended to denote nothing more than the imminency of the danger by figures borrowed from a case of drowning, the head alone being left above the water. Most writers suppose the figure of a stream to be exchanged in the last clause for that of a bird, or for the description of an army;

but others understand *wings* to be used here, as often elsewhere, in the sense of sides or lateral extremities, and applied to the river itself.

9. He now turns to the enemies of Judah and assures them of the failure of their hostile plans. The prediction, as in ch. 6 : 9, is clothed in the form of an ironical command or exhortation. *Be wicked* (i. e. indulge your malice, do your worst) *and be broken* (disappointed and confounded), *and* (that not only Syria and Israel, but) *give ear all remote parts of the earth* (whoever may attack the chosen people), *gird yourselves* (i. e. arm and equip yourselves for action) *and be broken, gird yourselves and be broken* (the repetition implying the certainty of the event). The failure or disappointment threatened is of course that of their ultimate design to overthrow the kingdom of Judah, and does not exclude the possibility of partial and temporary successes.

10. Not only their strength but their sagacity should be confounded. *Devise a plan, and it shall be defeated* (nullified or brought to nought), *speak a word* (whether a proposition or an order), *and it shall not stand* (or be carried into execution), *for* (*Immanuel*) *God* (*is*) *with us.* Even as a name Immanuel contains a proposition, and here this proposition is distinctly announced, but with a designed allusion to the person whom the name describes. As if he had said, 'the assurance of your safety is the great truth expressed by the name of your deliverer, to wit, that God is with us.' The mere retention of the Hebrew word could not convey its sense in this connection to the English reader.

11. The triumphant apostrophe in v. 10 is now justified by an appeal to the divine authority. I have reason to address our enemies in this tone, *for thus said Jehovah to me in strength*

of hand (i. e. when his hand was strong upon me, when I was under the influence of inspiration), *and instructed me away from walking in the way of this people* (i. e. warned me not to follow the example of the unbelieving Jews). When one is spoken of in Scripture as inspired, it is said not only that the *spirit* was upon him (Ezek. 11 : 5), but also that the *hand* of Jehovah was upon him (Ezek. 1 : 3. 3 : 22. 33 : 22. 37 : 1), and in one case at least that it was *strong* upon him (Ezek. 3 : 14). Hence *strength of hand* may have the sense of inspiration, and the whole phrase here employed be equivalent in meaning to the New Testament expressions ἐν πνεύματι (Rev. 1 : 10), ἐν ἐκστάσει (Acts 11 : 5), ἐν δύναμει καὶ πνεύματι ἁγίῳ (1 Thess. 1 : 5).

12. The words of God himself are now recorded. *Saying, ye shall not call conspiracy (or treason) every thing which this people calleth conspiracy (or treason), and its fear ye shall not fear nor be afraid.* The correct view of the passage seems to be this. The unbelieving fears of the people led them to seek foreign aid. From this they were dissuaded by the Prophet and his followers, who regarded it as a violation of their duty to Jehovah. This opposition, like the conduct of Jeremiah during the Babylonian siege, was regarded by the king and his adherents as a treasonable combination to betray them to their enemies. But God himself commands the Prophet and the true believers not to be affected by this false reproach, not to regard the cry of treason or conspiracy, nor share in the real or pretended terrors of the unbelievers.

13. *Jehovah of Hosts, him shall ye sanctify* (i. e. regard and treat as a Holy God, and as the Holy One of Israel), *and he shall be your fear, and he your dread,* i. e. the object of these feelings. If they felt as they ought towards God, as supreme and almighty, and as their own peculiar God, with whom they

were united in a national covenant, they could not so distrust him as to be alarmed at the approach of any earthly danger. The collocation of the words makes the sentence more emphatic. *Him shall ye fear* is substantially equivalent to *Him alone shall ye fear.* Thus explained, the passage is at once a condemnation of the terror inspired by the approach of the two kings, and of the application, which it had occasioned, to Assyria for aid against them.

14. *And he* (Jehovah) *shall be for* (or become) *a holy thing* (an object to be sanctified) *and for a stone of stumbling and for a rock of offence* (i. e. a stone to strike against and stumble over) *to the two houses of Israel* (Ephraim and Judah), *for a gin* (or trap) *and for a snare to the inhabitants of Jerusalem.* God was the only proper object to be dreaded, feared, and sanctified, i. e. regarded as a holy being in the widest and the most emphatic sense. Thus explained, the Hebrew word corresponds almost exactly to the Greek *τὸ ἅγιον*, the term applied to Christ by the angel who announced his birth (Luke 1 : 35). In 1 Peter 2 : 7, where this very passage is applied to Christ, *ἡ τιμή* seems to be employed as an equivalent to the word as here used. To others he is a stone of stumbling, but to you who believe he is *ἡ τιμή*, something precious, something honoured, something looked upon as holy. The same application of the words is made by Paul in Rom. 9 : 33. These quotations seem to show that the Prophet's words have an extensive import, and are not to be restricted either to his own times or the time of Christ. The doctrine of the text is, that even the most glorious exhibitions of God's holiness, i. e. of his infinite perfection, may occasion the destruction of the unbeliever. The most signal illustration of this general truth was that afforded in the advent of the Saviour. It was frequently exemplified, however, in the interval, and one of these exemplifications was afforded by the conduct of the unbelieving Jews in the reign of Ahaz, to whom

the only power that could save them was converted by their own unbelief into a stone of stumbling and a rock of offence. The same idea is then expressed by another simple and familiar figure, that of a snare or trap. Both figures naturally suggest the idea of inadvertence and unforeseen ruin. The sense is not that Jehovah would be sanctified by Judah, and become a stumbling-block to Israel; but that to some in either house or family these opposite events would happen. The inhabitants of Jerusalem are distinctly mentioned as the most conspicuous and influential members of the nation, just as Jerusalem itself is sometimes mentioned in connection with Judah, which really included it.

15. This verse completes the threatening by an explicit declaration that Jehovah would not only be a stumbling-block and snare to the houses of Israel, but that many should actually fall and be ensnared and broken. *And many shall stumble over them* (the stone and snare) or *among them* (the children of Israel) *and fall, and be broken, and be snared, and be taken.*

16. *Bind up the testimony, seal the law, in my disciples* These are not the words of the Prophet speaking in his own person, but a command addressed to him by God, or as some suppose by the Messiah. It is commonly agreed, that the Prophet is commanded to tie up a roll or volume, and to seal it, thereby closing it. By law and testimony here we may either understand the prophetic inscription in v. 1, or the whole preceding context, considered as included in the general sense of *revelation*, as God's *testimony* to the truth and as a *law* or declaration of his will. The *disciples*, or those taught of God, probably mean the better portion of the people, those truly enlightened because taught of God (ch. 54 : 13), to whom the knowledge of this revelation, or at least of its true meaning, was to be restricted. The act described is not that of literally bind-

ing and sealing up a material record, but that of spiritually closing and depositing the revelation of God's will in the hearts of those who were able and willing to receive it, with allusion at the same time to its concealment from all others.

17. *And I* (the Messiah) *will wait for Jehovah that hideth his face from the house of Jacob, and will expect him.* Most writers make these the words of the Prophet; but since he is addressed in the verse preceding, without any intimation of a change of speaker here, and since the next verse is quoted in Heb. 2 : 13, as the words of the Messiah, it seems better to assume, that throughout this passage the Messiah is the speaker. The phrase to *wait upon* has changed its meaning since the date of the English version, the prominent idea being now that of service and attendance, not as of old that of expectation, which is the meaning of the Hebrew verb. God's hiding his face from the house of Jacob implies not only outward troubles but the withholding of divine illumination, indirectly threatened in the verse preceding. The house of Jacob is the whole race of Israel, perhaps with special reference to Judah. The thing to be expected is the fulness of time when the Messiah, no longer revealed merely to a few, should openly appear. For a time the import of God's promises shall be concealed from the majority, and during that interval Messiah shall wait patiently until the set time has arrived.

18. *Behold, I and the children which Jehovah hath given me* (are) *for signs and for wonders in Israel from Jehovah of Hosts, the* (*One*) *dwelling in Mount Zion.* Of the whole verse there are two distinct interpretations. 1. According to some Isaiah is the speaker, and the children meant are his two sons *Shear-jashub* and *Maher-shalal-hash-baz*, to which some add *Immanuel.* As all these names, and that of the Prophet himself, are significant, it is supposed that for this reason he and his children

are said to be *signs and wonders*, personified prophecies to Israel, from Jehovah, who had caused the names to be imposed. 2. According to many writers, these are the words of the Messiah, and the children are his spiritual seed (Isai. 53 : 10), whom the Father had given him (John 6: 37, 39. 10:29. 17 : 6, 7, 9, 11, 12). The great argument in favour of this last interpretation is the application of the verse to Christ by Paul (Heb. 2 : 13), not as an illustration but an argument, a proof, that Christ partook of the same nature with the persons called his *children* and his *brethren.* It is true that many who regard Isaiah as the speaker suppose him to have been a type of Christ in this transaction. But a double sense ought not to be assumed where a single one is perfectly consistent with the context, and sufficient to explain all apparent contradictions, as in this case, where admitting that the Messiah is the speaker, we have no ellipsis to supply, and no occasion to resort to the hypothesis either of a type or an accommodation. It is not necessary, however, to restrict the terms, to the period of the advent, and to our Saviour's personal followers. Even before he came in the flesh, he and his disciples, i. e. all who looked for his appearing, were signs and wonders, objects of contemptuous astonishment, and at the same time pledges of the promise.

19. *And when they* (indefinitely *any one*, or definitely *the unbelievers*) *shall say to you* (the disciples and children of Messiah, who is still speaking), *seek unto* (i. e. consult as an oracle) *the spirits* (or the spirit-masters, those who have subject or *familiar* spirits at command) *and to the wizards* (wise or knowing ones), *the chirpers and the mutterers* (alluding to the way in which the heathen necromancers invoked their spirits, or uttered their responses) *should not a people seek to* (or consult) *its God, for the living* (i. e. in behalf of the living should it resort) *to the dead?* The last clause is the reply of the believing Jews to those who tempted them. 'When you, my disciples, are invited by su-

perstitious sinners to consult pretended wizards, consider (or reply) that as the heathen seek responses from their gods, so you ought to consult Jehovah, and not be guilty of the folly of consulting senseless idols or dead men for the instruction of the living.'

20. Instead of resorting to these unprofitable and forbidden sources, the disciples of Jehovah are instructed to resort *to the law and to the testimony* (i. e. to divine revelation, considered as a system of belief and as a rule of duty) *if they speak* (i. e. if any speak) *not according to this word* (another name for the revealed will of God), it is he *to whom there is no dawn*, or morning (i. e. no relief from the dark night of calamity). The first clause is elliptical. None can speak inconsistently with God's word—or, none can refuse to utter this word, viz. to the law and to the testimony—but one whom God has abandoned. "If our gospel be hid, it is hid to them that are lost." (2 Cor. 4 : 3.) As night is a common figure for calamity, the dawn will naturally signify its termination, the return of better times. (See ch. 58 : 8. 47 : 11. Job 11 : 17.) They may be said to have no *dawn*, for whom there is nothing better in reserve.

21. *And they* (the people) *shall pass through it* (the land) *hardly bestead* (i. e. distressed) *and hungry; and it shall be* (or come to pass) *that when they are hungry they shall fret themselves, and curse their king and their God, and shall look upward. His king* is Jehovah considered as the king of Israel. The last clause is really in close connection with the first of the next verse, and both together must be understood as indicating utter perplexity and absolute despair of help from God or man, from heaven or earth, from above or below.

22. *And to the earth he shall look, and behold distress and darkness, dimness of anguish, and* into *darkness* (he shall be) *driven*

—or, *the dimness of anguish and of darkness* is *dispelled.* Heaven and earth are here opposed to one another, as sea and land are in ch. 5 : 30. *Distress* and *darkness* are here identified, as *distress* and *light* are there contrasted.

23. This darkness is to be dispelled; *for* (there shall) *not* (be) *darkness* (forever) *to her who is now distressed* (literally, to whom there is distress). The present calamity, or that just predicted, is not to be perpetual. The future state of things shall exhibit a strange contrast with the former. *As the former time degraded the land of Zebulon and the land of Naphtali, so the latter glorifies the way of the sea, the bank of the Jordan, Galilee of the Gentiles.* The same region is described in both clauses, namely, the northern extremity of the land of Israel. This is designated, first, by the tribes which occupied it, then, by its relative position with respect to Jordan and the sea of Tiberias. This part of the country, from being the most degraded and afflicted, should receive peculiar honour. Its debasement and distress both arose from its remote and frontier situation, proximity to the heathen, intercourse and mixture with them, and constant exposure to the first attacks of enemies, who usually entered Canaan from the north. To the former of these reasons may be traced the expressions of contempt for Galilee recorded in the books of the New Testament (John 1 : 46. 7 : 52. Matt. 26 : 69. Acts 1 : 11. 2 : 7). How this disgrace was to be exchanged for honour, is explained in the next verse. The *sea* mentioned in the last clause is not the Mediterranean but the sea of Galilee, as appears from Matt. 4: 15, 16. The region spoken of was that *along the Jordan* (on one or both sides) near the sea of Galilee.

CHAPTER IX.

THE change for the better, which was promised at the close of the eighth chapter, is described in the ninth as consisting in the rise of a great light upon the darkness, in the increase of the nation and their joy, excited by deliverance from bondage and the universal prevalence of peace, arising from the advent of a divine successor to David, who should restore, establish, and enlarge his kingdom without any limitation, vs. 1–6.

From the times of the Messiah, the Prophet suddenly reverts to his own, and again predicts the punishment of Ephraim by repeated strokes. The people had been warned both by messages from God and by experience, but had continued to indulge their proud self-confidence, in consequence of which God allowed the Assyrians, after overthrowing Rezin, to attack them also, while at the same time they were harassed by perpetual assaults from their hostile neighbours, vs. 7–11.

Still they did not repent and return to God, who therefore cut off suddenly many of all classes, but especially the rulers of the nation and the false prophets, the flattering seducers of the wretched people, from whom he must now withhold even the ordinary proofs of his compassion, vs. 12–16.

All this was the natural effect of sin, like a fire in a thicket, which at last consumes the forest, and involves the land in smoke and flame. Yet amidst these strokes of the divine displeasure, they were still indulging mutual animosities and jealousies, insomuch that Israel was like a famished man devouring his own flesh. Manasseh thus devoured Ephraim and Ephraim Manasseh, while the two together tried to devour Judah, vs. 17–20.

It has been observed already that the division of the chapters is in this part of the book peculiarly unfortunate; the first part of the ninth (vs. 1–6) containing the conclusion of the eighth, and the first part of the tenth (vs. 1–4) the conclusion of the ninth.

The numbers of the verses in this chapter differ in the Hebrew and English Bibles; what is the last verse of the eighth in the former is the first of the ninth in the latter. The references in the commentary are all to the divisions of the Hebrew text.

1. *The people* (just described, i. e. the people of Galilee), *those walking in the dark* (expressive both of spiritual blindness and extreme distress), *have seen a great light* (the change being presented to the Prophet's view as already past)*: the dwellers in the land of the shadow of death* (i. e. of intense darkness), *light has beamed upon them.* These words, in a general sense, may be descriptive of any great and sudden change in the condition of the people, especially of one from ignorance and misery to illumination and enjoyment. They are still more appropriate to Christ as the *light of the world* (John 8:12), *a light to the nations* (Isai. 42 : 6. 49 : 6), and the *sun of righteousness* (Mal. 4 : 2), which rose upon the world when he *manifested forth his glory* by his teachings and his miracles in Galilee (John 2: 11). It was in this benighted and degraded region that he first appeared as a messenger from God; and in that appearance we are expressly taught that this prediction was fulfilled (Matt. 4: 12–17).

2. The Prophet now, by a sudden apostrophe, addresses God himself, who, by bestowing on the Galileans this *great light*, would not only honour them, but afford occasion of great joy to all the true Israel, including those who should be gathered from the gentiles. *Thou hast enlarged the nation* (i. e. Israel in

general), *thou hast increased its joy* (literally, to it thou hast increased the joy); they *rejoice before thee like the joy in harvest, as* men *rejoice when they divide the spoil.* The increase of the nation means the increase of the people in their own land, not a mere growth of population, but an increase of the true Israel by the calling of the gentiles. To the promise here given there is probably allusion in the language of the angel who announced the birth of Jesus to the shepherds (Luke 2:10): *Behold, I bring you good tidings of great joy, which shall be to all the people,* i. e. to the whole nation, all the Israel of God.

3. This verse assigns the reason or occasion of the promised joy. They shall rejoice before thee, *that* (or because) *the yoke of his burden* (his burdensome yoke), *and the rod of his shoulder* (or back) *and the staff of the one driving him* (his task-master, slave-driver) *thou hast broken, like the day* (as in the day) *of Midian,* as Gideon routed Midian, i. e. suddenly, totally, and by special aid from heaven. This promise was fulfilled in the glorious deliverance of the Galileans (the first converts to Christianity), and of all who with them made up the true Israel, from the heavy burden of the covenant of works, the galling yoke of the Mosaic law, the service of the devil, and the bondage of corruption. Outward deliverance is only promised, so far as it accompanied the spiritual change or was included in it. The *day* of any one in Hebrew often means the day in which something memorable happens to him, or is done by him (vide supra, ch. 2:12) and in Arabic is absolutely used for a day of battle. The rout of the Midianites, recorded in the seventh chapter of Judges, is here referred to, because it was a wonderful display of divine power, without the use of any adequate human means—and also, because it took place in the same part of the country which this prophecy refers to. Jezreel, where the battle was fought (Judg. 6:33), was in the territory of Manasseh, to which tribe Gideon himself belonged (Judg.

6 : 15) ; but he was aided by the neighbouring tribes of Asher, Zebulon, and Naphtali (Judg. 6 : 35).

4. The destruction of the oppressing power shall be followed by profound and universal peace. To express this idea, the Prophet describes the equipments of the soldier as consumed with fire. *For all the armour of the armed man* (or the man-at-arms, who mingles) *in the tumult* (of battle), *and the garment rolled in blood, shall be for burning* (and for) *food* (or fuel) *of fire.* In other words, the usual accompaniments of battle shall be utterly destroyed, and by implication, war itself shall cease. It is not the weapons of the enemy alone, but all weapons of war, that are to be consumed; not merely because they have been used for a bad purpose, but because they are hereafter to be useless. It is not so much a prophecy of conquest as of peace; a peace however which is not to be expected till the enemies of God are overcome; and therefore the prediction may be said to include both events, the final overthrow of all opposing powers and the subsequent prevalence of universal peace. This last is uniformly spoken of in Scripture as characteristic of Messiah's reign, both internal and external, in society at large and in the hearts of his people. With respect to the latter, the prediction has been verified with more or less distinctness, in every case of true conversion. With respect to the former, its fulfilment is inchoate, but will one day be complete, when the lion and the lamb shall lie down together, and He who is the Prince of Peace shall have dominion from sea to sea, and from the river to the ends of the earth. An allusion to this promise and its final consummation may be found in the words of the heavenly host who celebrated the Saviour's birth (Luke 2 : 14), *Glory to God in the highest, and on earth* PEACE, *good will to men.* Fire is mentioned simply as a powerful consuming agent, to express the abolition of the implements of war, and, as a necessary consequence, of war itself.

5. This verse gives a further reason for the joy of the people, by bringing into view the person who was to effect the great deliverance. *For a child is born to us* (or *for us*, i. e. for our benefit), *a son is given to us* (i. e. by Jehovah, an expression frequently applied in the New Testament to Christ's incarnation), *and the government is upon his shoulder* (as a burden or a robe of office), *and his name is called Wonderful* (literally *Wonder*), *Counsellor*, *Mighty God*, *Everlasting Father*, *Prince of Peace*. When it is said that his name should be so called, it does not mean that he should actually bear these names in real life, but merely that he should deserve them, and that they would be descriptive of his character. These words are strikingly appropriate to Jesus Christ, as the promised *child*, emphatically *born for us* and *given to us*, as the *Son* of God and the *Son* of Man, as being *wonderful* in his person, works and sufferings; a *counsellor*, prophet, authoritative teacher of the truth, a wise administrator of the church, and confidential adviser of the individual believer—a real man, and yet the *Mighty God; eternal* in his own existence, and the *giver of eternal life* to others; the great *peace-maker* between God and man, between Jew and gentile, the umpire between nations, the abolisher of war, and the giver of internal peace to all who *being justified by faith have peace with God through our Lord Jesus Christ* (Rom. 5 : 1).

6. The reign of this king shall be progressive and perpetual, because founded in justice and secured by the distinguishing favour of Jehovah. *To the increase of the government* (or power) *and to the peace* (or prosperity of this reign) *there shall be no end, upon the throne of David and upon his kingdom, to establish it and to confirm it, in justice and in righteousness, from henceforth and forever, the zeal of Jehovah of Hosts shall do this.* A striking parallel is furnished by the prophecy in Micah 5 : 2–4. There, as here, a king is promised who should be the son of David, and should reign over all the earth in peace and righteousness

forever. It is there expressed, and here implied, that this king should re-unite the divided house of Israel, although this is but a small part of the increase promised, which includes the calling of the gentiles also. *Peace* here denotes not only *peace* as opposed to war, intestine strife, or turbulence, but welfare and prosperity in general as opposed to want and sorrow. The reign here predicted was to be not only peaceful but in every respect prosperous. And this prosperity, like the reign of which it is predicted, is to have no limit either temporal or local. It is to be both universal and eternal. There is nothing to preclude the very widest explanation of the terms employed. The endless increase of power and prosperity *on the throne of David* means of course that the Prince, whose reign was to be thus powerful and prosperous, would be a descendant of David. This is indeed a repetition and explanation of a promise given to David (2 Sam. 7: 11–16. 1 Kings 8: 25) and repeatedly referred to by him (2 Sam. 23: 1–5. Ps. 2, 45, 72, 89, 132). Hence the Messiah is not only called the *Branch* or *Son of David* (2 Sam. 7: 12, 13. Jer. 23: 5. 33: 15), but David himself (Jer. 30: 9. Ezek. 34: 23, 24. 37: 24. Hos. 3: 5). The two reigns are identified, not merely on account of an external resemblance or a typical relation, but because the one was really a restoration or continuation of the other. Both kings were heads of the same body, the one a temporal head, the other spiritual, the one temporary, the other eternal. The Jewish nation, as a spiritual body, is really continued in the Christian church. The subject of the prophecy is the reign of the Messiah; the effect predicted, its stability and increase; the means to be employed, judgment and justice; the efficient cause, the zeal of Jehovah. The justice spoken of is that of the Messiah and his subjects. All the acts of his administration will be righteous, and the effect of this upon his people will be righteousness on their part, and this prevalence of righteousness will naturally generate the increase and stability here promised. The word translated *zeal* expresses the complex idea of strong affection comprehending or attended by a jealous preference of one above another. It is used in the Old Testament to signify not only God's intense love for his people but his jealousy in their behalf, that is to say, his disposition to protect and favour them at the expense of others. Sometimes, moreover, it includes the idea of a jealous care of his own honour, or a readiness to take offence at any thing opposed to it, and a determination to avenge it when insulted. The expressions are derived from the dialect of human passion, but describe something absolutely right on God's part for the very reasons which demonstrate its absurdity and wickedness on man's. These two ideas of God's jealous partiality for his own people, and his jealous sensibility respecting his own honour, are promiscuously blended in the usage of the word, and are perhaps both included in the case before us. Both for his own sake and his people's, he would bring these events to pass. Or rather the two motives are identical, that is to say, the one includes the other. The welfare of the church is only to be sought so far as it promotes God's glory, and a zeal which makes the glory of the church an object to be aimed at for its own sake, cannot be a zeal for God, or is at best *a zeal for God but not according to knowledge.* The mention of God's jealousy or zeal as the procuring cause of this result affords a sure foundation for the hopes of all believers. His zeal is not a passion but a principle of powerful and certain operation. The astonishing effect produced by feeble means in the promotion, preservation, and extension of Christ's kingdom, can only be explained upon the principle that the zeal of the Lord of Hosts effected it. The expressions of the verse before us were applied to Christ, before his birth, by Gabriel, when he said to Mary (Luke 1 : 32–34), *He shall be great, and shall be called the Son of the Highest, and the Lord God shall give unto him the throne of his father David, and he shall reign over the house of Jacob forever, and of his kingdom there shall be no end.*

7. Having repeatedly interchanged the three great subjects of this prophecy, the deliverance of Judah from the power of Syria and Israel, its subsequent punishment by means of the Assyrians, and the reign of the Messiah, for whose sake the kingdom was to be preserved, the Prophet passes here abruptly from the last to the first, and again predicts the punishment of Ephraim. He reverts to this event, which had already been repeatedly foretold, for the purpose of declaring that the blows would be repeated as often and as long as might be needed for the absolute fulfilment of God's threatenings. He begins by showing that Israel had already been sufficiently forewarned. *The Lord sent a word into Jacob, and it came down into Israel.* The two names of the patriarch are here used as equivalents, denoting his descendants, and especially the larger part, the kingdom of the ten tribes, to which the national name *Israel* is wont to be distinctively applied.

8. The word which God had sent had reached the people; they had heard and understood it, but continued to indulge their pride and self-security. *And they know* (the divine threatening), *the people, all of them* (literally *all of it*, the noun being singular but used collectively), *Ephraim and the inhabitants of Samaria* (a limitation of the general terms preceding, so as to prevent their application to Judah), *in pride and in greatness of heart* (an equivalent expression), *saying* (the words recorded in the next verse).

9. The very words of the self-confident Ephraimites are now recorded. Instead of being warned and instructed by what they had already suffered, they presumptuously look for greater prosperity than ever. *Bricks are fallen, and hewn stone will we build; sycamores are felled, and cedars will we substitute.* The oriental bricks are unburnt, so that most of their brick structures are as little durable as mud walls. The sycamore is

durable, but too light and spongy to be used in solid building. The latter is accordingly contrasted with the cedar, and the former with hewn stone, the two most highly valued building materials. This verse is a metaphorical description of a change from worse to better, by a substitution of the precious for the vile. Bricks and sycamores are proverbial expressions for that which is inferior, and cedars and hewn stone for that which is superior. An illustrative parallel is found in ch. 60 : 17, where the same general idea is expressed by the exchange of stones for iron, iron for silver, wood for brass, brass for gold, of course without allusion to a literal exchange or mutual substitution.

10. Here begins a second stage in the progress of God's judgments. He had sent a warning prophecy before (v. 7), and they had been taught its meaning by experience (v. 8), but without effect upon their proud self-confidence. *And* (now) *Jehovah raises up above him* (i. e. Ephraim) *the* (victorious) *enemies of Rezin* (his late ally), *and* (besides these) *he will instigate his own* (accustomed) *enemies* (to wit, those mentioned in the next verse). They who were to conquer Israel are called the *enemies of Rezin*, to remind the Israelites of their alliance with him, and to intimate that they who had so lately conquered Syria were soon to conquer Israel.

11. This verse contains a more particular description of Ephraim's *own enemies* who were to be stirred up against him, with a declaration that this was not to be the end of the infliction. *Aram* (or Syria in the widest sense) *before, and Philistia* (or *the Philistines*) *behind, and they devour Israel with open mouth* (i. e. ravenously). *For all this* (or notwithstanding all this) *his wrath does not turn back* (from the pursuit or the attack), *and still his hand is stretched out.* On the meaning of this last clause, see above, ch. 5 : 25. The Syrians and Philis-

tines are supposed by some to be referred to, as forming part of the Assyrian army. The reference may however be to separate attacks from these two powers. *Before* and *behind* may simply mean on opposite sides, or more specifically to the east and west, which are often thus described in Hebrew.

12. These continued and repeated strokes are still without effect in bringing the people to repentance. *And the people has not turned to him that smote them, and Jehovah of Hosts they have not sought.* Sin is described in Scripture as departure from God. Repentance, therefore, is returning to him. To *seek* God, in the idiom of Scripture, is to pray to him (Isai 55 : 6), to consult him (Isai. 8 : 19), to resort to him for help (Isai. 31 : 1), to hold communion with him (Amos 5 : 4, 5). Hence it is sometimes descriptive of a godly life in general (Psalm 14 : 2). So here it includes repentance, conversion, and new obedience. This verse does not assign the reason of the fact recorded in the one preceding, but continues the description. God went on punishing, *and* the people went on sinning.

13. The next stroke mentioned is a sudden destruction among all ranks of the people, the extremes being designated by two figures drawn from the animal and vegetable world. *And Jehovah has cut off from Israel head and tail, branch and rush, in one day.* The allusion here is to a branch of the palmtree or the tree itself This tree, though now rare in the Holy Land, abounded there of old, especially in the southern part, where several places were named after it (Deut. 34 : 3. 2 Chron. 20 : 2). Hence it appears on Roman coins as the symbol of Judea. It is highly esteemed in the east, both for beauty and utility. Its branches grow near the top of its lofty trunk and bend towards the ground, as its leaves do also, with a gentle curvature, resembling that of a hand partly closed, from which peculiarity the Hebrew name and the Latin *palma*

seem to be derived. *Palm* and *rush* denote that which is superior and inferior, including every class in the community.

14. To the descriptive figures of the preceding verse, the Prophet now adds a specific application of the first. Jehovah had cut off from Israel, not only in a general sense the upper and lower classes of society, but in a more restricted sense the wicked rulers, who were the corrupt *head* of the body politic, and the false prophets who, as their abject adherents, and on account of their hypocrisy and false pretensions to divine authority, must be regarded as its *tail*, because contemptible and odious, even in comparison with other wicked men, who laid no claim to a religious character. *The elder and the favourite* (or honourable person), *he* (*is*) *the head, and the prophet teaching falsehood, he* (*is*) *the tail.* The teaching of falsehood means teaching in the name of God what he has not revealed. The false prophets are called the *tail*, because the false prophets were morally the basest of the people, and because they were the servile adherents and supporters of the wicked rulers. With respect both to the head which they followed, and the body of which they were the vilest part, they might be justly called the tail.

15. This verse gives a reason, not why all classes were to be destroyed, but why the rulers and false prophets had been specially mentioned. It arises, therefore, naturally out of the fourteenth, and thus incidentally proves it to be genuine. The truth expressed and implied is, that the leaders of the people had destroyed them and should perish with them. *The leaders of this people have been seducers, and those led by them* (are) *swallowed up* (*or ruined*).

16. *Therefore* (because the people are thus incorrigibly impenitent) *the Lord will not rejoice over their young men* (literally

chosen ones, i. e. for military service, the word being used in the general sense of *youths*, but seldom without reference to war), *and on their orphans and their widows* (elsewhere represented as peculiarly the objects of God's care) *he will not have mercy* (expressing in the strongest form the extent and severity of the threatened judgments); *for every one of them* (literally *of it*, referring to the singular noun *people*) *is profane* (or impious) *and an evil doer, and every mouth* (is) *speaking folly* (in the strong Hebrew sense of wickedness). *For all this his wrath is not turned back, and still is his hand outstretched.*

17. This verse assigns a reason why God's hand is still stretched out for the destruction of his people, by describing that destruction as the natural effect of their own wickedness, here likened to a fire beginning near the ground among the thorns and briers, then extending to the undergrowth or brushwood of the forest, which, as it consumes away, ascends in a volume of smoke. *For wickedness burneth as the fire, thorns and briers it consumes, then kindles in the thickets of the forest, and they roll themselves upwards, a column* (literally, *an ascent*) *of smoke.* Thorns and briers are often used as emblems of the wicked (Mic. 7 : 4. Nah. 1 : 10. 2 Sam. 23 : 6), and their burning as a figure for the punishment of sinners (Isai. 33 : 12. Ps. 118 : 12. 2 Sam. 23 : 7), especially by means of foreign enemies (Isai. 10 : 17. 32 : 13).

18. The figure of a general conflagration is continued in this verse, and then exchanged for a literal description of the miseries produced by civil war. *In the wrath of Jehovah of Hosts, the land is darkened* (with the smoke, or *heated* by the flame) *and the people is like food* (or fuel) *of fire; one another* (literally, *man his brother*) *they do not spare.*

19. The horrors of civil war are now presented under the

fearful image of insatiable hunger, leading men to devour their own flesh. *And he tears on the right hand and is hungry* (still), *and devours on the left and* (still) *they are not satisfied; each the flesh of his* (own) *arm, they devour.* The words *right* and *left* simply denote that the devouring should be mutual and extend in all directions. The special mention of the arm may imply that the mutual destroyers ought to have been mutual protectors.

20. The application of the figures in v. 19 is now made plain by the Prophet himself, who has been drawing no imaginary scene. It is Israel, the chosen race, that feeds on its own flesh. *They devour each the flesh of his own arm—Manasseh* (devours) *Ephraim, and Ephraim Manasseh*—and *together they* (are) *against Judah. For all this his wrath is not turned back and still his hand* (is) *stretched out.* The tribes here specified are chosen for two reasons: first, because Judah and Joseph were the most important branches of the stock of Israel, as well before as after the disruption; and secondly, because the tribes of Ephraim and Manasseh were more nearly related to each other than to any of the rest, and therefore their hostility afforded the most striking illustration of the mutual rancour which the Prophet had described as prevalent. *Together* implies unity of time, place, and action. Not only is it common for intestine wars to give occasion and give place to foreign ones, but this clause really continues the description and adds greatly to its force, by suggesting the idea that the mutual enmity of these two kindred tribes could only be exceeded by their common hatred to their common relative, the tribe of Judah. The allusions of the verse are not to one exclusive period, but to a protracted series of events. The intestine strifes of Ephraim and Manasseh, although not recorded in detail, may be inferred from various incidental statements. Of their ancient rivalry we have examples in the history of Gideon (Judges 8: 1–3) and

Jephtha (Judges 12: 1–6); and as to later times, it has been observed that of all who succeeded Jeroboam the Second on the throne of Israel, Pekahiah alone appears to have attained it without treachery or bloodshed. That Manasseh and Ephraim were both against Judah, may refer either to their constant enmity or to particular attacks. No sooner did one party gain the upper hand in the kingdom of the ten tribes, than it seems to have addressed itself to the favourite work of harassing or conquering Judah, as in the case of Pekah, who invaded it almost as soon as he had waded to the throne through the blood of Pekahiah. The repetition in the last clause intimates that even these extreme evils should be followed by still worse; that these were but the beginning of sorrows; that the end was not yet.

CHAPTER X.

THE Prophet first completes his description of the prevalent iniquity, with special reference to injustice and oppression, as a punishment of which he threatens death and deportation by the hands of the Assyrians, vs. 1–4. He then turns to the Assyrians themselves, God's chosen instruments, whom he had commissioned against Israel, to punish and degrade it, but whose own views were directed to universal conquest, to illustrate which the Assyrian himself is introduced as boasting of his tributary princes and his rapid conquests, which had met with no resistance from the people or their gods, and threatening Judah with a like fate, unaware of the destruction which awaits himself, imputing his success to his own strength and wisdom, and glorying, though a mere created instrument, over his maker and his mover, vs. 5–15. His approaching doom is then described under the figure of a forest suddenly and almost totally consumed by fire, vs. 16–19. This succession of events is to have the effect of curing the propensity to trust in man rather than God, at least among the elect remnant who survive; for though the ancient promises of great increase shall certainly be verified, only a remnant shall escape God's righteous judgments, vs. 20–23. To these the Prophet now addresses words of strong encouragement, with a renewed prediction of a judgment on Assyria similar to that on Midian at Oreb and on Egypt at the Red Sea, which is then described, in the most vivid manner, by an exhibition of the enemy's approach, from post to post, until he stands before Jerusalem, and then, with a resumption of the metaphor before used, his destruction is described as the prostration of a forest—trees and thickets—by a mighty axe, vs. 24–34.

1. In these four verses, as in the different divisions of the ninth chapter, there is an accusation followed by a threatening of punishment. The sin denounced in the first two verses is that of oppression and injustice. The punishment threatened is desolation by a foreign foe, and its effect, captivity and death. *Woe unto them that decree decrees of injustice, and that write oppression which they have prescribed.* The metaphor of *writing* is used elsewhere to describe the decrees and providential purposes of God (Isai. 65 : 6. Job 13 : 26). Here the terms may include both legislative and judicial functions, which are not so nicely distinguished in ancient as in modern theories of government. The divine displeasure is expressed against all abuse of power.

2. As the first verse describes the sinners and their sin, so the second sets forth its effect upon the people. *To turn aside* (or exclude) *from judgment the weak, and to take away* (by violence) *the right of the poor* (or afflicted) *of my people, that widows*

may be (or so that widows are) *their spoil, and the fatherless they plunder.* The infinitive indicates the tendency and actual effect of their conduct The phrase here used is to turn one aside *from* the judgment, and seems intended to express not so much the idea of judging wrongfully as that of refusing to judge at all. The same charge is brought against the rulers of Judah in ch. 1 : 23. The expression *of my people* intimates, not only that the sufferers were Israelites, but that they sustained a peculiar relation to Jehovah, who is frequently described in Scripture as the protector of the helpless, and especially of widows and orphans (Ps. 68: 5).

3. The wicked rulers are themselves addressed, and warned of an approaching crisis, when they must be deprived of all that they now glory in. *And* (though you are now powerful and rich) *what will ye do in the day of visitation, and in the ruin* (which) *shall come from far* (though all may appear safe at home)? *To whom will ye flee for help, and where will ye leave your glory* (for safe-keeping)? The questions imply negation, as if he had said, you can do nothing to protect yourselves, there is no place of concealment for your glory. According to the usage of the Old Testament, the *day of visitation* is a time when God manifests his presence specially, whether in mercy or in wrath, but most frequently the latter. The word translated *ruin* originally signifies a noise or tumult, and is therefore peculiarly appropriate to the ruin caused by foreign invasions, such as those of the Assyrians and Babylonians, which appear to be alluded to. By *glory* we are to understand whatever they now boasted of and trusted in.

4. *It* (your glory) *does not bow beneath the prisoners, and* (yet) *they shall fall beneath the slain*—i. e. if they do not bow under the captives they shall fall under the slain—or, such of them as do not bow, etc. *Beneath* may either be strictly understood as

meaning under their feet, or simply among them. The most natural interpretation of this difficult and much disputed verse is that which explains it as a solemn declaration that their glory and especially their noble chiefs must either go into captivity or fall in battle. The concluding formula (*for all this his wrath is not turned back and still his hand is stretched out*) again suggests the fearful thought that all these accumulated judgments would be insufficient to arrest the progress of the sinner or appease the wrath of God.

5. The Assyrian is now distinctly brought into view, as the instrument which God would use in punishing his people. But instead of simply executing this task, the Assyrians would seek their own ends and exceed their commission, and for this they must themselves be punished. The Prophet begins therefore with a woe against them. *Woe unto Asshur* (the *Assyrian* or *Assyria* itself), *the rod of my anger, and the staff in their* (the Assyrians') *hand is my indignation*, i. e. its instrument.

6. *Upon* (or against) *an impious nation* (i. e. Israel, including Ephraim and Judah) *will I send him* (the Assyrian), *and against the people of my wrath* (i. e. the people that provokes it and deserves it and is to experience it) *I will commission him* (or give him his orders), *to take spoil and to seize prey* (literally to *spoil spoil* and to *prey prey*), *and to place* (or render) *it* (the people) *a trampling* (a thing to be trodden under foot, a common figure for extreme degradation) *like the mire of streets.* See the same comparison in ch. 5 : 25 and Ps. 18 : 42.

7. The Assyrian is now described as an unconscious instrument in God's hand, and as entertaining in his own mind nothing but ambitious plans of universal conquest. *And he* (Assyria personified, or the king of Assyria) *not so will think* (will not *imagine* for what purpose he was raised up, or will not *in-*

tend to execute my will), *and his heart not so will think* (or purpose); *for* (on the contrary) *to destroy* (is) *in his heart; and to cut off nations not a few*, i. e. *very many nations.*

8. This verse introduces the proof and illustration of his selfishness and pride. *For he will say* (or giving it a descriptive form, *he says*) *are not my princes altogether kings*, or *at the same time kings*, mere princes with respect to me, but kings as to all the world besides? By exalting his tributary princes or the nobles of his court, he magnifies himself the more. The oriental monarchs, both in ancient and modern times, have affected the title of *Great King* (Isai. 36 : 4. Hos. 8 : 10) and *King of kings* (Ezek. 26 : 7. Dan. 2 : 37).

9. Having boasted of his princes, he now boasts of his achievements. *Is not Calno like Carchemish?* Have they not been equally subdued by me? *Or (is) not Hamath like Arpad? Or (is) not Samaria like Damascus?* Similar boastings were uttered by Rabshakeh (ch. 36 : 19, 20. 37 : 12, 13). These conquests were the more remarkable because so speedily achieved, and because the Assyrians had before confined themselves within their own limits. All the towns named were further north than Jerusalem, and probably commanded the navigation of the two great rivers, Tigris and Euphrates. *Carchemish* was a fortified town on an island in the Euphrates, at the mouth of the Chaboras, called by the Greeks *Κιρκήσιον*, and in Latin *Cercusium.* It had its own king (Isai. 37 : 13) and its own gods (Isai. 36 : 19), and was taken by Tiglath-pileser (2 Kings 15 : 29). *Calno* was the *Ctesiphon* of the Greeks, on the east bank of the Tigris, opposite Seleucia. *Hamath* was a city of Syria, on the Orontes, the mouth of which river, according to Keith (Land of Israel, ch. 2. § 3), is the *entering into Hamath*, sometimes mentioned as the northern boundary of Canaan in its widest extent (Num. 34 : 8. Josh. 13 : 5). It was also by the Greeks *Epipha-*

nia. Abulfeda, the Arabian historian, reigned there about the beginning of the fourteenth century. It is now one of the largest towns in Asiatic Turkey, having about 100,000 inhabitants. *Arpad*, another town of Syria, near Hamath, with which it is several times named. It is mentioned last in Jer. 49 : 23, and is probably no longer in existence.

10. *As my hand hath found* (i. e. reached and seized) *the idol-kingdoms* (worshippers of idols)—*and their images* (i. e. whose images were more) *than* (those of) *Jerusalem and Samaria*—the apodosis of the sentence follows in the next verse.

11. *Shall I not, as I have done to Samaria and to her idols, so do to Jerusalem and her gods?* The interrogative particle, which properly belongs to the second verb, is placed at the beginning of the sentence, in order to give prominence to its interrogative form, which involves an affirmation.

12. To the boastful speech of the Assyrian succeeds a prediction of his fate. Although he had been suffered to proceed so far, and would be suffered to proceed still further in the work of subjugation, till he reached the very verge of Zion and the portals of Jerusalem, God had determined that the work should go no further, but be there cut short by the infliction of a signal vengeance on the selfishness and pride of the invader. *And it shall be* (i. e. the end of all this glorying shall be) *that the Lord will cut his work short at Mount Zion and at Jerusalem.* (Yes, even there) *will I visit* (i. e. manifest my presence for the purpose of inflicting punishment) *on the fruit* (or outward exhibition) *of the greatness of heart* (i. e. arrogance and pride) *of the king of Assyria, and on the ostentation* (or display) *of his loftiness of eyes* (or looks, a common scriptural expression for great haughtiness). *His work* may mean the Assyrian's work of conquest, or the Lord's own work of punishment, in

reference either to Assyria or Israel. Either of these senses may be preferred without effect upon the meaning of the sentence. By the destruction of Sennacherib's army, God may be said to have cut short the work of that invader, or to have cut short his own work by accomplishing his purpose of destruction, or to have cut short his own work of punishing his people, by relieving them from danger.

13. The Assyrian is again introduced as speaking, and as arrogating to himself the two most necessary qualities of a successful ruler, energy and wisdom, military prowess and political sagacity. The last clause gives the proofs of the assertion in the first, and mentions three things which the boaster had disposed of at his pleasure, political arrangements, money, and men. *For he saith* (in heart and life, if not in words), *by the strength of my* (own) *hand I have done* (all this), *and by my* (own) *wisdom, for I am wise* (as well as strong), *and* (in the exercise of these two attributes) *I remove the bounds of the nations, and rob their hoards, and bring down, like a mighty man* (as I am), *the inhabitants.* By removing the bounds is to be understood destroying the distinctions between nations by incorporation in a single empire.

14. The rapidity and ease of the Assyrian conquests are expressed by a natural and beautiful comparison. In seizing on the riches of the nations, the conqueror had encountered no more difficulty than if he had been merely taking eggs from a forsaken nest, without even the impotent resistance which the bird, if present, might have offered, by its cries and by the flapping of its wings. *My hand has found* (i. e. reached and seized) *the strength* (or more specifically, the pecuniary strength, the *wealth*) *of the nations, and like the gathering of* (or as one gathers) *eggs forsaken, so have I gathered all the earth* (i. e. all its inhabitants and their possessions), *and there was none that*

moved a wing, or opened a mouth, or chirped. The word *peeped* used in the English version is not only obsolete but liable to be confounded with another of the same form.

15. Yet in all this the Assyrian was but an instrument in God's hands, and his proud self-confidence is therefore as absurd as if an axe or a saw or a rod or a staff should exalt itself above the person wielding it. *Shall the axe glorify itself above the* (person) *hewing with it? Or shall the saw magnify itself above the* (person) *handling it?* (This is indeed) *like a rod's wielding those who wield it, like a staff's lifting* (that which is) *no wood* (but a man). The idea is not merely that of boastful opposition but of preposterous inversion of the true relation between agent and instrument, between mind and matter. The last clause of this verse has not only been very variously explained by modern writers, but given great difficulty to the old translators, as appears from the inconsistent and unmeaning versions of it.

16. *Therefore* (on account of this impious self-confidence) *the Lord, the Lord of Hosts, will send upon his fat ones leanness, and under his glory shall burn a burning like the burning of fire.* The accumulation of divine names calls attention to the source of the threatened evil, and reminds the Assyrian that Jehovah is the only rightful Sovereign and the God of battles. The sending of leanness upon them seems to be a figure for the reduction of their strength, with or without allusion to the health of individuals. Some suppose an exclusive reference to the slaughter of Sennacherib's army, others a more general one to the decline of the Assyrian power. Both are probably included, the first as one of the most striking indications of the last. By *glory* we are to understand magnificence and greatness in the general, civil and military, moral and material. The last

clause is a lively figure for the suddenness, completeness, and rapidity of the destruction.

17. *And the Light of Israel shall be for a fire* (i. e. shall become one, or shall act as one), *and his Holy One for a flame, and it shall burn and devour his* (the Assyrian's) *thorns and briers in one day* (i. e. in a very short time). The Light of Israel is no doubt intended as an epithet of God himself, so called because he enlightened Israel by his Word and Spirit, and cheered them by the light of his countenance. There may be an allusion to the pillar of the cloud, and some think to the angel of God's presence who was in it. The thorns and the briers are explained by most interpreters as a figure for the whole body, either in allusion to their pointed weapons or to the malice and vexation of the Jews, or to their combustible nature and fitness for the fire. Here, as in the foregoing verse, fire is mentioned as a rapid and powerful consuming agent, without express allusion to the manner or the means of the destruction threatened.

18. *And the glory* (i. e. beauty) *of his* (the Assyrian's) *forest and his fruitful field, from soul to body* (i. e. totally), *will he* (the Lord) *consume, and it shall be like the wasting away of a sick man.* The Prophet meant to represent the greatness of Assyria under figures borrowed from the vegetable world, and for that purpose uses terms descriptive of the most impressive aspects under which a fruitful land presents itself, forests and harvest-fields, the two together making a complete picture, without the necessity of giving to each part a distinctive import. The *forest* and the *fruitful field*, here applied to Assyria, are applied by Sennacherib himself to Israel (ch. 37 : 24). As the terms *soul* and *flesh* are strictly inapplicable to the trees and fields, we must either suppose that the Prophet here discards his metaphor, and goes on to speak of the Assyrians as men, or that the

phrase is a proverbial one, meaning *body and soul*, i. e. altogether, and is here applied without regard to the primary import of the terms, or their agreement with the foregoing figures. The various ways in which the last clause is explained may serve to show how difficult and doubtful it has seemed to all interpreters, ancient and modern.

19. *And the rest* (or *remnant*) *of the trees of his forest shall be few, and a child shall write them*, i. e. make a list or catalogue, and by implication *number* them.

20. *And it shall be* (or come to pass) *in that day* (that is, after these events have taken place), *that the remnant of Israel, and the escaped of the house of Jacob, shall no longer add* (i. e. continue) *to lean upon their smiter* (him that smote them), *but shall lean upon Jehovah, the Holy One of Israel, in truth.* There is here an allusion to the circumstances which gave rise to this whole prophecy. Ahaz, renouncing his dependence upon God, had sought the aid of Assyria, which secured his deliverance from present danger, but subjected the kingdom to worse evils from the very power to which they had resorted. But even these oppressions were to have an end in the destruction of the hostile power; and when this should take place, Judah, now instructed by experience, would no longer trust in tyrants but sincerely in Jehovah. The reference is not to a sudden and immediate effect, but to a gradual result of the divine dispensations, so that what is here predicted, though it began to be fulfilled from the time of that catastrophe, did not receive its final consummation before Christ's appearance. On this supposition, we are better able to explain the *remnant of Israel*, as meaning not merely those left in Judah after the carrying away of the ten tribes—nor the Jews themselves who should outlive the Assyrian oppressions, and to whom the same phrase is applied 2 Kings 19 : 4, 31. 21 : 14—nor merely the Jews who

should return from the Babylonish exile, and to whom it is applied Hagg. 1 : 12. Zech. 8 : 6—nor merely the spiritual Israel, the *remnant according to the election of grace*, Rom. 11 : 5—but all these at once, or rather in succession, should be taught the lesson of exclusive reliance upon God, by his judgments on his enemies. The verb *stay* used in the English Version is equivocal, like *peep* in v. 14, because now employed chiefly in another sense. The idea expressed by the Hebrew word is simply that of leaning for support. The phrase *in truth* means that they should trust God in *sincerity*, as opposed to a mere hypocritical profession, and with *constancy*, as opposed to capricious vacillation.

21. *A remnant shall return, a remnant of Jacob, to God Almighty.* There is an obvious allusion in these words to the name of the Prophet's son *Shear-jashub*, mentioned in ch. 7 : 3. As the people were probably familiar with this name, its introduction here would be the more significant. The *remnant of Jacob* means those who should survive God's judgments threatened in this prophecy, not merely the Assyrian invasion or the Babylonish exile, but the whole series of remarkable events, by which the history of the chosen people would be marked, including the destruction and dispersion of the nation by the Romans. The return here spoken of is one that was to take place at various times and in various circumstances. Under the old dispensation, the prophecy was verified in the conversion of idolatrous Jews to the worship of Jehovah, or of wicked Jews to a godly life, by means of their afflictions; under the new, in the admission of believing Jews to the Christian church, and prospectively in the general conversion of Israel to God, which is yet to be expected.

22. The Prophet now explains the use of the word *remnant*, and shows that the threatening which it involves is not incon-

sistent with the ancient promises. *For though thy people, oh Israel* (or Jacob), *shall be like the sand of the sea* (in multitude), (only) *a remnant of them shall return. A consumption is decreed, overflowing* (with) *righteousness.* The first clause relates to a certain event, but one still future (*though thy people shall be* or *is to be*). There seems, as Calvin says, to be allusion to the promises given to the Patriarchs (e. g. Gen. 13 : 16. 22 : 17), and repeated by the Prophets (e. g. Hos. 1 : 10.), the fulfilment of which might have seemed to be precluded by the threatening in v. 21; to prevent which false conclusion, Isaiah here repeats the threatening with the promise, 'though thy people shall indeed be numerous, *yet*' etc. The name *Israel* may be understood as that of the nation; but there is more force in the language if we suppose an apostrophe to Israel or Jacob as the common ancestor, thus keeping up a distinct allusion to the ancient promises. *Thy people* will then mean *thy posterity*, not the ten tribes exclusively, nor Judah exclusively, but the whole race without distinction. The return predicted is not merely that from the Babylonish exile, but a return to God by true repentance and conversion as the only means of salvation. That a remnant only should escape, implies of course a general destruction, which is positively foretold in the last clause.

23. This verse contains a further explanation. *For a consumption, even* (the one) *determined,* (is) *the Lord, Jehovah of Hosts, making* (or *about to make*) *in the midst of all the earth.* This verse and the one before it are quoted by Paul (Rom. 9 : 27, 28) to show that the Jews, as such, were not the heirs of the promise, which was intended for the remnant according to the election of grace.

24. The logical connection of this verse is not with that immediately preceding, but with v. 19. Having there declared

the fate impending over the Assyrian, the Prophet, as it were, turned aside to describe the effect of their destruction on the remnant of Israel, and now, having done so, he resumes the thread of his discourse, as if there had been no interruption. *Therefore* (since this is soon to be the fate of the Assyrians) *be not afraid, oh my people inhabiting Zion, of Asshur* (or *the Assyrian*). *He shall smite thee* (it is true) *with the rod, and shall lift up his staff upon* (or *over*) *thee in the way of Egypt.* As Zion was the seat of the true religion, and the people of God are often said to inhabit Zion, not in a local but a spiritual sense, most interpreters understand the object of address to be Israel in general, while some restrict it to the pious and believing Jews, the remnant of Israel, who were now to be consoled and reassured amidst the judgments which were coming on the nation. The last words, *in the way of Egypt*, are ambiguous, and admit of two distinct interpretations. Some early writers, quoted by Calvin, make the phrase to mean, *on the way to* (or *from*) *Egypt*, in allusion to the fact, that Sennacherib attacked Judea in the course of an expedition against Egypt. The weight of exegetical authority preponderates in favour of a figurative exposition, making *in the way* synonymous with *in the manner*, *after the example*, as in Amos 4 : 10. The sense will then be this : 'Assyria shall oppress thee as Egypt did before.'

25. This verse assigns a reason for the exhortation not to fear in v. 24. *For yet a very little, and wrath is at an end, and my anger* (shall go forth or tend) *to their destruction*, i. e. the destruction of the enemy. The first clause may have reference to that destruction also, or to the restoration of God's people to his favour.

26. The suddenness and completeness of the ruin threatened are expressed by a comparison with two remarkable events in

sacred history, the slaughter of the Midianites by Gideon, and the overthrow of Pharaoh in the Red Sea. *And Jehovah of Hosts shall raise up against him* (the Assyrian) *a scourge* (or instrument of vengeance), *like the smiting of Midian at the rock Oreb, and his rod* (Jehovah's) shall again be *over the sea, and he shall lift it up* (again) *as he did in Egypt* (literally, *in the way of Egypt*, as in v. 24). The *rock Oreb* is particularly mentioned because one of the Midianitish princes, who had escaped from the field of battle, was there slain by Gideon ; and so Sennacherib, although he should survive the slaughter of his host, was to be slain at home (ch. 37 : 38). In the last clause there is a beautiful allusion to v. 24. As the Assyrians lifted up the rod over Israel in the manner of Egypt, so God would lift up the rod over them in the manner of Egypt. As they were like the Egyptians in their sin, so should they now be like them in their punishment. The construction of the last clause in the English Bible—*and* (as) *his rod was upon the sea,* (so) *shall he lift it up* etc.—puts an arbitrary meaning on the particles. According to the first construction given, *his rod* (shall be again) *upon the sea* is a poetical expression for 'his power shall again be miraculously displayed.'

27. *And it shall be* (happen or come to pass) *in that day* (when this prediction is fulfilled) that *his burden* (the burden imposed by him, the heavy load of Assyrian oppression, perhaps with special reference to the tribute imposed upon Hezekiah) *shall depart* (be removed) *from thy shoulder, and his yoke* (a poetical equivalent to *burden*) *from thy neck* (oh Israel!) *and the yoke* (itself) *shall be destroyed* (or broken off) *because of* (literally, *from the face of*) *oil* (or *fatness* or *anointing*). The only difficulty lies in the concluding words, which have been variously understood. Some suppose an allusion to the softening of the yoke with oil, or to its preservation by it. But in this interpretation, the explanatory fact is arbitrarily assumed.

Others take the word in the sense of *fat* or *fatness*, and suppose an allusion to the rejection of the yoke by a fat bullock, Deut. 32 : 15. Hos. 4 : 16. 10 : 11, or to the bursting of the yoke by the increasing fatness of the bullock's neck, or to the wearing away of the yoke by the neck, instead of the neck by the yoke. The general meaning of the verse is plain, as a prediction of deliverance from Assyrian bondage.

28. From the time of the Assyrian's overthrow the Prophet now reverts to that of his invasion, which he describes in the most vivid manner by rapidly enumerating the main points of his march from the frontier of Judah to the gates of Jerusalem. Some regard the description as ideal and intended to express, in a poetical manner, the quarter from which the invasion was to come and its general direction, by specifying certain places as the points through which it was to pass. The same position is maintained in Robinson's Researches (vol. 2. p. 149), on the ground that the road here traced could never have been commonly used, because impracticable from the nature of the ground. If passable at all, however, it may well have been adopted in a case of bold invasion, where surprise was a main object. The difficulties of the route in question must be slight compared with those by which Hannibal and Napoleon crossed the Alps. It is therefore not impossible nor even improbable, that Isaiah intended to delineate the actual course taken by Sennacherib. At the same time this is not a necessary supposition, since we may conceive the Prophet standing in vision on the walls of Jerusalem, and looking towards the quarter from which the invasion was to come, enumerating certain intervening points, without intending to predict that he would really pass through them. In this case, the more difficult the route described, the better suited would it be to express the idea that the enemy would come in spite of all opposing obstacles. The places here enumerated seem to

have belonged chiefly or wholly to the tribes of Benjamin and Judah. Some of them are still in existence, and the site of several has been recently determined by the personal observations and inquiries of Robinson and Smith. The catalogue begins at the frontier of the kingdom of Judah, and at the first place conquered by the Israelites on taking possession of the land. The language is precisely that of an eye-witness describing at the moment what he actually sees. *He is come to Aiath —he is passed to Migron—to Michmash he intrusts his baggage.* Although the form *Aiath* nowhere else occurs, it is commonly supposed to be the same with *Ai*, the ancient royal city of the Canaanites, destroyed by Joshua (Josh. 8 : 1), and afterwards rebuilt (Ezra 2 : 28. Neh. 7 : 32). The ancient Ai was situated on a height to the north-east of Jerusalem. According to Dr. Robinson, its site is probably still marked by certain ruins, south of Deir Diwan, an hour from Bethel. The present form, *he passes*, represents the thing as actually taking place; the preterite, *he has passed*, implies that he has scarcely reached a place before he leaves it, and is therefore more expressive of his rapid movements. The precise situation of Migron is now unknown, as it is mentioned only here and in 1 Sam. 14 : 2, from which text it would seem to have been near to Gibeah. *Michmash* is still in existence under the almost unchanged name of Mukhmas, to the north-east of Jeba, on the slope of a steep valley. The place is now desolate, but exhibits signs of former strength, foundations of hewn stone and prostrate columns.

29. *They have passed the pass*, a narrow passage between Michmash and Geba (1 Sam. 13 : 3, 5 etc.), a spot no doubt easily maintained against an enemy. Their passing it implies that they met with no resistance, or had overcome it, and that there was now little or nothing to impede their march. *In Geba they have taken up their lodging* (literally, lodged a lodg-

ing). *Geba* appears from 1 Kings 15 : 22 to have been on or near the line between Benjamin and Judah. There is a small village now called *Jeba*, half in ruins, with large hewn stones and the remains of a square tower, on the opposite side of the valley from the ancient Michmash. This place Robinson and Smith supposed at first to be *Geba*, but afterwards concluded that it must be *Gibeah* of Saul, and that the site of Geba must be further down, where they heard of ruins, but had not time to explore (vol. 2. pp. 114, 115). Thus far he has described what the Assyrians themselves do—they cross the line at Ajath—pass through Migron—leave their baggage at Michmash—lodge at Geba. Now he describes what the places themselves do; *Ramah trembles—Gibeah of Saul flees.* Ramah was a city of Benjamin, near Gibeah, but further from Jerusalem. It is still in existence as *Er-ram.* It is about half a mile nearly due west of Jeba, but hidden from it by intervening heights (Robinson, vol. 2. pp. 108—114). It is two hours north of Jerusalem, on the eastern side of the road to Nablus. The identity of this place with the ancient Ramah was long lost sight of, but has been clearly ascertained by Smith and Robinson. *Ramah trembles* (or *is afraid*) at the enemy's approach, a strong and beautiful personification, or the place may be simply put for its inhabitants. The trembling and flight of these towns is naturally represented as occurring while the enemy was resting at Geba. It may imply, either that Ramah was not in the direct line of the march but within sight and hearing of it, or on the contrary, that it was the next place to be reached, and trembling in apprehension of it. A still stronger metaphor is used as to the next place. *Gibeah of Saul*, so called because it was his birth-place and residence, and to distinguish it from others of the same name, *is fled.* There is here a rapid but marked climax. While Ramah trembles, Gibeah flees.

30. To terror and flight he now adds an audible expression

of distress, representing one place as crying, another as listening, and according to some writers, a third as responding. At the same time he exchanges the language of description for that of direct personal address. *Cry aloud, daughter Gallim* (or daughter of Gallim), *hearken Laishah,* (ah) *poor Anathoth!* The site of Gallim is no longer known, but it was no doubt somewhere in the neighbourhood of Gibeah. The personification is made more distinct by the use of the word *daughter,* whether employed simply for that purpose and applied to the town itself, or, as in many other cases, to the population, as an individual.

31. *Madmenah wanders* (or removes from her place), *the inhabitants of Gebim flee* (or *cause to flee* i. e. *carry off* their goods). These places are no longer in existence, nor are they mentioned elsewhere. In this verse, for the first time, the inhabitants are expressly mentioned and distinguished from the place itself.

32. This verse conducts him to the last stage of his progress, to a point so near the Holy City that he may defy it thence. *Yet to-day in Nob* (he is) *to stand* (and there) *will shake his hand* (a gesture of menace and defiance) *against the mountain of the house* (or daughter) *of Zion* (i. e. Mount Zion itself), *the hill of Jerusalem.* Nob was a sacerdotal city of Benjamin near Anathoth (Neh. 11 : 32), and according to some, within sight of Jerusalem. Robinson and Smith explored the ridge of Olivet for traces of this town, but without success. The Nob here mentioned is no doubt the same that Saul destroyed, although there was another in the plain towards Lydda.

33. To the triumphant march and proud defiance now succeeds abruptly the tremendous downfall of the enemy himself, in describing which the Prophet resumes the figure dropped at v. 19, and represents the catastrophe as the sudden and violent

prostration of a forest. *Behold, the Lord, Jehovah of Hosts* (is) *lopping* (or about to lop) *the branch* (of this great tree) *with terror* (or tremendous violence), *and the* (trees) *high of stature* (shall be) *felled, and the lofty ones brought low. Lofty of stature* is not to be applied to men directly, as descriptive either of their pride or their appearance, but to trees, as representing the Assyrians in general or their chief men in particular.

34. *And he* (Jehovah) *shall cut down* (or away) *the thickets of the forest* (the Assyrian army) *with iron,* (i. e. with an instrument of iron, as an axe), *and this Lebanon* (this wooded mountain, this enormous forest, still referring to the host of the Assyrians) *with* (or by) *a mighty one.* It is clear that the *iron* of this verse and the *fire* of v. 17 denote one and the same thing, both implying that the forest was to perish, not by slow decay, but by sudden violence, which shows the absurdity of giving a specific sense to all the particulars in such a picture. Thus the *thickets* are probably mentioned only to complete the picture of a forest totally destroyed. The general figure of a forest is made more specific by referring to Lebanon, a mountain celebrated for its woods.

CHAPTER XI.

This chapter is occupied with promises of restoration and deliverance, external safety and internal peace, to God's own people, as contrasted with the ruin previously threatened to their enemies. Borrowing his imagery from the fall of the Assyrian forest, just before predicted, the Prophet represents a shoot as springing from the prostrate trunk of Jesse, or rather from his roots, and invested by the Spirit of Jehovah with all the necessary attributes of a righteous judge and ruler, vs. 1–4. The pacific effect of the Messiah's reign is then described by the beautiful figure of wild and domestic animals dwelling and feeding together, and of children unhurt by the most venomous reptiles; to which is added an express prediction that all mutual injuries shall cease in consequence of the universal prevalence of the knowledge of Jehovah, vs. 5–9. To these figures borrowed from the animal creation, the Prophet now adds others from the history of Israel, but intended to express the same idea. The Messiah is here represented as a signal set up to the nations, gathering the outcasts of his people from all quarters, and uniting them again into one undivided body, free from all sectional and party animosities, vs. 10–13. Under figures of the same kind, the triumph of the church is then represented as a conquest over the old enemies of Israel, especially those nearest to the Holy Land; while the interposition of God's power to effect this and the preceding promises is vividly described as a division of the Red Sea and Euphrates, and a deliverance from Egypt and Assyria, vs. 14–16. The evidently figurative character of some parts of this chapter seems to furnish a sufficient key to the interpretation of those parts which in themselves would be more doubtful.

1. The figure of the preceding verse is continued but applied to a new subject, the downfall of the house of David and the Jewish state, which is contrasted with the downfall of Assyria. The Assyrian forest was to fall forever, but that of Judah was to sprout again. *And there shall come forth a twig* (or shoot) *from the stock* (or stump) *of Jesse, and a branch from his roots shall grow.* The only application of this passage that can be sustained is that to Jesus Christ, who sprang from the family of Jesse when reduced to its lowest estate, and to whom alone the subsequent description is literally applicable. The fact of Christ's descent from David is not only repeatedly affirmed, but

constantly presupposed in the New Testament, as a fact too notorious to be called in question or to call for proof. Jesse is supposed by some to be named instead of David, because Jesse resided at Bethlehem where Christ was to be born, and because the family is here considered as reduced to the same obscure condition in which Jesse lived, as contrasted with that to which David was exalted, and which the mention of the latter would naturally have recalled to mind.

2. The person, whose origin and descent are metaphorically described in the preceding verse, is here described by his personal qualities, as one endowed with the highest intellectual and moral gifts by the direct influences of the Holy Spirit. *And upon him shall rest the Spirit of Jehovah, a Spirit of wisdom and understanding, a Spirit of counsel and strength, a Spirit of knowledge and of the fear of Jehovah.* The genitives do not denote qualities but effects of the Spirit. The Spirit of Jehovah is not here described as being himself wise etc. but as the author of wisdom in others. This is evident from the last clause, where the fear of Jehovah cannot be an attribute of his Spirit, but must be a fruit of his influence. The qualities enumerated are not to be confounded as mere synonymes, nor on the other hand distinguished with metaphysical precision. None of these terms is entirely exclusive of the others. Wisdom, understanding, the knowledge of God, the fear of God, are all familiar scriptural descriptions of religion or piety in general. Wisdom and understanding are often joined as equivalent expressions. The latter, according to its etymology, strictly denotes the power of discernment or discrimination. Both are applied to theoretical and practical wisdom, and especially to moral and religious subjects. Counsel and strength are the ability to plan and the ability to execute, neither of which can avail without the other. The knowledge of God does not in itself mean the love of him, although it may infer it as a necessary consequence.

The correct knowledge of him certainly produces godly fear or holy reverence, and the two are probably put here for religion in the general. The only person in whom the terms of this prediction have been verified is Jesus Christ, whose wisdom displayed itself in early life and is expressly ascribed to a special divine influence; who proved himself a discerner of the thoughts and intents of the heart; whose ministry was not only characterized by fortitude and boldness, but attested by miracles and mighty deeds; whose knowledge of divine things far surpassed that of all other men; and who was himself a living model of all piety.

3. The Messiah is now described as taking pleasure in true piety and recognizing its existence by an infallible sagacity or power of discerning good and evil, which would render him superior to the illusions of the senses and to every external influence. This faculty is figuratively described as an exquisite olfactory perception, such as enables its possessor to distinguish between different odours. *And his sense of smelling* (i. e. his power of perception, with a seeming reference to the pleasure it affords him, shall be exercised) *in* (or upon) *the fear of Jehovah* (as an attribute of others), *and* (being thus infallible) *not by the sight* (or *according to the sight*) *of his eyes shall he judge, and not by the hearing of his ears shall he decide.* He shall take delight in goodness, and be able to distinguish it without fail from its counterfeits. The sight of the eyes and the hearing of the ears are put for the testimony of those senses by which men are chiefly governed in their judgments. He should not judge of character at all by the senses, but by an infallible sagacity or power of discerning good and evil. *His consolation shall be in the fear of the Lord* i. e. afforded by religion. *He shall not judge according to the sight of his eyes* i. e. shall not despair even under the most discouraging appearances. *He shall not reason according to the hearing of his ears* i. e. he shall

draw no conclusions from the rumours that may reach him, but believe the declarations of the Prophets.

4. The Messiah, as a righteous judge, is now exhibited in contrast with the unjust magistrates of Judah, as described in ch. 1 : 23. 10 : 2. 5 : 23. *And he shall judge in righteousness the weak* (or poor) *and do justice with equity* (or impartiality) *to the meek of the earth, and shall smite the earth with the rod of his mouth, and with the breath of his lips shall slay the wicked.* By the *earth* to be smitten, some understand the inhabitants of the earth. But the expression seems at least to include the smiting of the earth itself, which is elsewhere represented as the object of God's wrath, and is here described as cursed on man's account. By a *breath of his lips*, we are to understand a mere word, or a mere breath, as something even less than a word, and yet sufficient to effect his purpose. Paul, in 2 Thess. 2 : 8, applies these words, with little change, to the destruction of Antichrist at the coming of Christ. It does not follow, however, that this is a specific and exclusive prophecy of that event, but only that it comprehends it, as it evidently does. If one of the Messiah's works is to destroy his enemies, it cannot be fulfilled without the destruction of the last and greatest of those enemies to whom the Scriptures make allusion. If the promise in the first clause is of general import, the threatening in the last must be coextensive with it.

5. *And righteousness shall be the girdle of his loins, and faithfulness the girdle of his reins*, i. e. he shall be clothed or invested with these attributes, and they shall adhere closely to him. The metaphor of putting on or clothing one's self with moral attributes is not unfrequent in the Scriptures. The girdle is mentioned as an essential part of oriental dress, and that which keeps the others in their proper place, and qualifies the wearer for exertion.

6. Here, as in ch. 2 : 4 and 9 : 5, 6, universal peace is represented as a consequence of the Messiah's reign, but under a new and striking figure. *And the wolf shall dwell with the lamb, and the leopard shall lie down with the kid, and the calf and young lion and fatling together, and a little child shall lead them.* The third Hebrew noun includes the leopard and the panther, and perhaps the tiger. Calf denotes probably any fatted beast, and may here be mentioned because beasts of prey select such as their victims. The wolf is introduced as the natural enemy of the lamb, and the leopard, as some allege, sustains the same relation to the kid. *Dwell* does not mean to dwell in general, but to sojourn as a stranger or a guest, and implies that the lamb should, as it were, receive the wolf into its home. The verb translated *lie down* is especially appropriated to express the lying down of sheep and other animals. Here it may denote that the leopard, accustomed to crouch while waiting for its prey, shall now lie down peaceably beside it; or there may be an allusion to the restlessness and fleetness of the wild beast, now to be succeeded by the quiet habits of the ruminating species. Most Christian writers, ancient and modern, explain the prophecy as wholly metaphorical, and descriptive of the peace to be enjoyed by God's people under the new dispensation. Some apply the passage to the external peace between the church and the world, but it is commonly regarded as descriptive of the change wrought by Christianity in wicked men themselves. To give a specific meaning to each figure in the landscape, making the lamb, the calf, and the fatted beast, denote successive stages in the Christian's progress, the lion open enemies, the leopard more disguised ones, the wolf treacherous and malignant ones, the little child the ministry, not only mars the beauty but obscures the real meaning of the prophecy.

7. *And the cow and the bear shall feed—together shall their*

young lie down—and the lion like the ox shall eat straw. The lion's eating straw implies not only cohabitation with domestic cattle, but a change of his carnivorous habits. It denotes a total change of habit, and indeed of nature, and is therefore a fit emblem for the revolution which the gospel, in proportion to its influence, effects in the condition of society, with some allusion possibly, as before suggested, to the ultimate deliverance of the inferior creation from that bondage of corruption, to which, for man's sake, it is now subjected.

8. To express the idea still more strongly, venomous serpents are represented as innoxious, not to other beasts, but to the human species, and to the most helpless and unthinking of that species. *And the sucking child shall play on* (or *over*) *the hole of the asp, and on the den of the basilisk* (or *cerastes*) *shall the weaned child stretch* (or *place*) *its hand.* The precise discrimination of the species of serpents here referred to, is of no importance to the exegesis. All that is necessary to a correct understanding of the verse is that both words denote extremely venomous and deadly reptiles. The weaned child means of course a child just weaned. This verse is a mere continuation of the metaphor begun in v. 7, and expresses, by an additional figure, the change to be effected in society by the prevalence of true religion, destroying noxious influences and rendering it possible to live in safety.

9. The strong figures of the foregoing context are now resolved into literal expressions. *They* (indefinitely, men in general) *shall not hurt nor destroy in all my holy mountain, because the land is full of the knowledge of Jehovah* (literally, of knowing him) *like the waters covering the sea.* This is not so much a direct continuation of the previous description as a summary explanation of it. *My holy mountain* means Zion, or Moriah, or the city built upon them, not considered simply as

a capital city, but as the seat of the true religion, and at that time the local habitation of the church. What was true of the church there is true of the church everywhere. The first clause clearly shows that the foregoing description is to be figuratively understood. That the wolf and the lamb should lie down together, means in other words, that none should hurt or destroy in the Messiah's kingdom. The reason is given in the last clause. The point of comparison in the last clause is not the mere extent of surface, nor the depth but the fulness of the land to the extent of its capacity. This passage is descriptive of the reign of the Messiah, not at any one period, but as a whole. A historian, in giving a general description of the reign of David, would not use language applicable only to its beginning. The prophecy is therefore one of gradual fulfilment. So far as the cause operates, the effect follows, and when the cause shall operate without restraint, the effect will be complete and universal. The use of the future in the first clause and the preterite in the second may imply, that the prevalence of the knowledge of Jehovah must precede that of universal peace. It is not till the land *has been filled* with that knowledge, that men *will cease* to injure and destroy.

10. Having described the Messiah's reign and its effects, he now brings his person into view again. *And in that day shall the root of Jesse which* (is) *standing* (or set up) *be for a signal to the nations; unto him shall the gentiles seek, and his rest* (or residence) *shall be glorious.* The family of Jesse now under ground shall reappear and become a signal, raised to mark a place of rendezvous, for which purpose lofty trees are said to have been sometimes used. A signal of the nations then is one displayed to gather them. The reference is to Christ's manifestation to the gentiles through the preaching of the gospel. To *seek to* is not merely to inquire about, through curiosity, or to seek one's favour in the general, or to pay religious honours,

but more specifically to consult as an oracle or depository of religious truth. By *his rest* we are to understand his place of rest, his residence. The church, Christ's home, shall be glorious from his presence and the accession of the gentiles.

11. *And it shall be* (or come to pass) *in that day* (the days of the Messiah) *the Lord shall add his hand* (or add to apply his hand) *a second time*, not second in reference to the overthrow of Pekah and Rezin, or the return from Babylon, but to the deliverance from Egypt. *The remnant of his people*, not the survivors of the original captives, but those living at the time of the deliverance, or still more strictly, the remnant according to the election of grace. The countries mentioned are put for all in which the Jews should be scattered. There is no importance to be attached to the order in which they are enumerated, nor is the precise extent of each material. Assyria and Egypt are named first and together, as the two great foreign powers, with which the Jews were best acquainted. *Pathros* is Thebais or Upper Egypt, as appears not only from Scriptural usage, but also from the Egyptian etymology of the name, as denoting the region of the south. *Cush* is not merely Ethiopia proper, but Ethiopia, perhaps including part of Arabia, from which it appears to have been settled. *Shinar* is properly the plain in which Babylon was built, thence put for Babylonia. *Elam* is Elymais, a province of Persia, contiguous to Media, sometimes put for the whole country. *Hamath* is a city of Syria on the Orontes (see above, ch. 10 : 9). *Islands of the sea*, not merely islands in the strict sense, but the shores of the Mediterranean, whether insular or continental, and substantially equivalent to Europe, meaning the part of it then known, and here put last, as being the most important. This prophecy does not relate to the Gentiles or the Christian church, but to the Jews. The dispersions spoken of are not merely such as had already taken place at the date of the prediction

but others then still future, including not only the Babylonish exile but the present dispersion. The prophecy was not fulfilled in the return of the refugees after Sennacherib's discomfiture, nor in the return from Babylon, and but partially in the preaching of the gospel to the Jews. The complete fulfilment is to be expected when *all Israel shall be saved.* The prediction must be figuratively understood, because the nations mentioned in this verse have long ceased to exist. The event prefigured is, according to some, the return of the Jews to Palestine; but according to others, their admission to Christ's kingdom on repentance and reception of the Christian faith.

12. *And he* (Jehovah) *shall set up a signal to the nations, and shall gather the outcasts of Israel, and the dispersed of Judah shall he bring together from the four wings of the earth. To the nations,* i. e. in their sight. The nations thus addressed are not the Jews but the Gentiles, and, as most interpreters suppose, those Gentiles among whom the Jews were scattered, and who are summoned by the signal here displayed to set the captives free, or to assist them in returning. The verse then contains two successive predictions; first, that the gentiles shall be called, and then that the Jews shall be restored, which agrees exactly with Paul's account of the connection between these events. *Blindness in part is happened to Israel until the fulness of the gentiles be come in* (Rom. 11 : 25, 26). On this hypothesis, the signal is displayed to the gentiles, not that they may send or bring the Jews back, but that they may come themselves, and then the gathering of Israel and Judah is added, as a distinct if not a subsequent event. Israel and Judah are put together to denote the race in general. If this verse be understood as predicting the agency of the Gentiles in restoring the Jews, it may be said to have been partially fulfilled in the return from Babylon under the auspices of Cyrus, and again in all efforts made by gentile Christians to convert the Jews; but

its full accomplishment is still prospective, and God may even now be lifting up a signal to the gentiles for this very purpose.

13. *And the envy of Ephraim shall depart* (or cease), *and the enemies of Judah shall be cut off. Ephraim shall not envy Judah, and Judah shall not vex* (oppress or harass) *Ephraim.* Jacob, in his prophetic statement of the fortunes of his sons, disregards the rights of primogeniture and gives the pre-eminence to Judah and Joseph (Gen. 49 : 8–12. 22–26), and in the family of the latter to the younger son Ephraim (Gen 48 : 19). Hence from the time of the exodus, these two were regarded as the leading tribes of Israel. Judah was much more numerous than Ephraim (Num. 1 : 27, 33), took precedence during the journey in the wilderness (Num. 2 : 3. 10 : 14), and received the largest portion in the promised land. But Joshua was an Ephraimite (Num. 13 : 8), and Shiloh, where the tabernacle long stood (Jos. 18 : 1. 1 Sam. 4 : 3), was probably within the limits of the same tribe. The ambitious jealousy of the Ephraimites towards other tribes appears in their conduct to Gideon and Jephthah (Judges 8 : 1. 12 : 1). Their special jealousy of Judah showed itself in their temporary refusal to submit to David after the death of Saul, in their adherence to Absalom against his father, and in the readiness with which they joined in the revolt of Jeroboam, who was himself of the tribe of Ephraim (1 Kings 11 : 26). This schism was, therefore, not a sudden or fortuitous occurrence, but the natural result of causes which had long been working. The mutual relation of the two kingdoms is expressed in the recorded fact, that *there was war between Rehoboam and Jeroboam, and between Asa and Baasha, all their days* (1 Kings 14 : 30. 15 : 16). Exceptions to the general rule, as in the case of Ahab and Jehoshaphat, were rare, and a departure from the principles and ordinary feelings of the parties. The ten tribes, which assumed the name of Israel after the division, and perhaps be-

fore it, regarded the smaller and less warlike state with a contempt which is well expressed by Jehoash in his parable of the cedar and the thistle (2 Kings 14 : 9), unless the feeling there displayed be rather personal than national. On the other hand, Judah justly regarded Israel as guilty, not only of political revolt, but of religious apostasy (Ps. 78 : 9–11), and the jealousy of Ephraim towards Judah would of course be increased by the fact that Jehovah had *forsaken the tabernacle of Shiloh* (Ps. 78 : 60), *refused the tabernacle of Joseph, and chose not the tribe of Ephraim, but chose the tribe of Judah, the Mount Zion which he loved* (ib. vs. 67, 68). This view of the matter will serve to explain why it is that when the Prophet would foretell a state of harmony and peace, he does so by declaring that the hereditary and proverbial enmity of Judah and Israel should cease. It also explains why he lays so much more stress upon the envy of Ephraim than upon the enmity of Judah, viz. because the latter was only an indulgence of unhallowed feeling, to which, in the other case, were superadded open rebellion and apostasy from God. Hence the first three members of the verse before us speak of Ephraim's enmity to Judah, and only the fourth of Judah's enmity to Ephraim; as if it had occurred to the Prophet, that although it was Ephraim whose disposition needed chiefly to be changed, yet Judah also had a change to undergo, which is therefore intimated in the last clause, as a kind of after-thought. The envy of Ephraim against Judah shall depart; the enemies of Judah (in the kingdom of the ten tribes) shall be cut off; Ephraim shall no more envy Judah; yes, and Judah in its turn shall cease to vex Ephraim. That this prophecy was not fulfilled in the return from exile, is sufficiently notorious. That it had not been fulfilled when Christ came, is plain from the continued enmity between the Jews, Samaritans, and Galileans. The only fulfilment it has ever had is in the abolition of all national and sectional distinctions in the Christian church (Gal 3 : 27, 29.

5 : 6), to which converted Jews as well as others must submit. Its full accomplishment is yet to come, in the re-union of the tribes of Israel under Christ their common head (Hos. 1 : 11).

14. Instead of assailing or annoying one another, they are represented as making common cause against a common enemy. *And they* (Ephraim and Judah, undivided Israel) *shall fly* (like a bird of prey) *upon the shoulder of the Philistines towards the sea* (or *westward*) *; together they shall spoil the sons of the east* (the Arabians and perhaps the Syrians) ; *Edom and Moab the stretching out of their hand* (i. e. the object of that action) *and the children of Ammon their obedience* (i. e. their subjects). All the names are those of neighbouring nations with whom the Hebrews were accustomed to wage war. Edom, Moab, and Ammon, may be specially named for an additional reason, viz. that they were nearly related to Israel, and yet among his most inveterate enemies. The Jews explain this as a literal prediction having respect to the countries formerly possessed by the races here enumerated. Most Christian writers understand it spiritually of the conquests to be achieved by the true religion, and suppose the nations here named to be simply put for enemies in general, or for the heathen world ; this method of description being rendered more emphatic by the historical associations which the names awaken. To *fly upon* means here to *fly at*, or to *pounce upon*, the figure being that of an eagle or other bird of prey.

15. To the destruction of the enemies of Israel is added a prediction that all obstacles, even the most formidable, to the restoration of God's people, shall be overcome or taken away by his almighty power. This idea is naturally expressed by the dividing of the Red Sea and Euphrates, because Egypt and Assyria are the two great powers from which Israel had suffered and was yet to be delivered. *And Jehovah will destroy*

(by drying up) *the tongue* (or bay) *of the sea of Egypt* (i. e. the Red Sea), *and he will wave his hand* (as a gesture of menace or a symbol of miraculous power) *over the river* (Euphrates), *in the violence of his wind* (or breath), *and smite it* (the Euphrates) *into seven streams, and make* (his people) *tread* (it) *in shoes* (i. e. dry-shod). *Tongue*, which is applied in other languages to projecting points of land, is here descriptive of a bay or indentation in a shore. The *sea of Egypt* is not the Nile, as some suppose, although the name *sea* has been certainly applied to it from the earliest times, but the Red Sea, called the Sea of Egypt for the same reason that it is called the Arabian Gulf. The *tongue* of this sea is the narrow gulf or bay in which it terminates to the north-west near Suez, called by the old writers the *Sinus Heroopolitanus*, to distinguish it from the *Sinus Elaniticus*, the north-east extremity. Through the former the Israelites passed when they left Egypt, and it is now predicted that it shall be utterly destroyed, i. e. dried up. At the same time the Euphrates is to be smitten into seven streams, and so made fordable, as Cyrus is said to have reduced the Gyndes by diverting its water into many artificial channels. The terms are probably strong figures drawn from the early history and experience of Israel.

16. *And there shall be a highway for the remnant of my people, which shall be left, from Assyria, as there was for Israel, in the day of his coming up from the land of Egypt.* This verse admits of two interpretations. According to one, it is a comparison of the former deliverance from Egypt with the future one from Assyria and the neighbouring countries, where most Jewish exiles were to be found. According to the other, it is a repetition of the preceding promise, that previous deliverances, particularly those from Egypt and Assyria, should be repeated in the future history of the church. The fulfilment has been sought by different interpreters, in the return from Babylon,

in the general progress of the gospel, and in the future restoration of the Jews. The first of these can at most be regarded only as a partial or inchoate fulfilment, and against the last lies the obvious objection, that the context contains promises and threatenings which are obviously figurative, although so expressed as to contain allusion to remarkable events in the experience of Israel. Such is the dividing or drying up of the tongue of the Red Sea, which must either be figuratively understood, or supposed to refer to a future miracle, which last hypothesis is certainly not necessary, and therefore can be fully justified by nothing but the actual event.

CHAPTER XII.

TAKING occasion from the reference to Egypt and the exodus in the close of the preceding chapter, the Prophet now puts into the mouth of Israel a song analogous to that of Moses, from which some of the expressions are directly borrowed. The structure of this Psalm is very regular, consisting of two parts, in each of which the Prophet first tells the people what they will say, or have a right to say, when the foregoing promises are verified, and then addresses them again in his own person and in the usual language of prediction. In the first stanza, they are made to acknowledge the divine compassion and to express their confidence in God as the source of all their strength, and therefore the rightful object of their praise, vs. 1–3. In the second stanza, they exhort one another to make known what God has done for them, not only at home but among all nations, and are exhorted by the Prophet to rejoice in the manifested presence of Jehovah, vs. 4–6.

1. *And thou* (Israel, the people of God) *shalt say in that day* (when the foregoing promise is accomplished) *I will praise thee* (strictly, *acknowledge thee* as worthy, and as a benefactor) *for thou wast angry with me, but thine anger is turned away and thou comfortest me.*—The apparent incongruity of thanking God because he was angry, is removed by considering that the subject of the thanksgiving is the whole complex idea expressed in the remainder of the verse, of which God's being angry is only one element. It was not simply because God was angry that the people praise him, but because he was angry and his anger ceased. The same idea is expressed by the English Version in another form, by intimating early in the sentence the relation of its parts, whereas it is characteristic of the Hebrew style to state things absolutely first, and qualify them afterwards. The same mode of expression is used by Paul in Greek, when he says (Romans 6 : 17), God be thanked that ye were the servants of sin, but ye have from the heart obeyed etc. *Thou comfortest me*, not by words only but by deeds.

2. *Behold, God is my salvation. I will trust, and not be afraid; for my strength and song is Jah Jehovah, and he is become my salvation.* The first verb may be rendered in the present (*I trust*), as describing an actual state of mind; but the future form, while it sufficiently implies this, at the same time expresses a fixed determination, I will trust, be confident, secure. The next words contain a negative expression of the same idea. *My strength and my song*, i. e. the source of my protection and the subject of my praise.

3. *And ye shall draw water with joy from the springs of salvation.* This is a natural and common figure for obtaining and enjoying divine favour.

4. *And ye shall say* (to one another) *in that day, praise* (or give thanks to) *Jehovah, call upon his name* (proclaim it), *make known among the nations his exploits* (or achievements), *remind* (them) *that his name is exalted. Name* is here used in the pregnant sense of that whereby God makes himself known, including explicit revelation and the exhibition of his attributes in all.

5. *Praise Jehovah* (by singing, and perhaps with instruments) *because he has done elevation* (or sublimity, i. e. a sublime deed). *Known is this* (or *be* this) *in all the earth,* means properly to play upon stringed instruments, then to sing with an accompaniment, then to sing in general, then to praise by singing or by music generally. In this last sense it may govern the noun directly. The English Version, *excellent things*, is too indefinite. The English Version supplies *is*, and makes the last clause an appeal to the whole world for the truth of the thing celebrated. Most of the recent versions make it an imperative expression, exhorting to a general diffusion of the truth.

6. *Cry out and shout* (or sing), *oh inhabitant of Zion* (the people or the church personified as a woman), *for great in the midst of thee* (residing in thee by a special manifestation of his presence) *is the Holy One of Israel* (that Holy Being who has bound himself to Israel, in a peculiar and extraordinary manner, as their covenant God).

CHAPTERS XIII, XIV.

HERE begins a series of prophecies (chap. XIII–XXIII) against certain foreign powers, from the enmity of which Israel had been more or less a sufferer. The first in the series is a memorable prophecy of the fall of the Babylonian empire and the destruction of Babylon itself (chap. XIII, XIV). The Medes are expressly named as the instruments of its subjection, and the prophecy contains several other remarkable coincidences with history both sacred and profane. Hence it was justly regarded by the older writers, both Jews and Christians, as an extraordinary instance of prophetic foresight. The great majority of Christian writers understand these chapters as a specific prophecy of the downfall of the Babylonian empire occasioned by the conquests of the Medes and Persians. To this event there are repeated unequivocal allusions. There are some points, however, in which the coincidence of prophecy and history, on this hypothesis, is not so clear. This is especially the case with respect to the total destruction and annihilation of the city itself, which was brought about by a gradual process through a course of ages. The true solution of this difficulty is that the prediction is generic, not specific; that it is not a detailed account of one event exclusively, but a prophetic picture of the fall of Babylon considered as a whole, some of the traits being taken from the first and some from the last stage of the fatal process, while others are indefinite or common to all. The same idea may be otherwise expressed by saying, that the king of Babylon, whose fall is here predicted, is neither Nebuchadnezzar nor Belshazzar, but the kings of Babylon collectively, or rather an ideal king of Babylon, in whom the character and fate of the whole empire are concentrated. Some of the terms applied to him may therefore be literally true of one king, some of another, some individually of none, although descriptive of the whole. This hypothesis, while it removes all discrepancies, still retains the wonderful coincidences of the prophecy with history, and makes them more remarkable by scattering them through so vast a field. It is universally admitted that the thirteenth chapter, and the greater part if not the whole of the fourteenth, constitute a single prophecy. The division of the chapters is, however, not a wrong one. Both parts relate to the destruction of Babylon, setting out from God's decree and winding up with the threatening of total desolation. Ch. XIV is therefore not a mere continuation of ch. XIII, but a repetition of the same matter in another form. The difference of form is chiefly this, that while ch. XIII is more historical in its arrangement, ch. XIV is dramatic or at least poetical. Another point of difference is that in ch. XIII the downfall of Babylon is represented rather as an act of divine vengeance, in ch. XIV as a means of deliverance to Israel, the denunciations of divine wrath being there clothed in the form of a triumphant song to be sung by Israel when Babylon is fallen. The downfall of Babylon, as a great antitheocratic power, an opponent and persecutor of the ancient church, affords a type or emblem of the destiny of all opposing powers under the New Testament; and in consequence of this analogy, the Apocalyptic prophecies apply the name Babylon to the Antichristian power. But these Apocalyptic prophecies are new ones, not interpretations of the one before us.

CHAPTER XIII.

AFTER a title, the prophecy opens with a summons to the chosen instruments of God's righteous judgments upon Babylon, who are described as mustered by the Lord himself, and then appearing, to the terror and amazement of the Babylonians, who are unable to resist their doom, vs. 1–9. The great catastrophe is then described in a series of beautiful figures, as an extinction of the heavenly bodies, and a general commotion in the frame of nature, explained by the prophet himself to mean a fearful visitation of Jehovah, making men more rare than gold, dispersing the strangers resident at Babylon, and subjecting the inhabitants to the worst inflictions at the hands of the Medes, who are expressly mentioned as the instruments of the divine vengeance, and described as indifferent to gain and relentless in their cruelty, vs. 1–18. From this beginning of the process of destruction, we are then hurried on to its final consummation, the completeness of which is expressed by a comparison with the overthrow of Sodom and Gomorrah, and by a prediction that the site of Babylon shall not be frequented even by the wandering Arab, or by shepherds and their flocks, but only by solitary animals whose presence is itself a sign of utter desolation, vs. 19–22.

1. *The Burden of Babylon* (or threatening prophecy respecting it), *which Isaiah the son of Amoz saw* (received by revelation). There are two interpretations of the word translated burden, both very ancient. The one makes it simply mean a *declaration*, or more specifically a divine declaration, a prophecy, oracle, or vision. The other explanation gives the word the sense of a minatory prophecy. Because in other connections it always means a *burden*, it is best to retain the common explanation. This word occurs in the titles of all the distinct prophecies of this second part.

2. The attack of the Medes and Persians upon Babylon is now foretold, not in the proper form of a prediction, nor even in that of a description, which is often substituted for it, but in that

of an order from Jehovah to his ministers to summon the invaders, first by an elevated signal, and then as they draw nearer by gestures and the voice. *Upon a bare hill* (i. e. one with a clear summit, not concealed by trees) *set up a signal, raise the voice* (shout or cry aloud) *to them* (the Medes and Persians), *and let them enter the gates of the* (Babylonian) *nobles.* Some suppose the angels to be here addressed; others, the captive Jews; but it is best to understand the words indefinitely as addressed to those whose proper work it was to do the thing commanded. Jehovah being here represented as a military leader, the order is of course to be conceived as given to his heralds or other officers. They are not commanded to display a banner as a sign of victory, but to erect a signal for the purpose of collecting troops. The nobles are those of Babylon.

3. The enemies thus summoned are described as chosen, designated instruments of the divine vengeance, and as already exulting in the certainty of their success. *I* (myself) *have given command* (or a commission) *to my consecrated* (chosen and appointed instruments). *Yes* (literally, *also*), *I have called* (forth) *my mighty ones* (or heroes) *for* (the execution of) *my wrath, my proud exulters.* Consecrated is here used in its primary and proper sense of separating, setting apart, or consecrating to a special use or service. To *call* out is here explained by some as denoting specially a call to military service. It may, however, have the general sense of summoning or calling upon by name. The last words of the verse, may be understood as a description of the confidence with which they anticipated victory; but most interpreters suppose an allusion to the natural character of the Persians as described by Croesus in Herodotus, by Herodotus himself and others.

4. The Prophet, in his own person, now describes the enemies of Babylon who had just been summoned, as actually on

their way. He hears a confused noise, which he soon finds to be that of confederated nations forming the army of Jehovah against Babylon. *The voice* (or sound) *of a multitude in the mountains! the likeness of much people! the sound of a tumult of kingdoms of nations gathered* (or gathering themselves)*! Jehovah of Hosts mustering* (i. e. inspecting and numbering) *a host of battle* (i. e. a military host)! The absence of verbs adds greatly to the vividness of the description. The sentence really consists of a series of exclamations, describing the impressions made successively upon the senses of an eye and ear-witness. By the mountains some suppose Media to be meant, to which others add Armenia and the other hilly countries from which Cyrus drew his forces. This supposes the movement here described to be that of the levy or conscription. But it seems more natural to understand it, as most writers do, of the actual advance of the invaders. The mountains then will be those dividing Babylonia from Media or Persia. The expression *likeness of much people* some refer to the indistinct view of a great multitude approaching from a distance. The reference to sound before and afterwards, makes the reference of this clause to the sense of sight improbable. It is commonly agreed that there is here a direct reference to the mixture of nations in the army of Cyrus. Besides the Persians and the Medes, Xenophon speaks of the Armenians, and Jeremiah adds the names of other nations (Jer. 50 : 9. 51 : 27). Most interpreters suppose the event here predicted to be subsequent in date to the overthrow of Croesus, while some refer it to the first attack of Cyrus upon Babylonia, recorded in the third book of the Cyropedia. But these distinctions seem to rest upon a false view of the passage as a description of particular marches, battles, etc., rather than a generic picture of the whole series of events which ended in the downfall of Babylon. For a just view of the principles on which such prophecies should be explained, with particular reference to that before us, see Stuart on the Apocalypse, vol 2, p. 143. The title *Jehovah of Hosts*, may here seem to be used unequivocally, in the sense of *God of Battles*, on account of the obvious allusion to the word *host* following. But as this explanation of the title is not justified by scriptural usage (see above, ch. 1 : 9), it is better to understand the words as meaning that the Lord of the Hosts of Heaven is now mustering a host on earth. He who controls the *hosts of heaven* is now engaged in mustering a *host of war*, i. e. an army. The substitution of the present for the participle in the English Version (*mustereth*) and most others, greatly impairs the force and uniformity of the expression by converting a lively exclamation into a dispassionate assertion.

5. *Coming from a distant land* (literally, *a land of distance*), *from the* (visible or apparent) *end of the heavens—Jehovah and the instruments* (or weapons) *of his wrath—to lay waste* (or destroy) *the whole land* (of Babylonia). The *end of heaven* is a strong but natural hyperbole. The best explanation is that the Prophet refers to the *horizon* or *bounding line* of vision. He is not deliberately stating from what region they set out, but from what point he sees them actually coming, viz. from the remotest point in sight. This view of the expression, not as a geographical description, but as a vivid representation of appearances, removes the necessity of explaining how Media or Persia could be called a distant land or the extremity of heaven. The host which Jehovah was before said to be mustering is now represented as consisting of himself *and* the weapons of his wrath. This intimation of his presence, his co-operation, and even his incorporation, with the invading host, adds greatly to the force of the threatening. The Hebrew word translated *implements* includes *instruments* and *vessels*. It has here the active sense of weapons, while in Rom. 9 : 22, Paul employs a corresponding Greek phrase in the passive sense of vessels.

Weapons of wrath are the weapons which execute it, *vessels of wrath* the vessels which contain it.

6. *Howl* (ye Babylonians, with distress and fear), *for the day of Jehovah* (his appointed time of judgment) *is near. Like might* (i. e. a mighty stroke or desolation) *from the Almighty it shall come.* A destruction as complete and overwhelming *as if* it were an act of reckless violence. This day is said to be *near*, not absolutely with respect to the date of the prediction, but relatively, either with respect to the perceptions of the Prophet, or with respect to what had gone before. For ages Babylon might be secure; but after the premonitory signs just mentioned should be seen, there would be no delay. The words of the verse are supposed to be uttered in the midst of the tumult and alarm of the invasion.

7. *Therefore* (because of this sudden and irresistible attack) *all hands shall sink* (fall down, be slackened or relaxed), *and every heart of man shall melt.* Both the clauses, in their strict sense, are descriptive of bodily effects, and both indicative of mental states. Each of the figures is repeatedly used elsewhere. (See Jos. 7 : 5. Ps. 22 : 14. Jer. 50 : 43. Job 4 : 3.)

8. *And they* (the Babylonians) *shall be confounded, pangs and throes shall seize* (them), *like the travailing* (woman) *they shall writhe, each at his neighbour, they shall wonder, faces of flames* (shall be) *their faces.* The expression *wonder at each other* occurs once in historical prose (Gen. 43 : 33). It seems here to denote not simply consternation and dismay, but stupefaction at each other's aspect and condition, q. d. *each man at his friend shall stand aghast.* The last clause is a continued description of the terror and distress of the Chaldeans. In the expression faces of flame, the point of comparison according to some is *redness*, here referred to as a natural symptom of confusion and shame.

But as this seems inappropriate in the case before us, others understand the aspect indicated to be one of *paleness*, as produced by fear. Others understand the *glow* or *flush* produced by anguish and despair to be intended.

9. All this must happen and at a set time, for *behold the day of Jehovah cometh, terrible, and wrath and heat of anger, to place* (or make) *the land a waste, and its sinners he* (or *it*, the day) *will destroy from it* (or *out of it*). The moral causes of the ruin threatened are significantly intimated by the Prophet's calling the people of the earth or land *its sinners.*

10. The day of Jehovah is now described as one of preternatural and awful darkness, in which the very sources of light shall be obscured. This natural and striking figure for sudden and disastrous change is of frequent occurrence in Scripture (see Isai. 24 : 23. 34 : 4. Ezek. 32 : 7, 8. Joel 2 : 10. 3 : 15. Amos 8 : 9. Matth. 24 : 29). Well may it be called a day of wrath and terror, *for the stars of the heavens and their signs* (or constellations) *shall not shed their light, the sun is darkened in his going forth, and the moon shall not cause its light to shine.* Some understand the image here presented to be that of a terrific storm, veiling the heavens, and concealing its luminaries. But grand as this conception is, it falls short of the Prophet's vivid description, which is not that of transient obscuration but of sudden and total extinction. The abrupt change from the future to the preterite and back again, has been retained in the translation, although most modern versions render all the verbs as present. From simply *foretelling* the extinction of the stars, the Prophet suddenly *describes* that of the sun as if he saw it, and then adds that of the moon as a necessary consequence.

11. The Prophet according to his custom (see above, ch.

1 : 22. 5 : 7. 11 : 9), now resolves his figures into literal expressions, showing that the natural convulsions just predicted are to be understood as metaphorical descriptions of the divine judgments. *And I will visit upon the world* (*its*) *wickedness* (i. e. manifest my presence for the purpose of punishing it), *and upon the wicked their iniquity, and I will cause to cease the arrogance of presumptuous sinners, and the pride of tyrants* (or oppressors) *I will humble.* World is here applied to the Babylonian empire, as embracing most of the known world.

12. To the general description in the foregoing verse he now adds a more specific threatening of extensive slaughter, and a consequent diminution of the population, expressed by a strong comparison. *I will make men more scarce* (or rare) *than pure gold, and a human being than the ore of Ophir.* The disputed question as to the locality of Ophir, although not without historical and archaeological importance, can have no effect upon the meaning of this passage. Whether the place meant be Ceylon, or some part of continental India, or of Arabia, or of Africa, it is here named simply as an *Eldorado*, as a place where gold abounded, either as a native product or an article of commerce, from which it was brought, and with which it was associated in the mind of every Hebrew reader.

13. The figurative form of speech is here resumed, and what was before expressed by the obscuration of the heavenly bodies is now denoted by a general commotion of the frame of nature. *Therefore I will make the heavens tremble, and the earth shall shake* (or be shaken) *out of its place in the wrath of Jehovah of Hosts and in the day of the heat* (or *fierceness*) *of his anger. Therefore* may either mean because of the wickedness mentioned in v. 11, or for the purpose of producing the effect described in v. 12.

14. *And it shall be* (or come to pass, that) *like a roe* (or antelope) *chased* (or driven by the hunters) *and like sheep with none to gather them* (literally, *like sheep and there is no one gathering*), *each to his people, they shall turn, and each to his country, they shall flee.* The points of comparison to antelopes are their timidity and fleetness. The figure of scattered sheep, without a gatherer or shepherd, is a common one in Scripture.

15. The flight of the strangers from Babylon is not without reason, *for every one found* (there) *shall be stabbed* (or thrust through), *and every one joined* (or joining himself to the Babylonians) *shall fall by the sword.* All interpreters agree that a general massacre is here described, although they differ as to the precise sense and connection of the clauses.

16. The horrors of the conquest shall extend not only to the men, but to their wives and children. *And their children shall be dashed to pieces before their eyes, their houses shall be plundered and their wives ravished.* The same thing is threatened against Babylon in Ps. 137 : 9, in retaliation for the barbarities practised in Jerusalem (2 Chr. 36 : 17. Lam. 5 : 11). The horror of the threatening is enhanced by the addition of *before their eyes.* (Compare ch. 1 : 7 and Deut. 28 : 31, 32.)

17. The Prophet now, for the first time, names the chosen instruments of Babylon's destruction. *Behold I (am) stirring up against them Madai* (Media or the Medes), *who will not regard silver, and (as for) gold, they will not take pleasure in it* (or desire it). Here, as in Jer. 51 : 11, 28, the Medes alone are mentioned, as the more numerous and hitherto more powerful nation, to which the Persians had long been subject, and were still auxiliary. Or the name may be understood as comprehending both, which has been clearly shown to be the usage of the classical historians. Indeed, all the names of the great

oriental powers are used, with more or less latitude and license, by the ancient writers, sacred and profane. As the Medes did not become an independent monarchy till after the date of this prediction, it affords a striking instance of prophetic foresight. At the date of this prediction they formed a part of the Assyrian empire, but revolted at the time of the Assyrian invasion of Syria and Israel. Their first king Dejoces was elected about 700 years before the birth of Christ. His son Phraortes conquered Persia, and the united Medes and Persians, with the aid of the Babylonians, subdued Assyria under the conduct of Cyaxares I. The conquest of Babylon was effected in the reign of Cyaxares II by the Median army, with an auxiliary force of thirty thousand Persians, under the command of Cyrus, the king's nephew. The thirst of blood would supersede the thirst of gold in the conquerors of Babylon, so that no one would be able to secure his life by ransom.

18. *And bows shall dash boys in pieces, and the fruit of the womb they shall not pity, on children their eye shall not have mercy.* The strong term *dash in pieces* is employed instead of one more strictly appropriate, with evident allusion to its use in v. 16. The cruelty of the Medes seems to have been proverbial in the ancient world.

19. From the very height of greatness and renown, Babylon shall be reduced not only to subjection but to annihilation. *And Babylon, the beauty* (or glory) *of kingdoms, the ornament, the pride, of the Chaldees, shall be like God's overthrowing Sodom and Gomorrah,* i. e. shall be totally destroyed in execution of a special divine judgment. The *beauty of kingdoms* is by most writers understood comparatively as denoting the most beautiful of kingdoms, either in the proper sense or in that of royal cities (see 1 Sam 27 : 5). But some understand the words more strictly as denoting the ornament of an empire which in

cluded various tributary kingdoms. This agrees well with the next clause, which describes the city as the ornament and pride of the Chaldees. The origin of this name, and of the people whom it designates, is doubtful and disputed. But whether the Chaldees were of Semitic origin or not, and whether they were the indigenous inhabitants of Babylonia or a foreign race imported from Armenia and the neighbouring countries, it is plain that the word here denotes the *nation* of which Babylon was the capital. The exact sense of the last clause is that already given, like God's overthrowing Sodom and Gomorrah. This is a common formula in Scripture for complete destruction, viewed as a special punishment of sin. (See above, ch. 1 : 7, 9.) It is certain that the destruction of Babylon was gradual, successively promoted by the conquests of Cyrus, Darius Hystaspes, Alexander the Great, Antigonus, Demetrius, the Parthians, and the founding of the cities of Seleucia and Ctesiphon. From this apparent disagreement of the prophecy with history, some seem disposed to infer that it relates not to the literal but spiritual Babylon. The true conclusion is that the prophecy does not relate to any one invasion or attack exclusively, but to the whole process of subjection and decay, so completely carried out through a course of ages, that the very site of ancient Babylon is now disputed. This hypothesis accounts for many traits in the description which appear inconsistent only in consequence of being all applied to one point of time and one catastrophe exclusively.

20. *It shall not be inhabited forever* (i. e. it shall never again or no more be inhabited) *and it shall not be dwelt in from generation to generation* (literally, to generation and generation), *neither shall the Arab pitch tent there, neither shall shepherds cause* (their flocks) *to lie there.* The conversion of a populous and fertile district into a vast pasture-ground, however rich and well frequented, implies extensive ruin, but not such ruin

as is here denounced. Babylon was not even to be visited by shepherds, nor to serve as the encamping ground of wandering Arabs. The completeness of the threatened desolation will be seen by comparing these expressions with ch. 5 : 5, 17. 7 : 21. 17 : 2, where it is predicted that the place in question should be *for flocks to lie down with none to make them afraid.* So fully has this prophecy been verified that the Bedouins, according to the latest travellers, are even superstitiously afraid of passing a single night upon the site of Babylon. The simplest version of the first clause would be, *she shall not dwell forever*, *she shall not abide* etc. And this construction is actually given by some. But the great majority of writers follow the Septuagint and Vulgate in ascribing to the active verbs a passive or intransitive sense.

21. Having excluded men and the domesticated animals from Babylon, the Prophet now tells how it shall be occupied, viz. by creatures which are only found in deserts, and the presence of which therefore is a sign of desolation. In the first clause these solitary creatures are referred to in the general; the other clause specifies two kinds out of the many which are elsewhere spoken of as dwelling in the wilderness *But there* (instead of flocks) *shall lie down desert creatures, and their houses*, (those of the Babylonians) *shall be filled with howls or yells, and there shall dwell the daughters of the ostrich, and shaggy* beasts (or *wild goats*) *shall gambol there.* The contrast is heightened by the obvious allusion to v. 20. As if he had said, flocks shall not lie down there, but wild beasts shall; man shall not dwell there, but the ostrich shall. The meaning evidently is that the populous and splendid city should become the home of animals found only in the wildest solitudes. To express this idea, other species might have been selected with the same effect. The endless discussions therefore as to the identity of those here named, however laudable as tending to promote

exact lexicography and natural history, have little or no bearing on the interpretation of the passage. Nothing more will be here attempted than to settle one or two points of comparative importance. Many interpreters regard the whole verse as an enumeration of particular animals. This has arisen from the assumption of a perfect parallelism in the clauses. It is altogether natural, however, to suppose that the writer would first make use of general expressions and afterwards descend to particulars. The *daughter of the ostrich* is an oriental idiom for ostriches in general, or for the female ostrich in particular. The old translation *owls* seems to be now universally abandoned. The most interesting point in the interpretation of this verse has reference to the word translated *satyrs* in the English Version; its original and proper sense is *hairy*, and its usual specific sense *he-goats*. In two places (Lev. 17 : 7. 2 Chron. 11 : 15), it is used to denote objects of idolatrous worship, probably images of goats, which according to Herodotus were worshipped in Egypt. In Chronicles especially this supposition is the natural one, because the word is joined with *calves*. Both there and in Leviticus, the Septuagint renders it ματαίοις *vain things*, i. e. false gods, idols. It is elsewhere explained to mean *demons*, and the same interpretation is given in the case before us by several of the ancient versions. From this traditional interpretation of the word here and in ch. 34 : 14, appears to have arisen, at an early period, a popular belief among the Jews, that *demons* or *evil spirits* were accustomed to haunt desert places in the shape of goats or other animals. And this belief is said to be actually cherished by the natives near the site of Babylon at the present day. To some, the combination of the two meanings, *goats* and *demons*, seems to have suggested the Pans, Fauns, and Satyrs of the classical mythology, imaginary beings represented as a mixture of the human form with that of goats, and supposed to frequent forests and other lonely places. Others explain the passage as relating to actual appearances of Satan under such disguises. Others understand the language as a mere concession or allusion to the popular belief, equivalent to saying, the solitude of Babylon shall be as awful *as if* occupied by Fauns and Satyrs, there, *if anywhere*, such beings may be looked for. But the great majority of modern writers adhere to the original meaning of the Hebrew word, *wild goats.* And even on the supposition of a reference to evil spirits, there is no need of assuming any concession or accommodation to the current superstitions. If the word denotes demons, this text is a proof, not of a popular belief, but of a fact, of a real apparition of such spirits under certain forms. The Jewish tradition warrants the application of the Hebrew term to *demons*, but not to the *fauns* or *satyrs* of the Greek and Roman fabulists. The popular belief of the Jews and other orientals may be traced to the traditional interpretation of this passage, and this to the Septuagint version. The mention of *demons* in a list of beasts and birds is at variance not only with the parallelism, but with the natural and ordinary usages of language. Such a combination and arrangement as the one supposed—ostriches, demons, wolves, jackals—would of itself be a reason for suspecting that the second term must really denote some kind of animal, even if no such usage existed. But the usage of the Hebrew word, as the name of an animal, is perfectly well defined and certain. Even in Lev. 17 : 7 and 2 Chron. 11 : 15, this, as we have seen, is the only natural interpretation. The result appears to be that if the question is determined by tradition and authority, it denotes *demons ;* if by the context and the usage of the word, it signifies *wild goats*, or more generically *hairy*, *shaggy* animals. According to the principles of modern exegesis, the latter is clearly entitled to the preference ; but even if the former be adopted, the language of the text should be regarded as the prediction of a real fact, which, though it should not be assumed without necessity, is altogether possible, and therefore, if alleged in Scripture, altogether credible.

22. *And wolves shall howl in his* (the king of Babylon's) *palaces, and jackals in the temples of pleasure. And near to come is her* (Babylon's) *time, and her days shall not be prolonged.* The latest writers seem to be agreed that these are different appellations of the jackal, but in order to retain the original variety of expression, substitute another animal in one of the clauses, such as *wolves*, *wild-cats*, etc. Whatever be the species here intended, the essential idea is the same as in the foregoing verse, viz. that Babylon should one day be inhabited exclusively by animals peculiar to the wilderness, implying that it should become a wilderness itself. The contrast is heightened here by the particular mention of palaces and abodes of pleasure, as about to be converted into dens and haunts of solitary animals. This fine poetical conception is adopted by Milton in his sublime description of the flood:

> And in their palaces,
> Where luxury late reigned, sea-monsters whelped
> And stabled.

The meaning of the word translated *palaces*, in every other case where it occurs, is *widows*, in which sense some rabbinical and other writers understand it here. It is possible that the two forms were designedly confounded by the writer, in order to suggest both ideas, that of palaces and that of widowhood or desolation. This explanation is adopted in the English Version, which has *palaces* in the margin, but in the text *desolate houses.* The last clause of the verse may be strictly understood, but in application to the Jewish captives in the Babylonian exile, for whose consolation the prophecy was partly intended. Or we may understand it as denoting proximity in reference to the events which had been passing in the Prophet's view. He sees the signals erected, he hears a noise in the mountains, and regarding these as actually present, he exclaims, *her time is near to come!* It may, however, mean, as similar expressions do in other cases, that when the appointed time should come, the event would certainly take place, there could be no postponement or delay.

CHAPTER XIV.

The destruction of Babylon is again foretold, and more explicitly connected with the deliverance of Israel from bondage. After a general assurance of God's favour to his people, and of an exchange of conditions between them and their oppressors, they are represented as joining in a song of triumph over their fallen enemy. In this song, which is universally admitted to possess the highest literary merit, they describe the earth as again reposing from its agitation and affliction, and then breaking forth into a shout of exultation, in which the very trees of the forest join, vs. 1–8. By a still bolder figure, the unseen world is represented as perturbed at the approach of the fallen tyrant, who is met, as he enters, by the kings already there, amazed to find him sunk as low as themselves and from a still greater height of actual elevation and of impious pretensions, which are strongly contrasted with his present condition, as deprived not only of regal honours but of decent burial, vs. 9–20. The threatening is then extended to the whole race, and the prophecy closes as before with a prediction of the total desolation of Babylon, vs. 21–23.

Vs. 24–27 are regarded by the latest writers as a distinct prophecy, unconnected with what goes before, and misplaced in the arrangement of the book. The reasons for believing that it is rather an appendix or conclusion, added by the Prophet himself, will be stated in the exposition.

Vs. 28–32 are regarded by a still greater number of writers as a distinct prophecy against Philistia. The traditional arrangement of the text, however, creates a strong presumption that this passage stands in some close connection with what goes before. The true state of the case may be, that the Prophet, having reverted from the downfall of Babylon to that of Assyria, now closes with a warning apostrophe to the Philistines who had also suffered from the latter power, and were disposed to exult unduly in its overthrow. If the later application of the name Philistia (Palestine), to the whole land of Canaan could be justified by Scriptural usage, these verses might be understood as a warning to the Jews themselves not to exult too much in their escape from Assyrian oppression, since they were yet to be subjected to the heavier yoke of Babylonian bondage. Either of these suppositions is more reasonable than that this passage is an independent prophecy subjoined to the foregoing one by caprice or accident.

1. This verse declares God's purpose in destroying the Babylonian power. *For Jehovah will pity* (or *have mercy upon*) *Jacob, and will again* (or still) *choose Israel and cause them to rest on their* (*own*) *land, and the stranger shall be joined to them; and they* (the strangers) *shall be attached to the house of Jacob.* Jacob and Israel are here used for the whole race. The plural pronoun *them* does not refer to Jacob and Israel as the names of different persons, but to each of them as a collective. By God's *still* choosing Israel we are to understand his continuing to treat them as his chosen people. Or we may render it *again*, in which case the idea will be, that having for a time or in appearance cast them off and given them up to *other lords*, he would now take them to himself again. This is not a mere promise of temporal deliverance and increase to Israel as a nation, but an assurance that the preservation of the chosen people was a necessary means for the fulfilment of God's purposes of mercy

to mankind in general. The literal fulfilment of the last clause in its primary sense is clear from such statements as the one in Esther 8 : 17.

2. *And nations shall take them and bring them to their place, and the house of Israel shall take possession of them on Jehovah's land for male and female servants, and* (thus) *they* (the Israelites) *shall be the captors of their captors, and rule over their oppressors.* The first clause is rendered somewhat obscure by the reference of the pronoun *them* to different subjects, first the Jews and then the gentiles. Most interpreters are agreed that it relates to the part taken by the gentiles in the restoration of the Jews. To a Hebrew reader the word would convey the idea, not of bare possession merely, but of permanent possession, rendered perpetual by hereditary succession. The word is used in this sense, and with special reference to slaves or servants, in Lev. 25 : 46. The simple meaning of this promise seems to be that the church or chosen people and the other nations should change places, the oppressed becoming the oppressor, and the slave the master. This of course admits both an external and internal fulfilment. In a lower sense and on a smaller scale it was accomplished in the restoration of the Jews from exile; but its full accomplishment is yet to come.

3. *And it shall be* (or *come to pass*) *in the day of Jehovah's causing thee to rest from thy toil* (or *suffering*), *and from thy commotion* (or *disquietude*), *and from the hard service which was wrought by thee* (or *imposed upon thee*). In this verse and the following context, the Prophet, in order to reduce the general promise of the foregoing verse to a more graphic and impressive form, recurs to the downfall of Babylon, as the beginning of the series of deliverances which he had predicted, and describes the effect upon those most concerned, by putting into the mouth of Israel a song of triumph over their oppressor.

This is universally admitted to be one of the finest specimens of Hebrew and indeed of ancient composition.

4. *Then thou shalt raise this song over the king of Babylon and say, How hath the oppressor ceased, the golden (city) ceased!* The meaning of the first clause is of course that Israel would have occasion to express such feelings. The king here introduced is an ideal personage, whose downfall represents that of the Babylonian monarchy.

5. This verse contains the answer to the question in the one before it. *Jehovah hath broken the staff of the wicked, the rod of the rulers.* The rod and staff are common figures for dominion, and their being broken for its destruction.

6. *Smiting nations in anger by a stroke without cessation, ruling nations in wrath by a rule without restraint*, literally, which *he* (or *one* indefinitely) *did not restrain.* The participles may agree grammatically either with the *rod* or with the king who wields it. The English Version applies the last clause only to the punishment. But the great majority both of the oldest and the latest writers make the whole descriptive of the Babylonian tyranny.

7. *At rest, quiet, is the whole earth. They burst forth into singing* (or a shout of joy). There is no inconsistency between the clauses, as the first is not descriptive of *silence*, but of tranquillity and rest. *The land had rest* is a phrase employed in the book of Judges (e. g. ch. 5 : 31) to describe the condition of the country after a great national deliverance. The verb to *burst* is peculiarly descriptive of an ebullition of joy long suppressed or suddenly succeeding grief.

8. Not only the earth and its inhabitants take part in this

triumphant song or shout, but the trees of the forest. *Also* (or *even*) *the cypresses rejoice with respect to thee*, the cedars of *Lebanon* (saying) *now that thou art fallen* (literally *lain down*), *the feller* (or woodman, literally *the cutter*) *shall not come up against us.* Now that we are safe from thee, we fear no other enemy. As to the meaning of the figures in this verse, there are various opinions; but the only one that seems consistent with a pure taste, is that which supposes this to be merely a part of one great picture, representing universal nature as rejoicing. Both here and elsewhere in the sacred books, inanimate nature is personified, and speaks herself instead of being merely spoken of.

> Ipsi laetitia voces ad sidera jactant
> Intonsi montes; ipsae jam carmina rupes,
> Ipsa sonant arbusta.

9. The bold personification is now extended from the earth and its forests to the invisible or lower world, the inhabitants of which are represented as aroused at the approach of the new victim and as coming forth to meet him. *Hell from beneath is moved* (or *in commotion*) *for thee* (i. e. on account of thee) *to meet thee* (*at*) *thy coming; it rouses for thee the giants* (the gigantic shades or spectres), *all the chief ones* (literally *he-goats*) *of the earth; it raises from their thrones all the kings of the nations.* The word translated Hell has already been explained (see above, ch. 5 : 14) as meaning first *a grave* or individual sepulchre, and then *the grave* as a general receptacle, indiscriminately occupied by all the dead without respect to character, as when we say, the rich and the poor, the evil and the good, lie together in *the grave*, not in a single tomb, which would be false, but *under ground* and in a common state of death and burial. The English word *Hell*, though now appropriated to the condition or the place of future torments, corresponds, in etymology and early usage, to the Hebrew word in question.

The passage comprehends two elements and only two, religious verities or certain facts, and poetical embellishments. It may not be easy to distinguish clearly between these; but it is only between these that we are able or have any occasion to distinguish. The admission of a third in the shape of superstitious fables, is as false in rhetoric as in theology. The shades or spectres of the dead might naturally be conceived as actually larger than the living man, since that which is shadowy and indistinct is commonly exaggerated by the fancy. Or there may be an allusion to the Canaanitish giants who were exterminated by divine command, and might well be chosen to represent the whole class of departed sinners. Or in this particular case, we may suppose the kings and great ones of the earth to be distinguished from the vulgar dead as giants or gigantic forms.

10. *All of them shall answer and say to thee: thou also art made weak as we, to us art likened!* This is a natural expression of surprise that one so far superior to themselves should now be a partaker of their weakness and disgrace. The interrogative form given to the last clause by all the English versions is entirely arbitrary, and much less expressive than the simple assertion or exclamation preferred by the oldest and latest writers.

11. *Down to the grave is brought thy pride* (or *pomp*), *the music of thy harps; under thee is spread the worm; thy covering is vermin.* The word harp is evidently put for musical instruments or music in general, and this for mirth and revelry. (See above, ch. 5 : 12.) Some suppose an allusion to the practice of embalming; but the words seem naturally only to suggest the common end of all mankind, even the greatest not excepted. The imagery of the clause is vividly exhibited in

Gill's homely paraphrase—'nothing but worms over him and worms under him, worms his bed and worms his bed-clothes.'

12. *How art thou fallen from heaven, Lucifer, son of the morning—felled to the ground, thou that didst lord it over the nations.* In the two other places where the word translated *Lucifer* occurs, it is an imperative signifying *howl.* This sense is also put upon it here by the Peshito, but all the other ancient versions and all the leading Rabbins make the word a noun denoting *bright one*, or more specifically, *bright star*, or according to the ancients more specifically still, the *morning star* or harbinger of day-light, called in Greek ἑωσφόρος and in Latin *lucifer.* The same derivation and interpretation is adopted by the latest writers. Some of the Fathers, regarding Luke 10 : 18 as an explanation of this verse, apply it to the fall of Satan, from which has arisen the popular perversion of the beautiful name *Lucifer* to signify the Devil. In the last clause the figure of a fallen star is exchanged for that of a prostrate tree. The last clause is a description of the Babylonian tyranny.

13. His fall is aggravated by the impious extravagance of his pretensions. *And* (yet) *thou hadst said in thy heart* (or to thyself), *the heavens will I mount* (or *scale*), *above the stars of God will I raise my throne, and I will sit in the mount of meeting* (or *assembly*), *in the sides of the north.* He is here described as aiming at equality with God himself. There are two distinct interpretations of the last clause, one held by the early writers, the other by the moderns. According to the first, it relates to the mountain where God agreed to meet the people, to commune with them, and to make himself known to them (Ex. 25 : 22. 29 : 42, 43). According to this view of the passage, it describes the king of Babylon as insulting God by threatening to erect his throne upon those consecrated hills, or even affecting to be God, like Antichrist, of whom Paul says, with obvious

allusion to this passage, that he opposeth and exalteth himself above all that is called God, or that is worshipped, so that he, as God, sitteth in the temple of God, showing himself that he is God (2 Thess. 2 : 4). Whether the weight of argument preponderates in favour of the old interpretation or against it, that of authority is now altogether on the side of the new one. This makes the Babylonian speak the language of a heathen, and with reference to the old and wide-spread oriental notion of a very high mountain in the extreme north, where the gods were believed to reside, as in the Greek Olympus. This is the Meru of the Hindoo mythology, and the Elborz or Elborj of the old Zend books. The meaning of the clause, as thus explained, is, 'I will take my seat among or above the gods upon their holy mountain.' This interpretation is supposed to be obscurely hinted in the Septuagint version. As the mythological allusion is in this case put into the mouth of a heathen, there is not the same objection to it as in other cases, where it seems to be recognized and sanctioned by the writer. The general meaning of the verse is of course the same on either hypothesis. The expression *stars of God* does not merely describe them as his creatures, but as being near him, in the upper world or heaven.

14. *I will mount above the cloud-heights; I will make myself like the Most High.* This is commonly regarded as a simple expression of unbounded arrogance ; but there may be an allusion to the oriental custom of calling their kings gods, or to the fact that Syrian and Phenician kings did actually so describe themselves (Ezek. 28 : 2. 6. 9. 2 Macc. 9 : 12). According to some writers, the singular noun cloud is here used to designate the cloud of the divine presence in the tabernacle and temple. This would agree well with the old interpretation of v. 13 ; but according to the other, *cloud* is a collective, meaning clouds in general.

15. But instead of being exalted to heaven, *thou shalt only be brought down to hell, to the depths of the pit.* Against the strict application of the last clause to the grave is the subsequent description of the royal body as unburied. But the imagery is unquestionably borrowed from the grave. Some understand by *sides* the horizontal excavations in the oriental sepulchres or catacombs. But according to its probable etymology the Hebrew word does not mean *sides* in the ordinary sense, but rather *hinder parts* and then *remote parts* or *extremities*, as it is explained by the Targum here and in v. 13. The specific reference may be either to extreme height, extreme distance, or extreme depth, according to the context. Here the last sense is required by the mention of the *pit*, and the word is accordingly translated in the Vulgate *profundum.*

16. *Those seeing thee shall gaze* (or stare) *at thee, they shall look at thee attentively,* (and say) *is this the man that made the earth shake, that made kingdoms tremble?* The scene in the other world is closed, and the Prophet, or triumphant Israel, is now describing what shall take place above ground. The gazing mentioned in the first clause is not merely the effect of curiosity but of incredulous surprise.

17. *Made a* (fruitful or habitable) *world like the desert, destroyed its cities, and its captives did not set free homewards.* These are still the words of the astonished spectators as they behold the body of the slain king. The construction of the last clause is somewhat difficult; but the general meaning evidently is that he did not release his prisoners.

18. *All kings of nations, all of them, lie in state* (or glory), *each in his house.* There is here a special reference to the peculiar oriental feeling with respect to burial. The Egyptians paid far more attention to the dwellings of the dead

than of the living. Some of the greatest national works have been intended for this purpose, such as the pyramids, the temple of Belus, and the cemetery at Persepolis. The environs of Jerusalem are full of ancient sepulchres. The want of burial is spoken of in Scripture as disgraceful even to a private person (1 Kings 13:22), much more to a sovereign (2 Chr. 21 : 20). The ancient oriental practice of burying above ground and in solid structures, often reared by those who were to occupy them (see below, ch. 22:16) will account for the use of *house* here in the sense of *sepulchre*, without supposing any reference to the burial of kings within their palaces. *To lie in state* may seem inappropriate to burial, but is in fact happily descriptive of the oriental method of sepulture.

19. With the customary burial of kings he now contrasts the treatment of the Babylonian's body. *And thou art cast out from thy grave, like a despised branch, the raiment of the slain, pierced with the sword, going down to the stones of the pit,* (even) *like a trampled carcass* (as thou art). That the terms of the prediction were literally fulfilled in the last king of Babylon, is highly probable, from the hatred with which this impious king (as Xenophon calls him) was regarded by the people. Such a supposition is not precluded by the same historian's statement that Cyrus gave a general permission to bury the dead; for his silence in relation to the king rather favours the conclusion that he was made an exception, either by the people or the conqueror. There is no need however of seeking historical details in this passage, which is rather a prediction of the downfall of the empire than of the fate of any individual monarch.

20. *Thou shalt not be joined with them* (the other kings of the nations) *in burial, because thy land thou hast destroyed, thy people thou hast slain. Let the seed of evil-doers be named no more forever.* The only natural interpretation of these words is that which

applies them to the Babylonian tyranny as generally exercised. The charge here brought against the king implies that his power was given him for a very different purpose. The older writers read the last clause as a simple prediction. Thus the English version is, *the seed of evil-doers shall never be renowned.* But the later writers seem to make it more emphatic by giving the future the force of an imperative or optative. Some of the older writers understand the clause to mean that the names of the wicked shall not be perpetuated by transmission in the line of their descendants. Others explain the verb as meaning to *be called*, i. e. proclaimed or celebrated. It is now pretty generally understood to mean, or to express a wish, that the posterity of such should not be spoken of at all, implying both extinction and oblivion.

21. That the downfall of the Babylonian power shall be perpetual, is now expressed by a command to slaughter the children of the king. *Prepare for his sons a slaughter, for the iniquity of their fathers. Let them not arise and possess the earth, and fill the face of the world with cities.* The dramatic form of the prediction is repeatedly shifted, so that the words of the triumphant Jews, of the Dead, of the Prophet, and of God himself, succeed each other as it were insensibly, and without any attempt to make the points of the transition prominent. The command in the first clause is not addressed specifically to the Medes and Persians, but more indefinitely to the executioners of God's decree against Babylon. The Hebrew construction is, they shall not arise (or let them not arise), and the negative may either be confined to the first two verbs or extended to the third. The last, however, is more natural on account of the exact resemblance in the form of the two members. The best sense, on the whole, is afforded by the old interpretation which understands the clause to mean, lest they overspread and colonize the earth.

22. This verse contains an intimation that the destruction just predicted is to be the work not of man merely but of God, and is to comprehend not only the royal family but the whole population. *And I (myself) will rise up against them* (or *upon them*), *saith Jehovah of Hosts, and will cut off from Babylon* (literally, *as to Babylon*) *name and remnant and progeny and offspring.* The last four nouns are put together to express posterity in the most general and universal manner. The threatening is applied to the king of Babylon, not as a collective appellation merely, but as an ideal person representing the whole line of kings. The agreement of the prophecy with history is argued from the facts, that none of the ancient royal family of Babylon ever regained a throne, and that no Babylonian empire ever rose after the destruction of the first, Alexander the Great's project of restoring it having been defeated by his death.

23. *And I will render it* (literally, *place it for*) *a possession* (or inheritance) *of the porcupine, and pools of water, and will sweep it with the broom* (or *besom*) *of destruction.* The porcupine is here mentioned only as a solitary animal frequenting marshy grounds. The construction is not, I will make the pools of water a possession, etc. by drying them up—nor, I will make it a possession for pools of water—but, I will make it a possession for the porcupine and (will convert it into) pools of water. The exposure of the level plains of Babylonia to continual inundation without great preventive care, and the actual promotion of its desolation by this very cause, are facts distinctly stated by the ancient writers. Some suppose this evil to have had its origin in the diversion of the waters of the Euphrates by Cyrus.

24. From the distant view of the destruction of Babylon, the Prophet suddenly reverts to that of the Assyrian host, either

for the purpose of making one of these events accredit the prediction of the other, or for the purpose of assuring true believers, that while God had decreed the deliverance of his people from remoter dangers, he would also protect them from those near at hand. *Jehovah of Hosts hath sworn, saying, Surely* (literally, *if not*) *as I have planned* (or imagined) *it has come to pass, and as I have devised, it shall stand* (or be established). On the elliptical formula of swearing, see above, ch. 5 : 9. The true force of the preterite and future forms, as here employed, is that according to God's purpose, it has come to pass and will come to pass hereafter. This view of the matter makes the mention of Assyria in this connection altogether natural, as if he had said, of the truth of these predictions against Babylon a proof has been afforded in the execution of the threatenings against Assyria. Another method of expounding the verse is to apply both verbs to the same events, but in a somewhat different sense. As I intended it has come to pass, and as I purposed it shall continue. The Assyrian power is already broken and shall never be restored. This interpretation of the preterite does not necessarily imply that the prophecy was actually uttered after the destruction of Sennacherib's army. Such would indeed be the natural inference from this verse alone, but for reasons which will be explained below, it is more probable that the Prophet merely takes his stand in vision at a point of time between the two events of which he speaks, so that both verbs are really prophetic, the one of a remote the other of a proximate futurity. We have here a signal instance of prophetic foresight exercised at least two centuries before the event.

25. He now declares what the purpose is, which is so certainly to be accomplished, namely, God's determination *to break Assyria* (or the Assyrian) *in my land, and on my mountains I will trample him ; and his yoke shall depart from off them, and his*

burden from off his back (or *shoulder*) *shall depart. My mountains* some have understood to be Mount Zion, others more generally the mountains of Jerusalem; but it seems to be rather a description of the whole land of Israel, or at least of Judah, as a mountainous region. (See Ezek. 38 : 21. 39 : 2, 4.)

26. The Prophet now explains his previous conjunction of events so remote as the Assyrian overthrow and the fall of Babylon, by declaring both to be partial executions of one general decree against all hostile and opposing powers. *This is the purpose that is purposed upon all the earth, and this the hand that is stretched out over all the nations.* The outstretched hand is a gesture of threatening.

27. As the preceding verse declares the extent of God's avenging purpose, so this affirms the certainty of its execution, as a necessary consequence of his almighty power. *For Jehovah of Hosts hath purposed* (this), *and who shall annul* (his purpose)? *And his hand* (*is*) *the* (*one*) *stretched out, and who shall turn it back?* The meaning of the last clause is not simply that *his hand is stretched out*, but that *the hand stretched out is his.*

28. *In the year of the death of king Ahaz, was this burden*, or threatening prophecy, against Philistia. This is a title forming part of the text as far as we can trace it back. There is an erroneous division of the text in some editions of the English Bible, by prefixing the paragraph mark to v. 29, so as to apply the date here given to what goes before, whereas dates are always placed at the beginning.

29. *Rejoice not, O Philistia, all of thee* (or all Philistia), *because the rod that smote thee is broken, for out of the root of the serpent shall come forth a basilisk, and its root a flying fiery serpent.* The name Philistia is applied in Hebrew to the southwestern

part of Canaan on the Mediterranean coast, nominally belonging to the tribe of Judah, but for ages occupied by the Philistines, a race of Egyptian origin who came to Canaan from Caphtor, i. e. according to the ancients Cappadocia, but according to the moderns either Cyprus or Crete, most probably the latter. The name is now traced to an Ethiopic root meaning to wander, and probably denotes wanderers or emigrants. Hence it is commonly rendered in the Septuagint ἀλλόφυλοι. The Philistines are spoken of above in ch. 9 : 11. 11 : 14, and throughout the historical books of the Old Testament, as the hereditary enemies of Israel. They were subdued by David (2 Sam. 5 : 17–25. 21 : 15), and still paid tribute in the reign of Jehoshaphat (2 Chron. 17 : 11), but rebelled against Jehoram (2 Chr. 21 : 16, 17), were again subdued by Uzziah (2 Chr. 26 : 6), and again shook off the yoke in the reign of Ahaz (2 Chr. 28 : 18). The Greek modification of the Hebrew name is applied by Josephus and other ancient writers to the whole land of Israel, from which comes our *Palestine*, employed in the same manner. The expression *all* (or *the whole*) *of thee*, may have reference to Philistia as a union of several principalities. All interpreters agree that the Philistines are here spoken of as having recently escaped from the ascendency of some superior power, but at the same time threatened with a more complete subjection. The first of these ideas is expressed by the figure of a broken rod or staff, for the meaning of which see above, ad v. 5. The other is expressed by the very different figure of an ordinary serpent producing or succeeded by other varieties more venomous and deadly. Whatever be the particular species intended, the essential idea is the same, and has never been disputed. Some indeed suppose a gradation or climax in the third term also, the fiery flying serpent being assumed to be more deadly than the basilisk, as this is more so than the ordinary serpent. But most writers regard the other two names as correlative or parallel. The transition in the last clause from the figure of an animal to that of a plant may serve the double purpose of reminding us that what we read is figurative, and of showing how unsafe it is to tamper with the text on the ground of mere rhetorical punctilios. As to the application of the figures, there are different opinions, but their essential meaning is obvious enough.

30. *And the first-born of the poor shall feed, and the needy in security lie down, and I will kill thy root with famine, and thy remnant it shall slay.* The future condition of the Jews is here contrasted with that of the Philistines. The figures in the first clause are borrowed from a flock, in the second from a tree, but with obvious allusion to a human subject. The first-born of the poor is a superlative expression for the poorest and most wretched. An allusion to the next generation leaves the promise too remote and the expression *first-born* unexplained. The figurative part of the last clause is borrowed from a tree, here divided into two parts, the *root* and the *rest* or remainder. What is first mentioned as an instrument in God's hand, reappears in the last member of the sentence as an agent.

31. *Howl, oh gate! cry, oh city! dissolved, oh Philistia, is the whole of thee; for out of the north a smoke comes, and there is no straggler in his forces.* The Philistines are not only forbidden to rejoice, but exhorted to lament. The object of address is a single city representing all the rest. *Gate* is not here put for the judges or nobles who were wont to sit there, nor is it even mentioned as the chief place of concourse, but rather with allusion to the defences of the city, as a parallel expression to *city* itself. According to some writers, the *smoke* here meant is that of conflagrations kindled by the enemy. Some of the older writers understood it simply as an emblem for wrath or trouble. Lowth cites Virgil's *fumantes pulvere campos*, and supposes an allusion to the clouds of dust raised by an army on the march. Others refer it to the practice of literally carrying fire in front

of caravans to mark the course. It may be doubted, notwithstanding the allusion in the last clause, whether it was intended to refer to an army at all. If not, we may suppose with Calvin that smoke is mentioned merely as a sign of distant and approaching fire, a natural and common metaphor for any powerful destroying agent. The diversity of judgments as to the particular enemy here meant, and the slightness of the grounds on which they severally rest, may suffice to show that the prophecy is really generic, not specific, and includes all the agencies and means by which the Philistines were punished for their constant and inveterate enmity to the chosen people, as well as for idolatry and other crimes.

32. *And what shall one answer* (what answer shall be given to) *the ambassadors of a nation? That Jehovah has founded Zion, and in it the afflicted of his people shall seek refuge.* The meaning of the last clause is too clear to be disputed, viz. that God is the protector of his people. This is evidently stated as the result and sum of the whole prophecy, and as such is sufficiently intelligible. It is also given, however, as an answer to ambassadors or messengers, and this has given rise to a great diversity of explanations, which seems to show that the expression is indefinite, as the very absence of the article implies, and that the whole sense meant to be conveyed is this, that such may be the answer given to the inquiries made from any quarter. Of all the specific applications, the most probable is that which supposes an allusion to Rabshakeh's argument with Hezekiah against trusting in Jehovah. But this seems precluded by the want of any natural connection with Philistia, which is the subject of the previous context.

CHAPTERS XV, XVI.

These chapters contain a prediction of the downfall of Moab. Some writers regard the last two verses of ch. XVI as an addition made by Isaiah to an earlier prediction of his own, or an addition made to a prophecy of Isaiah by a later prophet. The simplest view of the passage is that which regards the whole as a continuous composition, and supposes the Prophet at the close to fix the date of the prediction which he had just uttered. The particular event referred to in these chapters has been variously explained to be the invasion of Moab by Jeroboam II. king of Israel, by Tirhaka king of Ethiopia, by Tiglath-Pileser king of Assyria, by his successors Shalmaneser, Sennacherib, and Esarhaddon, by Nebuchadnezzar king of Babylon etc. The safest conclusion seems to be, that the prediction is generic and intended to describe the destruction of Moab, without exclusive reference to any one of the events by which it was occasioned or promoted, but with special allusions possibly to all of them. Compare the introduction to ch. XIII—XIV.

CHAPTER XV.

This chapter is occupied with a description of the general grief, occasioned by the conquest of the chief towns and the desolation of the country at large. Its chief peculiarities of form are the numerous names of places introduced, and the strong personification by which they are represented as grieving for the public calamity. The chapter closes with an intimation of still greater evils.

1. (This is) *the burden of Moab, that in a night Ar-Moab is laid waste, is destroyed; that in a night Kir-Moab is laid waste, is destroyed.* The English Version understands the first verse as assigning a reason for the second. *Because in a night* etc. *he ascends* etc. But so long a sentence is at variance, not only with the general usage of the language, but with the style of this particular prophecy. *Ar* originally meant a *city*, and *Ar-Moab* the city of Moab, i. e. the capital city, perhaps as the only real city of the Moabites. It was on the south side of the Arnon (Num. 22 : 36). The Greeks called it *Areopolis* or City of Mars, according to their favourite practice of corrupting foreign names so as to give them the appearance of significant Greek words. Ptolemy calls it *Rhabmathmom*, a corruption of the Hebrew *Rabbath-Moab* i. e. chief city of Moab. Jerome says that the place was destroyed in one night by an earthquake when he was a boy. The Arabs call it *Mab* and *Er-rabba.* It is now in ruins. In connection with the capital city, the Prophet names the principal or only fortress in the land of Moab. *Kir* originally means a *wall*, then a walled town or fortress. The place here meant is a few miles south-east of Ar, on a rocky hill, strongly fortified by nature, and provided with a castle. The Chaldee Paraphrase of this verse calls it *Kerakka de Moab*, the fortress of Moab, which name it has retained among the orientals, who extend it to the whole of ancient Moab.

2. The destruction of the chief cities causes general grief. *They* (indefinitely) *go up to the house* (i. e. the temple), *and Dibon* (*to*) *the high places for* (the purpose of) *weeping. On Nebo and on Medeba, Moab howls—on all his heads baldness—*

every beard cut off. The ancient heathen built their temples upon heights (ch. 65 : 7). Solomon built one to the Moabitish god Chemosh on the mountain before Jerusalem (1 Kings 11 : 7). *Dibon*, a town north of the Arnon, rebuilt by the tribe of Gad, and thence called *Dibon-gad* (Num. 33 : 45), although it had formerly belonged to Moab, and would seem from this passage to have been recovered by them. The same place is called *Dimon* in v. 9, in order to assimilate it to the Hebrew word for blood. The modern name is Diban. There is no preposition before it here in Hebrew. Hence it may be either the object or the subject of the verb. The first construction is preferred by the older writers; those of modern date are almost unanimous in favour of the other, which makes Dibon itself go up to the high places. The objection to the first is that Dibon was situated in a plain; to which it may be answered that the phrase *go up* has reference in many cases not to geographical position but to sacredness and dignity.

3. *In its streets they are girded with sackcloth; on its roofs and in its squares* (or broad places) *all* (literally, *all of it*) *howls, coming down with weeping* (from the house-tops or the temples). In the Hebrew of this verse there is a singular alternation of masculine and feminine forms, all relating to Moab, sometimes considered as a country and sometimes as a nation. The last clause is explained by most modern writers, to mean melting into tears, as the eye is elsewhere said to run down tears or water (Jer. 9 : 18. Lam. 3 : 48). But as the eye is not here mentioned, and the preposition is inserted, making a marked difference between this and the alleged expressions, it is better to adhere to the old construction which supposes an antithesis between this clause and the ascent to the temples or the house-tops. Sackcloth is mentioned as the usual mourning dress and a badge of deep humiliation.

4. *And Heshbon cries and Elealeh—even to Jahaz is their voice heard—therefore the warriors of Moab cry—his soul is distressed to him* (or in him). Heshbon, a royal city of the Amorites, assigned to Reuben and to Gad at different times, or to both jointly, famous for its fish-pools, a celebrated town in the days of Eusebius, the ruins of which are still in existence under the slightly altered name of *Hesbân.* Elealeh, often mentioned with it, was also assigned to the tribe of Reuben. Eusebius describes these towns as near together in the highlands of Gilead, opposite to Jericho. Robinson and Smith, while at the latter place, conversed with an Arab chief, who pointed out to them the Wady Hesbân, near which far up in the mountain is the ruined place of the same name, the ancient Heshbon. Half an hour north-east of this lies another ruin called El Al, the ancient Elealeh. (Palestine II. 278.)

5. *My heart for Moab cries out—her fugitives* (are fled) *as far as Zoar—an heifer of three years old—for he that goes up Luhith with weeping goes up by it—for in the way of Horonaim a cry of destruction they lift up.* Every part of this obscure verse has given rise to some diversity of exposition. Zoar, one of the cities of the plain, preserved by Lot's intercession, is now ascertained to have been situated on the eastern shore of the Dead Sea, at the foot of the mountains near its southern extremity. (Robinson's Palestine II. 480, 648.) It is here mentioned as an extreme southern point, but not without allusion to Lot's escape from the destruction of Sodom.—The next phrase is famous as the subject of discordant explanations. These may however be reduced to two classes, those which regard the words as proper names, and those which regard them as appellatives. All the ancient versions, and the great majority of modern writers, regard the words in question as appellatives, and all agree in rendering the first of the two *heifer.* The other is explained to mean *three years old*, or retaining the

form of the original more closely, *a heifer of the third* (year). By *a heifer three years old*, we may understand one that has never yet been tamed or broken, according to Pliny's maxim, *domitura boum in trimatu, postea sera, antea praematura.* Now as personal afflictions are sometimes likened to the taming of animals (Jer. 31 : 18. Hos. 10 : 11), and as communities and governments are often represented by the figure of a heifer (Jer. 46 : 20. 50 : 11. Hos. 4 : 16), the expressions thus interpreted would not be inappropriate to the state of Moab, hitherto flourishing and uncontrolled, but now *three years old* and subjected to the yoke. Some of the older interpreters suppose this statement of the age to have reference to the voice of the animal, which is said to be deepest at that age. There is still a doubt, however, with respect to the application of the simile, as last explained. Some refer it to the Prophet himself. Others to the fugitives of Moab, who escape to Zoar, crying like a heifer three years old. Luhith is mentioned only here and in Jeremiah 48 : 5. Eusebius describes it as a village still called *Λουείθ*, between Areopolis and Zoar. Horonaim is mentioned only here and in Jer. 48 : 3, 5, 34. The name originally means *two caverns*, and is near akin to Beth-horon. It is not improbable that Luhith and Horonaim were on opposite faces of the same hill, so that the fugitives on their way to Zoar, after going up the ascent of Luhith, are seen going down the descent of Horonaim. A *cry of breaking* is explained by some of the rabbinical interpreters as meaning the explosive sound produced by clapping the hands or smiting the thigh. Others understand it to mean *a cry of contrition*, i. e. a penitent and humble cry. Gill suggests that it may mean *a broken cry*, i. e. one interrupted by sighs and sobs. It is possible however that it may be mentioned as the very word uttered.

6. *For the waters of Nimrim* (are and) *shall be desolations; for withered is the grass, gone is the herbage, verdure there is none.*

The description is continued, the desolation of the country being added to the capture of the cities and the flight of the inhabitants. The *waters* meant may be streams which met there, or the springs and running streams of that locality. The translation of the first verb as a future and the others as preterites seems to make the desolation of the waters not the cause but the effect of the decay of vegetation. It is better, therefore, to adopt the present or descriptive form throughout the verse, as all the latest writers do.

7. *Therefore* (because the country can no longer be inhabited) *the remainder of what* (*each*) *one has made* (i. e. acquired), and their *hoard* (or store), *over the brook of the willows they carry them away.* Not one of the ancient versions has given a coherent or intelligible rendering of this obscure sentence. It is now commonly agreed that the brook mentioned is the Wady el Ahsa of Burckhardt (the Wady el Ahsy of Robinson and Smith), running into the Dead Sea near its southern extremity, and forming the boundary between Kerek and Gebal, corresponding to the ancient Moab and Edom. On the whole, the most probable meaning of the verse is that the Moabites shall carry what they can save of their possessions into the ancient land of Edom.

8. The lamentation is not confined to any one part of the country. *For the cry goes round the border of Moab* (i. e. entirely surrounds it); *even to Eglaim* (is) *its howling* (heard), *and to Beer Elim its howling.* The meaning is not that the land is externally surrounded by lamentation, but that lamentation fills it.

9. The expressions grow still stronger. Not only is the land full of tumult and disorder, fear and flight; it is also stained with carnage and threatened with new evils. *For the waters of Dimon are full of blood; for I will bring upon Dimon additions*

(i. e. additional evils), *on the escaped* (literally, *the escape*) *of Moab a lion; and on the remnant of the land* (those left in it, or remaining of its population). By the waters of Dimon or Dibon, most writers understand the Arnon, near the north bank of which the town was built, as the river Kishon is called *the waters of Megiddo* (Judg. 5 : 19).

CHAPTER XVI.

THIS chapter opens with an exhortation to the Moabites to seek protection from their enemies by renewing their allegiance to the house of David, accompanied by an intimation that this prospect of deliverance would not in fact be realized, vs. 1–6. From this transient gleam of hope, the prophecy reverts to a description of the general desolation and distress, in form almost identical with that in the foregoing chapter, vs. 7–12. The prophecy then closes with a specification of the time at which it was to be fulfilled, vs. 13, 14.

The needless division of the prophecy at this point seems to have some connection with an old opinion that the lamb mentioned in v. 1 is Christ. A similar cause appears to have affected the division of the second, third, and fourth chapters.

1. In their extremity, the Moabites exhort one another to return to their allegiance to the family of David, by whom they were subdued and rendered tributary (2 Sam. 8 : 2). When the kingdom was divided, they continued in subjection to the ten tribes till the death of Ahab, paying yearly, or perhaps at the accession of every new king, a tribute of a hundred thousand lambs and as many rams with the wool (2 Kings 3 4, 5).

After the kingdom of the ten tribes was destroyed, their allegiance could be paid only to Judah, who had indeed been all along entitled to it. *Send ye the lamb* (i. e. the customary tribute) *to the ruler of the land* (your rightful sovereign), *from Sela* (or Petra) *to the wilderness, to the mountain of the daughter of Zion.* The verse then really continues the description of the foregoing chapter. Jerome understands the verse as a prayer or a prediction, that God would send forth Christ, *the lamb, the ruler of the land* (or earth). *Sela,* which properly denotes a *rock,* is now commonly agreed to be here used as the name of the city *Petra,* the ancient capital of Idumea, so called because surrounded by impassable rocks, and to a great extent hewn in the rock itself. It is described by Strabo, Diodorus, and Josephus, as a place of extensive trade. The Greek form *Πέτρα* is supposed to have given name to *Arabia Petraea* in the old geography. If so, the explanation of that name as meaning *stony,* and as descriptive of the soil of the whole country, must be incorrect. Petra was conquered by Trajan, and rebuilt by Hadrian, on whose coins its name is still extant. It was afterwards a bishop's see, but had ceased to be inhabited before the time of the crusades. It was then entirely lost sight of, until Burckhardt in 1812 verified a conjecture of Seetzen's, that the site of Petra was to be sought in the valley called the *Wada Musa,* one or two days' journey southeast of the Dead Sea. It was afterwards explored by Irby and Mangles, and has since been often visited and described. See in particular Robinson's Palestine II. 573–580. Jerome explains the whole verse as a prediction of Christ's descent from Ruth the Moabitess, the *lamb, the ruler of the land, sent forth from the rock of the wilderness!*

2. This verse assigns the ground or reason of the exhortation in the one before it. *And it shall be* (or come to pass, that) *like a bird wandering,* (like) *a nest cast out, shall be the daughters of Moab, the fords of Arnon.* The construction *cast out from the*

nest is inconsistent with the form of the original. *Nest* may be understood as a poetical term for its contents. There are three interpretations of the phrase *daughters of Moab.* The first gives the words the geographical sense of villages or dependent towns. (See above ch. 3 : 16. 4 : 4.) The second explanation makes it mean the people generally, here called *daughters*, as the whole population is elsewhere called *daughter.* The third gives the words their strict sense as denoting the female inhabitants of Moab, whose flight and sufferings are a sufficient index to the state of things. In the absence of any conclusive reason for dissenting from this strict and proper sense of the expressions, it is entitled to the preference. The Arnon is mentioned as the principal stream of Moab.

3. Most of the older writers from Jerome downwards, understand this verse as a continuation of the advice to the Moabites, in which they are urged to act with *prudence* as well as *justice*, to take counsel (i. e. provide for their own safety) as well as execute judgment (i. e. act right towards others). In other words, they are exhorted to prepare for the day of their own calamity, by exercising mercy towards the Jews in theirs. But the explanation of the verse as the words of the Moabites addressed to the Jews, is favoured by the foregoing context, which relates throughout to the sufferings of Moab, whereas on the other supposition, the prophet suddenly exhorts the sufferers to harbour the fugitives of that very nation, with whom they had themselves been exhorted to seek refuge. This interpretation also relieves us from the necessity of determining historically what particular affliction of the Israelites or Jews is here referred to, a question which has occasioned much perplexity, and which can be solved only by conjecture. As noonday heat is a common oriental figure to denote distress (Isai. 4 : 6. 25 : 4. 32 : 2), so a shadow is a relief from it. Possibly, however, the allusion here is to the *light* of noonday, and the shadow dark

as night denotes concealment. If so, the clause is equivalent in meaning to the one which follows.

4. *Let my outcasts, Moab, sojourn with thee, be thou a covert* (refuge or hiding-place) *to them from the face* (or presence) *of the spoiler* (or oppressor)*; for the extortioner is at an end, oppression has ceased, consumed are the tramplers out of the land.* Here, as in the preceding verse, the sense depends upon the object of address. If it be Moab, as the older writers held, the outcasts referred to are the outcasts of Israel. If the address be to Israel, the outcasts are those of Moab. The latter interpretation seems to be irreconcilable with the form of expression. Most interpreters, ancient and modern, give the verbs in this last clause a future sense. As if he had said, 'Give the fugitives a shelter; they will not need it long, for the extortioner will soon cease,' etc. This gives an appropriate sense, whether the words be addressed to Israel or Moab.

5. This verse contains a promise, that if the Jews afforded shelter to the fugitives of Moab, their own government should be strengthened by this exercise of mercy, and their national prosperity promoted by the appearance of a king in the family of David, who should possess the highest qualifications of a moral kind for the regal office. *And a throne shall be established in mercy, and one shall sit upon it in truth in the tent of David, judging and seeking justice and prompt in equity.*

6. *We have heard of the pride of Moab, the very proud, his haughtiness and his pride and his wrath, the falsehood of his pretensions.* Those writers who suppose Moab to be addressed in the preceding verses, understand this as a reason for believing that he will not follow the advice just given. As if he had said: 'it is vain to recommend this merciful and just course, for we have heard etc.' But the modern writers who regard

what immediately precedes as the language addressed by the Moabitish fugitives to Judah, explain this as a reason for rejecting their petition.

7. *Therefore* (because thus rejected) *Moab shall howl for Moab; all of it shall howl; for the grapes* (or raisin-cakes) *of Kir-hareseth shall ye sigh* (or moan), *only* (i. e. altogether) *smitten.* The idea may be that the nation of Moab mourns for the land of Moab, but the simplest supposition is that *Moab for Moab* means *Moab for itself.*

8. *For the fields of Heshbon are withered—the vine of Sibmah—the lords of the nations broke down its choice plants—unto Jazer they reached—they strayed into* (or *through*) *the desert—its branches—they were stretched out—they reached to* (or *over*) *the sea. Sibmah* is mentioned Num. 32 : 38. Josh. 13 : 19, and in the former place joined with Nebo, which occurs above, ch. 15 : 2. It had been taken by the Amorites, but was probably again recovered. Eusebius speaks of it as a town of Gilead, and Jerome describes it as not more than half a mile from Heshbon. According to the English Version, it would seem to be the lords of the nations who came to Jazer, wandered through the wilderness, etc. All this, however, is really predicated of the vines, the luxuriant growth of which is the subject of the following clauses. It may either mean that the vines covered the shore and overhung the water, or that the luxuriant vineyards of Moab really extended beyond the northern point of the Dead Sea. In the parallel passage, Jer. 48 : 32, we read of the *sea of Jazer*, which may have been a lake in its vicinity, or even a reservoir, such as Seetzen found there. The same traveller found an abundant growth of vines in the region here described, while at Szalt (the ancient Ramoth) Burckhardt and Buckingham both speak, not only of the multitude of grapes, but of an active trade in raisins.

9. *Therefore I will weep with the weeping of Jazer (for) the vine of Sibmah. I will wet thee (with) my tears, Heshbon and (thee) Elealeh! For upon thy fruit and upon thy harvest a cry has fallen.* Some suppose these to be the words of a Moabite bewailing the general calamity. There is no objection, however, to the supposition, that the Prophet here expresses his own sympathy with the distress of Moab, as an indirect method of describing its intensity. The emphasis does not lie merely in the Prophet's feeling for a foreign nation, but in his feeling for a guilty race, on whom he was inspired to denounce the wrath of God.

10. *And taken away is joy and gladness from the fruitful field, and in the vineyards shall no (more) be sung, no (more) be shouted: wine in the presses shall the treader not tread; the cry have I stilled* (or *caused to cease*). The English Version, on the other hand, by using the expression *no wine*, seems to imply that the treading of the grapes would not be followed by its usual result, whereas the meaning is that the grapes would not be trodden at all. The same version needlessly puts *treaders* in the plural. The idiomatic combination of the verb and its participle or derivative noun, is not uncommon in Hebrew. The ancient mode of treading grapes is still preserved in some of the monuments of Egypt.

11. *Therefore my bowels for Moab like the harp shall sound, and my inwards for Kirhares.* The viscera are evidently mentioned as the seat of the affections. Modern usage would require *heart* and *bosom.* The distinction which philologists have made between the ancient usage of *bowels* to denote the upper viscera and its modern restriction to the lower viscera, sufficiently accounts for the different associations excited by the same or equivalent expressions, then and now. The comparison is either with the sad notes of a harp, or with the striking of its strings,

which may be used to represent the beating of the heart or the commotion of the nerves. *Sound* is not an adequate translation of the Hebrew word which conveys the idea of tumultuous agitation.

12. From the impending ruin Moab attempts in vain to save himself by supplication to his gods. They are powerless and he is desperate. *And it shall be* (or come to pass), *when Moab has appeared* (before his gods), *when he has wearied himself* (with vain oblations) *on the high place, then* (literally *and*) *he shall enter into his sanctuary to pray, and shall not be able* (to obtain an answer). Another construction, equally grammatical, though not so natural, is, 'when he has appeared etc. and enters into his sanctuary to pray, he shall not be able.' The *weariness* here spoken of is understood by some as referring to the complicated and laborious ritual of the heathen worship; by others, simply to the multitude of offerings; by others, still more simply, to the multitude of prayers put up in vain. The last clause may either represent the worshipper as passing from the open high place to the shrine or temple where his god resided, in continuation of the same religious service, or it may represent him as abandoning the ordinary altars, and resorting to some noted temple, or to the shrine of some chief idol, such as Chemosh (1 Kings 11 : 7). It does not mean that he should not be able to reach or to enter the sanctuary on account of his exhaustion, but that he should not be able to obtain what he desired, or indeed to effect anything whatever by his prayers.

13. *This is the word which Jehovah spake concerning Moab of old.* The reference is not to what follows but to what precedes. It may be of old applied either to a remote or a recent period, and is frequently used by Isaiah elsewhere, in reference to earlier predictions.

14. *And now Jehovah speaks* (or *has spoken*) *saying, in three*

years, like the years of an hireling, the glory of Moab shall be disgraced, with all the great throng, and the remnant (shall be) small and few, not much. By the years of an hireling most writers understand years computed strictly and exactly, with or without allusion to the eager expectation with which hirelings await their time, and their joy at its arrival, or to the hardships of the time of servitude. The glory of Moab is neither its wealth, its army, its people, nor its nobility exclusively, but all in which the nation gloried. As the date of this prediction is not given, the time of its fulfilment is of course uncertain. Some suppose it to have been executed by Tirhakah, king of Ethiopia (2 Kings 19:9); others by Shalmaneser; others by Sennacherib; others by Esarhaddon; others by Nebuchadnezzar. These last of course suppose that the verses are of later date than the time of Isaiah. That the final downfall of Moab was to be effected by the Babylonians, seems clear from the repetition of Isaiah's threatenings by Jeremiah (ch. 48). The only safe conclusion is that these two verses were added by divine command in the days of Nebuchadnezzar, or that if written by Isaiah they were verified in some of the Assyrian expeditions which were frequent at that period, although the conquest of Moab is not explicitly recorded in the history.

CHAPTER XVII.

THIS chapter is chiefly occupied with a prophecy of desolation to the kingdoms of Syria and Ephraim, vs. 1–11. It closes with a more general threatening against the enemies of Judah, vs. 12–14. The most satisfactory view of the whole passage is that it was meant to be a prophetic picture of the doom which awaited the enemies of Judah, and that while many of its expressions admit of a general application, some traits in the description are derived from particular invasions and attacks. Thus Syria and Ephraim are expressly mentioned in the first part, while the terms of the last three verses are more appropriate to the slaughter of the Assyrian host; but as this is not explicitly referred to, there is no need of regarding it as the exclusive subject even of that passage. The eighteenth chapter may then be treated as a part of the same context. In the first part of ch. 17, the Prophet represents the kingdoms of Syria and Ephraim as sharing the same fate, both being brought to desolation, vs. 1–3. He then describes the desolation of Ephraim especially, by the figures of a harvest and a gathering of olives, in which little is left to be afterwards gleaned, vs. 4–6. As the effect of these judgments, he describes the people as renouncing their idols and returning to Jehovah, vs. 7, 8. He then resumes his description of the threatened desolation, and ascribes it to the general oblivion of God, and cultivation of strange doctrines and practices, vs. 9–11. In the close of the chapter, the Prophet first describes a gathering of nations, and then their dispersion by divine rebuke, which he declares to be the doom of all who attack or oppress God's people, vs. 12–14.

1. *The Burden of Damascus. Behold, Damascus is removed from (being) a city, and is a heap, a ruin.* For the meaning of *burden*, see above, on ch. 13 : 1. The title is equivalent to saying, 'I have a threatening to announce against Damascus.' The idiomatic phrase *removed from a city* means *removed from* (the state or condition of) *a city*, or, *from* (being) *a city*. Compare ch. 7 : 8, and 1 Sam. 15 : 26. Some regard this and the next two verses as a description of the past, and infer that the prophecy is subsequent in date to the conquest of Damascus and Syria. But as the form of expression leaves this undeter-

mined, it is better to regard the whole as a prediction. Damascus is still the most flourishing city in Western Asia. It is also one of the most ancient. It is here mentioned as the capital of a kingdom, called *Syria of Damascus* to distinguish it from other Syrian principalities, and founded in the reign of David by Rezon (1 Kings 11 : 23, 24). It was commonly at war with Israel, particularly during the reign of Benhadad and Hazael, so that a three years' peace is recorded as a long one (1 Kings 22 : 1). Under Rezin, its last king, Syria joined with Ephraim against Judah, during which confederacy, i. e. in the first years of the reign of Ahaz, this prophecy was probably uttered. Damascus appears to have experienced more vicissitudes than any other ancient city except Jerusalem. After the desolation here predicted it was again rebuilt, and again destroyed by Nebuchadnezzar, notwithstanding which it reappears in the New Testament as a flourishing city and a seat of government. In the verse before us, the reference may be chiefly to its downfall as a royal residence.

2. *Forsaken* (*are*) *the cities of Aroer; for flocks shall they be, and they shall lie down, and there shall be no making* (*them*) *afraid.* There are three Aroers distinctly mentioned in the Bible; one in the territory of Judah (1 Sam. 30 : 28), one at the southern extremity of the land of Israel east of Jordan (Jos. 12 : 2. 13 : 16), and a third further north near to Rabbah (Jos 13 : 25. Num. 32 : 34). It is now commonly agreed that the place meant is the northern Aroer east of Jordan, and that *its cities* are the towns around it and perhaps dependent on it. An analogous expression is the *cities of Heshbon* (Jos. 13 : 17). At all times, it is probable, the boundaries between these adjacent states were fluctuating and uncertain. This accounts for the fact that the same place is spoken of at different times as belonging to Israel, to Moab, to Ammon, and to Syria.

Forsaken probably means emptied of their people and left desolate. There is then a specific reference to deportation and exile.

3. *Then shall cease defence from Ephraim and royalty from Damascus and the rest of Syria. Like the glory of the children of Israel shall they be, saith Jehovah of Hosts.* The *defence* may be either Damascus (as a protection of the ten tribes) or Samaria (Mic. 1 : 5). The *rest of Syria* may either mean the whole of Syria besides Damascus, or the *remnant* left by the Assyrian invaders. The latter agrees best with the terms of the comparison. What was left of Syria should resemble what was left of the glory of Israel. The *glory of Israel* includes all that constitutes the greatness of a people. (See above, ch. 5 : 14)

4. *And it shall be* (or come to pass) *in that day, the glory of Jacob shall be brought low* (or made weak), *and the fatness of his flesh shall be made lean.* This is an explanation of the comparison in the verse preceding. The remnant of Ephraim was to be like the glory of Israel; but how was that? This verse contains the answer. *Glory*, as before, includes all that constitutes the strength of a people, and is here contrasted with a state of weakness. The same idea is expressed in the last clause by the figure of emaciation.

5. *And it shall be like the gathering of* (or *as one gathers*) *the harvest, the standing corn, and his arm reaps the ears. And it shall be like one collecting ears in the valley of Rephaim.* The first verb is not to be rendered *he shall be* (i. e. Israel, or the king of Assyria), but to be construed impersonally, *it shall be* or *come to pass.* The valley of Rephaim or the Giants extends from Jerusalem to the south-west in the direction of Bethlehem. It is here mentioned as a spot near to Jerusalem and

well known to the people, for the purpose of giving a specific character to the general description or allusion of the first clause. There is no proof that it was remarkable either for fertility or barrenness. Some of the commentators represent it as now waste; but Robinson speaks of it, *en passant*, as "the cultivated valley or plain of Rephaim." (Palestine I. 323.)

6. *And gleanings shall be left therein like the beating* (or *shaking*) *of an olive tree, two* (*or*) *three berries in the top of a high bough, four* (*or*) *five in the branches of the fruit-tree, saith Jehovah God of Israel.* There is here an allusion to the custom of beating the unripe olives from the tree for the purpose of making oil. Those described as left may either be the few left to ripen for eating, or the few overlooked by the gatherer or beyond his reach. The common version (*gleaning grapes*) is too restricted, and presents the incongruity of grapes upon an olive-tree. The transition from the figure of a harvest to that of an olive-gathering may be intended simply to vary and multiply the images, or, as some suppose, to complete the illustration which would otherwise have been defective, because the reaper is followed by the gleaner who completes the ingathering at once, whereas the olive-gatherer leaves some of course. Two, three, four, and five, are used, as in other languages, for an indefinite small number or *a few.* This verse is regarded by most interpreters as describing the extent to which the threatened judgment would be carried. The gleanings, then, are not the pious remnant, but the ignoble refuse who survived the deportation of the ten tribes by the Assyrians.

7. *In that day man shall turn to his Maker, and his eyes to the Holy One of Israel shall look. Maker* is here used in a pregnant sense to describe God, not merely as the natural creator of mankind, but as the maker of Israel, the author of their privileges, and their covenant God. (Compare Deut.

32 : 6.) The same idea is expressed by the parallel phrase, *Holy One of Israel*, for the import of which see above, ch. 1 : 4. It is matter of history, that after the Assyrian conquest and the general deportation of the people, many accepted Hezekiah's invitation and returned to the worship of Jehovah at Jerusalem (2 Chron. 30 : 11); and this reformation is alluded to as still continued in the times of Josiah (2 Chron. 34 : 9). At the same time the words may be intended to suggest that a similar effect might be expected to result from similar causes in later times.

8. *And he shall not turn* (or *look*) *to the altars, the work of his own hands, and that which his own fingers have made shall he not regard, and the groves* (or *images of Ashtoreth*) *and the pillars* (or *images*) *of the sun.* The positive declaration of the preceding verse is negatively expressed in this, with a particular mention of the objects which had usurped the place of God. Idol-altars are described as the work of men's hands, because erected by their sole authority, whereas the altar at Jerusalem was, in the highest sense, the work of God himself. The old translation *groves*, i. e. such as were used for idol-worship, has been shown to be in some places inadmissible, as when the grove is said to have stood upon an altar, or under a tree, or to have been brought out of a temple (1 Kings 14 : 23. 2 Chron. 34 : 4). The modern writers, therefore, understand it as denoting the goddess of fortune or happiness, otherwise called *Ashtoreth*, the Phenician Venus, extensively worshipped in conjunction with Baal.

9. *In that day shall his fortified cities be like what is left in the thicket and the lofty branch* (namely the cities), *which they leave* (as they retire) *from before the children of Israel, and* (the land) *shall be a waste.* It is universally agreed that the desolation of the ten tribes is here described by a comparison, but as to

the precise form and meaning of the sentence there is great diversity of judgment. Some suppose the strongest towns to be here represented as no better defended than an open forest. Others on the contrary understand the strong towns alone to be left, the others being utterly destroyed. These are the principal interpretations of the whole verse, or at least of the comparison which it contains. The first supposes the forsaken cities of Ephraim to be here compared with those which the Canaanites forsook when they fled before the Israelites under Joshua, or with the forests which the Israelites left unoccupied after the conquest of the country. The other interpretation supposes no historical allusion, but a comparison of the approaching desolation with the neglected branches of a tree or forest that is felled, or a resumption of the figure of the olive-tree in v. 6. This last is strongly recommended by its great simplicity by its superseding all gratuitous assumptions beyond what is expressed.

10. *Because thou hast forgotten the God of thy salvation, and the Rock of thy strength hast not remembered, therefore thou wilt plant plants of pleasantness* (or pleasant plantations) *and with a strange slip set it.* The planting here described is the sin of the people, not their punishment. Those who think a literal planting to be meant, understand *strange* to signify exotic, foreign, and by implication valuable, costly; but upon the supposition that a moral or spiritual planting is intended, it has its frequent emphatic sense of *alien from God*, i. e. *wicked*, or more specifically *idolatrous.* The foreign growth introduced is understood by some to be idolatry, by others foreign alliance; but these two things, as we have seen before, were inseparably blended in the history and policy of Israel. (See above, ch. 2 : 6–8.)

11. *In the day of thy planting thou wilt hedge it in, and in the*

morning thou wilt make thy seed to blossom, (but) *away flies the crop in a day of grief and desperate sorrow. In the morning* is an idiomatic phrase for *early,* which some refer to the rapidity of growth, and others to the assiduity of the cultivator, neither of which senses is exclusive of the other.

12. *Hark! the noise of many nations! Like the noise of the sea they make a noise. And the rush of peoples! Like the rush of mighty waters they are rushing.* The diversity of judgments, as to the connection of these verses (12–14) with the context, has been already stated in the introduction. On the whole, the safest ground to assume is that already stated in the introduction, viz. that the two chapters form a single prophecy or prophetic picture of the doom awaiting all the enemies of Judah, with particular allusion to particular enemies in certain parts. To the poetical images of this verse a beautiful parallel is found in Ovid's Metamorphoses:

> Qualia fluctus
> Aequorei faciunt, si quis procul audiat ipsos,
> Tale sonat populus.

13. *Nations, like the rush of many waters, rush; and he rebukes it, and it flees from afar, and is chased like the chaff of hills before a wind, and like a rolling thing before a whirlwind.* While there seems to be an obvious allusion to the flight of Sennacherib and the remnant of his host (ch. 37 : 36, 37), the terms are so selected as to admit of a wider application to all Jehovah's enemies, and thus prepare the way for the general declaration in the following verse.

14. *At evening-tide, and behold terror; before morning he is not. This is* (or *be*) *the portion of our plunderers, and the lot of our spoilers.* The Prophet is the speaker, and he uses the plural pronouns only to identify himself with the people.

CHAPTER XVIII.

The two great powers of western Asia, in the days of Isaiah, were Assyria and Egypt or Ethiopia, the last two being wholly or partially united under Tirhakah, whose name and exploits are recorded in Egyptian monuments still extant, and who is expressly said in Scripture (2 Kings 19:9) to have come out against Sennacherib. With one or the other of these great contending powers, Judah was commonly confederate, and of course at war with the other. Hezekiah is explicitly reproached by Rabshakeh (Is. 36:9) with relying upon Egypt, i. e. the Ethiopico-Egyptian empire. These historical facts, together with the mention of Cush in v. 1, and the appropriateness of the figures in vs. 4, 5, to the destruction of Sennacherib's army, give great probability to the hypothesis now commonly adopted, that the Prophet here announces that event to Ethiopia, as about to be effected by a direct interposition of Jehovah, and without human aid. On this supposition, although not without its difficulties, the chapter before us is much clearer in itself and in its connection with the one before it, than if we assume with some interpreters, both Jews and Christians, that it relates to the restoration of the Jews, or to the overthrow of the Egyptians or Ethiopians themselves as the enemies of Israel. At the same time, some of the expressions here employed admit of so many interpretations, that it is best to give the whole as wide an application as the language will admit, on the ground before suggested, that it constitutes a part of a generic prophecy or picture of God's dealings with the foes of his people, including illustrations drawn from particular events, such as the downfall of Syria and Israel, and the slaughter of Sennacherib's army.

The Prophet first invites the attention of the Ethiopians and of the whole world to a great catastrophe as near at hand, vs. 1–3. He then describes the catastrophe itself, by the beautiful figure of a vine or vineyard suffered to blossom and bear fruit, and then, when almost ready to be gathered, suddenly destroyed, vs. 4–6. In consequence of this event, the same people, who had been invoked in the beginning of the chapter, are described as bringing presents to Jehovah at Jerusalem, v. 7.

1. *Ho! land of rustling wings, which art beyond the rivers of Cush* (or Ethiopia)! Instead of *rustling* some read *shadowy wings*. But as the Hebrew word in every other case has reference to sound, some suppose an allusion to the noise made by locusts, some to the rushing sound of rivers, others to the clash of arms or other noises made by armies on the march, here called *wings* by a common figure. The *rivers of Cush* are supposed by some to be the Nile and its branches; by others, the Astaboras, Astapus, and Astasobas, mentioned by Strabo as the rivers of Meroe.

2. *Sending by sea ambassadors, and in vessels of papyrus on the face of the waters. Go ye light* (or *swift*) *messengers, to a nation drawn and shorn, to a people terrible since it existed and onwards, a nation of double strength, and trampling, whose land the streams divide.* Nearly every word and phrase of this difficult verse has been the subject of discordant explanations. The word *sea* is variously explained to mean the Red Sea, the Mediterranean, and the Nile (Is. 19:5. Nah. 3:8). The use of vessels made of the papyrus plant upon the Nile, is expressly mentioned by Theophrastus, Pliny, Lucan, and Plutarch. The second clause of the verse is regarded by some writers as the language of the people who had just been addressed, as if he had said, 'sending ambassadors (and saying to them) go etc.' More probably, however, the Prophet is still speaking in the name of God. The following epithets are applied by some to the Jews, and sup-

posed to be descriptive of their degraded and oppressed condition, by others as descriptive of their warlike qualities. Shorn or shaven, is applied by some to the Egyptian and Ethiopian practice of shaving the head and beard, while others understand it as a figure for robbery and spoliation. By rivers, in the last clause, some suppose nations to be meant, or the Assyrians in particular; but most writers understand it literally as a description of the country.

3. *All ye inhabitants of the world and dwellers on the earth shall see as it were the raising of a standard on the mountains, and shall hear as it were the blowing of a trumpet.* Another construction, more generally adopted, makes the verbs imperative. So the English Version: *see ye when he lifteth up an ensign on the mountains, and when he bloweth a trumpet hear ye.* There seems, however, to be no sufficient reason for departing from the strict translation of the verbs as future. In either case, the verse invites the attention of the world to some great event.

4. *For thus said* (or *saith*) *Jehovah to me, I will rest* (remain quiet), *and will look on* (as a mere spectator) *in my dwelling place, like a serene heat upon herbs, like a cloud of dew* (or dewy cloud), *in the heat of harvest* (i. e. the heat preceding harvest, or the heat by which the crop is ripened). This verse assigns a reason for the preceding invitation to attend. The obvious meaning of the figure is, that God would let the enemy proceed in the execution of his purposes until they were nearly accomplished.

5. *For before the harvest, as the bloom is finished, and the flower becomes a ripening grape, he cuts down the branches with the pruning knives, and the tendrils he removes, he cuts away.* The obvious meaning of the figures is, that although God would suffer the designs of the enemy to approach completion, he would never-

theless interfere at the last moment and destroy both him and them. As if he had said, let all the world await the great catastrophe—*for* I will let the enemy almost attain his end—but let them still attend—*for* before it is attained, I will destroy him. The verbs in the last clause may either be referred directly to *Jehovah* as their subject, or construed indefinitely, one shall cut them down.

6. *They shall be left together to the wild bird of the mountains and to the wild beasts of the earth* (or *land*), *and the wild bird shall summer thereon, and every wild beast of the earth* (or *land*) *thereon shall winter.* It is commonly supposed that there is here a transition from the figure of a vineyard to that of a dead body, the branches cut off and thrown away being suddenly transformed into carcasses devoured by beasts and birds. For a like combination, see above, ch. 14 : 19. But this interpretation, though perhaps the most natural, is not absolutely necessary. As the act of devouring is not expressly mentioned, the reference may be, not to the carnivorous habits of the animals, but to their wild and solitary life. In that case the sense would be that the amputated branches, and the desolated vineyard itself, shall furnish lairs and nests for beasts and birds which commonly frequent the wildest solitudes, implying abandonment and utter desolation. The only reason for preferring this interpretation is that it precludes the necessity of assuming a mixed metaphor, or an abrupt exchange of one for another, both which, however, are too common in Isaiah to excite surprise. On either supposition, the general meaning of the verse is obvious. The form of the last clause is idiomatic, the birds being said to spend the summer and the beasts the winter, not with reference to any real difference in their habits, but for the purpose of expressing the idea, that beasts and birds shall occupy the spot throughout the year. According to the common explanation of the verse as referring to dead bodies, it is a hyper-

bolical description of their multitude, as furnishing repast for a whole year to the beasts and birds of prey.

7. *At that time shall be brought a gift to Jehovah of Hosts, a people drawn out and shorn, and from a people terrible since it has been and onward* (or still more terrible and still further off), a *nation of double power and trampling, whose land streams divide, to the place of the name of Jehovah of Hosts, Mount Zion.* Here, as in v. 2, the sense of some particular expressions is so doubtful, that it seems better to retain, as far as possible, the form of the original, with all its ambiguity, than to attempt an explanatory paraphrase. All are agreed that we have here the prediction of an act of homage to Jehovah, occasioned by the great event described in the preceding verses. The Jews, who understand the second verse as a description of the sufferings endured by Israel, explain this as a prophecy of their return from exile and dispersion, aided and as it were presented as an offering to Jehovah by the heathen. (see below, ch. 66 : 20.) The older Christian writers understand it as predicting the conversion of the Egyptians or Ethiopians to the true religion. The most natural construction of the words would seem to be that the gift to Jehovah should consist of one people offered by another. The place of God's name is not merely the place called by his name, but the place where his name, i. e. the manifestation of his attributes resides.

CHAPTER XIX.

THIS chapter admits of a well-defined division into two parts, one of which contains threatenings (vs. 1–17), and the other promises (vs. 18–25). The first part may again be subdivided.

In vs. 1–4, the Egyptians are threatened with a penal visitation from Jehovah, with the downfall of their idols, with intestine commotions, with the disappointment of their superstitious hopes, and with subjection to hard masters. In vs. 5–10 they are threatened with physical calamities, the drying up of their streams, the decay of vegetation, the loss of their fisheries, and the destruction of their manufactures. In vs. 11–17, the wisdom of their wise men is converted into folly, the courage of their brave men into cowardice, industry universally suspended, and the people filled with dread of the anger of Jehovah. The second part may be also subdivided. In vs. 18–21, the Egyptians are described as acknowledging the true God in consequence of what they had suffered at his hand, and the deliverance which he had granted them. In vs. 22–25, the same cause is described as leading to an intimate union between Egypt, Assyria, and Israel, in the service of Jehovah, and the enjoyment of his favor. The Prophet wishing to announce to the Jews the decline and fall of that great heathen power, in which they were so constantly disposed to trust (30 : 1. 31 : 1), describes the event under figures borrowed from the actual condition of Egypt. As a writer, who should now predict the downfall of the British empire, in a poetical and figurative style, would naturally speak of its fleets as sunk or scattered, its colonies dismembered, its factories destroyed, its railways abandoned, its universities abolished, so the Prophet vividly portrays the fall of Egypt by describing the waters of the Nile as failing, its meadows withering, its fisheries ceasing, and the peculiar manufactures of the country expiring, the proverbial wisdom of the nation changed to folly, its courage to cowardice, its strength to weakness Whether particular parts of the description were intended to have a more specific application, is a question not affecting the truth of the hypothesis, that the first part is a metaphorical description of the downfall of the great Egyptian monarchy. So too in the second part, the introduction of the true religion, and its effect as well on the internal state as on the international relations of the different countries, is expressed by figures drawn from the civil and religious institutions of the old economy.

1. *The Burden of Egypt. Behold! Jehovah riding on a light cloud, and he comes to* (or *into*) *Egypt, and the idols of Egypt move at his presence, and the heart of Egypt melts within him.* This verse describes God as the author of the judgments afterwards detailed. His visible appearance on a cloud, and the personification of the idols, prepare the mind for a poetical description. The act of riding on a light cloud implies that he comes from heaven, and that he comes swiftly. On the contemptuous import of the word translated *idols*, see above, ch. 2 : 8 ; on the meaning of *burden*, ch. 13 : 1.

2. *And I will excite Egypt against Egypt, and they shall fight, a man with his brother, and a man with his fellow, city with city, kingdom with kingdom.* The first verb is by some rendered *arm*, by others *join* or engage in conflict ; but the sense of *stirring up* or *rousing* is preferred both by the oldest and the latest writers. The version usually given, *Egyptians against Egyptians*, though substantially correct, is neither so expressive nor so true to the original as *Egypt against Egypt*, which involves an allusion to the internal divisions of the kingdom, or rather the existence of contemporary kingdoms, more explicitly referred to in the other clause. Some understand this verse as referring specifically to the civil wars of Egypt in the days of Sethos or Psammetichus. But while the coincidence with history adds greatly to the propriety and force of the description, there is no sufficient reason for departing from its obvious import, as a description of internal strife and anarchy in general. The expressions bear a strong resemblance to those used in the description of the state of Judah, ch. 3 : 5. Some regard these

as the words to be uttered by Jehovah when he enters Egypt. It may, however, be a simple continuation of the prophecy, with a sudden change from the third to the first person, of which there are many other examples.

3. *And the spirit of Egypt shall be emptied out* (or *exhausted*) *in the midst thereof, and the counsel* (or *sagacity*) *thereof I will swallow up* (annihilate or render useless), *and they will seek to the idols, and to the mutterers, and to the familiar spirits, and to the wizards.* By *spirit*, in the first clause, we are not to understand courage but intellect. As to the ancient mode of incantation, see above, ch. 8 : 19.

4. *And I will shut up Egypt in the hands of a hard master, and a strong king shall rule over them, saith the Lord, Jehovah of Hosts.* *Master*, literally *masters*, a *pluralis majestaticus*, elsewhere applied to individual men (Gen. 42 : 30, 33. 2 Kings 2 : 3, 5, 16). The king here mentioned is identified, according to various hypotheses, with Sethos, Psammetichus, Sennacherib, Sargon, Nebuchadnezzar, Cambyses, Ochus, and Charlemagne! The very multiplicity of these explanations shows how fanciful they are, and naturally leads us to conclude that the Prophet is describing in a general way the political vicissitudes of Egypt, one of which would be subjection to an arbitrary power, whether foreign or domestic, or to both at different periods of its history.

5. *And the waters shall be dried up from the sea, and the river shall fail and be dried up.* Three distinct verbs are here used in the sense of drying up, for which our language does not furnish equivalents. As the Nile has in all ages been called a sea by the Egyptians, most interpreters suppose it to be here referred to, in both clauses. According to the exegetical hypothesis laid down in the introduction to the chapter, this is a prediction of Egypt's national decline and fall,

clothed in figures drawn from the characteristic features of its actual condition. As the desolation of our own western territory might be poetically represented as the drying up of the Mississippi and its branches, so a like event in the history of Egypt would be still more naturally described as a desiccation of the Nile, because that river is still more essential to the prosperity of the country which it waters. In favour of this figurative exposition is the difficulty of applying the description to particular historical events, and also the whole tenor of the context, as will be more clearly seen hereafter.

6. *And the rivers shall stink* (or become putrid), *the streams of Egypt are emptied and dried up, reed and rush sicken* (pine or wither). The streams meant are the natural and artificial branches of the Nile. The reed and rush are mentioned as a common growth in marshy situations.

7. *The meadows by the river, by the mouth of the river, and all the sown ground of the river, shall wither, being driven away, and it is not* (or shall be no more). The first word in Hebrew means bare or open places, i. e. meadows, as distinguished from woodland. The English and some other versions treat it as the name of the papyrus, but without authority. The word translated *river* is the one already mentioned as the common name in Scripture for the Nile, nor is there any need of departing from this sense in the case before us. Calvin explains *mouth* to mean source or fountain, which is wholly arbitrary. Others regard it as synonymous with *lip*, used elsewhere (Gen. 41 : 3. Exod. 2 : 3) to denote the brink or margin of the Nile. Some of the older writers give the word its geographical sense, as denoting the place where the waters of a stream are discharged into another or the sea. The *place of seed* or *sowing*, i. e. cultivated ground, is here distinguished from the meadows or uncultivated pastures.

8. *And the fishermen shall mourn, and they shall lament, all the throwers of a hook into the river and the spreaders of a net upon the surface of the water languish.* Having described the effect of the drought on vegetation, he now describes its effect upon those classes of the people who were otherwise dependent on the river for subsistence. The multitude of fishes in the Nile, and of people engaged in catching them, is attested both by ancient and modern writers. The use of fish in ancient Egypt was promoted by the popular superstitions with respect to other animals. The net is said to be not now used in the fisheries of Egypt. It is remarkable, however, that the implement itself appears on some of the old monuments. This verse is not to be applied to an actual distress among the fishermen at any one time, but to be viewed as a characteristic trait in the prophetic picture. When he speaks of a wine-growing country, the Prophet renders vineyards and vine-dressers prominent objects. So here, when he speaks of a country abounding in fisheries and fishermen, he describes their condition as an index or symbol of the state of the country. In like manner, a general distress in our southern states might be described as a distress among the sugar, cotton, or tobacco planters.

9. *And ashamed* (disappointed or confounded) *are the workers of combed* (or hatchelled) *flax, and the weavers of white* (stuffs). The older writers supposed the class of persons here described to be the manufacturers of nets for fishing. The moderns understand the verse as having reference to the working of flax and manufacture of linen.

10. *And her pillars* (or *foundations*) *are broken down, all labourers for hire are grieved at heart.* The simplest exposition of the verse is that which regards this as a general description of distress, extending to the two great classes of society, the pillars or chief men and the labourers or commonalty.

11. *Only foolish* (i. e. entirely foolish) *are the princes of Zoan, the sages of the counsellors of Pharaoh,* (their) *counsel is become brutish* (or irrational). *How can ye say to Pharaoh, I am the son of wise* (fathers), *I am the son of kings of old?* The reference is not merely to perplexity in actual distress, but also to an unwise policy as one of the causes of the distress itself. Zoan, the Tanis of the Greeks, was one of the most ancient cities of Lower Egypt (Num. 13 : 22) and a royal residence. The name is of Egyptian origin and signifies a low situation. *Pharaoh* was a common title of the Egyptian kings. It is originally an Egyptian noun with the article prefixed. The statesmen and courtiers of ancient Egypt belonged to the sacerdotal caste, from which many of the kings were also taken. The *wisdom of Egypt* seems to have been proverbial in the ancient world (1 Kings 4 : 30. Acts 7 : 22). The last clause is addressed to the counsellors themselves. The interrogation implies the absurdity of their pretensions.

12. *Where* (*are*) *they? Where* (*are*) *thy wise men? Pray let them tell thee, and* (if that is too much) *let them* (at least) *know, what Jehovah of Hosts hath purposed against* (or *concerning*) *Egypt.* It was a proof of their false pretensions that so far from being able to avert the evil, they could not even foresee it. The repetition of the interrogative *where* is highly emphatic.

13. *Infatuated are the chiefs of Zoan, deceived are the chiefs of Noph, and they have misled Egypt, the corner* (or *corner-stone*) *of her tribes. Noph* is the *Memphis* of the Greek geographers, called *Moph,* Hos. 9 : 6. It was one of the chief cities of ancient Egypt, the royal seat of Psammetichus. After Alexandria was built it declined. Arabian writers in the twelfth and thirteenth centuries speak of its extensive and magnificent ruins, which have now almost wholly disappeared.

14. *Jehovah hath mingled in the midst of her a spirit of confusion, and they have misled Egypt in all its work, like the misleading of a drunkard in his vomit.* This verse describes the folly before mentioned as the effect not of natural causes or of accident but of a judicial infliction. *Spirit* here means a supernatural influence. By *work* we are to understand affairs and interests. The last verb in Hebrew is used elsewhere in reference to the unsteady motions of a drunken man (Job 12 : 25. Isai. 28 : 7).

15. *And there shall not be to Egypt a work which head and tail, branch and rush, may do.* Work here means anything done or to be done, including private business and public affairs. The figures of head and tail, branch and rush, are used, as in ch. 9 : 14, to denote all classes of society, or rather the extremes between which the others are included.

16. *In that day shall Egypt be like a woman, and shall fear and tremble from before the shaking of the hand of Jehovah of Hosts, which he (is) shaking over it.* The comparison in the first clause is a common one for terror and the loss of courage. The reference is not to the slaughter of Sennacherib's army, but more generally to the indications of divine displeasure.

17. *And the land of Judah shall be for a terror* (or *become a terror*) *unto Egypt; every person to whom one mentions it* (or every one who recalls it to his own mind) *shall fear before the purpose of Jehovah of Hosts which he is purposing against it.* This verse relates to the new feelings which would be entertained by the Egyptians towards the God of the Jews and the true religion. Judah, in a political and military sense, might still appear contemptible; but in another aspect, and for other reasons, it would be an object of respect and even fear to the Egyptians.

18. *In that day there shall be five cities in the land of Egypt speaking the lip* (i. e. language) *of Canaan, and swearing to Jehovah of Hosts. The city of destruction shall be said to one* (i. e. shall one be called). *In that day*, according to prophetic usage, is a somewhat indefinite expression, and may either mean *during* or *after* the distresses just described. *Canaan* is here put for the land of Canaan (as in Ex. 15 : 15), and the *language of Canaan* for the Hebrew language, not because it was the language of the old Canaanites, but because it was spoken in the land which they once occupied. Some of the later writers understand what is here said strictly as denoting an actual prevalence of the Hebrew language, while others take it as a strong expression for such intimate union, social, commercial, and political, as would seem to imply a community of language. The older writers very generally apply the terms to religious union and communion. The simplest interpretation of the phrase is, that in itself it denotes intimate intercourse and union generally, but that the idea of religious unity is here suggested by the context and especially by the following clause. Many interpreters appear to regard the phrases *swearing by* and *swearing to* as perfectly synonymous. The former act does certainly imply the recognition of the deity by whom one swears, especially if *oaths* be regarded (as they are in Scripture) as solemn acts of religious worship. But the phrase *swearing to* conveys the additional idea of doing homage and acknowledging a sovereign by swearing fealty or allegiance to him. This is the only meaning that the words can bear in 2 Chr. 15 : 14, and in Isai. 45 : 23 the two phrases seem to be very clearly distinguished. The act of thus professing the true faith and submitting to the true God is ascribed in the verse before us to *five towns*, or *cities*. What appears to be meant is that five sixths, i. e. a very large proportion, shall profess the true religion, while the remaining sixth persists in unbelief. *It shall be said to one*, i. e. one shall be addressed as follows, or called by the following name. For

one town which shall perish in its unbelief five shall profess the true faith and swear fealty to Jehovah.

19. *In that day there shall be an altar to Jehovah in the midst of the land of Egypt, and a pillar at* (or *near*) *its border to Jehovah.* It has been disputed whether we are here to understand an altar for sacrifice or an altar to serve as a memorial (Josh. 22:26, 27). It has also been disputed whether the prohibition of altars and consecrated pillars (Lev. 26:1. Deut. 12:5, 16:22) was applicable only to the Jews or to Palestine, leaving foreign Jews or proselytes at liberty to rear these sacred structures as the Patriarchs did of old (Gen. 28:18. 35:14). The necessity of answering these questions is removed by a just view of the passage, as predicting the prevalence of the true religion and the practice of its rites, in language borrowed from the Mosaic or rather from the patriarchal institutions. As we might now speak of a missionary *pitching his tent* at Hebron or at Shechem, without intending to describe the precise form of his habitation, so the Prophet represents the converts to the true faith as erecting an altar and a pillar to the Lord in Egypt, as Abraham and Jacob did of old in Canaan. A still more exact illustration is afforded by the frequent use among ourselves of the word *altar* to denote the practice of devotion, especially in families. There is a double propriety and beauty in the use of the word *pillar*, because while it instantly recalls to mind the patriarchal practice, it is at the same time finely descriptive of the obelisk, an object so characteristic of Egypt that it may be regarded as its emblem. Both the obelisk and the patriarchal pillar, being never in the human form, are to be carefully distinguished from statues or images, although the latter word is sometimes used to represent the Hebrew one in the English Version. (See 2 Kings 3:2. 10:26. Mic. 5:13.)

20. *And it shall be for a sign and for a testimony to Jehovah of*

Hosts in the land of Egypt, that they shall cry to Jehovah from the presence of oppressors, and he will send them a deliverer and a mighty one and save them. This shall be a sign and a witness to (i. e. with respect to, in behalf of) Jehovah in the land of Egypt, viz. that when they cry, he will afford a providential testimony in behalf of his own being, presence, and supremacy, by saving those who cry to him. If, as we have seen reason to believe, the chapter is a prophecy, not of a single event but of a great progressive change to be wrought in the condition of Egypt by the introduction of the true religion, the promise of the verse before us must be that when they cried God would send them a deliverer, a promise verified not once but often, not only by Ptolemy or Alexander, but by others, and in the highest sense by Christ himself. In the language of this verse there is an obvious allusion to the frequent statement in the book of Judges, that the people cried to God and he raised them up deliverers who saved them from their oppressors (Judg. 2:16. 3:9 etc.).

21. *And Jehovah shall be known to Egypt, and Egypt* (or the Egyptians) *shall know Jehovah in that day, and shall serve (with) sacrifice and offering, and shall vow a vow to Jehovah and perform* it. This is not the prediction of a new event, but a repetition in another form of the preceding promise. What is first described as the knowledge of the true God, is afterwards represented as his service, the expressions being borrowed from the ancient ritual. If the last clause be literally understood, we must either regard it as an unfounded expectation of the Prophet which was never fulfilled, or suppose that it relates to an express violation of the law of Moses, or assume that the ancient rites and forms are hereafter to be re-established. On the other hand, the figurative explanation is in perfect agreement with the usage of both testaments and with the tenor of the prophecy itself. Bloody and unbloody sacrifice is here combined with vows in order to express the totality of ritual services as a fig-

ure for those of a more spiritual nature. The express mention of the Egyptians themselves as worshipping Jehovah shows that they are also meant in the preceding verse.

22. *And Jehovah shall smite Egypt* (or *the Egyptians*), *smiting and healing, and they shall return unto Jehovah, and he shall be entreated of them and shall heal them.* Here again the second clause contains no advance upon the first, and the whole verse no advance upon the foregoing context, but an iteration of the same idea in another form. This verse may indeed be regarded as a recapitulation of the whole preceding prophecy, consisting as it does of an extended threatening (vs. 1–17) followed by an ample promise (vs. 18–21). As if he had said, thus will God smite Egypt and then heal it. That great heathen power, with respect to which the Jews so often sinned both by undue confidence and undue dread, was to be broken and reduced; but in exchange for this political decline, and partly as a consequence of it, the Egyptians should experience benefits far greater than they ever before knew. Thus would Jehovah *smite and heal*, or smite but so as afterwards to heal, which seems to be the force of the reduplicated verb. The meaning is not simply that the stroke should be followed by healing, nor is it simply that the stroke should itself possess a healing virtue; but both ideas seem to be included. Returning to Jehovah is a common figure for repentance and conversion, even in reference to the heathen. (See Psalm 22:27.)

23. *In that day there shall be a highway from Egypt to Assyria, and Assyria shall come into Egypt and Egypt into Assyria, and Egypt* (or *the Egyptians*) *shall serve with Assyria.* No translation will convey the precise form of the original, in which the ancestral names are put not only for their descendants but for the countries which they occupied. No one, it is probable, has ever yet maintained that a road was literally opened between

Egypt and Assyria, or that Isaiah expected it. All classes of interpreters agree that the opening of the highway is a figure for easy, free, and intimate communication. This unanimous admission of a metaphor in this place not only shows that the same mode of interpretation is admissible in the other parts of the same prophecy, but makes it highly probable that what is said of altar and sacrifices is to be likewise so understood.

24. *In that day shall Israel be a third with respect to Egypt and Assyria, a blessing in the midst of the earth.* The meaning obviously is that Israel should be *one of three* or a party to a triple union. The idea meant to be conveyed, is not merely that of equality in magnitude or power, but also that of intimate conjunction, as in the preceding verse. *Blessing* is here used in a comprehensive sense, as denoting at the same time a source of blessing, a means of blessing, and an object to be blessed.

25. *Which Jehovah of Hosts has blessed* (or *with which Jehovah of Hosts has blessed it*) *saying, Blessed be my people Egypt, and the work of my hands Assyria, and my heritage* (or peculiar people) *Israel.* The perfect union of the three great powers in the service of God and the enjoyment of his favour is now expressed by a solemn benediction on the three, in which language commonly applied to Israel exclusively is extended to Egypt and Assyria. The force of the expressions would be much enhanced by the habitual associations of a Jewish reader. It arises very much from the surprise excited by the unexpected termination of the clauses. Instead of *Blessed be my people Israel*, the formula is *Blessed be my people Egypt.* That *the work of my hands* does not merely mean *my creature*, or a creature perfectly at my disposal, but my creature in a special and a spiritual sense, the same in which God is said to be the maker or founder of Israel (Deut. 32 : 6. Isai. 43 : 6, 7), is evident from this consideration, that the clause would otherwise say

nothing peculiar or distinctive of Assyria, as those before and after it do of Egypt and Israel. In order to express once more and in the most emphatic manner the admission of Egypt and Assyria to the privileges of the chosen people, he selects three titles commonly bestowed upon the latter exclusively, to wit, *God's people*, the *work of his hands*, and his *inheritance*, and these three he distributes to the three united powers without discrimination or invidious distinction. As to the application of the prophecy there are three distinct opinions. One is, that the Prophet here anticipates a state of peace and international communion between Egypt, Israel, and Assyria in his own times, which may or may not have been actually realized. Another is, that he predicts what actually did take place under the reign of Alexander and the two great powers that succeeded him, viz. the Graeco-Syrian and Egyptian monarchies, by which the true religion was protected and diffused and the way prepared for the preaching of the gospel. A third is, that Egypt and Assyria are here named as the two great heathen powers known to the Jews, whose country lay between them and was often the scene if not the subject of their contests, so that for ages they were commonly in league with the one against the other. To describe these two great belligerent powers as at peace with Israel and one another, was not only to foretell a most surprising revolution in the state of the world, but to intimate at least a future change in the relation of the Jews and the Gentiles. When he goes still further and describes these representatives of heathenism as received into the covenant and sharing with the church of God its most distinctive titles, we have one of the clearest and most striking predictions of the calling of the Gentiles that the word of God contains. One advantage of this exposition is that, while it thus extends and elevates the scope of the prediction, it retains unaltered whatever there may be of more specific prophecy or of coincidence with history. If Alexander is referred to, and the spread of Judaism under him and his successors, and the general pacification of the world and progress of refinement, these are so many masterly strokes added to the great prophetic picture; but they cannot be extracted from it and made to constitute a picture by themselves.

CHAPTER XX.

About the time of the Assyrian attack on Ashdod, the Prophet is directed to walk naked and barefoot as a sign of the defeat and captivity of the Egyptians and Ethiopians who were at war with Assyria. The first verse fixes the date of this symbolical transaction; the second contains the divine command and the record of its execution; the third and fourth explain the meaning of the symbol; the fifth and sixth predict its effect, or rather that of the event which it prefigured. The questions which have been raised, as to the date of the composition and the fulfilment of the prophecy, will be most conveniently considered in the course of the detailed interpretation.

1. *In the year of Tartan's coming to Ashdod, in Sargon king of Assyria's sending him* (i. e. when Sargon king of Assyria sent him), *and he fought with Ashdod* (i. e. besieged it) *and took it.* Ashdod was one of the five cities of the Philistines (Josh. 11 : 22. 15 : 46. 1 Sam. 5 : 1), considered on account of its strong fortifications (from which its name is supposed to be derived) the key of Egypt, and therefore frequently attacked in the wars between Egypt and Assyria. According to Herodotus, Psammetichus besieged it twenty-nine years. This, if not an exaggeration, is the longest siege in history, and probably took place after what is here recorded, to recover Ashdod from Assyria. Its site is marked by a village still called Esdûd

(Robinson's Palestine II. 368). The name of Sargon nowhere else occurs. Tartan appears again as a general under Sennacherib (2 Kings 18 : 17). From this some infer that Sargon and Sennacherib are one and the same person. Others identify Sargon with Esarhaddon, or with Shalmaneser. All these suppositions are less probable than the obvious one, that Sargon was a king of Assyria mentioned only here, because his reign was very short, and this was the only occurrence that brought him into contact with the Jews. That he was not the immediate successor of Sennacherib, is clear from ch. 37 : 38, and from the fact which seems to be implied in 2 Chr. 32 : 21, that Tartan perished in the great catastrophe. The most plausible hypothesis, and that now commonly adopted, is that he reigned three or four years between Shalmaneser and Sennacherib. It is disputed whether *in the year of Tartan's coming* means before or after that occurrence. The truth is, it means neither, but leaves that question undetermined, or at most to be determined by the context.

2. *At that time spake Jehovah by the hand of Isaiah the son of Amoz, saying, Go, and thou shalt open* (i. e. loose) *the sackcloth from upon thy loins, and thy shoe thou shalt pull off from upon thy foot. And he did so, going naked and barefoot.* The word *naked* is used to express partial denudation in all languages. As biblical examples, may be cited 1 Sam. 19 : 24. 2 Sam. 6 : 20. Amos 2 : 16. John 21 : 7. In the case before us, we may either suppose that the sackcloth was an upper garment which he threw entirely off, or an inner garment which he opened by ungirding it, or a girdle itself which he loosened and perhaps removed. Sackcloth was a common mourning dress, and some suppose that Isaiah was now wearing it in token of his grief for the exile of the ten tribes. Others understand it as an official or ascetic dress worn by the Prophets (Zech. 13 : 4), as for instance by Elijah (2 Kings 1 : 8) and by John the Baptist

(Matt. 3 : 4). Others again suppose that it is mentioned as a cheap coarse dress worn by the Prophet in common with the humbler class of people. *By the hand* denotes ministerial agency or intervention, and is often used in reference to communications made to the people *through* the prophets. (Ex. 4 : 13. 1 Sam. 16 : 20. Jer. 37 : 2.) So in this case, the divine communication was really addressed to the people, though the words immediately ensuing are addressed to the Prophet himself. It is not necessary to suppose that the phrase has exclusive reference to the symbolical action. What was said *to* the Prophet was obviously said *through* him to the people.

3. *And Jehovah said, As my servant Isaiah hath gone naked and barefoot three years a sign and symbol concerning Egypt and concerning Ethiopia.* Here begins the divine explanation of the symbolical act before commanded. The design of this transaction was to draw attention by exciting surprise. In the prophecies belonging to the reign of Hezekiah, Egypt and Ethiopia are frequently combined, either because they were in close alliance, or because an Ethiopian dynasty then reigned in Upper Egypt. The Prophet probably exposed himself but once in the way described, after which he continued to be a sign and wonder for three years, i. e. till the fulfilment of the prophecy. The three years have been variously understood, as the duration of the siege of Ashdod, as the duration of the exile threatened in the next verse, and as the interval which should elapse between the prophecy and its fulfilment. Of these three hypotheses the second is the least probable, while the first and third may be combined.

4. *So shall the king of Assyria lead the captivity* (i. e. *the captives*) *of Egypt and the exiles of Ethiopia, young and old, naked and barefoot, with their buttocks uncovered, the nakedness* (or *disgrace*) *of Egypt.* This verse completes the comparison begun

in that before it. It is also clear from a comparison of the type and antitype, that the nakedness of v. 2 was a partial one, since captives were not commonly reduced to a state of absolute nudity. This is confirmed by the addition of the word *barefoot* in both cases, which would be superfluous if *naked* had its strictest sense. Connected as Egypt and Ethiopia were in fact and in the foregoing context, either name includes the other. The *King of Assyria* here meant is either Sennacherib or Sargon himself. Some suppose this prediction to have been fulfilled in the conquest of No-Ammon (i. e. Diospolis or Thebes) mentioned in Nah. 3 : 8 as a recent event. How long beforehand the prediction was uttered, is a question of small moment and one which cannot be decided. There is no ground, however, for the supposition that the interval was so short as to convert the prophecy into a mere conjecture or an act of sagacious forecast.

5. *And they shall be afraid and ashamed of Ethiopia their expectation and of Egypt their boast.* This is the effect to be produced by the catastrophe just threatened. The full sense of the first verb is that they shall be confounded, filled with consternation, at the fate of those in whom they trusted for deliverance. The meaning of the verse is, that they who had relied on Egypt and its ally Ethiopia for aid against Assyria, whether Jews or Philistines or both, should be confounded at beholding Egypt and Ethiopia themselves subdued.

6. *And the inhabitant of this isle* (or *coast*) *shall say in that day, Behold, thus* (or *such*) *is our expectation, whither we fled for help, to be delivered from the presence of the king of Assyria. And how shall we* (*ourselves*) *escape?* The disappointment described in the foregoing verse is now expressed by those who felt it. The argument is one *a fortiori.* If the protectors were subdued, what must become of the protected? The pronoun in

the last clause is emphatic, as it usually is when not essential to the sense. The Hebrew word for *island* has no exact equivalent in English. Three distinct shades or gradations of meaning seem to be clearly marked in usage. The first is that of *land* as opposed to water; the second that of *coast* as opposed to inland; the third that of *island* as opposed to mainland. The last, although commonly expressed in most translations, is perhaps the least frequent of the three. The word here denotes the south-eastern shore of the Mediterranean, called *this coast*, in order to distinguish it from *that coast*, viz. Ethiopia and Egypt, which had just before been mentioned. As to the extent of country meant to be included, nothing of course can be determined from the word itself, which is designedly indefinite. *Thus or such is our expectation*, i. e. this is the end of it, you see what has become of it, you see the fate of that to which we looked for help; how then can we ourselves be delivered or escape? See a similar expression 2 Kings 10 : 4.

CHAPTER XXI.

As three of the verses of this chapter begin with the word *burden* (vs. 1, 11, 13), it is now commonly supposed to consist of three distinct prophecies. Taking the language in its obvious meaning and excluding all gratuitous assumptions, we shall be constrained to look upon the first of these divisions (vs. 1–10) as one of the most striking instances of strict agreement between prophecy and history. As to the remainder of the chapter, while it cannot be denied that the connection of the parts, and the meaning of each in itself, are exceedingly obscure, it may be doubted whether there is sufficient ground for their entire separation as distinct and independent prophecies. The extreme brevity, especially of the second part (vs. 11, 12), makes this very dubious, and the doubt is strengthened by the recurrence of the figure of a watchman in v. 11. In the case before us, as in ch. 14 : 28, it is safer to assume the unity of the composition than rashly to dismember it. However difficult it may be to determine the connection of these parts, they may safely be regarded as composing one obscure but continuous prediction. This is the less improbable because they can all be brought into connection, if not unity, by simply supposing that the tribes or races, to which vs. 11–17 relate, were sharers with the Jews in the Babylonian tyranny, and therefore interested in its downfall. This hypothesis, it is true, is not susceptible of demonstration; but it is strongly recommended by the very fact that it explains the juxtaposition of these prophecies, or rather entitles them to be considered one. The first part of the prophecy opens with an emphatic intimation of its alarming character, vs. 1–4. We have then a graphic representation of the march of the Medes and Persians upon Babylon, vs. 5–9. This is followed by a hint of the effect which this event would have upon the people of Jehovah, v. 10. The remainder of the chapter represents the neighboring nations as involved in the same sufferings with the Jews, but without any consolatory promise of deliverance, vs. 11–17.

1. *The burden of the desert of the sea. Like whirlwinds in the south, as to rushing* (or *driving*), *from the wilderness it comes, from a terrible land.* Most interpreters are agreed that the phrase *desert of the sea* is an enigmatical description of Babylonia as a great plain (Gen. 11 : 1. Isai. 23 : 13), watered by a great river which, like the Nile (ch. 19 : 5), is sometimes called a sea (ch. 27 : 1). This designation was the more appropriate because the plain of Babylon, according to Herodotus, was often overflowed before Semiramis took measures to prevent it, and

an ancient writer says expressly that it then had the appearance of a sea. The threatened danger is compared to the approach of a tempest from the south, i. e. from the great Arabian desert, in which quarter the most violent winds are elsewhere represented as prevailing.

2. *A hard vision—it is revealed to me—the deceiver deceiving and the spoiler spoiling—go up, oh Elam—besiege, oh Media—all sighing* (or *all its sighing*) *I have made to cease.* The first phrase means a vision of severe and awful judgments. If the next clause be applied to Cyrus, one of the terms may describe the stratagems of war, as the other does its violence. This is the more natural as Babylon was actually taken by stratagem. *Go up*, i. e. against Babylon, either in reference to its lofty defences (ch. 26 : 5), or according to a more general military usage of the phrase. (See above, ch. 7 : 1.) The Medes and Persians were united under Cyrus, but the latter are here named first, as some think, because they were now in the ascendant.

3. *Therefore my loins are filled with pain; pangs have seized me like the pangs of a travailing* (*woman*)*; I writhe* (or *am convulsed*) *from hearing; I am shocked* (or *agitated*) *from seeing.* Some regard these as the words of a captive Jew, or of a Babylonian; but there is no objection to explaining them as expressive of the Prophet's own emotions, a very common method of enhancing the description even of deserved and righteous judgments.

4. *My heart wanders* (reels, or is bewildered); *horror appals me; the twilight* (night or evening) *of my pleasure* (or desire) *he has put for* (or converted into) *fear* (or trembling) *for me.* There are two interpretations of the last clause. One supposes it to mean that the night desired as a time of rest is changed into a

time of terror; the other, that a night of festivity is changed into a time of terror. That the court was revelling when Cyrus took the city, is stated in the general by Herodotus and Xenophon, and in full detail by Daniel. That the two first, however, did not derive their information from the Prophet, may be inferred from their not mentioning the writing on the wall, which would have seemed incredible to neither of them.

5. *Set the table, spread the cloth, eat, drink, arise ye chiefs, anoint the shield!* The Hebrew verbs are not imperatives but infinitives, here used in the first clause for the historical tense in order to give brevity, rapidity, and life to the description. For the same purpose the English imperative may be employed, as the simplest form of the verb and unencumbered with the personal pronouns. The sense, however, is that while the table is set etc. the alarm is given. The anointing of the shield is supposed by some to be a means of preserving it or of repelling missiles from its surface, by others simply a means of cleansing and perhaps adorning it. Both agree that it is here poetically used to express the idea of arming or preparing for battle. There are two interpretations of the last clause. One makes it an address by Jehovah or the Prophet to the Medes and Persians, as in the last clause of v. 2; the other a sudden alarm to the Babylonians at their feast. Both explanations, but especially the last, seem to present a further allusion to the surprise of the king and court by Cyrus.

6. *For thus saith the Lord to me: Go set* (or *cause to stand*) *the watchman* (or *sentinel*); *that which he sees let him tell.* Instead of simply predicting or describing the approach of the enemy, the Prophet introduces an ideal watchman, as announcing what he actually sees.

7. *And should he see cavalry—a pair* (or *pairs of horsemen*)—

ass-riders—camel-riders—then shall he hearken with hearkening a great hearkening (i. e. listen attentively). This construction of the sentence supposes the divine instructions to be still continued. This verse contains the order and the ninth its execution, while the eighth, as a preface to the latter, is exactly in its proper place. It is a slight but obvious coincidence of prophecy and history that Xenophon represents the Persians advancing two by two.

8. *And he cries—a lion—on the watch-tower, Lord, I am standing always by day, and on my ward* (or *place of observation*) *I am stationed all the nights* (i. e. *all night*, or *every night*, or both). That the setting of the watch is an ideal process, seems to be intimated by the word *Lord*, one of the divine names (not *my lord* or *sir*), and also by the unremitted vigilance to which he here lays claim. According to the usual interpretation, these are the words of the delegated watchman, announcing that he is at his post and will remain there and announce whatever he may see. The word *lion* forms no part of the sentinel's report, but is rather a description of the way in which he makes it. The true sense of the words is given in a paraphrase in Rev. 10 : 3, *he cried with a loud voice as when a lion roareth.* As to the syntax, we may either supply *as* before *a lion*, of which ellipsis there are some examples, or still more simply read *the lion cries*, thus converting the simile into a metaphor. The first construction agrees best however with the masoretic accents.

9. *And behold, this comes* (or this is what is coming), *mounted men, pairs of horsemen. And he answers* (i. e. speaks again) *and says, Fallen, fallen, is Babylon, and all the images of her gods he has broken* (or *crushed*) *to the earth.* The last verb is indefinitely construed, but obviously refers to the enemy as the instrument of Babylon's destruction, rather than to God as the efficient cause. The description given in v. 7 is abbreviated here, be-

cause so much was to be added. Still the correspondence is sufficiently exact. The structure of the passage is highly dramatic. In the sixth verse, the prophet is commanded to set a watch. In the seventh, the sentinel is ordered to look out for an army of men, mounted on horses, camels, and asses. In the eighth, he reports himself as being at his post. In the ninth, he sees the very army which had been described approaching. *Answer* is used, both in Greek and Hebrew, for the resumption of discourse by the same speaker, especially after an interval. It is here equivalent to *spoke again.* During the interval implied, the city is supposed to have been taken, so that when the watchman speaks again, it is to say that Babylon is fallen. The omission of all the intermediate details, for the purpose of bringing the extremes together, is a masterly stroke of poetical description, which would never have occurred to an inferior writer. The allusion to idols in the last clause is not intended merely to remind us that the conquest was a triumph of the true God over false ones, but to bring into view the well-known aversion of the Persians to all images. Herodotus says they not only thought it unlawful to use images, but imputed folly to those who did it. Here is another incidental but remarkable coincidence of prophecy even with profane history.

10. *Oh my threshing and the son of my threshing-floor! What I have heard from Jehovah of hosts, the God of Israel, I have told you.* This part of the prophecy closes with an apostrophe, showing at once by whose power and for whose sake the downfall of Babylon was to be brought about. *Threshing* here means that which is threshed, and is synonymous with the following phrase, *son of the threshing-floor*, i. e. (according to the oriental idiom which uses *son* to signify almost any relation) *threshed grain.* The comparison of severe oppression or affliction to threshing is a common one, and though the terms here used are scarcely intelligible when literally rendered into English,

it is clear that they mean, *oh my oppressed and afflicted people*, and must therefore be addressed not to the Babylonians but the Jews, to whom the fall of Babylon would bring deliverance, and for whose consolation this prediction was originally uttered. The last clause assures them that their own God had sent this message to them.

11. *The burden of Dumah. To me (one is) calling from Seir, Watchman, what of the night? Watchman, what of the night?* It has been already stated that most interpreters regard this and the next verse as an ind pendent prophecy, but that the use of the word burden is an insufficient reason, while the extreme brevity of the passage, and the recurrence of the figure of a sentinel or watchman, seem to indicate that it is a continuation of what goes before, although a new subject is here introduced. Of *Dumah* there are two interpretations. Some understand it as the name of an Arabian tribe descended from Ishmael (Gen. 25:14. 1 Chr. 1:30), or of a place belonging to that tribe, perhaps the same now called *Dumah Eljandil* on the confines of Arabia and Syria. In that case, Seir, which lay between Judah and the desert of Arabia, is mentioned merely to denote the quarter whence the sound proceeded. But as Seir was itself the residence of the Edomites or children of Esau, others explain Dumah as a variation of the name Edom, intended at the same time to suggest the idea of *silence*, solitude, and desolation. In favour of the first interpretation is the mention of Arabia and of certain Arabian tribes in the following verses. But even Edom might be said to form part of Arabia. The greater importance of Edom and the frequency with which it is mentioned in the prophets, especially as an object of divine displeasure, also recommend this exegetical hypothesis. The Edomites were long subject to Israel, and might therefore naturally take part in its sufferings from Babylonian tyranny. The English Version seems to mean, what have you to say

of the night? Interpreters are commonly agreed, however, that the question is, what part of the night is it, equivalent to our question, what o'clock? This may have been a customary method of interrogating watchmen. Night is a common metaphor to represent calamity, as daybreak does relief from it. Some regard this as a taunting inquiry addressed to Judah by his heathen neighbours. It is much more natural, however, to explain it as an expression of anxiety arising from a personal concern in the result.

12. *The watchman says, Morning comes and also night; if ye will inquire, inquire; return, come.* Most writers understand this as relating to different subjects, morning comes (to one) and night (to another); which would seem to mean that while the Jewish night was about to be dispelled, that of Edom or Arabia should still continue. But connected as the words are with the foregoing prophecy, it is far more natural to understand them as referring to the Babylonian conquest of Judea and the neighbouring countries. The last clause intimates that the event was still uncertain. If you wish to know you must inquire again; you are come too soon; the time of your deliverance is not at hand; return or come again. On any hypothesis, however, these two verses still remain enigmatical and doubtful in their meaning.

13. *The burden of Arabia. In the forest in Arabia shall ye lodge, oh ye caravans of Dedanim.* The Prophet here passes from Edom to Arabia, or from one Arabian tribe or district to another. The answer in v. 12 is here explained. The country was to be in such a state that the caravans which usually travelled undisturbed would be obliged to leave the public road and pass the night among the bushes or thickets. Forests properly so called do not exist in the Arabian desert. The Dedanim are mentioned elsewhere in connection with Edom and Teman (Jer.

49 : 8. Ez. 25 : 13), to whom they were probably contiguous. Their precise situation is the less important as they are not the subjects of the prophecy, but spoken of as strangers passing through, the interruption of whose journey is mentioned as a proof of the condition of the country.

14. *To meet the thirsty they bring water, the inhabitants of the land of Tema; with his bread they prevent* (i. e. meet or anticipate) *the fugitive.* The men of Tema, another Arabian tribe, also engaged in trade (Jer. 25 : 23. Job 6 : 19), are described as bringing food and drink, not to the Dedanim mentioned in v. 13, but to the people of the wasted country. *His bread* is rendered in the English Version as a collective (*their bread*), referring to the men of Tema; but the pronoun relates rather to the fugitive himself, and the whole phrase means his portion of food, the food necessary for him, his *daily bread.*

15. *Because* (or *when*) *from the presence of swords they fled, from the presence of a drawn sword and from the presence of a bended bow, and from the presence of a weight of war.* This verse describes them as not only plundered but pursued by a bloodthirsty enemy.

16. *For thus saith the Lord to me, In yet a year* (or *in a year longer*) *like the years of a hireling* (i. e. strictly computed) *shall fail* (or *cease*) *all the glory of Kedar.* This verse seems to fix a time for the fulfilment of the foregoing prophecy. Here, as in chap. 17 : 3, glory comprehends all that constitutes the dignity or strength of a people. On the meaning of the phrase, *years of a hireling*, see above, ch. 16 : 14. Kedar was the second son of Ishmael (Gen. 25 : 13). The name is here put either for an Arab tribe or for Arabia in general (Isai. 42 : 11. 60 : 7. Ez. 27 : 21). The Rabbins call the Arabic the *language of Kedar.* The chronological specification in this verse makes it necessary either

to assume a later writer than Isaiah, as some do in ch. 16 : 14; or a *terminus a quo* posterior to his time, as if he had said, within a year after something else before predicted; or an abrupt recurrence from the days of Nebuchadnezzar or Cyrus to those of Hezekiah. The last would be wholly in accordance with the usage of the prophets; but the best solution seems to be afforded by the second hypothesis. The sense will then be that the Arabians who suffered with the Jews, so far from sharing their deliverance, should within a year after that event be entirely destroyed. At the same time, due allowance should be made for diversity of judgment in a case so doubtful.

17. *And the remnant of the number of bows* (or *archers*), *the mighty men* (or *heroes*) *of the children of Kedar, shall be few* (or *become few*), *for Jehovah God of Israel hath spoken it.* We read elsewhere of the archery of Ishmael (Gen. 21 : 20) and Kedar (Ps. 120 : 4). The last clause intimates that God, as the God of Israel, has a quarrel with Kedar, and at the same time that his power and omniscience will secure the fulfilment of the threatening. It is not impossible that future discoveries may yet throw light upon these brief and obscure prophecies.

CHAPTER XXII.

THIS chapter naturally falls into two parts. The first describes the conduct of the people of Jerusalem during a siege, vs. 1–14. The second predicts the removal of Shebna from his post as treasurer or steward of the royal household, vs. 15–25. The whole may be described as a prophecy against the people of Jerusalem in general, and against Shebna in particular, considered as their leader and example.

It has been disputed whether the description in the first part of this chapter was intended to apply to the siege of Jerusalem by Sennacherib, or by Esarhaddon in the reign of Manasseh, or by Nebuchadnezzar, or by Titus. If the whole must be applied to one specific point of time, it is probably the taking of Jerusalem by the king of Assyria in the days of Manasseh, (2 Chron. 33 : 11), when the latter was himself carried captive with his chief men, and Shebna possibly among the rest. The choice seems to lie between this hypothesis and that of a generic prediction, a prophetic picture of the conduct of the Jews in a certain conjuncture of affairs which happened more than once, particular strokes of the description being drawn from different memorable sieges, and especially from those of Sennacherib and Nebuchadnezzar.

1. *The burden of the Valley of Vision. What* (*is*) *to thee* (what hast thou? or what aileth thee?) *that thou art wholly* (literally *the whole of thee*) *gone up on the house-tops?* By the valley of vision we are to understand Jerusalem, as being surrounded by hills with valleys between them. There is allusion to Jerusalem as the seat of revelation, the abode of the prophets, and the place where God's presence was manifested. The oriental roofs are flat and used for various purposes. The ascent here mentioned is probably used as a lively description of an oriental city in commotion, without any intention to intimate as yet the cause or the occasion, just as we might say that the streets of our own cities were full of people, whether the concourse were occasioned by grief, joy, fear, or any other cause. Some suppose the Prophet to inquire as a stranger what is the matter; but he seems rather to express disapprobation of the stir which he describes.

2. *Full of stirs, a noisy town, a joyous city, thy slain are not slain with the sword nor dead in battle.* The first clause is com-

monly explained by the older writers as descriptive of the commotion and alarm occasioned by the enemy's approach. The latest writers are agreed in making it descriptive of the opposite condition of joyous excitement, frivolous gayety, and reckless indifference, described in v. 13. The expression *thy slain are not slain with the sword* cannot mean that none were slain, but necessarily implies mortality of another kind. The allusion is supposed by some to be to pestilence, by others to famine, such as prevailed in the siege of Jerusalem by Nebuchadnezzar and also by the Romans. As neither is specified, the words may be more generally understood as describing all kinds of mortality incident to sieges, excepting that of actual warfare.

3. *All thy chiefs fled together—from the bow—they were bound—all that were found of thee were bound together—from afar they fled.* This verse describes the people as flying from the enemy, and being nevertheless taken. We may either read, *they are bound* (i. e. made prisoners) *by the bow* (i. e. the archers, as light-armed troops), or *without the bow* (i. e. not in battle, as the slain were not slain with the sword); or it may mean *without resistance*, without drawing a bow. Some understand it to mean, *they are restrained* (by fear) *from* (using) *the bow. All that were found of thee* may be in antithesis to *thy chiefs*, as if he had said, not only thy chiefs but all the rest. Some understand this as describing the voluntary confinement of the people in Jerusalem during a siege; others apply it to their vain endeavours to escape from its privations and dangers. It is best to give the verse its largest meaning as descriptive of the hardships and concomitant evils, not of one siege merely but of sieges in general.

4. *Therefore I said* (or say), *Look away from me; let me be bitter in weeping* (or *weep bitterly*); *try not to comfort me for the desolation of the daughter of my people.* These are not the words

of Jerusalem in answer to the question in v. 1, but those of the Prophet expressing his sympathy with the sufferings which he foresees and foretells, as in ch. 16 : 11. *The daughter of my people* means the people itself, poetically represented as a woman, and affectionately spoken of as a daughter.

5. *For there is a day of confusion and trampling and perplexity to the Lord Jehovah of Hosts in the valley of vision—breaking the wall and crying to the mountain. He has a day* i. e. he has it appointed, or has it in reserve. (See above, ch. 2 : 12.) *Trampling* does not refer to the treading down of the fields and gardens, but of men in battle, or at least in a general commotion and confusion. *To the mountain* are not the words of the cry, but its direction. The mountain is not Jerusalem or Zion as the residence of God, but the mountains round about Jerusalem (Ps. 125 : 1.) The meaning is not that the people are heard crying on their way to the mountain, but rather that their cries are reverberated from it. The whole verse is a vivid poetical description of the confusion of a siege.

6. *And Elam bare a quiver, with chariots, men* (i. e. *infantry*), *horsemen, and Kir uncovered the shield.* Elam was a province of Persia, often put for the whole country. Its people were celebrated archers. The simplest and most natural construction seems to be that which supposes three kinds of troops to be here enumerated; cavalry, infantry, and men in chariots. Kir is now agreed to be identical with *Κύρος*, the name of a river rising in the Caucasus and emptying into the Caspian sea, from which Georgia (Girgistan) is supposed to derive its name. Kir was subject to Assyria in the time of Isaiah, as appears from the fact thas it was one of the regions to which the exiles of the ten tribes were transported. It may here be put for Media, as Elam is for Persia. The uncovering of the shield has reference to the leathern cases used to protect the shield or keep it bright.

The removal of these denotes preparation for battle. The ancient versions and some modern writers translate the clause, *the shield leaves the wall bare* by being taken down from the place where it hung, or the enemy *deprives the wall of its shield* i. e. its defenders. Some even suppose an allusion to the *testudo* or covered way of shields, under which the Roman soldiers used to advance to the walls of a besieged town. The verbs are in the past tense, which proves nothing however as to the date of the events described.

7. *And it came to pass* (that) *the choice of thy valleys* (thy choicest valleys) *were full of chariots, and the horsemen drew up* (or took up a position) *towards the gate.* The Prophet sees something which he did not see before. He had seen the chariots and horsemen coming; but now he sees the valleys around full of them. The future form adopted by some versions is entirely unauthorized. Whatever be the real date of the events described, the Prophet evidently meant to speak of them as past or present, and we have neither right nor reason to depart from his chosen form of expression. The address is to Jerusalem. The valleys are mentioned as the only places where the cavalry or chariots could be useful or could act at all. As the only level approach to Jerusalem is on the north, that quarter may be specially intended, and *the gate* may be a gate on that side of the city.

8. *And he removed the covering of Judah, and thou didst look in that day to the armour of the house of the forest.* The first verb, which some connect with *the enemy* and others with *Jehovah* understood, is really indefinite and may be resolved into an English passive, *the covering was removed.* This expression has been variously explained. The analogous expression of taking away the veil from the heart (2 Cor. 3 : 15, 16), and the immediate mention of the measures used for the defence

of the city, are perhaps decisive in favour of explaining the words to mean that the Jews' own eyes were opened. It is best to understand here an abrupt apostrophe to Judah, a figure of perpetual occurrence in Isaiah. *House of the forest* is the designation of a house built by Solomon, and elsewhere called the house of the forest of Lebanon, because erected on that mountain, as some writers think, but according to the common opinion, because built of cedar-wood from Lebanon. This house is commonly supposed to have been either intended for an arsenal by Solomon himself, or converted into one by some of his successors, and to be spoken of in Neh. 3 : 19. *Looking to* this arsenal implies dependence on its stores as the best means of defence against the enemy, unless we understand the words to signify *inspection*, which agrees well with what follows, but is not sufficiently sustained by the usage of the verb and preposition. *In that day* seems to mean *at length*, i. e. when made aware of their danger.

9. *And the breaches of the city of David ye saw, that they were many, and ye gathered the waters of the lower pool.* The breaches meant are not those made by the enemy in the siege here described, but those caused by previous neglect and decay. The city of David may be either taken as a poetical name for Jerusalem at large, or in its strict sense as denoting the upper town upon Mount Zion, which was surrounded by a wall of its own, and called the city of David because he took it from the Jebusites and afterwards resided there. *Ye saw* may either mean, ye saw them for the first time, at length became aware of them, or, ye looked at them, examined them, with a view to their repair. The last is more probably implied than expressed. The last clause describes a measure of defence peculiarly important at Jerusalem where there are very few perennial springs. This precaution (as well as the one previously hinted at) was actually taken by Hezekiah in the prospect of Sennacherib's approach

(2 Chr. 32 : 4), and has perhaps been repeated in every siege of any length which Jerusalem has since experienced. The *lower pool* is probably the tank or reservoir still in existence in the valley of Hinnom opposite the western side of Mount Zion. This name, which occurs only here, has reference to the *upper pool* higher up in the same valley near the Jaffa gate. (See above, ch. 7 : 3. Compare Robinson's Palestine, I. 483–487.)

10. *And the houses of Jerusalem ye numbered, and ye pulled down the houses to repair* (rebuild or fortify) *the wall.* The numbering of the houses probably has reference, not to the levying of men or of a tax, but to the measure mentioned in the last clause, for the purpose of determining what houses could be spared, and perhaps of estimating the expense. The houses are destroyed, not merely to make room for new erections, but to furnish materials. Ancient Jerusalem, like that of our day, was built of stone.

11. *And a reservoir ye made between the two walls* (or *the double wall*) *for the waters of the old pool, and ye did not look to the maker of it, and the former of it ye did not see.* The reference is probably to a wall built out from that of the city and returning to it, so as to enclose the tank or reservoir here mentioned. As this was a temporary measure, perhaps often repeated, there is no need of tracing it in other parts of history or in the present condition of Jerusalem. It is altogether probable, however, that the *old pool* here mentioned is the same with the *upper pool* of ch. 7 : 3. Some have identified it with the *lower pool* of the ninth verse, but this would hardly have been introduced so soon by another name. The last clause shows that the fault, with which the people of Jerusalem were chargeable, was not that of guarding themselves against attack, but that of relying upon human defences, without regard to God. The verbs *look* and *see* are evidently used in allusion to the last clause of v. 8 and

the first of v. 9. They looked to the arsenal but not to God. This seems to put the clause before us in antithesis to the whole foregoing context from v. 8. *Maker* and *former* are not distinctive terms referring to God's purpose or decree on one hand, and the execution of it on the other, but poetical equivalents both denoting the efficient cause.

12. *And the Lord Jehovah of Hosts called in that day to weeping and to mourning and to baldness and to girding sackcloth.* The meaning is not that he called or summoned grief to come, but that he called on men to mourn, not only by his providence, but by his word through the prophets. By *baldness* we may either understand the tearing of the hair, or the shaving of the head, or both, as customary signs of grief. The last phrase, rendered in the English Bible *girding with sackcloth*, does not mean girding up the other garments with a sackcloth girdle, but girding the body with a sackcloth dress, or girding on i. e. wearing sackcloth. The providential call to mourning here referred to must be the siege before described.

13. *And behold mirth and jollity, slaying of oxen and killing of sheep, eating of flesh and drinking of wine; eat and drink, for to-morrow we die.* This verse presents the contrast of their actual behaviour with that to which God called them by his providence. The common version, *let us eat and drink*, is perfectly correct as to sense, but needlessly departs from the peculiar and expressive form of the original. I have substituted *eat and drink*, not as imperatives, but as the simplest forms of the English verbs. (See above, ch. 21 : 5.) *To eat and to drink* might be considered more exact, but would not exhibit the compression and breviloquence of the original. It has been disputed whether these last words are expressive of contemptuous incredulity or of a desperate determination to spend the residue of life in pleasure. It is by no means clear that these two feelings are exclusive of

each other, since the same man might express his disbelief of the threatening, and his resolution, if it should prove true, to die in the enjoyment of his favourite indulgences. At all events, there can be no need of restricting the full import of the language, as adapted to express both states of mind, in different persons, if not in the same.

14. *And Jehovah of Hosts revealed himself in my ears* (i. e. made a revelation to me, saying) *If this iniquity shall be forgiven you* (i. e. it certainly shall not be forgiven you) *until you die.* The conditional form of expression, so far from expressing doubt or contingency, adds to the following declaration the solemnity of an oath. What is said is also sworn, so that by two immutable things in which it is impossible for God to lie, the truth of the threatening may be confirmed. On the elliptical formula of swearing, see above ch. 5:9. *This iniquity* of course means the presumptuous contempt of God's messages and providential warnings, with which the people had been charged in the preceding verse. This offence is here treated as the sin against the Holy Ghost is in the New Testament, and is indeed very much of the same nature. The word translated *shall be forgiven* strictly means *shall be atoned for* or expiated. *Until you die* is equivalent to *ever*, the impossibility of expiation afterwards being assumed. This use of *until* is common in all languages. 'As long as you live you shall not be forgiven' is equivalent to saying 'you shall never be forgiven.'

15. *Thus said the Lord Jehovah of Hosts, Go, go in to this treasurer* (or steward, or chamberlain), *to Shebna who* (*is*) *over the house.* From the people in general the threatening now passes to an individual, perhaps because he was particularly guilty of the crime alleged, and by his influence the means of leading others astray likewise. Some of the ancient versions give to *house* here the sense of *temple* or the house of God, and infer

that Shebna, if not High Priest or a Priest at all, was at least the treasurer of the temple. But the phrase here used is nowhere else employed in reference to the temple, whereas it repeatedly occurs as the description of an officer of state or of the royal household, a major-domo, chamberlain, or steward. As the modern distinction between state and household officers is not an ancient or an oriental one, it is not unlikely that the functionary thus described, like the medieval *maires du palais*, was in fact prime-minister. This would account for the influence tacitly ascribed to Shebna in this chapter, as well as for his being made the subject of a prophecy. The phrase *this treasurer* may either be expressive of disapprobation or contempt, or simply designate the man as well known to the Prophet and his readers. These familiar allusions to things and persons now forgotten, while they add to the obscurity of the passage, furnish an incidental proof of its antiquity and genuineness. *Go in,* i. e. into Shebna's house, or into the sepulchre which he was preparing, and in which some suppose him to have been accosted by the Prophet.

16. *What hast thou here, and whom hast thou here, that thou hast hewn thee here a sepulchre? Hewing on high his sepulchre, graving in the rock a habitation for himself!* The negation implied in the interrogation is not that he had none to protect and aid him, or that none of his kindred should be buried there because they should be banished with him, but rather that he had none buried there before him; it was not his birth-place or the home of his fathers. What interest, what part or lot, what personal or hereditary claim, hast thou in Judah? *Here* then refers not to the sepulchre, but to Jerusalem. The foreign form of the name *Shebna,* which occurs only in the history of Hezekiah, and for which no satisfactory Hebrew etymology has been proposed, seems to confirm this explanation of the first clause as representing him to be a foreigner, perhaps a heathen. Another

confirmation is afforded by the otherwise unimportant circumstance, that the name of Shebna's father is nowhere added to his own, as in the case of Eliakim and Joah (v. 20. ch. 36 : 3). These seem to be sufficient reasons for concluding that the Prophet is directed to upbraid him, not with seeking to be buried in the royal sepulchres although of mean extraction, but with making provision for himself and his posterity in a land to which he was an alien, and from which he was so soon to be expelled. The Prophet, after putting to him the prescribed question, was to express his own contemptuous surprise at what he saw, or to let his eyes pass from the man to the sepulchre which he was hewing. It is not necessarily implied however in this explanation that the conversation was to take place at the sepulchre. The labour and expense bestowed on ancient sepulchres (of far later date however than Isaiah's time), is still attested by the tombs remaining at Jerusalem, Petra, and Persepolis, where some are excavated near the tops of lofty rocks in order to be less accessible, to which practice there may be allusion in the verse before us, and also in the words of 2 Chr. 32 : 33, as explained by most interpreters, viz. that Hezekiah was buried in the *highest* of the tombs of the sons of David. (See Robinson's Palestine, I. 516–539. II. 525.) The word *habitation* is supposed by some to have allusion to the oriental practice of making tombs in shape (and frequently in size) like houses, by others more poetically to the idea of the grave, as a *long home* (Ecc. 12 : 5). In this case, as in many others, the ideal and material allusion may have both been present to the writer's mind. *What (is) to thee* and *who is to thee* are the usual unavoidable periphrases for *what and whom hast thou*, the verb *to have* being wholly wanting in this family of languages.

17. *Behold, Jehovah is casting thee a cast, oh man! and covering thee a covering.* The idea is that he is *certainly* about to cast and cover thee, or to do it *completely* and with violence.

18. *Rolling he will roll thee in a roll, like a ball (thrown) into a spacious ground—there shalt thou die—and there the chariots of thy glory—shame of thy master's house.* The ejection of Shebna from the country is compared to the rolling of a ball into an open space where there is nothing to obstruct its progress. The ideas suggested are those of violence, rapidity, and distance. All the interpreters appear to apply this directly to Shebna, and are thence led to raise the question, what land is meant? It seems to me that the phrase in question has relation not to Shebna as a man but to the ball with which he is compared, and that *land* should be taken in the sense of *ground.* There are several different constructions of the last clause, of which this is one: *thither shalt thou die* (i. e. thither shalt thou go to die) *and thither shall thy splendid chariots* (*convey thee*). The allusion will then be simply to Shebna's return to his own country (whether Syria, Phenicia, Mesopotamia, or Assyria), and not to captivity in war or to suffering in exile, of which there is no intimation in the text. All that the Prophet clearly threatens Shebna with, is the loss of rank and influence in Judah and a return to his own country. An analogous incident in modern history (so far as these circumstances are concerned) is Necker's retreat from France to Switzerland at the beginning of the French Revolution.

19. *And it shall come to pass in that day that I will call for my servant, for Eliakim the son of Hilkiah*, i. e. will personally designate him. Eliakim appears again in ch. 36 : 3, and there as here in connection with Shebna. The epithet *my servant* seems to be intended to describe him as a faithful follower of Jehovah, and as such to contrast him with Shebna, who may have been a heathen. The employment of such a man by such a king as Hezekiah is explained by some upon the supposition that he had been promoted by Ahaz and then suffered to remain by his

successor. It is just as easy to suppose however that he had raised himself by his abilities for public business.

20. *And I will thrust thee from thy post, and from thy station shall he pull thee down.* The verb in the last clause is indefinite and really equivalent to a passive (thou shalt be pulled down).

21. *And I will clothe him with thy dress, and with thy girdle will I strengthen him, and thy power will I give into his hand, and he shall be for a father* (or *become a father*) *to the dweller in Jerusalem and to the house of Judah.* We may either suppose a reference to an official dress, or a metaphor analogous to that of filling another's shoes in colloquial English. *Father* is not a mere oriental synonyme of *ruler*, but an emphatic designation of a wise and benevolent ruler. It seems therefore to imply that Shebna's administration was of an opposite character. The inhabitants of Jerusalem and the family of Judah comprehended the whole nation.

22. *And I will put the key of the house of David on his shoulder; he shall open and there shall be no one shutting, he shall shut and there shall be no one opening.* In other words, he shall have unlimited control over the royal house and household, which according to oriental usages implies a high political authority. Some suppose a reference to the actual bearing of the key by the royal steward or chamberlain, and explain its being carried on the shoulder by the fact that large wooden locks and keys of corresponding size are still used in some countries, the latter being sometimes curved like a sickle so as to be hung around the neck. Against this explanation it may be objected, that the phrase *house of David* seems to imply a metaphorical rather than a literal palace, and that the word translated shoulder includes the upper part of the back, as the place for

bearing burdens. (See above, ch. 9 : 4. 10 : 27.) The best interpreters appear to be agreed that the government or administration is here represented by the figure of a burden, not merely in the general as in ch. 9 : 6, but the specific burden of a key, chosen in order to express the idea of control *over the royal house*, which was the title of the office in question. The application of the same terms to Peter (Matt. 16 : 19) and to Christ himself (Rev. 3 : 7) does not prove that they here refer to either, or that Eliakim was a type of Christ, but merely that the same words admit of different applications.

23. *And I will fasten him a nail in a sure place, and he shall be for a throne of glory to his father's house.* The figure in the first clause naturally conveys the idea of security and permanence. The reference is not to the stakes or centre post of a tent, but to the large pegs, pins or nails often built into the walls of oriental houses for the purpose of suspending clothes or vessels. The last clause is obscure. The most natural interpretation of the words, and that most commonly adopted, is that the figure of a nail is here exchanged for that of a seat, this being common to the two, that they alike suggest the idea of support though in different ways. Those whom Eliakim was the means of promoting might be said, with a change of figure but without a change of meaning, both to sit and hang upon him. He was to be not only a seat but a *seat of honour*, which is nearer to the meaning of the Hebrew phrase than *throne of glory*.

24. *And they shall hang upon him all the honour of his father's house—the offspring and the issue—all vessels of small quantity—from vessels of cups even to all vessels of flagons.* Here the figure of a nail is resumed. The dependents of Eliakim are represented as suspended on him as their sole support. The words translated *offspring* and *issue*, are expressions borrowed from

the vegetable world. It is commonly assumed by interpreters that the two words are in antithesis, denoting either different sexes (sons and daughters), or different generations (sons and grandsons), or different ranks, which last is the usual explanation. The next phrase is designed to show that even the least are not to be excepted. The two expressions in the last clause may be taken either as equivalent or as contrasting the gold and silver vessels of the altar (Ex. 24 : 6) with common earthen utensils (Jer. 48 : 12. Lam. 4 : 2).

25. *In that day, saith Jehovah of Hosts, shall the nail fastened in a sure place be removed, and be cut down, and fall, and the burden which was on it shall be cut off, for Jehovah speaks.* The most natural and obvious application of these words is to Eliakim, who had just been represented as a nail in a sure place. But as this would predict his fall, without the slightest intimation of the reason, and in seeming contradiction to the previous context, most interpreters reject this exposition as untenable. Most writers seem to be agreed, that the twenty-fifth verse relates to Shebna, and that the Prophet, after likening Eliakim to a nail fastened in a sure place, tacitly applies the same comparison to Shebna, and declares that the nail which now seems to be securely fastened shall soon yield to make way for the other. Those who refer the verse to Eliakim suppose his fall to have been occasioned by his nepotism or excessive patronage of his relations, a conjectural inference from v. 24. The partial fulfilment of this prophecy is commonly supposed to be recorded in ch. 36 : 3, where Eliakim actually fills the place here promised to him, and Shebna appears in the inferior character of a scribe or secretary. Some indeed suppose two persons of the name of Shebna, which is not only arbitrary in itself, but rendered more improbable by this consideration, that Shebna is probably a foreign name, and certainly occurs only in these and the parallel places, whereas

Hilkiah is of frequent occurrence, and yet is admitted upon all hands to denote the same person. It seems improbable no doubt that Shebna, after such a threatening, should be transferred to another office. But the threatening may not have been public, and the transfer may have been merely the beginning of his degradation. But even supposing that the Shebna of ch. 36 · 3 is a different person, and that the execution of this judgment is nowhere explicitly recorded, there is no need of concluding that it was revoked or that it was meant to be conditional, much less that it was falsified by the event. It is a common usage of the Scriptures, and of this book in particular, to record a divine command and not its execution, leaving the latter to be inferred from the former as a matter of course. Of this we have had repeated examples, such as ch 7 : 4 and 8 : 1\ Nay in this very case, we are merely told what Isaiah was commanded to say to Shebna, without being told that he obeyed the order. If the execution of this order may be taken for granted, so may the fulfilment of the prophecy. If it had failed, it would not have been recorded or preserved among the prophecies.

CHAPTER XXIII.

This prophecy consists of two parts. The first predicts the fall of Tyre, vs. 1–14. The second promises its restoration and conversion, vs. 15–18. The fall of Tyre is predicted, not directly, but in the form of apostrophes, addressed to her own people or her colonies, vs. 1–7. The destruction is referred to God as its author, and to the Chaldees as his instruments, vs. 8–14. The prediction in the latter part includes three events. Tyre shall be forsaken and forgotten for seventy years, v. 15. She shall then be restored to her former activity and wealth, vs. 16, 17. Thenceforth her gains shall be devoted to the Lord, v. 18.

Tyre, one of the chief cities of Phenicia, was situated partly on a rocky island near the coast, and partly in a wide and fertile plain upon the coast itself. It was long a current opinion that the insular Tyre had no existence before the time of Nebuchadnezzar; but Hengstenberg has made it probable that from the beginning the chief part of the city was situated on the island, or rather a peninsula connected with the mainland by a narrow isthmus. Tyre is remarkable in history for two things; its maritime trade, and the many sieges it has undergone. The first of these on record was by Shalmaneser king of Assyria, who according to Menander, a historian now lost but quoted by Josephus, blockaded Tyre for five years, so as to cut off the supply of water from the mainland, but without being able to reduce the city. The next was by Nebuchadnezzar king of Babylon, who besieged it thirteen years; with what result, is not expressly mentioned either in profane or sacred history. A third siege was by Alexander the Great, who after seven months and with the utmost difficulty finally reduced it. It was afterwards besieged by the Syrian king Antigonus, and more than once during the Crusades, both by Franks and Saracens. After this period it entirely decayed, and has now disappeared, its site being marked by the insulated rock, by the causeway between it and the mainland still existing as a bar of sand, and by columns and other architectural remains mostly lying under water.

It has been much disputed which of these events is the subject of the prophecy before us. Some see the fulfilment in the days of Isaiah himself, and refer the prediction to the siege by Shalmaneser. Others give it a wider scope, and seem to make the siege by Alexander its main subject. But the great body of the older writers refer it to an intermediate event, the siege by Nebuchadnezzar. Most probably the prophecy before us is generic not specific, a panoramic picture of the downfall of Tyre, from the beginning to the end of the destroying process, with particular allusions to particular sieges, as for instance to that of the Chaldees in v. 13, and perhaps to that of Alexander in v. 6.

1. *The burden of Tyre. Howl, ships of Tarshish, for it is laid waste—no house, no entrance—from the land of Chittim it is revealed to them.* The command or exhortation to howl implies that those to whom it is addressed have peculiar cause for grief. By ships of Tarshish we are not to understand merchant-ships in general, but strictly those which carried on the trade between Phenicia and its Spanish colony Tartessus. *It is laid waste* may be indefinitely taken to mean *desolation has been wrought*, or *something has been desolated*, without saying what. The expressions *no house*, *no entrance*, may refer particularly to the mariners returning from their long voyage and finding their homes destroyed. *Chittim* is the island of Cyprus, in which there was a city *Citium*, which Cicero expressly mentions as a Phenician settlement. *It is revealed* (i. e. the event announced in the preceding clause) *to them* (the Tyrian mariners on their way home from Tarshish). The meaning seems to be, that the news of the fall of Tyre has reached the Phenician settlements in Cyprus, and through them the Tyrian mariners that touch there.

2. *Be silent oh inhabitants of the isle* (or *coast*), *the merchants of Sidon crossing the sea filled thee.* This may either be addressed to the coasts and islands of the Mediterranean which had long been frequented by the Phenician traders, or to Phenicia itself, which foreign commerce had enriched. The last explanation is commonly preferred; but the first is recommended by the fact that it assigns a reason for the mention of the foreign trade

of Sidon, as accounting for the interest which other nations are supposed to feel in the fall of Tyre. On either supposition, Sidon, the other great city of Phenicia, is put for the whole country.

3. *And in great waters* (*was*) *the seed of the Nile; the harvest of the river* (*was*) *her revenue; and she was a mart of nations.* The Hebrew and Egyptian names of the Nile are here combined. The first, according to its etymology, means *black*, and corresponds to *Μέλας* and *Melo*, Greek and Latin names of the same river, all derived from the colour of the water or the mud which it deposits. Of the whole verse there are three interpretations. The first supposes an allusion to the fact that the grain of Egypt was exported in Phenician vessels *on the great waters* i. e. over the sea. The objection that Phenicia is described by Ezekiel as trading not with Egypt but with Palestine in grain, though entitled to some weight, is not conclusive. A stronger objection may be drawn from the apparent incongruity of naming this one branch of commerce as a proof that Tyre was *a mart of nations.* A second interpretation understands what is said of Egypt figuratively, or as a comparison; as if he had said that the wealth which Egypt derived from the Nile, Phenicia derived from the great waters i. e. by her maritime trade. The third differs from this only by supposing a distinct allusion to the insular situation of Tyre, which, though planted on a rock and girt by mighty waters, reaped as rich a harvest as the fertile land of Egypt. This last interpretation is much more poetical than either of the others, and at least in that respect entitled to the preference.

4. *Be ashamed* (or *confounded*) *Zidon, for the sea saith, the strength of the sea, saying, I have not travailed, and I have not borne, and I have not reared young men* (*or*) *brought up virgins.* One of the great cities of Phenicia is here called upon to be

confounded at the desolation of the other; or Zidon may be put for the whole country, as in the preceding verse. The Prophet hears a voice from the sea, which he then describes more exactly as coming from the stronghold or fortress of the sea, i. e. insular Tyre as viewed from the mainland. The rest of the verse is intended to express the idea that the city thus personified was childless, was as if she had never borne children. The whole metaphor is clearly intended to express the idea of depopulation.

5. *When the report (comes) to Egypt, they are pained at the report of Tyre.* There are three distinct interpretations of this verse. The first refers the pronoun to the Sidonians or Phenicians generally, and understands the verse to mean that they would be as much grieved to hear of the fall of Tyre as if they should hear of that of Egypt. The second makes the verb indefinite, or understands it of the nations generally, who are then said to be as much astounded at the fall of Tyre as they once were at the judgments of Jehovah upon Egypt. The third, which is the one now commonly adopted, makes Egypt itself or the Egyptians the subject of the verb. This last supposes the Egyptians to lament for the loss of their great mart and commercial ally. The idea expressed by the second construction is a much more elevated one. Either of these interpretations appears preferable to the first, which yields an unnatural and inappropriate sense.

6. *Pass over to Tarshish; howl, ye inhabitants of the isle (or coast).* The mother country is exhorted to take refuge in her distant colonies.

7. *Is this your joyous city* (literally, *is this to you a joyous one?*) *from the days of old is her antiquity; her feet shall carry her afar off to sojourn.* Most writers understand the last clause as ap-

plying, either to the flight of the Tyrians to their colonies, or to their being carried into exile.

8. *Who hath purposed this against Tyre the crowning (city), whose merchants (are) princes, her traffickers the honoured of the earth?* Most writers seem to be agreed that the word here translated *crowning* denotes the *crowner* or *crown-giver*, in allusion to the fact that crowned heads were among the tributaries of Phenicia, according to the testimony of the Greek historians. The question in this verse implies that no ordinary power could have done it.

9. *Jehovah of Hosts hath purposed it, to profane the elevation of all beauty, to degrade all the honoured of the earth.* This is the answer to the question in v. 8. Not only in poetry, but in animated prose, the writers of all languages ask questions to be answered by themselves. The word translated *profane* means strictly to desecrate that which is reckoned holy, but is here used to express the making common of that which was distinguished by magnificence or beauty.

10. *Pass through thy land like the river (Nile). Daughter of Tarshish, there is no girdle (any) longer.* It is commonly agreed that the phrase means, *as the Nile passes*, i. e. quickly or without restraint. The *daughter of Tarshish* is Tarshish itself. *There is no more girdle*, may be taken in opposite senses, as denoting the failure of strength and general dissolution, or the absence of restraint and freedom from oppression.

11. *His hand he stretched out over the sea; he made kingdoms tremble; Jehovah commanded respecting Canaan to destroy her strongholds.* The subject of the verbs in the first clause is the same as in the last.

12. *And he said, Thou shalt not add longer (or continue) to*

triumph, oppressed (or violated) virgin daughter of Zidon; to Chittim arise, pass over; there also there shall be no rest to thee. The address is not to Chittim, nor to Tyre as a daughter of the older city, but to Zidon itself. Zidon is here put for Phenicia in general. This exhortation corresponds exactly to the one in v. 6, Tarshish and Chittim being both Phenician colonies. The last clause implies, either that the colonists would not receive them, or that the enemy would still pursue them, probably the latter.

13. *Behold the land of the Chaldees; this people was not; Assyria founded it for dwellers in the wilderness; they have set up his towers; they have roused up her palaces; he has put it for* (or *rendered it*) *a ruin.* This difficult verse has been very variously understood. Some apply it exclusively to the destruction of Tyre by the Assyrians; but this can only be effected by an arbitrary change of text. The great majority, both of the older and the later writers, leave the text unaltered, and suppose that the Prophet here brings the Chaldees into view as the instruments of Tyre's destruction. The second clause will then be a parenthesis, containing an allusion to a historical fact not expressly mentioned elsewhere, but agreeing well with other facts of history, to wit, that the Chaldees were not the aborignal inhabitants of Babylonia, but were brought thither from the mountains of Armenia or Kurdistan by the Assyrians in the days of their supremacy. This accounts for the fact that Xenophon speaks of the Chaldees as northern mountaineers, while in the sacred history we find them in possession of the great plain of Shinar. The former statement has respect, no doubt, to that portion of the people who were left behind in their original territory. This incidental statement, it may also be observed, is in strict accordance with the Assyrian policy of peopling their own provinces with conquered nations. But why should this fact in the history of the Chaldees be referred

to here? Because the recent origin and present insignificance of the chosen instruments made the conquest more humiliating to the Tyrians. When Isaiah wrote, Assyria was the ruling power of the world; whatever changes were expected, were expected from that quarter. But here the conquest of Phenicia is ascribed to a people then but little known, if known at all. It was perfectly natural therefore to say negatively, that it was not to be effected by Assyria, as well as positively, that it was to be effected by Chaldea. In like manner, if the fall of the Roman state had been foretold during the period of the Persian wars, how naturally might the Prophet have said that it should fall, *not before the Carthaginians*, but before the Goths.

14. *Howl, ships of Tarshish, for destroyed is your stronghold.* The first part of the prophecy here closes very much as it began. The description of Tyre is the same as in v. 4, except that it was there called the fortress of the sea, and here the fortress of the Tyrian ships.

15. *And it shall come to pass in that day that Tyre shall be forgotten seventy years, as the days of the king; from the end of seventy years shall be* (or *happen*) *to Tyre like the harlot's song.* The remainder of the chapter predicts the restoration of Tyre, not to its former dignity, but to its wealth and commercial activity, the fruits of which should thenceforth be consecrated to Jehovah. There is no difference of opinion with respect to the meaning of the words or the grammatical construction of the sentence, but the utmost diversity of judgment in relation to the general sense and application of the whole, and especially of the words, *seventy years as the days of one king.* That Tyre was a flourishing city in the time of Alexander the Great, is matter of history. When it again became so, is not. But since the fact is certain and the prophecy explicit, the most rational conclusion is that they chronologically coincide, or in other

words, that Tyre did begin to recover from the effects of the Babylonian conquest about seventy years after the catastrophe itself. This of course supposes that the words are to be definitely understood. If, on the other hand, they are indefinite, there can be still less difficulty in supposing their fulfilment. In either case, the words *seventy days* etc. remain so enigmatical, and all the explanations of them so unsatisfactory, that some may be tempted to refer them to the future, and to look for their fulfilment hereafter. When Zechariah wrote, the Babylonian conquest predicted by Isaiah and Ezekiel had already taken place. The change for the better, predicted by Isaiah alone, was then already visible. The prophecies of both respecting the total destruction of the city are renewed by Zechariah and referred to a period still future, with particular reference, as some suppose, to the time of Alexander but it may be with a scope still more extensive. The last clause foretells the restoration of Tyre in a very peculiar and significant form. Instead of a queen reinstated on the throne, she now appears as a forgotten harlot, suing once more for admiration and reward. Although this metaphor, as we shall see below, does not necessarily imply moral turpitude, it does necessarily impart a contemptuous tone to the prediction. The best explanation of this change of tone is that the restoration here predicted was to be a restoration to commercial prosperity and wealth, but not to regal dignity or national importance. The *song of a harlot* (or *the harlot*) is now commonly agreed to mean a particular song well known to the contemporaries of the Prophet. *It shall be to her like this song* can only mean that what the song presents as an ideal situation should be realized in the experience of Tyre. The Hebrew words will scarcely bear the meaning put upon them in the text of the English Version.

16. *Take a harp, go about the city, oh forgotten harlot, play*

well, sing much, that thou mayest be remembered. These are now commonly explained as the words of the song itself, describing the only way in which the harlot could recover her lost place in the memory of men, viz. by soliciting their notice and their favour. The application of the song to Tyre implies not only that she had lost her former position in the sight of the nations, but that exertion would be needed to recover it. *Play well, sing much*, literally, *make good playing, multiply song.*

17. *And it shall be* (or *come to pass*), *from* (or *at*) *the end of seventy years, Jehovah will visit Tyre, and she shall return to her hire* (or *gain*), *and shall play the harlot with all the kingdoms of the earth upon the face of the ground.* As God is said to *visit* men both in wrath and mercy, and as the figure here employed is at first sight a revolting one, some of the older writers understand this verse as describing the continued wickedness of Tyre requiring further judgments. The figure indeed is now commonly agreed to denote nothing more than commercial intercourse without necessarily implying guilt. In ancient times, when international commerce was a strange thing and nearly monopolized by a single nation, and especially among the Jews, whose law discouraged it for wise but temporary purposes, there were probably ideas attached to such promiscuous intercourse entirely different from our own. Certain it is that the Scriptures more than once compare the mutual solicitations of commercial enterprise to illicit love. That the comparison does not necessarily involve the idea of unlawful or dishonest trade, is sufficiently apparent from the following verse.

18. *And her gain and her hire shall be holiness* (or *holy* i. e. consecrated) *to Jehovah; it shall not be stored and it shall not be hoarded; for her gain shall be for those who sit* (or *dwell*) *before Jehovah, to eat to satiety, and for substantial clothing.* By those who dwell before Jehovah we are probably to understand his

worshippers in general and his official servants in particular. There may be an allusion to the chambers around the temple which were occupied by priests and Levites when in actual service. The general sense of the prediction evidently is, that the commercial gains of Tyre should redound to the advantage of the servants of Jehovah.

CHAPTER XXIV.

Here begins a series of prophecies (ch. xxiv–xxxv), having reference chiefly to Judah. It is not divided into parts by any titles or express intimations of a change of subject. The style is also homogeneous and uniform. The attempts which have been made to subdivide this portion of the book are for the most part arbitrary. The conventional division into chapters may be retained as a matter of convenience. The first four chapters (xxiv–xxvii) are now universally regarded as forming one continuous composition. What is said of ch. xxiv is therefore in some degree applicable to the whole. This chapter contains a description of a country filled with confusion and distress by a visitation from Jehovah in consequence of its iniquities, vs. 1–12. It then speaks of a remnant scattered among the nations and glorifying God in distant lands, vs. 13–16. The Prophet then resumes his description of the judgments coming on the same land or another, winding up with a prophecy of Jehovah's exaltation in Jerusalem, vs. 16–23. The endless diversity of judgment with regard to this chapter, both among the older and later writers, shows that the prediction is generic. In this case, as in many others, the exclusive restriction of the prophecy to one event is wholly arbitrary. What the Prophet has left indefinite we have no right to make specific. Particular allusions there may be; but this, as we have seen in other cases, does not limit the application of the whole.

1. *Behold, Jehovah (is) pouring out the land and emptying it, and he will turn down its face, and he will scatter its inhabitants.* The figure is that of a bottle or other vessel drained of its contents by being turned upside down. The allusion in this last clause may be both to flight and deportation. Isaiah here speaks of the Babylonian conquest as still distant, but at the same time as infallibly certain.

2. *And it shall be, as the people so the priest, as the servant so his master, as the buyer so the seller, as the borrower so the lender, as the debtor so the creditor.* That is, all ranks and classes shall fare alike.

3. *The land shall be utterly emptied and utterly spoiled, for Jehovah speaks* (or *hath spoken*) *this word.* The last clause denotes the certainty of the event because predicted by Jehovah.

4. *The earth mourneth, fadeth; the world languisheth, fadeth; the highest of the people of the earth languish.* *Earth* and *world* are not to be taken in their widest sense, but as poetical descriptions of the country.

5. *And the land has been profaned under its inhabitants, because they have transgressed the laws, violated the statute, broken the everlasting covenant.* Almost all writers seem to apply the passage to the Jews, and to understand it as referring their calamities to their transgressions. The land is said to be profaned as being a holy land or consecrated to Jehovah. Most interpreters suppose a special reference to pollution by blood or the guilt of murder. The reference in this verse is to the divine law generally. The three terms used are substantially

synonymous, *law*, *statute*, *covenant*, being continually interchanged. The simple meaning of the verse is that they disobeyed the will of God.

6. *Therefore a curse devoured the earth, and those dwelling in it were reckoned guilty* (and so treated). *Therefore the inhabitants of the earth burned, and there are few men left.*

7. *The new wine mourneth; the vine languisheth; all the merry-hearted do sigh.*

8. *Still is the mirth of drums; ceased is the noise of revellers; still is the mirth of the harp.* Music is here mentioned as a common token and accompaniment of mirth.

9. *With the song they shall not drink wine; bitter shall strong drink be to them that drink it.* The last clause means of course that they should lose the appetite for such enjoyments.

10. *Broken down is the city of confusion* (emptiness or desolation), *shut up is every house from entering* (i. e. so that it is not or cannot be entered). The city meant is Jerusalem. The last clause might be understood to refer to the closing of the houses by the inhabitants against the enemy, or to their being left unoccupied; but the first clause seems to show that it rather relates to the obstruction of the entrance by the ruins.

11. *A cry for wine in the streets—darkened is all joy—departed is the gladness of the earth.* The cry meant is that of the perishing inhabitants for necessary refreshment, perhaps with special reference to the sick and wounded or to children.

12. (What is) *left in the city is desolation, and into ruins is the gate beaten down.* The first clause is in opposition to the last

of v. 11. Joy is gone and desolation is left behind. The gate is here named as the most important part of the city; but it does not directly mean the city itself.

13. *For so shall it be in the midst of the earth among the nations, like the beating of an olive-tree, like gleanings when the gathering is done.* The Prophet is stating more distinctly the extent of the desolation which he had before described. *In the midst of the nations* is explained as actual dispersion among foreign nations.

14. *They shall raise their voice, they shall sing* (or *shout*), *for the majesty of Jehovah they cry aloud from the sea.* The pronoun at the beginning is emphatic. *They*, the few dispersed survivors of these judgments.

15. *Therefore in the fires glorify Jehovah, in the islands of the sea the name of Jehovah God of Israel.* This seems to be an address to the persons who had already been described as praising God, exhorting them to do so still. The word translated *fires* is now commonly agreed to be a local designation The weight of exegetical authority preponderates in favour of the meaning *in the east* (as the region of sunrise or of dawning light) in opposition to the sea or west.

16. *From the wing* (*skirt* or *edge*) *of the earth we have heard songs, praise to the righteous, and I said, woe to me, woe to me, alas for me! The deceivers deceive, with deceit the deceivers deceive.* We hear promises and praise to the righteous, but our experience is that of misery.

17. *Fear and pit and snare upon thee, oh inhabitant of the land!* This may be either a warning (*are upon thee*) or the expression of a wish (*be upon thee*). It is a probable though

not a necessary supposition, that the terms here used are borrowed from the ancient art of hunting.

18. *And it shall be (that) the (one) flying from the voice of the fear shall fall into the pit, and the (one) coming up from the midst of the pit shall be taken in the snare; for windows from on high are opened, and the foundations of the earth are shaken.* The first clause carries out the figures of the foregoing verse; the second introduces those of a deluge and an earthquake. The allusion to the flood is acknowledged by almost all writers, and is rendered certain by the resemblance of the language to that used in Gen. 7 : 11.

19. *Broken, broken is the earth; shattered, shattered is the earth; shaken, shaken is the earth.*

20. *The earth reels, reels like a drunken man, and is shaken like a hammock. And heavy upon her is her guilt, and she shall fall and rise no more.* The ideas *earth* and *land*, both which are expressed by the Hebrew word, run into one another and are interchanged in a manner not to be expressed in a translation. The old translation of the second clause (*removed like a cottage*) is now commonly abandoned. The Hebrew word denotes properly a temporary lodging-place. In ch. 1 : 8 it was applied to a watch-shed in a melon-field. Here it seems to signify something more moveable and something suspended in the air. The latest writers are accordingly agreed in retaining the interpretation which makes it mean a cloth or mat suspended between trees or boughs of trees for the use of nocturnal watchers. Such are described by Niebuhr as common in Arabia, and are known throughout the east by a name essentially identical with those used in the Chaldee, Syriac, and Arabic versions of this sentence.

21. *And it shall be in that day (that) Jehovah shall visit* (for the purpose of inflicting punishment) *upon the host of the high place in the high place and upon the kings of the earth upon the earth.* Interpreters have commonly assumed that the *host of the high place* is the same with the *host of heaven*, and must therefore mean either stars or angels or both. It may be doubted however whether there is any reference to the host of heaven at all. *High* is a relative expression, and although applied to heaven in v. 18, is applied to earth or to human society in v. 4. The former sense may seem to be here required by the antithesis; but it is not clear that any antithesis was intended, which is the less probable because earth is not the customary opposite of heaven. The sense may simply be that God will judge the high or lofty host viz. the kings of the land upon the land. But even if there be an antithesis, and even if the host of heaven in the usual sense of the expression be alluded to, the analogy of this whole context would seem to indicate that this is merely a strong figure for different ranks or degrees of dignity on earth.

22. *And they shall be gathered with a gathering as prisoners in a pit, and shall be shut up in a dungeon, and after many days they shall be visited.* The sense of the first clause evidently is that they shall be imprisoned. The persons meant are the principalities and powers of the verse preceding. There are two interpretations of the verb *visited.* According to one it means *they shall be punished*, or at least brought forth to judgment. The other is, *they shall be visited in mercy.*

23. *And the moon shall be confounded and the sun ashamed, for Jehovah of Hosts is king in Mount Zion and in Jerusalem, and before his elders there is glory.* Before the splendour of Jehovah's reign all lesser principalities and powers shall fade away. The *elders* are the rulers of Israel as the church. The simple meaning of the verse appears to be that Jehovah's reign over

his people shall be more august than that of any created sovereign. This is true of the church in various periods of history, but more especially in those when the presence and power of God are peculiarly manifested. The affinity between this verse and the last of the preceding chapter seems to show that their juxtaposition is by no means fortuitous.

CHAPTER XXV.

THIS chapter consists of three distinguishable parts. The first is a thanksgiving to God for the destruction of Babylon and the deliverance of the Jews, vs. 1–5. The second is a promise of favour to the gentiles and the people of God, when united on Mount Zion, vs. 6–9. The third is a threatening of disgraceful ruin to Moab, vs. 10–12.

1. *Jehovah, my God (art) thou; I will exalt thee; I will praise thy name; for thou hast done a wonder, counsels from afar off, truth, certainty.* The song of praise opens in the usual lyric style. (See Ex. 15:2, 11. Ps. 118:28. 145:1.) The whole phrase may either mean, I will acknowledge thy goodness towards me, or I will confess thee to be what thy name imports, I will acknowledge thy acts to be consistent with the previous revelations of thine attributes. What wonder is especially referred to, the next verse explains. The last clause admits of several different constructions. Many of the older writers make it an independent proposition. Thus the English Version: *thy counsels of old are faithfulness and truth.* Others simplify the same construction still more by making all the nouns in the last clause objects of the verb in the first: thou hast brought to pass a wonder, ancient counsels, faithfulness, truth. *From afar*

off seems to imply, not only that the plans were formed of old, but that they were long ago revealed. Even long before the event they are certain.

2, 3. *For thou hast turned* (*it*) *from a city to a heap, a fortified town to a ruin, a palace of strangers from* (*being*) *a city; forever it shall not be built. Therefore a powerful people shall honour thee, a city of terrible nations shall fear thee.* The destruction of Babylon, and the fulfilment of prophecy thereby, shall lead even the boldest and wildest of the heathen to acknowledge Jehovah as the true God. It is usual to apply the terms of this verse specifically to the Medes and Persians as the conquerors of Babylon. There seems to be no need of applying the verse to a cordial voluntary recognition of Jehovah. It may just as well denote a compulsory extorted homage, *fear* being taken in its proper sense. The verse will then be an apt description of the effect produced by Jehovah's overthrow of Babylon on the Babylonians themselves. There is something unusual in the expression *city of nations.* It must either be explained as implying a plurality of subject nations, or the word translated nations must be taken in its secondary sense of *gentiles, heathen,* as applied to individuals or to one community.

4. *For thou hast been a strength* (or *stronghold*) *to the weak, a strength* (or *stronghold*) *to the poor in his distress, a refuge from the storm, a shadow from the heat, when the blast of the terrible* (or *of the tyrants*) was *like a storm against a wall.* The nations shall reverence Jehovah, not merely as the destroyer of Babylon, but as the deliverer of his people, for whose sake that catastrophe was brought about. *Weak* and *poor,* are epithets often applied to Israel considered as a sufferer. The two figures of extreme heat and a storm of rain are combined to express the idea of persecution or affliction. The last phrase in the Hebrew

naturally signifies precisely what the English Version has expressed, to wit, *a storm against a wall*, denoting the direction and the object of the violence, but not its issue. As a storm of rain beats upon a wall, so the Babylonian persecution beat upon the captive Jews.

5. *As the heat in a drought* (or *in a dry place*), *the noise of strangers wilt thou bring down;* (*as*) *heat by the shadow of a cloud,* (*so*) *shall the song of the tyrants be brought low.* The sufferings of Israel under oppression shall be mitigated and relieved as easily and quietly as the intense heat of the sun by an intervening cloud. The *noise* mentioned in the first clause is probably the tumult of battle and conquest, and the *song* in the last clause the triumphal song of the victorious enemy. The meaning *branch* is more agreeable to usage, but not so appropriate in this connection.

6. *And Jehovah of Hosts will make, for all nations, in this mountain, a feast of fat things, a feast of wines on the lees, of fat things full of marrow, of wines on the lees well refined.* Jerusalem, hitherto despised and oppressed, shall yet be a source of attraction, nourishment, and exhilaration, to mankind. This verse resumes the thread of the discourse, which was interrupted at the end of the last chapter, for the purpose of inserting the triumphal song (vs. 1–5). Having there said that Jehovah and his elders should appear in glory on Mount Zion, he now shows what is there to be bestowed upon the nations. This verse contains a general statement of the relation which Jerusalem or Zion should sustain to the whole world, as a source of moral influence. There is nothing to indicate the time when the promise should be fulfilled, nor indeed to restrict it to one time exclusively. As the ancient seat of the true religion, and as the cradle of the church which has since overspread the nations, it has always more or less fulfilled the office here ascribed to it.

7. *And he will swallow up* (i. e. destroy) *in this mountain the face of the veil, the veil upon all peoples, and the web, the (one) woven over all the nations.* The influence to go forth from this centre shall dispel the darkness, both of ignorance and sorrow, which now broods over the world. The subject of the verb is Jehovah. By the *face of the veil* some understand the veil itself. Others suppose a metathesis for the *veil of the face.* Others, with more probability, infer from the analogous expression in Job 41 : 13, that the veil or covering is here described as being the *surface* or upper side of the object covered. Most interpreters suppose an allusion to the practice of veiling the face as a sign of mourning, which agrees well with the next verse and is no doubt included, but the words seem also to express the idea of a veil upon the understanding. (See above, ch. 22 : 8.)

8. *He has swallowed up death forever, and the Lord Jehovah wipes away tears from off all faces, and the reproach of his people he will take away from off all the earth, for Jehovah hath spoken (it).* The people of God, who seemed to be extinct, shall be restored to life, their grief exchanged for joy, and their disgrace for honour in the presence of the world, a result for which he pledges both his power and foreknowledge. The true sense seems to be that all misery and suffering, comprehended under the generic name of *death*, should be completely done away. It is then a description of the ultimate effects of the influence before described as flowing from Mount Zion or the church of God. In its highest sense this may never be realized by any individual till after death. Paul says accordingly (1 Cor. 15 . 54), that when this corruptible shall have put on incorruption, and this mortal shall have put on immortality, then shall be brought to pass the saying that is written, *κατεπόθη ὁ θάνατος εἰς νῖκος.* As this is not an explanation of the text before us, nor even a citation of it in the way of argument, but merely a sublime description, all that it was necessary to express was the final, per-

13*

petual, triumphant abolition of death. The phrase εἰς νῖκος therefore, although not a strict translation, is no departure from its essential meaning. In its primary import, the clause is a promise to God's people, corresponding to the foregoing promise to the nations. While on the one hand he would lift the veil from the latter, and admit them to a feast upon Zion, on the other he would abolish death and wipe tears from the faces of his people. The restriction of these last expressions to the pains of death, or to the sorrow of bereavement, detracts from the exquisite beauty of the passage, which the poet Burns, it is said, could not read without weeping.

9. *And one shall say* (or *they shall say*) *in that day, Lo, this is our God; we have waited for him, and he will save us; this is Jehovah; we have waited for him; let us rejoice and be glad in his salvation.* When these gracious promises shall be fulfilled, those who have trusted in them shall no longer be ashamed of their strong confidence, because it will be justified by the event, and they will have nothing left but to rejoice in the fulfilment of their hopes. *This is our God, this is Jehovah;* as if they had said, this is the God of whom we have spoken, and for trusting in whom we have so often been derided. We have waited long, but he is come at last, to vindicate his truth and our reliance on him.

10. *For the hand of Jehovah shall rest upon this mountain, and Moab shall be trodden down under him* (or *in his place*) *as straw is trodden in the water of the dunghill.* While Israel shall thus enjoy the permanent protection of Jehovah, his inveterate enemies shall experience ignominious destruction. God's hand is the symbol of his power. Its resting on an object is the continued exercise of that power, whether for good or evil. This is determined by the nature of the object, as *this mountain* cannot well mean anything but what is meant in vs. 6, 7, to wit,

Mount Zion or the church of God, and the promise of the foregoing context must of course be continued here. Moab and Edom were the two hereditary and inveterate enemies of Israel, their hatred being rendered more annoying and conspicuous by their affinity and neighbouring situation. Hence they are repeatedly mentioned, separately or together, as the representatives of obstinate and malignant enemies in general. As the name *British*, in our own revolutionary war, became equivalent to *hostile*, without losing its specific sense, so might the Prophets threaten Moab with God's vengeance, without meaning to exclude from the denunciation other like-minded enemies. This wide interpretation, both of Moab and Edom, is confirmed by the fact that one of them is often mentioned where both would seem to be equally included. The figure in the last clause is strongly expressive both of degradation and destruction. Moab is likened not only to straw, but to straw left to rot for the dunghill. The idea of subjection and ruin is expressed by the figure of treading down or trampling under foot. The Hebrew word is commonly translated *thresh;* but as the oriental threshing was performed for the most part by the feet of cattle, this sense and that of *treading down* are really coincident. *Under him* may either mean *under Jehovah* or *under himself*, that is, in his own place, in the country of Moab, or wherever he is found.

11. *And he shall spread forth his hands in the midst of it, as the swimmer spreadeth forth his hands to swim; and he shall humble his pride, together with the spoils* (or *devices*) *of his hands.* From this ignominious doom Moab shall try in vain to save himself; his pride shall be humbled, and his struggles only serve to precipitate his ruin. Having compared the fall of Moab to the treading down of straw in a filthy pool, the Prophet carries out his figure here, but with a change so slight and at the same time so natural as almost to escape observation, while it greatly adds to the life of the description. The down-trodden straw now

becomes a living person, and struggles in the filthy pool to save himself from drowning, but in vain.

12. *And the fortress of the high fort of thy walls he hath cast down, humbled, brought to the ground, to the very dust* (or *even to the dust*). The specific fulfilment of this prophecy cannot be distinctly traced in history. It was certainly verified, however, in the downfall of the Moabitish nation, whenever it took place.

CHAPTER XXVI.

THIS chapter contains a song of praise and thanksgiving to be sung by Israel after his deliverance, vs. 1–19. To this is added a postscript, intimating that the time for such rejoicing was not yet at hand, vs. 20, 21.

The song opens with an acknowledgment of God's protection and an exhortation to confide therein, vs. 1–4. This is founded on the exhibition of his righteousness and power in the destruction of his foes and the oppressors of his people, vs. 5–11. The church abjures the service of all other sovereigns, and vows perpetual devotion to him by whom it has been delivered and restored, vs. 12–15. Her utter incapacity to save herself is then contrasted with God's power to restore his people to new life, with a joyful anticipation of which the song concludes, vs. 16–19. The additional sentences contain a beautiful and tender intimation of the trials, which must be endured before these glorious events take place, with a solemn assurance that Jehovah is about to visit both his people and their enemies with chastisement, vs. 20, 21.

1. *In that day shall this song be sung in the land of Judah:*

We have a strong city; salvation will he place (as) walls and breastwork. The condition and feelings of the people after their return from exile are expressed by putting an ideal song into their mouths. Though the first clause does not necessarily mean that this should actually be sung, but merely that it might be sung, that it would be appropriate to the times and to the feelings of the people, it is not at all improbable that it was actually used for this purpose, which could more readily be done as it is written in the form and manner of the Psalms, to which it exhibits many points of resemblance. The day meant is the day of deliverance which had just been promised.

2. *Open ye the gates, and let the righteous nation enter, keeping truth* (or *faith*). The supposition of responsive choirs gives a needless complexity to the structure of the passage. The speakers are the same as in the first verse, and the words are addressed to those who kept the doors.

3. *The mind stayed (on thee) thou wilt preserve in peace (in) peace* (i. e. in perfect peace), *because in thee (it is) confident* (literally *confided*). This is a general truth deduced from the experience of those who are supposed to be the speakers. The elliptical construction in the English Bible (*him whose mind is stayed on thee*) is not very natural.

4. *Trust ye in Jehovah forever* (literally, *even to eternity*), *for in Jah Jehovah is a rock of ages* (or *an everlasting rock*). To the general truth stated in v. 3, a general exhortation is now added, not addressed by one chorus to another, but by the same ideal speakers to all who hear them or are willing to receive the admonition. This is one of the few places in which the name *Jehovah* is retained by the common English Version. On the origin and usage of the name *Jah*, see above, ch. 12 : 2. The occurrence of the combination here confirms its genuine-

ness there. The figurative name *rock*, as applied to God, includes the two ideas of a *hiding place* and a *foundation*, or the one complex idea of a *permanent asylum.*

5. *For he hath brought down the inhabitants of the high place, the exalted city; he will lay it low, he will lay it low, to the very ground; he will bring it to the very dust.* He has proved himself able to protect his people, and consequently worthy to be trusted by them, in his signal overthrow of that great power by which they were oppressed. The alternation of the tenses here is somewhat remarkable. The English Version treats them all as presents, which is often allowable where the forms are intermingled. But in this case, a reason can be given for the use of the two tenses, even if strictly understood. The Prophet looks at the events from two distinct points of observation, his own and that of the ideal speakers. With respect to the latter, the fall of Babylon was past; with respect to the former it was still future. He might therefore naturally say, even in the same sentence, *he has brought it low* and *he shall bring it to the dust.*

6. *The foot shall trample on it, the feet of the afflicted, the steps of the weak.* The ruins of the fallen city shall be trodden underfoot, not only by its conquerors, but by those whom it oppressed. *Steps* is here a poetical equivalent to *feet.*

7. *The way for the righteous is straight* (or *level*)*; thou most upright wilt level* (or *rectify*) *the path of the righteous.* A man's way is a common scriptural figure for his course of life. A straight or level way is a prosperous life. It is here declared that the course of the righteous is a prosperous one, because God makes it so. The primary idea of the word here translated *level*, is to render even ; it is therefore applied both to balances and paths; but the two applications are not to be

confounded; paths may be made even, but they cannot be weighed.

8. *Also in the way of thy judgments, oh Jehovah, we have waited for thee; to thy name and thy remembrance (was our) soul's desire.* For this manifestation of thy righteousness and goodness we have long been waiting *in the way of thy judgments*, i. e. to see thee come forth as a judge, for the vindication of thy people and the destruction of their enemies. *Name* and *remembrance* or *memorial* denote the manifestation of God's attributes in his works.

9. (*With*) *my soul have I desired thee in the night; yea* (*with*) *my spirit within me will I seek thee early: for when thy judgments* (*come*) *to the earth, the inhabitants of the world learn righteousness.* The desire here expressed is not a general desire for the knowledge and favour of God, but a special desire that he would manifest his righteousness by appearing as a judge. This explanation is required by the connection with what goes before and with what follows in this very verse. The night is mentioned for the purpose of expressing the idea, that he feels this wish at all times, by night and by day. The question whether these are the words of the Prophet, or of each of the people, or of a choir or chorus representing them, proceeds upon the supposition of an artificial structure and a strict adherence to rhetorical propriety, which have no real existence in the writings of the Prophet. The sentiments, which it was his purpose and his duty to express, are sometimes uttered in his own person, sometimes in that of another, and these different forms of speech are interchanged, without regard to the figments of an artificial rhetoric. By *judgments*, here as in the foregoing context, we can only understand judicial providences. The doctrine of the verse is, that a view of God's severity is necessary to convince men of his justice.

10. *Let the wicked be favoured, he does not learn righteousness: in the land of right he will do wrong, and will not see the exaltation of Jehovah.* The reasoning of the preceding verse is here continued. As it was there said that God's judgments were necessary to teach men righteousness, so it is here said that continued prosperity is insufficient for that purpose. The wicked man will go on to do wickedly, even in the very place where right conduct is peculiarly incumbent. Though the verse is in the form of a general proposition, and as such admits of various applications, there is obvious reference to the Babylonians, who were not only emboldened by impunity to do wrong in the general, but to do it even in the *land of right* or rectitude, the holy land, Jehovah's land, where such transgressions were peculiarly offensive.

11. *Jehovah, thy hand is high, they will not see;* (yes) *they will see (and be ashamed) thy zeal for thy people; yea, the fire of thine enemies shall devour them.* The seeming contradiction instantly explains itself, as being a kind of after-thought. *They will not see,* (but yes) *they will see. Fire* denotes the wrath of God, as a sudden, rapid, irresistible, and utterly destroying agent.

12. *Jehovah, thou wilt give us peace, for even all our works thou hast wrought for us.* This is an expression of strong confidence and hope, founded on what has already been experienced. God certainly would favour them in future, for he had done so already. *Peace* is, as often elsewhere, to be taken in the wide sense of prosperity or welfare. It is commonly agreed among interpreters, that *our works* here means not *the works done by us* but *the works done for us*, i. e. what we have experienced. The version of the last clause in the text of the English Bible (thou hast wrought all our works *in us*) is connected with an old interpretation of the verse, as directly teaching the doctrine of human dependence and efficacious grace. This translation, how-

ever, is equally at variance with the usage of the Hebrew preposition and with the connection here. The context, both before and after, has respect, not to spiritual exercises, but to providential dispensations.

13. *Jehovah, our God, (other) lords beside thee have ruled us; (but henceforth) thee, thy name, only will we celebrate.* The usual construction of the last clause is *through thee* i. e. through thy favour, by thy help, we are enabled now to praise thy name. But some regard the pronoun as in apposition with *thy name*, and the whole clause as describing only the object of their worship, not the means by which they were enabled to render it. As to the *lords* who are mentioned in the first clause, there are two opinions. One is, that they are the Chaldees or Babylonians, under whom the Jews had been in bondage. This is now the current explanation. The other is, that they are the false gods or idols, whom the Jews had served before the exile. Against the former and in favour of the latter supposition it may be suggested, first, that the Babylonian bondage did not hinder the Jews from mentioning Jehovah's name or praising him; secondly, that the whole verse looks like a confession of their own fault and a promise of amendment, rather than a reminiscence of their sufferings; and thirdly, that there seems to be an obvious comparison between the worship of Jehovah, as *our God*, with some other worship and some other deity. At the same time let it be observed, that the ideas of religious and political allegiance and apostasy, or of heathen rulers and of idol gods, were not so carefully distinguished by the ancient Jews as by ourselves, and it is therefore not impossible that both the kinds of servitude referred to may be here included, yet in such a manner that the spiritual one must be considered as the prominent idea, and the only one, if either must be fixed upon to the exclusion of the other. An additional argument, in favour of the reference of this verse to spiritual rulers, is its

exact correspondence with the singular fact in Jewish history, that since the Babylonish exile they had never been suspected of idolatry. That such a circumstance should be adverted to in this commemorative poem, is so natural that its omission would be almost unaccountable.

14. *Dead, they shall not live: ghosts, they shall not rise: therefore thou hast visited and destroyed them, and made all memory to perish with respect to them.* Those whom we lately served are now no more; thou hast destroyed them and consigned them to oblivion, for the very purpose of securing our freedom and devotion to thy service. It seems best to refer this verse to the strange lords of the foregoing verse, i. e. the idols themselves, but with some allusion, as in that case, to the idolatrous oppressors of the Jews. The sense is correctly given in the English Version: *they are dead, they shall not live; they are deceased, they shall not rise.* An attempt, however, has been made above to imitate more closely the concise and compact form of the original. For the meaning of *ghosts* see above, ch. 14 : 9. It is here a poetical equivalent to *dead*, and may be variously rendered, shades, shadows, spirits, or the like. The common version (*deceased*) leaves too entirely out of view the figurative character of the expression. *Therefore* may be used to introduce, not only the cause, but the design of an action. Though the words cannot mean, thou hast destroyed them *because* they are dead and powerless, they may naturally mean, thou hast destroyed them *that they might be* dead and powerless. The same two meanings are attached to the English phrase *for this reason*, which may either denote cause or purpose. The meaning of the verse, as connected with the one before it, is that the strange lords who had ruled them should not only cease to do so, but, so far as they were concerned, should cease to exist or be remembered.

15. *Thou hast added to the nation, oh Jehovah, thou hast added to the nation; thou hast glorified thyself; thou hast put far off all the ends of the land.* By this deliverance of thy people from the service both of idols and idolaters, thou hast added a great number to the remnant who were left in the Holy Land, so that larger territories will be needed for their occupation; and in doing all this, thou hast made an exhibition of thy power, justice, truth, and goodness. Thus understood, the whole verse is a grateful acknowledgment of what God had done for his suffering people. The enlargement of the boundaries may either be explained as a poetical description of the actual increase and expected growth of the nation (ch. 49 : 19), or literally understood as referring to the fact, that after the return from exile the Jews were no longer restricted to their own proper territory, but extended themselves more or less over the whole country. The translation of the verb as a reflexive, rather than a simple passive, greatly adds to the strength of the expression.

16. *Jehovah, in distress they visited thee; they uttered a whisper; thy chastisement was on them.* It was not merely after their deliverance that they turned from idols unto God. Their deliverance itself was owing to their humble prayers. *Visit* is here used in the unusual but natural sense of seeking God in supplication. The translation *they uttered a whisper* is not only admissible but beautifully expressive of submissive humble prayer, like that of Hannah when *she spake in her heart and only her lips moved, but her voice was not heard*, although, as she said herself, *she poured out her soul before God*, which is the exact sense of the word in this place. A like expression is applied to prayer in the title of Psalm 102. It is implied, though not expressed, that their prayer was humble and submissive *because* they felt that what they suffered was a chastisement from God.

17. *As when a pregnant* (*woman*) *draws near to the birth, she writhes, she cries out in her pangs; so have we been, from thy presence, oh Jehovah!* Before we thus cast ourselves upon thy mercy in submissive prayer, we tried to deliver ourselves, but only to the aggravation of our sufferings. The comparison here used is not intended simply to denote extreme pain, as it is in many other cases, but as the next verse clearly shows, the pain arising from ineffectual efforts to relieve themselves. The great majority of writers apply this verse to the condition of the exiles. The translation *from thy presence* is to be preferred; but whether with the accessory idea of removal, alienation, or with that of infliction, is a question not determined by the phrase itself, but either left uncertain or to be decided by the context.

18. *We were in travail, we were in pain, as it were we brought forth wind. Deliverances we could not make the land, nor would the inhabitants of the world fall.* The figure introduced in the preceding verse is here carried out and applied. The second clause admits of several different constructions. The simplest supplies a preposition before land, *in* or *for the land.* The one now commonly adopted is, *we could not make the land safety*, i. e. could not make it safe or save it. The future form of the verb has respect to the period described. As the people then might have said, *we shall not save the land*, so the same expression is here put into their mouths retrospectively. The best equivalent in English is the potential or subjunctive form, *we could not.* The foregoing context, as we have seen, relates to the period of captivity itself. Those who suppose the exile itself to be the time in question, understand by world the Babylonian empire as in ch. 13 : 11.

19. *Thy dead shall live, my corpses shall arise; (awake and sing ye that dwell in the dust!) for the dew of herbs is thy dew,*

and (on) the earth, (on) the dead, thou wilt cause it to fall This verse is in the strongest contrast with the one before it. To the ineffectual efforts of the people to save themselves, he now opposes their actual deliverance by God. They shall rise because they are *thy dead*, i e. thy dead people. Some supply a preposition (*with my dead body*), which construction is adopted in the English Version, but is now commonly abandoned as incongruous and wholly arbitrary. Neither the Prophet, nor the house of Israel, in whose name he is speaking, could refer to their own body as distinct from the bodies of Jehovah's dead ones. *Awake* etc. is a joyful apostrophe to the dead, after which the address to Jehovah is resumed. The reference to the dew is intended to illustrate the vivifying power of God. The obvious meaning of the words is an expression of strong confidence and hope, or rather of prophetic foresight, that God *will* raise the dead, that his life-giving influence will be exerted. The question now arises, what resurrection is referred to? All the answers to this question may be readily reduced to three. The first is, that the prophet means the general resurrection of the dead, or according to an old rabbinical tradition, the exclusive resurrection of the righteous, at the last day. The second is, that he refers to a resurrection of the Jews already dead, not as an actual or possible event, but as a passionate expression of desire that the depopulated land might be replenished with inhabitants. The third is, that he represents the restoration of the exiles and of the theocracy under the figure of a resurrection, as Paul says the restoration of Israel to God's favour will be *life from the dead.* The figurative exposition seems decidedly entitled to the preference. This national address to God could not be more suitably wound up, or in a manner more in keeping with the usage of the prophecies, than by a strong expression of belief, that God would raise his people from the dust of degradation and oppression, where they had long seemed dead though only sleeping.

20. *Go, my poeple, enter into thy chambers, and shut thy doors after thee, hide thyself for a little moment, till the wrath be past.* Having wound up the expectations of the people to a full belief of future restoration from their state of civil and religious death, the Prophet by an exquisite transition intimates, that this event is not yet immediately at hand, that this relief from the effects of God's displeasure with his people must be preceded by the experience of the displeasure itself, that it is still a time of indignation, and that till this is elapsed the promise cannot be fulfilled. This painful postponement of the promised resurrection could not be more tenderly or beautifully intimated than in this fine apostrophe. The English Version (*as it were*) is incorrect. The period of suffering is described as very small in comparison with what had gone before and what should follow it, as St. Paul says (Rom. 8 : 18) that *the sufferings of this present time are not worthy to be compared with the glory which shall be revealed in us.*

21. *For behold, Jehovah* (*is*) *coming out of his place, to visit the iniquity of the inhabitant of the earth upon him, and the earth shall disclose her blood, and shall no more cover her slain.* This is a reason both for expecting ultimate deliverance and for patiently awaiting it. The reason is that God has a work of chastisement to finish, first upon his own people, and then upon their enemies. During the former process, let the faithful hide themselves until the wrath be past. When the other begins, let them lift up their heads, for their redemption draweth nigh. This large interpretation of the verse is altogether natural and more satisfactory than those which restrict it either to the judgments upon Israel or to those upon Babylon. On the latter the eye of the Prophet chiefly rests, especially at last, so that the closing words may be applied almost exclusively to the retribution which awaited the Chaldean for the slaughter of God's people. The blood, which the earth had long since

drunk in, should as it were be vomited up, and the bodies of the murdered, which had long been buried, should be now disclosed to view.

CHAPTER XXVII.

THIS chapter is an amplification of the last verse of the one preceding, and contains a fuller statement both of Israel's chastisements and of Jehovah's judgments on his enemies. The destruction of the latter is foretold as the slaughter of a huge sea-monster, and contrasted with God's care of his own people even when afflicting them, vs. 1–5. Hereafter Israel shall flourish, and even in the mean time his sufferings are far less than those of his oppressors, vs. 6, 7. The former is visited in moderation, for a time, and with the happiest effect, vs. 8, 9. The latter is finally and totally destroyed, vs. 10, 11. This shall be followed by the restoration of the scattered Jews, vs. 12, 13.

1. *In that day shall Jehovah visit, with his sword, the hard, the great, the strong (sword), upon Leviathan the swift* (or *flying*) *serpent, and upon Leviathan the coiled* (or *crooked*) *serpent, and shall slay the dragon which (is) in the sea.* The leviathan and dragon of this verse are probably descriptive of a great oppressive power, with particular allusion to the Babylonian empire. Assuming this to be the general meaning of the verse, that of its mere details becomes either easy or comparatively unimportant. The word *leviathan*, which from its etymology appears to mean *contorted, coiled*, is sometimes used to denote particular species (e. g. the crocodile), and sometimes as a generic term for huge aquatic animals, or the larger kinds of ser-

pents, in which sense the corresponding term *serpent* is also used. They both appear to be employed in this case to express the indefinite idea of a formidable monster, which is in fact the sense now commonly attached to the word *dragon.* The second epithet means *tortuous*, either with respect to the motion of the serpent, or to its appearance when at rest. The only explanation of the other epithet which is fully justified by Hebrew usage is that of *fugitive* or *fleeing*, which may either be a poetical equivalent to *fleet*, or descriptive of the monster as a *flying* serpent. For the meaning of the phrase to *visit upon*, see above, ch. 13 : 11. The sword is a common emblem for the instruments of the divine vengeance.

2. On the explanation of this verse depends that of a large part of the chapter. The two points upon which all turns, are the meaning of the Hebrew word translated *sing*, and the reference of the pronoun *her.* The only supposition which will meet the difficulties of the case, is the one adopted by most of the old writers, to wit, that the pronoun refers to Jerusalem or the daughter of Zion, i. e. to the church or people of God considered as his spouse (ch. 1 : 21). This reference to a subject not expressly mentioned might be looked upon as arbitrary, but for the fact that the assumption of it is attended with fewer difficulties than the construction which it supersedes. As to the other word, tradition and authority are almost unanimous in giving it the sense of *sing* and regarding what follows as a *song.* To this exposition there are several objections. In the first place, no one has been able to determine with precision where the *song* concludes, some choosing one place for its termination, some another. This would of course prove nothing in a clear case, but in a case like this it raises a presumption that a song, of which the end cannot be found, has no beginning. But in the next place, it is easy to see why the end cannot be easily defined, to wit, because there is nothing in

the next three, four, or five verses to distinguish them as being any more a *song* than what precedes and follows, whether with respect to imagery, rhythm, or diction. In the third place, the presumption thus created and confirmed is corroborated further by the obvious incongruity of making the song, which the people are supposed to sing, begin with *I Jehovah keep it* etc. Out of fifty-six cases in which the Hebrew word occurs, there are only three in which the sense of *singing* is conceivable, and of these three one (Ps. 88 : 1) is the enigmatical title of a Psalm; another (Ex. 32 : 18) is so dubious that the one sense is almost as appropriate as the other, and the third is that before us. On such grounds the assumption of the meaning *sing* could hardly be justified, even if it were far more appropriate to the context than the common one. But in the last place, while the supposition of a song, as we have seen, embarrasses the exposition, the usual meaning of the verb is perfectly appropriate. This meaning is to *afflict*, and especially to afflict in an humbling and degrading manner. This may seem to be utterly at variance with the context as it is commonly explained; but the common explanation rests on the supposititious meaning of the verb, and cannot therefore be alleged in favour of that meaning. On the usual hypothesis, the verse exhorts the people to sing to the vineyard or the church; on the one now proposed, it challenges her enemies to do their worst, declaring that God still protects her. This explanation of the verse agrees well with the distinct allusions to the punishment of Israel in vs. 4, 7, 8, 9, which would be comparatively out of place in a song of triumph or gratulation. Against this explanation of the verse lies the undivided weight of tradition and authority, so far as I can trace the exposition of the passage. So unanimous a judgment might be looked upon as perfectly decisive of the question but for two considerations; first, that the proposed interpretation removes a variety of difficulties, not by forsaking usage but by returning to it; and secondly, that none of the interpreters consulted seem to have adverted to the facts already stated, with respect to the usage of the Hebrew word. As the result of this investigation, we may now translate the verse as follows. *In that day, as a vineyard of wine, afflict her*, or, *in that day afflict for her the vineyard of wine.* It is then a defiance or permission of the enemies of the church to afflict her, with an intimation that in carrying out this idea, the expressions will be borrowed from the figure of a vineyard, as in ch. 5 : 1–6.

3. *I Jehovah (am) keeping her ; every moment I will water her ; lest any hurt her, night and day will I keep her.* That is, in spite of the afflictions which befall her I will still preserve her from destruction. The antecedent of the pronouns is the same as in v. 2, viz. the church or nation considered as a vineyard. To *visit upon* has here its common meaning of *inflicting evil upon*, but without any special reference to crime or punishment. As the expression is a relative one, it must here be understood according to the context, as denoting fatal or at least excessive injury.

4. *Fury is not in me: who would set the briers and thorns against me in battle? I would go through them, I would burn them together.* Of all the senses put upon this difficult verse, there are only two which can be looked upon as natural or probable. The first may be paraphrased as follows ; it is not because I am cruel or revengeful that I thus afflict my people, but because she is a vineyard overrun with thorns or briers, on account of which I must pass through her and consume her (i. e. burn them out of her). The other is this : I am no longer angry with my people ; oh that their enemies (as thorns and briers) would array themselves against me, that I might rush upon them and consume them. This last is preferred by most of the

later writers. The objection that *no longer* has to be supplied is of little weight.

5. *Or let him lay hold of my strength and make peace with me; peace let him make with me.* The verbs are properly indefinite (let one take hold etc.) but referring to the enemy described in the preceding verse as thorns and briers. The word translated *strength* commonly denotes a strong place or fortress, and is here understood by most interpreters to signify a refuge or asylum, with allusion to the practice of laying hold upon the altar. The alternative presented to the enemy is that of destruction or submission. If the thorns and briers of v. 4 be referred to the internal condition of the church, this may be understood as having reference to the church itself, which is then called upon to make its peace with God as the only means of escaping further punishment.

6. *(In) coming (days) shall Jacob take root, Israel shall bud and blossom, and they shall fill the face of the earth with fruit.* The construction of the first clause in the English Bible (*them that come of Jacob shall he cause to take root*) is forbidden by the collocation of the words, and by the usage of the verb, which always means to *take root.*

7. *Like the smiting of his smiter did he smite him, or like the slaying of his slain was he slain?* Having declared in the preceding verse that Israel should hereafter flourish, he now adds that even in the meantime he should suffer vastly less than his oppressors. Negation, as in many other cases, is expressed by interrogation. Did the Lord smite Israel as he smote his smiters, or slay him as his murderers were slain?

8. *In measure, by sending her away, thou dost contend with her. He removes her by his hard wind in the day of the east wind.* The

negation implied in the preceding verse is here expressed more distinctly. The Prophet now proceeds to show that Israel was not dealt with like his enemies, by first describing what the former suffered, then what the latter. Israel was punished moderately, and for a time, by being removed out of his place, as if by a transient storm or blast of wind. The east wind is mentioned as the most tempestuous in Palestine. The *day* of the east wind is supposed by some to denote the season of the year when it prevails; but it is rather used to intimate the temporary nature of the chastisement, as if he had said, one day when the east wind chanced to blow.

9. *Therefore* (because his chastisement was temporary and remedial in design) *by this* (affliction) *shall Jacob's iniquity be expiated* (i. e. purged away), *and this is all* (its) *fruit* (or intended effect), *to take away his sin*, (as will appear) *in his placing all the stones of the* (idolatrous) *altar like limestones dashed in pieces*, (so that) *groves and solar images* (or images of Ashtoreth and Baal) *shall arise no more.* The contrast between Israel and Babylon is still continued. Having said that the affliction of the former was but moderate and temporary, he now adds that it was meant to produce a most beneficent effect, to wit, the purgation of the people from the foul stain of idolatry. The sense required by the connection is, not that the breaking of the altars, as a spontaneous act, atoned for Israel's previous idolatry, but that the exile cured them of that vice, and thereby led to the breaking of the altars.

10. *For a fenced* (or *fortified*) *city shall be desolate, a dwelling broken up and forsaken like the wilderness. There shall the calf feed, and there shall it lie and consume her branches.* Here begins the other part of the comparison. While Israel is chastised in measure and with the happiest effect, his oppressors are given up to final desolation. This explanation of the

verse, as referring to Babylon, is strongly recommended by the fact, that the comparison otherwise remains unfinished, only one side of it having been presented. Apart from this consideration, there are certainly strong reasons for supposing the city meant to be Jerusalem itself. One of these reasons is, that the figure of a vineyard seems to be still present to the writer's mind, at the close of this verse and throughout the text, although the terms used admit of a natural application to the figure of a tree. Another reason is, that the desolation here described is not so total as that threatened against Babylon in ch. 13 : 19–22, where instead of saying it shall be a pasture, it is said expressly that it shall not even be frequented by flocks or herds. But these two places may have reference to different degrees of desolation. In favour of the reference to Babylon may be alleged the natural consecution of the twelfth verse upon that hypothesis. On the whole, the question may be looked upon as doubtful, but as not materially affecting the interpretation of the chapter, since either of the two events supposed to be foretold would be appropriate in this connection.

11. *In the withering of its boughs* (or *when its boughs are withered*) *they shall be broken off, women coming and burning them; because it is not a people of understanding, therefore its creator shall not pity it, and its maker shall not have mercy on it.* The destruction of Babylon is still described, but under the figure of a tree, whose branches are withered and cast into the fire. Women are mentioned, not in allusion to the weakness of the instruments by which Babylon was to be destroyed, but because the gathering of firewood in the east is the work of women and children. According to the usage of the Scriptures, *not wise* here means foolish in the strongest sense, and God's *not pitying* and having mercy is equivalent to his being very wroth and taking vengeance.

12. *And it shall be in that day, that Jehovah shall beat off* (or gather in his fruit), *from the channel of the river to the stream of Egypt, and ye shall be gathered one by one* (or *one to another*), *oh ye children of Israel.* To the downfall of Babylon he now adds, as in ch. 11:1, its most important consequence, the restoration of the Jews. The idea meant to be conveyed is that of a careful and complete ingathering. *Stream of Egypt* is now commonly agreed to signify the Wady Elarish, anciently called *Rhinocorura*, which name is given to it here by the Septuagint. *The river* is as usual the Euphrates. The simple meaning of the whole expression is, *from Assyria to Egypt*, both which are expressly mentioned in the next verse. The precise sense of the Hebrew phrase in the latter part of the verse is not well expressed by the English *one by one*, which seems to represent the process as a gradual one. It rather denotes *one to one*, i. e. in our idiom, *one to another*, all together, or without exception. From what has been already said it will be seen, that the boundaries named are not intended to define the territory which should be occupied by those returning, but the regions whence they should return, which explanation is confirmed moreover by the explicit terms of the next verse.

13. *And it shall be* (or *come to pass*) *in that day,* (*that*) *a great trumpet shall be blown, and they shall come that were lost* (or *wandering*) *in the land of Assyria, and those cast out* (or *exiled*) *in the land of Egypt, and shall bow down to Jehovah, in the holy mountain, in Jerusalem.* The same event is here described as in the verse preceding, but with a change of figure. What is there represented as a gathering of olives by beating the tree, is now represented as a gathering of men by the blast of a trumpet, which here takes the place of a signal-pole or flag in ch. 11:12. This variety of forms, in which the same idea is expressed, clearly shows the whole description to be figurative. Assyria

and Egypt may be either put for foreign countries generally, or with particular allusion to the actual emigration and dispersion of the Jews in these two regions. Assyria may here be used as a comprehensive term, in order to include both the Assyrian and Babylonian deportations. For although the ten tribes never were restored, individual members of them found their way back with the Jews from Babylon. On the whole, however, it is probable that Egypt and Assyria are here named, just as Babylonia and the islands of the sea might have been named instead of them, and just as all these names and others are connected elsewhere, to denote the various lands where Jews were scattered. The emigration of the people, especially after Nebuchadnezzar's conquests, was of course not confined to their actual deportation by the enemy, nor was the restoration merely that of such as had been thus carried captive, but of all who, in consequence of that catastrophe or any other, had been transferred to foreign parts by exile, flight, or voluntary expatriation. The application of this verse to a future restoration of the Jews can neither be established nor disproved. If such a restoration can be otherwise shown to be a subject of prophecy, this passage may be naturally understood at least as comprehending it. But in itself considered, it appears to contain nothing which may not be naturally applied to events long past, or which has not found in those events an adequate fulfilment.

CHAPTER XXVIII.

SAMARIA, the crown of Ephraim, shall be cast down by a sudden and impetuous invasion, as a just judgment upon sensual and impious Israel, vs. 1–4. To the remnant of Israel, Jehovah will himself be a crown and a protection, a source of wisdom and of strength, vs. 5, 6. Yet even these imitate the example of apostate Israel, and in their self-indulgence cast off the authority of God and refuse the instructions of his prophet, to their own undoing, vs. 7–13. But their impious contempt of God and self-reliance shall but hasten their destruction. All who do not build upon the sure foundation laid in Zion, must inevitably perish as the enemies of Israel were destroyed of old, vs. 14–22. The delay of judgment no more proves that it will never come, than the patience of the husbandman, and his preparatory labours, prove that he expects no harvest; and the difference of God's dealings with different men is no more inconsistent with his general purposes of wrath or mercy, than the husbandman's treatment of the different grains is inconsistent with his general purpose of securing and enjoying them, vs. 23–29.

1. *Woe to the high crown of the drunkards of Ephraim, and the fading flower, his ornament of beauty, which (is) on the head of the fat valley of the wine-smitten.* Here, as in ch. 9 : 9, 21. 11 : 13, we are to understand by *Ephraim* the kingdom of the ten tribes, by the *drunkards of Ephraim* its vicious population, and by the *lofty crown* the city of Samaria, so called as the chief town and the royal residence, but also with allusion to its local situation on an insulated hill overlooking a rich plain or valley. "It would be difficult to find, in all Palestine, a situation of

equal strength, fertility, and beauty combined." (Robinson's Palestine, III. 146.) Most interpreters assume a further allusion to the practice of wearing wreaths or garlands at feasts. The reference to literal intoxication appears plain from a comparison of Amos 4 : 1, 6 : 1, 6. Drunkenness is mentioned, not as the only prevalent iniquity, but as a crying one, and one contributing to many others. The moral and spiritual consequences of this vice must be taken into view; but the exclusive reference of the words to spiritual drunkenness, whether delusion or stupidity or both, seems entirely untenable. This verse contains three examples of the Hebrew idiom, which, instead of an adjective, uses one substantive to qualify another; *crown of elevation* for lofty crown, *beauty of glory* for glorious beauty, and *valley of fatnesses* for fat valley. The latter member of the first clause is by some construed thus, *and the flower whose glorious beauty fades;* by others, for example the English Version, (*Ephraim*) *whose glorious beauty is a fading flower.* The analogy of v. 4 seems to show, however, that this member of the sentence is in apposition with the one before it, which construction is moreover the most obvious and simple. The English Version also mars the beauty of the first clause, by making *drunkards of Ephraim* not a genitive but a dative. The *fading flower* implies that the glory of Samaria was transient, with particular allusion to its approaching overthrow by Shalmaneser. *Wine-smitten* or *wine-stricken* is a strong description of the intellectual and moral effects of drunkenness. Gill's lively paraphrase is, "smitten, beaten, knocked down with it as with a hammer, and laid prostrate on the ground, where they lie fixed to it, not able to get up."

2. *Behold, there is to the Lord* (i. e. *the Lord has*) *a strong and mighty one, like a storm of hail, a destroying tempest, like a storm of mighty rushing waters, he has brought (it) to the ground with the hand.* The meaning *to the earth* or *to the ground* is clear

from ch. 63 : 6, and other cases. The crown of Ephraim is described as torn from his head and thrown upon the ground by the hand of a victorious enemy. To this explanation no objection can be drawn from the previous mention of the hail and rain; for these are mere comparisons, descriptive of the violence with which the enemy should make his attack. It is as if he had said, a strong and mighty enemy, rushing upon you like a hail-storm or a driving rain, shall cast your crown upon the earth with his hand.

3. *With the feet shall be trodden the lofty crown of the drunkards of Ephraim.* It is cast down by the hand and trampled under foot.

4. *And the fading flower of his glorious beauty, which is on the head of the fat valley, shall be like a first-ripe fig, which he that sees it sees, and while it is yet in his hand swallows it.* This comparison expresses the avidity with which the enemy would seize upon Samaria, and perhaps the completeness of its desolation. The fruit referred to is the early fig of Palestine which ripens in June, while the regular season of ingathering is from August to November, so that the former is regarded as a rarity and eaten with the greater relish. The figure is not here intended to express either ease or rapidity of conquest, for the siege of Samaria lasted three years (2 Kings 17 : 5). The immediate eating of the fruit is only mentioned as a sign of eagerness or greediness. The last clause, though singularly worded, evidently means that as soon as one sees it and lays hold of it he swallows it without delay, or as Gill expresses it in homespun English, "as soon as he has got it into his hand, he can't keep it there to look at, or forbear eating it, but greedily devours it and swallows it down at once."

5. *In that day shall Jehovah of Hosts be for* (or *become*) *a crown*

of beauty and a diadem of glory to the remnant of his people. The true sense appears to be that after Samaria, the pride of the apostate tribes, had fallen, they who still remained as members of the church or chosen people should glory and delight in the presence of Jehovah as their choicest privilege and highest honour. The expressions are borrowed from the first verse but presented in a new combination.

6. *And for a spirit of judgment to him that sitteth in judgment, and for strength to them that turn the battle to the gate.* This, which is the common English Version, coincides with that of the latest and best writers. *In judgment*, i. e. for the purpose of judging. The last words of the verse are applied by all the later writers to those who drive the war back to the enemy's own gates, or as it were carry it into his own country. The two great requisites of civil government are here described as coming from Jehovah. The *Spirit* of this verse is not a mere influence, but God himself.

7. *And (yet) these also* (or *even these*) *through wine have erred, and through strong drink have gone astray. Priest and Prophet have erred through strong drink, have been swallowed up of wine, have been led astray by strong drink, have erred in vision, have wavered in judgment.* Having predicted in the foregoing verse, that when Ephraim fell Judah should continue to enjoy the protection of Jehovah, the Prophet now describes even this favoured remnant as addicted to the same sins which had hastened the destruction of the ten tribes, viz. sensual indulgence and the spiritual evils which it generates. The meaning then is that the Jews, although distinguished from the ten tribes by God's sparing mercy, should nevertheless imitate them in their sins. There is great probability in the suggestion, that the prophecy refers to the national deterioration in the reign of Manasseh. The Priest and Prophet are named as the leaders

of the people, and as those who were peculiarly bound to set a better example. The reference to *judgment* in the last clause may be explained, either on the ground that the Priest and Prophet represent the rulers of the people in general, or because the Priests themselves exercised judicial functions in certain prescribed cases (Deut. 17 : 9. 19 : 17). The use of strong drinks was expressly forbidden to the priests in the discharge of their official functions (Lev. 10 : 9. Ezek. 44 : 21).

8. *For all tables are full of vomit, of filth, without a place* (i. e. a clean place). The only natural interpretation is that which supposes *tables* to denote the places where men eat and drink, and the other terms the natural though revolting consequences of excess. Whether the intoxication thus described is wholly spiritual, depends of course upon the meaning given to the preceding verse. The sense of the last clause is correctly though diffusely given in the English Version (*so that there is no place clean*).

9. *Whom will he teach knowledge? And whom will he make to understand doctrine? Those weaned from the milk and removed from the breasts.* The older Christian writers understand this as descriptive of the persons whom Jehovah, or the Prophet acting in his name, would choose as proper subjects of instruction, viz. simple and childlike disciples, who *as new-born babes desire the sincere milk of the word* (1 Pet. 2 : 2). But the children here described are weanlings not sucklings, and on this hypothesis the weaning, which is so particularly mentioned, would have no significancy. Besides, this explanation of the words would not suit the context, either before or after. It is therefore commonly agreed, that the last clause must be taken in a contemptuous or unfavourable sense, as denoting children not in malice merely but in understanding (1 Cor. 14 : 20). The verse has been explained by some, as the language not of the Prophet

but of the wicked men before described, expressing their indignation and contempt at the Prophet's undertaking to instruct them as if they were mere children. Whom does he undertake to teach? and whom would he make to understand his doctrine? Children weaned from the milk and removed from the breast? This interpretation has in substance been adopted by all later writers, as affording a good sense and one admirably suited both to the foregoing and the following context. It seems to be liable to only two objections; first, that it gratuitously gives the passage a dramatic form by supposing a new speaker to be introduced without any intimation in the text; and then, that it arbitrarily continues the interrogation through the sentence. The last objection may be obviated by adopting the construction, which supposes them to ask not whom he *would* but whom he *ought* to teach, and then to answer, little children just weaned from the breast, not men of mature age and equal to himself. The other objection, being wholly negative, must yield of course to the positive arguments in favour of an exposition which is otherwise coherent, satisfactory, and suited to the context.

10. *For (it is) rule upon rule, rule upon rule, line upon line, line upon line, a little here, a little there.* The interpretation of this verse varies of course with that of the one before it. As all the latest writers make v. 9 the language of the Jews themselves, complaining of the Prophet's perpetual reproofs and teachings, they are equally agreed in making v. 10 a direct continuation of the same complaint. The construction in the English Version (*precept upon precept*) is good, except that the word *precept* is too long to represent the chosen monosyllables of the original. *Here a little, there a little,* is expressive of minuteness and perpetual repetition.

11. *For with stammering lips and with another tongue will he*

speak unto this people. As the words translated *stammering lips* may denote either *foreign* or *scoffing* speech (the former being usually described in the Old Testament as *stammering*), some suppose a double allusion here, to wit, that as they had mocked at the divine instructions by their stammering speech, so he would speak to them in turn by the stammering lips of foreigners in another language than their own. This, though by no means an obvious construction in itself, is preferred by the latest writers and countenanced by several analogous expressions in the subsequent context.

12. *Who said to them, this is rest, give rest to the weary, and this is quiet, but they would not hear.* The judgments threatened in the foregoing verse were the more evidently just because he who threatened them had warned the people and pointed out to them the only way to happiness. The sense is not, that the true way to rest is to give rest to the weary; the latter expression is a kind of parenthesis, as if he had said, this is the true rest, let the weary enjoy it. By *this* we are therefore to understand, not compassion and kindness to the suffering, but obedience to the will of God in general. This is the true rest which I alone can give, and the way to which I have clearly marked out. To *give rest to the weary* means simply to reduce to practice the lesson which God had taught them. This is the way to peace, let those who wish it walk therein. In the last clause, *would* is not a mere auxiliary, but an independent and emphatic verb, *they were not willing.*

13. *And the word of Jehovah was to them rule upon rule, line upon line, a little here, a little there, that they might go, and fall backwards, and be broken, and be snared, and be taken.* The law was given that sin might abound. The only effect of the minute instructions, which they found so irksome, was to aggravate their guilt and condemnation. The terms of the first clause

are repeated from v. 10, and have of course the same meaning in both places.

14. *Therefore* (because your advantages have only made you more rebellious) *hear the word of Jehovah, ye scornful men* (literally *men of scorn*, i. e. despisers of the truth), *the rulers of this people which is in Jerusalem* (or ye rulers of this people who are in Jerusalem). *This people*, here as elsewhere, may be an expression of displeasure and contempt. Jerusalem is mentioned as the seat of government and source of influence. The whole verse invites attention to the solemn warning which follows.

15. *Because ye have said* (in thought or deed if not in word), *we have made a covenant with death, and with hell* (the grave, or the unseen world) *have formed a league; the overflowing scourge, when it passes through, shall not come upon us, for we have made falsehood our refuge, and in fraud we have hid ourselves.* The meaning evidently is, that if their actions were translated into words, this would be their import. The mixed metaphor of an *overflowing scourge* combines two natural and common figures for severe calamity. The *falsehood* mentioned in the last clause is unfaithfulness to God, i. e. wickedness in general, perhaps with an allusion to the falsity or treacherous nature of the hopes built upon it. The translation *under falsehood*, which is given in the English Bible and in some other versions, is neither justified by usage nor required by the connection.

16. *Therefore thus saith the Lord Jehovah, Behold I lay in Zion a stone, a stone of proof, a corner stone of value of a firm foundation; the believer will not be in haste.* To the words of the scoffers are now opposed the words of God himself. Because you say thus and thus, therefore the Lord says in reply what follows. You trust for safety in your own delusions; on the contrary I lay a sure foundation, and no other can be laid. This founda-

tion is the Messiah, to whom it is repeatedly and explicitly applied in the New Testament (Rom. 9: 33. 10: 11. 1 Peter 2: 6). The phrase literally rendered *stone of proof* admits of two interpretations. Some understand by it a stone which was to be the test or standard of comparison for others; but the common explanation is more natural, which makes it mean a stone that has itself been proved or tried and found sufficient. *Will not be in haste*, i. e. will not be impatient, but will trust the promise, even though its execution be delayed. The force of the figures in this verse is much enhanced by the statements of modern travellers in relation to the immense stones still remaining at the foundation of ancient walls. (See particularly Robinson's Palestine, I. 343, 351, 422.)

17. *And I will place judgment for a line and justice for a plummet, and hail shall sweep away the refuge of falsehood, and the hiding-place waters shall overflow.* The meaning of the first clause is, that God would deal with them in strict justice; he would make justice the rule of his proceedings, as the builder regulates his work by the line and plummet. The English Version seems to make judgment or justice not the measure but the thing to be measured. Hail and rain are here used, as in v. 2 above, to denote the divine visitations. The refuge and the hiding-place are those of which the scornful men had boasted in v. 15. To their confident assurance of safety God opposes, first, the only sure foundation which himself had laid, and then the utter destruction which was coming on their own chosen objects of reliance.

18. *And your covenant with death shall be annulled, and your league with hell shall not stand, and the overflowing scourge—for it shall pass through, and ye shall be for it to trample on.* In the last clause, the construction seems to be interrupted. Supposing it to be complete, it may be explained as in the Eng-

lish Version, which makes both the words in question particles of time meaning *when* and *then*. There can be no doubt that the idea of a human invader was before the Prophet's mind; but the mere rhetorical incongruity is not at all at variance with the Prophet's manner. The attempt to reconcile the language with the artificial rules of composition is in this case rendered hopeless by the combination of expressions which cannot be strictly applied to the same subject. An army might trample, but it could not literally overflow; a stream might overflow, but it could not literally trample down. The time perhaps is coming when, even as a matter of taste, the strength and vividness of such mixed metaphors will be considered as outweighing their inaccuracy in relation to an arbitrary standard of correctness or propriety.

19. *As soon* (or *as often*) *as it passes through, it shall take you* (or *carry you away*); *for in the morning, in the morning* (i. e. every morning), *it shall pass through, in the day and in the night, and only vexation* (or *distress*) *shall be the understanding of the thing heard.* The meaning may be that the threatened visitation shall come soon and be frequently repeated. There are three interpretations of the last clause, one of which supposes it to mean, that the mere report of the approaching scourge should fill them with distress; another, that the effect of the report should be unmixed distress; a third, that nothing but a painful experience would enable them to understand the lesson which the Prophet was commissioned to teach them. The last words may of course denote either rumour or revelation. The latter seems to be the meaning in v. 9, where the noun stands connected with the same verb as here. Whether this verb ever means simply to perceive or hear, may be considered doubtful; if not, the preference is due to the third interpretation above given, viz. that nothing but distress or suffering could make them understand or even attend to the message from Jehovah.

20. *For the bed is too short to stretch one's self, and the covering too narrow to wrap one's self.* This is probably a proverbial description of a perplexed and comfortless condition. The connection with the foregoing verse is this: you cannot fully understand the lessons which I teach you now until your bed becomes too short, etc.

21. *For like Mount Perazim shall Jehovah rise up, like the valley in Gibeon shall he rage, to do his work, his strange work; and to perform his task, his strange task.* Into such a condition as that just described they shall be brought, for some of the most fearful scenes of ancient history are yet to be repeated. Interpreters are not agreed as to the precise events referred to in the first clause. The common opinion is, that it alludes to the slaughter of the Philistines described in 2 Sam. 5 : 18–25 and 1 Chron. 14 : 9–16, in the latter of which places *Gibeon* is substituted for *Geba.* The valley meant will then be the valley of Rephaim. That these were foreigners and heathen, only adds to the force of the threatening, by making it to mean that as God had dealt with these in former times, he was now about to deal with the unbelieving and unfaithful sons of Israel. It is indeed not only implied but expressed, that he intended to depart from his usual mode of treating them, in which sense the judgments here denounced are called a *strange work*, i. e. foreign from the ordinary course of divine providence. The idea that punishment is God's strange work because at variance with his goodness, is not only less appropriate in this connection, but inconsistent with the tenor of Scripture, which describes his vindicatory justice as an essential attribute of his nature.

22. *And now scoff not lest your bands be strong; for a consumption and decree* (or *even a decreed consumption*) *I have heard from the Lord Jehovah of Hosts, against* (or *upon*) *the whole earth.*

Bands, i. e. bonds or chains, is a common figure for afflictions and especially for penal sufferings. To strengthen these bands is to aggravate the suffering. The last clause represents the threatened judgments as inevitable, because determined and revealed by God himself. The form of expression is partly borrowed from ch. 10 : 23.

23. *Give ear and hear my voice ; hearken and hear my speech.* This formula invites attention to what follows as a new view of the subject. The remainder of the chapter contains an extended illustration drawn from the processes of agriculture. Interpreters, although agreed as to the import of the figures, are divided with respect to their design and application. Some regard the passage as intended to illustrate, in a general way, the wisdom of the divine dispensations. Others refer it more specifically to the delay of judgment on the sinner, and conceive the doctrine of the passage to be this, that although God is not always punishing, any more than the husbandman is always ploughing or always threshing, he will punish at last. A third interpretation makes the prominent idea to be this, that although God chastises his own people, his ultimate design is not to destroy but to purify and save them. The preference is on the whole due to the second, which supposes the Prophet to explain by this comparison the long forbearance of Jehovah, and to show that this forbearance was no reason for believing that his threatenings would never be fulfilled. As the husbandman ploughs and harrows, sows and plants, before he reaps and threshes, and in threshing employs different modes and different implements, according to the nature of the grain, so God allows the actual infliction of his wrath to be preceded by what seems to be a period of inaction but is really one of preparation, and conforms the strokes themselves to the capacity and guilt of the transgressor.

24. *Does the ploughman plough every day to sow? Does he open and level his ground?* The common version, *all day*, though it seems to be a literal translation, does not convey the sense of the original expression, which is used both here and elsewhere to mean *all the time* or *always*. He may plough a whole day together when he is at it, but he does not plough every day in the year; he has other work to do besides ploughing. (Gill.) The interrogation may be confined to the first clause, and the second construed as an exhortation: (*no*) *let him open and level his ground*. But as there is a difficulty then in explaining what is meant by *opening* the ground, as distinct from opening the furrows with the plough, most interpreters suppose the interrogation to extend through the verse, and make the second clause a repetition of the first, with an additional reference to harrowing. As if he had said, is the ploughman always ploughing; is he always ploughing and harrowing?

25. *Does he not, when he has levelled the surface of it, cast abroad dill, and scatter cummin, and set wheat in rows, and barley (in the place) marked out, and spelt in his border?* That is to say, he attends to all these processes of husbandry successively, with due regard to time and place, and to the various crops to be produced. The words do not denote an indiscriminate sowing, but a careful planting, which is said to be still practised in the oriental culture of wheat, and is thought by many to have been one of the causes of the wonderful fertility of Palestine in ancient times.

26. *So teaches him aright his God instructs him.* This is the form of the Hebrew sentence, in which *his God* is the grammatical subject of both the verbs between which it stands. The English idiom requires the noun to be prefixed, as in the common version. The verse refers even agricultural skill to divine instruction.

27. *For not with the sledge must dill be threshed, or the cart-wheel turned upon cummin; for with the stick must dill be beaten, and cummin with the rod.* Having drawn an illustration from the husbandman's regard to times and seasons, he now derives another from his different modes of threshing out the different kinds of grain. The *semina infirmiora* are not to be separated by the use of the ponderous sledge or wagon, both of which are common in the east, but by that of the flail or switch, as better suited to their nature. The minute description of the oriental threshing-machines belongs more properly to books of archaeology, especially as nothing more is necessary here to the correct understanding of the verse than a just view of the contrast intended between heavy and light threshing.

28. *Bread-corn must be crushed, for he will not be always threshing it; so he drives the wheel of his cart (upon it), but with his horsemen* (or *horses*) *he does not crush it.* The sense of this verse is obscured by an apparent inconsistency between the opening and the closing words. The translation above given supposes a climax beginning in v. 27 and completed here. Dill and cummin must be threshed out with the flail; wheat and barley may be more severely dealt with; they will bear the wheel, but not the hoofs of horses. The first words and the last are then in strict agreement; bread-corn must be bruised, but not with horses' hoofs. This is merely suggested as an additional attempt to elucidate a passage in detail, the general sense of which is clear enough.

29. *Even this* (or *this also*) *from Jehovah of Hosts comes forth; he is wonderful in counsel, great in wisdom.* The literal translation of the last clause is, *he makes counsel wonderful, he makes wisdom great.* As to the meaning of the whole verse, some suppose that the preceding illustration is here applied to the divine dispensations; others, that this is the conclusion of the

illustration itself. On the latter hypothesis, the meaning of the verse is, that the husbandman's treatment of the crop, no less than his preparation of the soil, is a dictate of experience under divine teaching. In the other case, the sense is that the same mode of proceeding, which had just been described as that of a wise husbandman, is also practised by the Most High in the execution of his purposes. Against this, and in favour of the other explanation, it may be suggested, first, that *coming forth* from God is a phrase not so naturally suited to express his own way of acting as the influence which he exerts on others; secondly, that this verse seems to correspond, in form and sense, to v. 27, and to bear the same relation to the different modes of threshing that v. 27 does to the preparation of the ground and the sowing of the seed. Having there said of the latter, that the husbandman is taught of God, he now says of the former, that it also comes forth from the same celestial source. According to the view which has now been taken of v. 29, the general application of the parable to God's dispensations is not formally expressed, but left to the reflection of the reader.

CHAPTER XXIX.

This chapter consists of two parts, parallel to one another, i. e. each containing the same series of promises and threatenings, but in different forms. The prophetic substance or material of both is that Zion should be threatened and assailed yet not destroyed, but on the contrary strengthened and enlarged. These ideas are expressed in the second part much more fully and explicitly than in the first, which must therefore be interpreted according to what follows. In the first part, the threatening is that Zion shall be assailed by enemies and brought very low, vs. 1–4. The promise is that the assailants shall be scattered like dust and chaff, vanish like a dream, and be wholly disappointed in their hostile purpose, vs. 5–8. In the second part, the Prophet brings distinctly into view, as causes of the threatened judgments, the spiritual intoxication and stupor of the people, their blindness to revealed truth, their hypocritical formality, and their presumptuous contempt of God, vs. 9–16. The judgment itself is described as a confounding of their fancied wisdom, v. 14. The added promise is that of an entire revolution, including the destruction of the wicked, and especially of wicked rulers, the restoration of spiritual sight, joy to the meek and poor in spirit, and the final recovery of Israel from a state of alienation and disgrace to the service of Jehovah and to the saving knowledge of the truth, vs. 17–24. The only key to the consistent exposition of the chapter as a whole, is furnished by the hypothesis already stated, that the two parts are parallel, not merely successive, and that the second must explain the first. That the second part describes not physical but spiritual evils, is admitted on all hands, and indeed asserted by the Prophet himself. This description is directly and repeatedly applied in the New Testament to the Jews contemporary with our Saviour. It does not follow from this, that it is a specific and exclusive prophecy respecting them; but it does follow that it must be so interpreted as to include them, which can only be effected by regarding this last part of the chapter as descriptive of the Jews, not at one time merely, but throughout the period of the old dispensation, an assumption fully confirmed by history. The judgment threatened will then be the loss of their peculiar privileges and an exchange of state with others who had been less favoured, involving an extension of the church beyond its ancient bounds, the destruction of the old abuses, and the final restoration of the Jews themselves. If this be the meaning of the second part, it seems to determine that of the first as a figurative expression of the truth, that the church should suffer but not perish, the imagery used for this purpose being borrowed from the actual sieges of Jerusalem. Thus understood, the chapter is prophetic of two great events, the seeming destruction of the ancient church, and its reproduction in a new and far more glorious form, so as not only to include the gentiles in its bounds, but also the converted remnant of God's ancient people.

1. *Woe to Ariel* (or *alas for Ariel*), *Ariel, the city David encamped! Add year to year; let the feasts revolve.* All interpreters agree that *Ariel* is here a name for Zion or Jerusalem, although they greatly differ in the explanation of the name itself. There are two explanations between which interpreters are chiefly divided. One of these makes it mean *lion of God*, i. e. a lionlike champion or hero (2 Sam. 23 : 20. Isai. 33 : 7), here applied to Jerusalem as a city of heroes which should never be subdued. The other hypothesis explains it, from an Arabic analogy, to mean the *hearth* or *fire-place of God*, in which sense it seems to be applied to the altar by Ezekiel (43 : 15, 16), and the extension of the name to the whole city is the more natural because Isaiah himself says of Jehovah, that *his fire is in Zion and his furnace in Jerusalem* (ch. 31 : 9). *The city David encamped* is an elliptical expression not unlike the Hebrew one, in which the relative must be supplied. Here again there seems to be a twofold allusion to David's siege and conquest of Zion (2 Sam. 5 : 7), and to his afterwards encamping i. e. dwelling there (2 Sam. 5 : 9). Most interpreters explain the words *add year to year*, as simply meaning, let the years roll on with the accustomed routine of ceremonial services. The last phrase *let the feasts revolve*, corresponds exactly to the one preceding, *add year to year.*

2. *And I will distress Ariel, and there shall be sadness and sorrow, and it shall be to me as Ariel.* Let the years revolve and

the usual routine continue, but the time is coming when it shall be interrupted. The words translated *sadness and sorrow* are collateral derivatives from one root. The last clause may be either a continuation of the threatening or an added promise. If the former, the meaning probably is, *it shall be indeed a furnace* or *an altar*, i. e. when the fire of affliction or divine wrath shall be kindled on it. If the latter, *it shall still be a city of heroes*, and as such withstand its enemies. Or, combining both the senses of the enigmatical name, it shall burn like a furnace, but resist like a lion.

3. *And I will camp against thee round about* (literally, *as a ring* or *circle*), *and push against thee* (or *press upon thee with*) *a post* (or *body of troops*), *and raise against thee ramparts* (or *entrenchments*). The siege of Ariel is now represented as the work of God himself, which, although it admits of explanation as referring merely to his providential oversight and control, seems here to be significant, as intimating that the siege described is not a literal one.

4. *And thou shalt be brought down, out of the ground shalt thou speak, and thy speech shall be low out of the dust, and thy voice shall be like* (*the voice of*) *a spirit, out of the ground, and out of the dust shall thy speech mutter.* The simple meaning naturally suggested by the words is, that the person here addressed, to wit, the city or its population, should be weakened and humbled. The last verb properly denotes any feeble inarticulate sound, and is applied in ch. 10 : 14 and 38 : 14 to the chirping or twittering of birds.

5. *Then shall be like fine dust the multitude of thy strangers, and like passing chaff the multitude of the terrible ones, and it shall be in a moment suddenly.* It is now very commonly agreed, that this verse describes the sudden and complete dispersion of their

enemies. The absence of *but* at the beginning, or some other indication that the writer is about to pass from threats to promises, although it renders the connection more obscure, increases the effect of the description. The terms of this verse readily suggest the sudden fall of the Assyrian host, nor is there any reason for denying that the Prophet had a view to it in choosing his expressions. But that this is an explicit and specific prophecy of that event is much less probable, as well because the terms are in themselves appropriate to any case of sudden and complete dispersion, as because the context contains language wholly inappropriate to the slaughter of Sennacherib's army. These considerations, although negative and inconclusive in themselves, tend strongly to confirm the supposition founded on the last part of the chapter, that the first contains a strong metaphorical description of the evils which Jerusalem should suffer at the hands of enemies, but without exclusive reference to any one siege, or to sieges in the literal sense at all. That the evils which the last part of the chapter brings to light are of a spiritual nature, and not confined to any single period, is a fact which seems to warrant the conclusion, or at least to raise a strong presumption, that the Ariel of this passage is Zion or Jerusalem, considered only as the local habitation of the church.

6. *From with* (i. e. from the presence of) *Jehovah of hosts shall it be visited with thunder and earthquake and great noise, tempest and storm and flame of devouring fire.* Some refer this to the singular phenomena which are said to have preceded and accompanied the taking of Jerusalem by Titus. This application may be admitted, in the same sense and on the same ground with the allusion to Sennacherib's host in the foregoing verse. But that the prophecy is not a prophecy of either catastrophe, may be inferred from the fact that neither is described in the context. Indeed, the direct application of this

verse to the fall of Jerusalem is wholly inadmissible, since the preceding verse describes the assailants as dispersed, and this appears to continue the description.

7. *Then shall be as a dream, a vision of the night, the multitude of all the nations fighting against Ariel, even all that fight against her and her munition and distress her.* The modern writers generally understand both this verse and the next as meaning that the enemy himself should be wholly disappointed and his vain hopes vanish as a dream. But the true sense appears to be that these two verses are distinct though similar, the enemy being first compared to a dream and then to a dreamer. He who threatens your destruction shall vanish like a dream. He who threatens your destruction shall awake as from a dream, and find himself cheated of his expectations. These seem to be the two comparisons intended, both of which are perfectly appropriate, and one of which might readily suggest the other

8. *And it shall be as when the hungry dreams, and lo he eats, and he awakes, and his soul is empty; and as when the thirsty dreams, and lo he drinks, and he awakes, and lo he is faint and his soul craving: so shall be the multitude of all the nations that fight against Mount Zion.* In this verse *soul* is twice used in the not uncommon sense of *appetite*, first described as *empty* (i. e. unsatisfied) and then as *craving*. A striking and affecting parallel from real life has been quoted from Mungo Park's journals. "No sooner had I shut my eyes than fancy would convey me to the streams and rivers of my native land. There, as I wandered along the verdant bank, I surveyed the clear stream with transport, and hastened to swallow the delightful draught; but alas! disappointment awakened me, and I found myself a lonely captive, perishing of thirst amid the wilds of Africa."

9. *Waver and wonder! be merry and blind! They are drunk, but not with wine; they reel, but not with strong drink.* Here begins the description of the moral and spiritual evils which were the occasion of the judgments previously threatened. In the first clause, the Prophet describes the condition of the people by exhorting them ironically to continue in it; in the second, he seems to turn away from them and address the spectators. The terms of the first clause are very obscure. The second imperative may be understood as indicating the effect or consequence of that before it: refuse to believe, but you will only be the more astonished; continue to enjoy yourselves, but it will only be the means of blinding you. The express description of the drunkenness as spiritual shows that where no such explanation is added (as in ch. 28 : 1, 7), the terms are to be literally understood. By spiritual drunkenness we are probably to understand unsteadiness of conduct and a want of spiritual discernment.

10. *For Jehovah hath poured out upon you a spirit of deep sleep and hath shut your eyes; the prophets and your heads* (or *even your heads*) *the seers hath he covered.* On the agency here ascribed to God, see the exposition of ch. 6 : 9, 10. The two ideas expressed in the parallel clauses are those of bandaging the eyes and covering the head so as to obstruct the sight. In the latter case the Prophet makes a special application of the figure to the chiefs or religious leaders of the people, as if he had said, he hath shut your eyes, and covered your heads, viz. the prophets.

11. *And the vision of all* (or *of the whole*) *is* (or *has become*) *to you like the words of the sealed writing, which they give to one knowing writing, saying Pray read this, and he says, I cannot, for it is sealed.* The *vision of all* may either mean *of all the prophets*, or collectively *all vision*, or the *vision of all things*,

i. e. prophecy on all subjects. The English word *book* does not exactly represent the Hebrew word, which originally signifies writing in general or anything written, and is here used as we might use *document* or the still more general term *paper.* In the phrase *one knowing writing*, the last word seems to mean writing in general, and the whole phrase one who understands it or knows how to read it. The application of the simile becomes clear in the next verse.

12. *And the writing is given to one who knows not writing, saying, Pray read this, and he says, I know not writing.* The common version, *I am not learned*, is too comprehensive and indefinite. A man might read a letter without being learned, at least in the modern sense, although the word was once the opposite of illiterate or wholly ignorant. In this case it is necessary to the full effect of the comparison, that the phrase should be distinctly understood to mean, *I cannot read.* The comparison itself represents the people as alike incapable of understanding the divine communications, or rather as professing incapacity to understand them, some upon the general ground of ignorance, and others on the ground of their obscurity.

13. *And the Lord said, Because this people draws near with its mouth, and with its lips they honour me, and its heart it puts* (or *keeps*) *far from me, and their fearing me is* (or *has become*) *a precept of men,* (*a thing*) *taught.* The conclusion follows in the next verse. The singular and plural pronouns are promiscuously used in this verse with respect to Israel considered as a nation and an individual. At the end of the verse the English Version has, *taught by the precept of men;* but a simpler construction is the one given above. The last clause might be simply understood to mean, that they served God merely in obedience to human authority. It would then of course imply no censure

on the persons thus commanding, but only on the motives of those by whom they were obeyed. In our Saviour's application of the passage to the hypocrites of his day (Matthew 15 : 7–9), he explains their teachings as human corruptions of the truth, by which the commandment of God was made of none effect. The expressions of the Prophet may have been so chosen as to be applicable either to the reign of Hezekiah, when the worship of Jehovah was enforced by human authority, or to the time of Christ, when the rulers of the people had corrupted and made void the law by their additions. The apparent reference, in this description, to the Jews not at one time only but throughout their history, tends to confirm the supposition, that the subject of the prophecy is not any one specific juncture, and that the first part of the chapter is not a prediction of any one siege of Jerusalem exclusively.

14. *Therefore, behold, I will add* (or *continue*) *to treat this people strangely, very strangely, and with strangeness, and the wisdom of its wise ones shall be lost* (or *perish*), *and the prudence of its prudent ones shall hide itself*, i. e. for shame, or simply *disappear*. This is the conclusion of the sentence which begins with the preceding verse. *Because they draw near etc. therefore I will add etc.* The nature of the judgment here denounced seems to show that the corruption of the people was closely connected with undue reliance upon human wisdom. (Compare ch. 5 : 21.)

15. *Woe unto those* (or *alas for those*) *going deep from Jehovah to hide counsel* (i. e. laying their plans deep in the hope of hiding them from God), *and their works* (*are*) *in the dark, and they say, Who sees us and who knows us?* This is a further description of the people or their leaders, as not only wise in their own conceit, but as impiously hoping to deceive God or elude his notice. The absurdity of such an expectation is exposed

in the following verse. In the last clause of this, the interrogative form implies negation.

16. *Your perversion! Is the potter to be reckoned as the clay that the thing made should say of its maker, he made me not, and the thing formed say of its former, he does not understand?* The attempt to hide anything from God implies that he has not a perfect knowledge of his creatures, which is practically to reduce the maker and the thing made to a level. With this inversion or perversion of the natural relation between God and man, the Prophet charges them in one word. Most of the recent writers are agreed in construing the first word as an exclamation, *oh your perverseness!* i. e. how perverse you are! in which sense it had long before been paraphrased by Luther. Both the derivation of the word, however, and the context here seem to demand the sense *perversion* rather than *perverseness.* The verse seems intended not so much to rebuke their perverse disposition, as to show that by their conduct they subverted the distinction between creature and creator, or placed them in a preposterous relation to each other. Thus understood, the word may be thus paraphrased: (*this is*) *your* (*own*) *perversion* (*of the truth*, or of the true relation between God and man).

17. *Is it not yet a very little while, and Lebanon shall turn* (or *be turned*) *to the fruitful field, and the fruitful field be reckoned to the forest* (i. e. reckoned as belonging to it, or as being itself a forest)? The negative interrogation is one of the strongest forms of affirmation. The metaphors of this verse evidently signify a great revolution, a mutual change of condition, the first becoming last and the last first. If, as we have seen sufficient reason to believe, the previous context has respect to the Jews under the old dispensation, nothing can be more appropriate or natural than to understand the verse before as

foretelling the excision of the unbelieving Jews and the admission of the Gentiles to the church.

18. *And in that day shall the deaf hear the words of the book* (or *writing*), *and out of obscurity and darkness shall the eyes of the blind see.* This is a further description of the change just predicted under other figures. As the forest was to be transformed into a fruitful field, so the blind should be made to see and the deaf to hear. There is an obvious allusion to the figure of the sealed book or writing in vs. 13, 14. The Jews could only plead obscurity or ignorance as an excuse for not understanding the revealed will of God. The Gentiles, in their utter destitution, might be rather likened to the blind who cannot read, however clear the light or plain the writing, and the deaf who cannot even hear what is read by others. But the time was coming when they, who would not break the seal or learn the letters of the written word, should be abandoned to their chosen state of ignorance, while on the other hand, the blind and deaf, whose case before seemed hopeless, should begin to see and hear the revelation once entirely inaccessible. The perfect adaptation of this figurative language to express the new relation of the Jews and Gentiles after the end of the old economy affords a new proof that the prophecy relates to that event.

19. *And the humble shall add joy* (i. e. shall rejoice more and more) *in Jehovah, and the poor among men in the Holy One of Israel shall rejoice.* As the preceding verse describes the happy effect of the promised change upon the intellectual views of those who should experience it, so this describes its influence in the promotion of their happiness. Not only should the ignorant be taught of God, but the wretched should be rendered happy in the enjoyment of his favour.

20. *For the violent is at an end, and the scoffer ceaseth, and all*

the watchers for injustice are cut off. A main cause of the happiness foretold will be the weakening or destruction of all evil influences, here reduced to the three great classes of violent wrong-doing, impious contempt of truth and goodness, and malignant treachery or fraud, which watches for the opportunity of doing evil, with as constant vigilance as ought to be employed in watching for occasions of redressing wrong and doing justice. This is a change which, to some extent, has always attended the diffusion of the true religion.

21. *Making a man a sinner for a word, and for him disputing in the gate they laid a snare, and turned aside the righteous through deceit.* An amplification of the last phrase in the foregoing verse. Some understand the first clause to mean, *seducing people into sin by their words.* It is much more common to explain the whole phrase to mean unjustly condemning a man in his cause, which agrees well with the obvious allusion to forensic process in the remainder of the verse. The English and many other early versions explain the clause to mean accusing or condemning men for a mere error of the tongue or lips. The general sense is plain, viz. that they embrace all opportunities and use all arts to wrong the guiltless. Most of the modern writers take the word translated *disputing*, in the sense of arguing, pleading *in the gate*, i. e. the court, often held in the gates of oriental cities. The other explanation supposes the gate to be mentioned only as a place of public concourse. By the *turning aside* of the righteous (i. e. of the party who is in the right) we are here to understand the depriving him of that which is his due. For the meaning and usage of the figure, see the commentary on ch. 10:2. The last words have been variously understood to mean *through falsehood* (with particular reference to false testimony), or by means of a judgment which is null and void, or for nothing i. e. without just cause. In either case the phrase describes the perversion or abuse of jus-

tice by dishonest means, and thus agrees with the expressions used in the foregoing clauses.

22. *Therefore thus saith Jehovah to the house of Jacob, he who redeemed Abraham, Not now shall Jacob be ashamed, and not now shall his face turn pale.* The Hebrew phrase *not now* does not imply that it shall be so hereafter, but on the contrary that it shall be so no more. The phrase *redeemed Abraham* may be naturally understood, either as signifying deliverance from danger and the divine protection generally, or in a higher sense as signifying Abraham's conversion and salvation. Shame and fear are here combined as strong and painful emotions from which Jacob should be henceforth free. Some understand by Jacob here the patriarch himself, poetically represented as beholding and sympathizing with the fortunes of his own descendants. Most interpreters suppose the name to be employed like *Israel* in direct application to the race itself.

23. *For in his seeing* (i. e. when he sees) *his children, the work of my hands, in the midst of him, they shall sanctify my name, and sanctify* (or *yes they shall sanctify*) *the Holy One of Jacob, and the God of Israel they shall fear.* The verse thus translated according to its simplest and most obvious sense has much perplexed interpreters. The difficulties chiefly urged are, first, that Jacob should be said to see his children *in the midst of himself;* secondly, that *his* thus seeing them should be the occasion of *their* glorifying God. What follows is suggested as a possible solution of this exegetical enigma. We have seen reason, wholly independent of this verse, to believe that the immediately preceding context has respect to the excision of the Jews and the vocation of the Gentiles. Now the latter are described in the New Testament as Abraham's (and consequently Jacob's) spiritual progeny, as such distinguished from his natural descendants. May not these adventitious or adopted children of the patriarch,

constituted such by the electing grace of God, be here intended by the phrase, *the work of my hands?* If so, the whole may thus be paraphrased: when he (the patriarch, supposed to be again alive and gazing at his offspring) shall behold his children (not by nature but) created such by me, in the midst of him (i. e. in the midst, or in the place, of his natural descendants), they (i. e. he and his descendants jointly) shall unite in glorifying God as the author of this great revolution. This explanation of the verse is the more natural, because such would no doubt be the actual feelings of the patriarch and his descendants, if he should really be raised from the dead, and permitted to behold what God has wrought, with respect both to his natural and spiritual offspring. To the passage thus explained a striking parallel is found in ch. 49 : 18–21, where the same situation and emotions here ascribed to the patriarch are predicated of the church personified, to whom the Prophet says, 'Lift up thine eyes round about and behold, all these gather themselves together, they come to thee. The children which thou shalt have after thou hast lost the others shall say etc. Then shalt thou say in thine heart, who hath begotten me these, seeing I have lost my children, and am desolate, a captive, and removing to and fro? And who hath brought up these? Behold, I alone was left; these, where were they?' For the use of the word *sanctify* in reference to God as its object, see the note on ch. 8 : 13. The *Holy One of Jacob* is of course identical in meaning with the *Holy One of Israel*, which last phrase is explained in the note on ch. 1 : 4. The emphatic mention of the Holy One of Jacob and the God of Israel, as the object to be sanctified, implies a relation still existing between all believers and their spiritual ancestry, as well as a relation of identity between the Jewish and the Christian Church.

24. *Then shall the erring in spirit know wisdom, and the murmurers* (or *rebels*) *shall receive instruction.* These words would

be perfectly appropriate as a general description of the reclaiming and converting influence to be exerted upon men in general. But under this more vague and comprehensive sense, the context, and especially the verse immediately preceding, seems to show that there is one more specific and significant included. If the foregoing verse predicts the reception of the Gentiles into the family of Israel, and if this reception, as we learn from the New Testament, was connected with the disinheriting of most of the natural descendants, who are nevertheless to be restored hereafter, then the promise of this final restoration is a stroke still wanting to complete the fine prophetic picture now before us. That finishing stroke is given in this closing verse, which adds to the promise that the Gentiles shall become the heirs of Israel, another that the heirs of Israel according to the flesh shall themselves be restored to their long lost heritage, not by excluding their successors in their turn, but by peaceful and brotherly participation with them. This application of the last part of the chapter to the calling of the Gentiles and the restoration of the Jews has been founded, as the reader will observe, not on on any forced accommodation of particular expressions, but on various detached points, all combining to confirm this exegetical hypothesis, as the only one which furnishes a key to the consistent exposition of the chapter, as a concatenated prophecy without abrupt transitions or a mixture of incongruous materials.

CHAPTER XXX.

This chapter contains an exposure of the sin and folly of ancient Israel in seeking foreign aid against their enemies, to the neglect of God, their rightful sovereign and protector. The costume of the prophecy is borrowed from the circumstances and events of Isaiah's own times. Thus Egypt is mentioned in the first part of the chapter as the chosen ally of the people, and Assyria in the last part as the dreaded enemy. There is no need however of restricting what is said to that period exclusively. The presumption, as in all such cases, is that the description was designed to be more general, although it may contain allusions to particular emergencies. Reliance upon human aid, involving a distrust of the divine promises, was a crying sin of the ancient church, not at one time only, but throughout her history. To denounce such sins, and threaten them with condign punishment, was no small part of the prophetic office. The chronological hypotheses assumed by different writers with respect to this chapter are erroneous only because too specific and exclusive. It was clearly intended to reprove the sin of seeking foreign aid without divine permission; but there is nothing in the terms of the reproof confining it to any single case of the offence. The chapter may be divided into three parts. In the first, the Prophet shows the sin and folly of relying upon Egypt, no doubt for protection against Assyria, as these were the two great powers between which Israel was continually oscillating, almost constantly at war with one and in alliance with the other, vs. 1–7. In the last part, he describes the Assyrian power as broken by an immediate divine interposition, precluding the necessity of any human aid, vs. 27–33. In the larger intervening part, he shows the connection of this distrust of God and reliance on the creature with the general character and spiritual state of the people, as unwilling to receive instruction, as dishonest and oppressive, making severe judgments necessary as a prelude to the glorious change which God would eventually bring to pass, vs. 8–26.

1. *Woe to the disobedient children, saith Jehovah,* (so disobedient as) *to form* (or execute) *a plan and not from me, and to weave a web, but not* (*of*) *my Spirit, for the sake of adding sin to sin.* Here, as in ch. 1 : 2, Israel's filial relation to Jehovah is particularly mentioned as an aggravation of his ingratitude and disobedience. The infinitives express *the respect in which,* or the *result with which,* they had rebelled against Jehovah. The relative construction of the English Version does not materially change the sense. The simple meaning seems to be that of multiplying or accumulating guilt.

2. *Those walking to go down to Egypt, and my mouth they have not consulted* (literally *asked*), *to take refuge in the strength of Pharaoh, and to trust in the shadow of Egypt.* Motion towards Egypt is commonly spoken of in Scripture as downward. To *ask the mouth,* or *at the mouth,* of the Lord is a phrase used elsewhere in the sense of seeking a divine decision or response.

3, 4. *And the strength of Egypt shall be to you for shame and the trust in the shadow of Egypt for confusion. For his chiefs are in Zoan, and his ambassadors arrive at Hanes.* As to the site and political importance of *Zoan* or *Tains,* see the note on ch. 19 : 11.

5. *All are ashamed of a people who cannot profit them,* (*a people*) *not for help and not for profit, but for shame, and also for disgrace.* The Hebrew construction is, they are not a profit or a help, *for* (on the contrary) they are a disgrace and a reproach.

6. *The burden of the beasts of the south, in a land of suffering and distress, whence (are) the adder and the fiery flying serpent; they are carrying* (or *about to carry*) *on the shoulder of young asses their wealth, and on the hump of camels their treasures, to a people* (or *for the sake of a people*) *who cannot profit.* The Prophet sees the ambassadors of Israel carrying costly presents through the waste howling wilderness, for the purpose of securing the Egyptian alliance. Some apply the description to the emigration of the Jews into Egypt in the days of Jeremiah. This may be alluded to, but cannot be the exclusive subject of the passage. The most natural construction of the first clause is to take it as an exclamation (*oh the burden of the beasts! what a burden to the beasts!*) or as an absolute nominative (*as to the burden of the beasts*). The beasts meant are the asses and the camels of the following clause, called *beasts of the south* because travelling in that direction. The *land* meant is the interjacent desert described by Moses in similar terms (Deut. 1 : 19. 8 : 15). *Land of suffering* denotes a land of danger and privation, such as the great Arabian desert is to travellers. The lions and vipers of this verse belong to the poetical description of the desert.

7. *And Egypt* (or *the Egyptians*)—*in vain and to no purpose shall they help. Therefore I cry concerning this, their strength is to sit still.* Most of the modern writers understand the last clause as contrasting the pretensions of Egypt with its actual performances, the opposite ideas being those of arrogance or insolence and quiescence or in action. Tho general meaning may be considered as determined by the other clause.

8. *And now go, write it with them on a tablet and inscribe it in a book, and let it be for a future day, forever, to eternity.* This, like the similar precaution in ch. 8 : 1, was intended to verify the fact of the prediction after the event. Most interpreters

suppose two distinct inscriptions to be here required, one on a solid tablet for public exhibition, and the other on parchment or the like for preservation. But it is more natural to understand the words as equivalents.

9. *For a people of rebellion* (a rebellious people) *is it, lying* (or *denying*) *children, children* (*who*) *are not willing to learn the law of Jehovah.* The English Version makes this verse state the substance of the inscription, *that this is a rebellious people etc.*,

10. *Who say to the seers, Ye shall not see, and to the viewers, ye shall not view for us right things; speak unto us smooth things, view deceits.* There is great difficulty in translating this verse literally, as the two Hebrew verbs, meaning to *see*, have no equivalents in English, which of themselves suggest the idea of prophetic revelation. The common version (*see not, prophesy not*), although it conveys the true sense substantially, leaves out of view the near relation of the two verbs to each other in the original. In the translation above given, *view* is introduced merely as a synonyme of *see*, both being here used to express supernatural or prophetic vision. With this use of the verbal noun (*seer*) we are all familiar through the English Bible. This is of course not given as the actual language of the people, but as the tendency and spirit of their acts. *Smooth things* or *words* is a common figurative term for flatteries. Luther's expressive version is, *preach soft to us.*

11. *Depart from the way, swerve from the path, cause to cease from before us the Holy One of Israel.* The request is not that they would go out of the people's way, so as no longer to prevent their going on in sin, but that they would get out of their own way, i. e. wander from it or forsake it. *Cause to cease from before us*, i. e. remove from our sight. It was

a common opinion with the older writers, that this clause alludes to Isaiah's frequent repetition of the name *Holy One of Israel*, and contains a request that they might hear it no more. But the modern interpreters appear to be agreed that the allusion is not to the name but the person.

12. *Therefore thus saith the Holy One of Israel, Because of your rejecting* (or *despising*) *this word, and* (*because*) *ye have trusted in oppression and perverseness, and have relied thereon.* The *word* here mentioned is no doubt the *law* of v. 9, both being common epithets of revelation generally, and of particular divine communications. (See the note on ch. 2 : 3.)

13. *Therefore shall this iniquity be to you like a breach falling* (or *ready to fall*) *swelling out in a high wall, whose breaking may come suddenly, at* (*any*) *instant.* The image is that of a wall which is rent or cracked and bulges out. This interpretation conveys the idea of a gradual yet sudden catastrophe, which is admirably suited to the context. It is also true that the idea of a downfall springing from internal causes is more appropriate in this connection than that of mere external violence however overwhelming.

14. *And it* (the wall) *is broken like the breaking of a potter's vessel, broken unsparingly* (or *without mercy*), *so that there is not found in its fracture* (or *among its fragments*) *a sherd to take up fire from a hearth, and to skim* (or *dip up*) *water from a pool.* A potter's vessel, literally, *vessel of the potters. Sherd* is an old English word, now seldom used, meaning a broken piece of pottery or earthenware, and found more frequently in the compound form of *potsherd.*

15. *For thus saith the Lord Jehovah, the Holy One of Israel, in returning* (or *conversion*) *and rest shall ye be saved, in remain-*

ing quiet and in confidence shall be your strength; and ye would not (or *were not willing*). This overwhelming judgment would be strictly just because they had been fully admonished of the way of safety. For the spiritual usage of the verb *returning*, see the note on ch. 1 : 27.

16. *And ye said, No, for we will flee upon horses; therefore shall ye flee; and upon the swift will we ride; therefore shall your pursuers be swift.* The hope here ascribed to the people is not simply that of going swiftly, but of escaping from the dangers threatened.

17. *One thousand from before the rebuke* (or *menace*) *of one, from before the rebuke of five shall ye flee, until ye are left like a mast* (or *pole*) *on the top of the mountain, and like the signal on the hill.* The allusion may be simply to the similar appearance of a lofty and solitary tree, or the common idea may be that of a *flag-staff*, which might be found in either situation.

18. *And therefore will Jehovah wait to have mercy upon you, and therefore will he rise up* (or *be exalted*) *to pity you, for a God of judgment is Jehovah; blessed are all that wait for him.* The apparent incongruity of this promise with the threatening which immediately precedes, has led to various constructions of the first clause. The simplest and most probable conclusion seems to be that *therefore* refers, as in many other cases, to a remoter antecedent than the words immediately before it. As if the Prophet paused at this point and reviewing his denunciations said, Since this is so, since you must perish if now dealt with strictly, God will allow you space for repentance, he will wait to be gracious, he will exalt himself by showing mercy. Another difficulty of the same kind has arisen from the next clause, where the justice of God seems to be given as a reason for showing mercy. That the clause does not relate

to righteousness or justice in the strict sense, appears plain from the added benediction of those who trust Jehovah. One point is universally admitted, namely, that somewhere in this verse is the transition from the tone of threatening to that of promise. The question where it shall be fixed, though interesting, does not affect the general connection or the import of the passage as a whole.

19. *For the people in Zion shall dwell in Jerusalem; thou shalt weep no more; he will be very gracious unto thee at the voice of thy cry; as he hears it he will answer thee.* The position of the first verb in this English sentence leaves it doubtful whether it is to be construed with what follows or what goes before. Precisely the same ambiguity exists in the original, which may either mean that the people who are now in Zion shall dwell in Jerusalem, or that the people shall dwell in Zion, in Jerusalem. This last is the most natural construction. It is adopted in the English version, but with a needless variation of the particle, *in Zion at Jerusalem.* In the translation above given the Hebrew order is restored.

20. *And the Lord will give you bread of affliction and water of oppression, and no more shall thy teachers hide themselves, and thine eyes shall see thy teachers.* God would afflict them outwardly, but would not deprive them of their spiritual privileges; or, there should be a famine of bread, but not of the word of the Lord (Amos 8: 11). The word *teachers* is probably a designation or description of the prophets, with particular reference, as some suppose, to their reappearance after a period of severe persecution or oppression. (See Ezek. 33: 22.)

21. *And thine ears shall hear a word from behind thee, saying, This is the way, walk ye in it, when ye turn to the right and when ye turn to the left.* *Word* is an idiomatic expression used where

we should say *one speaking*. The direction of the voice *from behind* is commonly explained by saying, that the image is borrowed from the practice of shepherds going behind their flocks, or nurses behind children, to observe their motions. A much more natural solution is that their guides were to be before them, but that when they declined from the right way their backs would be turned to them, and consequently the warning voice would be heard behind them. The meaning of the call is, this is the way which you have left, come back to it. As if he had said, this warning will be necessary, *for* you will certainly depart at times from the path of safety. This idea may, however, be considered as included or implied in the usual translation *when*.

22. *And ye shall defile* (i. e. treat as unclean) *the covering of thy idols of silver and the case of thy image of gold; thou shalt scatter them* (or *abhor them*) *as an abominable thing. Away! shalt thou say to it.* The remarkable alternation of the singular and plural, both in the nouns and verbs of this sentence, is retained in the translation. The gold and silver, both in Hebrew and English, may qualify either the image or the covering. The latter is more probable, because the covering would scarcely have been mentioned, if it had not been commonly of greater value than the body of the idol. The words translated *idol* and *image* strictly denote *graven* and *molten* images respectively, but are constantly employed as poetical equivalents.

23. *And he shall give the rain of thy seed* (i. e. the rain necessary to its growth), *with which thou shalt sow the ground, and bread, the produce of the ground, and it shall be fat and rich; thy cattle shall feed that day in an enlarged pasture.* This is a promise of increased prosperity after a season of privation, and was often verified.

24. *And the oxen and the asses working the ground shall eat salted provender which has been winnowed* (literally, *which one winnows*) *with the sieve and fan.* The meaning is that the domesticated animals shall fare as well as men in other times. The word *ear*, used in the English Version, is an obsolete derivative of the Latin *aro* to plough. The word translated *provender* is commonly supposed to denote here a mixture of different kinds of grain, and the one joined with it a seasoning of salt or acid herbs, peculiarly grateful to the stomachs of cattle.

25. *And there shall be, on every high mountain, and on every elevated hill, channels, streams of water, in the day of great slaughter, in the falling of towers* (or *when towers fall*). The meaning seems to be, that water shall flow where it never flowed before, a common figure in the Prophets for a great change, and especially a change for the better. The same sense is no doubt to be attached to the previous descriptions of abundance and fertility. There are no sufficient data in the text itself for any specific and exclusive application. All that can certainly be gathered from the words is, that a period of war and carnage should be followed by one of abundance and prosperity.

26. *And the light of the moon shall be as the light of the sun, and the light of the sun shall be sevenfold, as the light of seven days, in the day of Jehovah's binding up the breach of his people, and the stroke of his wound he will heal.* Instead of the usual words for sun and moon, we have here two poetical expressions, one denoting *heat* and the other *white.* The Prophet's language is designed, not merely to express great joy, but to describe a change in the face of nature, as an emblem of some great revolution in the state of society. (Compare ch. 13 : 10, 13.) It is therefore another item added to the catalogue of previous similes or comparisons, all denoting the same thing, yet showing

by their very diversity that they denote it only in a tropical or figurative manner.

27. *Behold, the name of Jehovah cometh from afar, burning his anger and heavy the ascent* (of smoke): *his lips are full of wrath and his tongue as a devouring fire.* By the *name of Jehovah* we are not simply to understand Jehovah himself, but Jehovah as revealed in word or act, and therefore glorious.

28. *And his breath* (or *spirit*), *like an overflowing stream, shall divide as far as the neck, to sift the nations in the sieve of falsehood, and a misleading bridle on the jaws of the people.* There are here three metaphors employed to express the same general idea, those of a flood, a sieve, and a bridle. The whole verse is a threatening against Jehovah's enemies. The verb translated *divide* is here explained by the English Version in the sense of *reaching to the midst;* but most interpreters adopt the explanation that the water rising to the neck divides the body into two unequal parts. The metaphor itself, as in ch. 8 : 8, denotes extreme danger. The phrase *sieve of falsehood,* is ambiguous. It may either mean *wickedness* in general, i. e. the instrument by which the wicked and especially the false are to be punished; or the *sieve of ruin,* pointing out the issue of the process, as the other version does the object upon which it acts. Gill's paraphrase is, "they were to be sifted, not with a good and profitable sieve, which retains the corn and shakes out the chaff, or so as to have some taken out and spared, but with a sieve that lets all through, and so be brought to nothing." The last clause may be understood in the sense of *leading astray* or in the wrong direction.

29. *The song* (or *singing*) *shall be to you* (i. e. your song shall be) *like the night of the consecration of a feast, and joy of heart* (i. e. your joy shall be) *like* (that of) *one marching with the pipe*

(or *flute*) *to go into the mountain of Jehovah, to the Rock of Israel.* The night may be particularly mentioned in the first clause, either because all the Mosaic festivals began in the evening, or with special allusion to the Passover, which is described in the law (Ex. 12 : 42) as *a night to be much observed unto the Lord*, as *that night of the Lord to be observed of all the children of Israel in their generations.* This verse gives an interesting glimpse of ancient usage as to the visitation of the temple at the greater yearly festivals. The *Rock of Israel* is not Mount Zion or Moriah, but Jehovah himself, to whose presence they resorted, as appears from 2 Samuel 23 : 3.

30, 31. *And Jehovah shall cause to be heard the majesty of his voice, and the descent of his arm shall he cause to be seen, with indignation of anger and a flame of devouring fire, scattering and rain and hailstones* (literally *stone of hail*). *For at the voice of Jehovah shall Assyria* (or *the Assyrian*) *be broken, with the rod shall he smite.* The word translated *broken* is commonly applied, in a figurative sense, to the breaking of the spirit or the courage by alarm. Here some translate it *beaten down*, as in the English Version. There are two constructions of the last clause, one continuing *Assyria* as the subject of the verb, the other referring it to *Jehovah.* The past form given to the verb in the English Version (*smote*) seems entirely unauthorized by usage or the context. Even if Assyria be the subject of the clause, it is clear that the Prophet speaks of her oppression as being, in whole or in part, still future to his own perceptions. The express mention of Assyria in this verse, though it does not prove it to have been from the beginning the specific subject of the prophecy, does show that it was a conspicuous object in Isaiah's view, as an example both of danger and deliverance, and that at this point he concentrates his prophetic vision on this object as a signal illustration of the general truths which he has been announcing.

32. *And every passage of the rod of doom, which Jehovah will lay* (or *cause to rest*) *upon him, shall be with tabrets and harps, and with fights of shaking it is fought therein.* There is the same diversity of judgment here as in the foregoing verse, with respect to the question whether the rod mentioned in the first clause is the rod which the Assyrian wielded, or the rod which smote himself. On the former supposition, the sense would seem to be, that in every place through which the rod of the oppressor had before passed there should now be heard the sound of joyful music. The reference to Jehovah's judgments on Assyria is recommended by the reasons above given for applying the last words of v. 31 to the same catastrophe. Assuming therefore that the clause before us was likewise intended to be so applied, the sense would seem to be that every passage of Jehovah's rod (i. e. every stroke which passes from it to the object) will be hailed, by those whom the Assyrian had oppressed, with joy and exultation. The common version, *grounded staff*, is almost unintelligible.

33. *For arranged since yesterday is Tophet; even it for the king is prepared; he has deepened, he has widened* (*it*); *its pile fire and wood in plenty; the breath of Jehovah, like a stream of brimstone, kindles it.* It is universally agreed that the destruction of the Assyrian king is here described as a burning of his body at a stake or on a funeral-pile. But whether the king mentioned be an individual king or an ideal representative of all, and whether this be a mere figurative representation of his temporal destruction or a premonition of his doom hereafter, are disputed questions. Tophet is well known to have been the name of a place in the valley of Hinnom where children were sacrificed to Moloch, and on that account afterwards defiled by the deposit of the filth of the city, to consume which constant fires were maintained. Hence, by a natural association, Tophet, as well as the more general name, Valley of Hinnom, was applied by

the later Jews to the place of future torment. The question whether it is here used to describe the place of future torments or as a mere poetical description of the temporal destruction of the king of Assyria, is the less important, as the language must in either case be figurative, and can teach us nothing therefore as to the real circumstances either of the first or second death. Considering however the appalling grandeur of the images presented, and our Saviour's use of similar expressions to describe the place of everlasting punishment, and also the certainty deducible from other scriptures, that a wicked king destroyed in the act of fighting against God must be punished in the other world as well as this, we need not hesitate to understand the passage as at least including a denunciation of eternal misery, although the general idea which the figures were intended to express is that of sudden terrible destruction.

CHAPTER XXXI.

Reliance upon Egypt is distrust of God, who will avenge himself by destroying both the helper and the helped, vs. 1–3. His determination and ability to save those who confide in his protection are expressed by two comparisons, vs. 4–5. The people are therefore invited to return to him, from every false dependence, human or idolatrous, as they will be constrained to do with shame, when they shall witness the destruction of their enemies by the resistless fire of his wrath, vs. 6–9. This chapter seems to be a direct continuation, or at most a repetition, of the threatenings and reproofs which had just been uttered.

1. *Woe to those going down to Egypt for help, and on horses they lean* (or *rely*), *and trust in cavalry, because it is numerous, and in horsemen, because they are very strong, and they look not to the Holy One of Israel, and Jehovah they seek not.* The abundance of horses in Egypt is attested, not only in other parts of Scripture, but by profane writers. Homer describes Thebes as having a hundred gates, out of each of which two hundred warriors went forth with chariots and horses. Diodorus speaks of the whole country between Thebes and Memphis as filled with royal stables. The horses of Solomon are expressly said to have been brought out of Egypt. This kind of military force was more highly valued, in comparison with infantry, by the ancients than the moderns, and especially by those who, like the Hebrews, were almost entirely deprived of it themselves. Hence their reliance upon foreign aid is frequently identified with confidence in horses, and contrasted with simple trust in God (Psalm 20: 7). To *seek Jehovah* is not merely to consult him, but to seek his aid, resort to him, implying the strongest confidence. For the meaning of the phrase *look to*, see the note on ch. 17 : 8.

2. *And* (yet) *he too is wise, and brings evil, and his words he removes not, and he rises up against the house of evil-doers, and against the help of the workers of iniquity.* The word *yet* is required by our idiom in this connection. *Too* implies a comparison with the Egyptians, upon whose wisdom, as well as strength, the Jews may have relied, or with the Jews themselves, who no doubt reckoned it a masterpiece of wisdom to secure such powerful assistance. The comparison may be explained as comprehending both. God was as wise as the Egyptians, and ought therefore to have been consulted; he was as wise as the Jews, and could therefore thwart their boasted policy. There is in this sentence an obvious irony. The *house of evil-doers* is their family or race (ch. 1 : 4), here applied to the unbelieving Jews. The Egyptians are called their *help*, and both are threat-

ened with destruction. To *rise up* is to show one's self, address one's self to action, and implies a state of previous forbearance or neglect.

3. *And Egypt (is) man and not God, and their horses flesh and not spirit, and Jehovah shall stretch out his hand, and the helper shall stumble and the helped fall, and together all of them shall cease* (or be destroyed). This verse repeats the contrast between human and divine aid, and the threatening that the unbelievers and their foreign helpers should be involved in the same destruction. The antithesis of *flesh* and *spirit*, like that of *God* and *man*, is not metaphysical but rhetorical, and is intended simply to express extreme dissimilitude or inequality. Reliance upon Egypt is again sarcastically represented as reliance upon horses, and as such opposed to confidence in God. As Egypt here means the Egyptians, it is afterwards referred to as a plural. *Stumble* and *fall* are here poetical equivalents.

4. *For thus saith Jehovah unto me, As a lion growls, and a young lion, over his prey, against whom a multitude of shepherds is called forth, at their voice he is not frightened, and at their noise he is not humbled, so will Jehovah of Hosts come down, to fight upon Mount Zion and upon her hill.* This is still another form of the same contrast. The comparison is a favourite one with Homer, and occurs in the eighteenth book of the Iliad, in terms almost identical. *Growl* is to be preferred to *roar*, because the Hebrew word more properly denotes a suppressed or feeble sound. Most interpreters have *for Mount Zion*. Others regard this as a threatening that God will take part with the Assyrians against Jerusalem, the promise of deliverance beginning with the next verse. By supposing the particle to mean *concerning*, we can explain its use both in a hostile and a favourable sense. The *for* at the beginning of this verse introduces the ground or reason of the declaration that

the seeking of foreign aid was both unlawful and unnecessary The *hill* is by some supposed to be Moriah, as an appendage of Mount Zion; but it may just as well be simply parallel to *mountain*, the mountain of Zion and the hill thereof.

5. *As birds flying* (over or around their nests), *so will Jehovah cover over* (or protect) *Jerusalem, cover and rescue, pass over and save.* The verb here is the one used to denote the passing over of the houses in Egypt by the destroying angel to which there may be an allusion here.

6. Since you need no protection but Jehovah's, therefore, *return unto him from whom* (or *with respect to whom*) *the children of Israel have deeply revolted* (literally, *have deepened revolt*). The last words may also be read, *from whom they* (i. e. men indefinitely) *have deeply revolted, oh ye children of Israel. Deep* may be here used to convey the specific idea of debasement, or the more general one of distance, or still more generally, as a mere intensive, like our common phrases *deeply grieved* or *deeply injured.* The analogy of ch. 29: 15, however, would suggest the idea of deep contrivance or design, which is equally appropriate.

7. This acknowledgment you will be constrained to make sooner or later. *For in that day* (of miraculous deliverance) *they shall reject* (cast away with contempt), *a man* (i. e. each) *his idols of silver and his idols of gold, which your sinful hands have made for you*, or, *which your own hands have made for you as sin*, i. e. as an occasion and a means of sin. In like manner the golden calves are called the sin of Israel (Deut. 9:21. Am. 8: 14). For the true construction of *his silver* and *his gold*, see the note on ch. 2:20. Trust in idols and reliance upon human helpers are here, and often elsewhere, put together, as identical

in principle, and closely connected in the experience of ancient Israel. (See the notes on ch. 2. 8, 22.)

8. This future abandonment of all false confidences is described as springing from the demonstration of Jehovah's willingness and power to save. *And Assyria shall fall by no man's sword, and no mortal's sword shall devour him, and (yet) he shall flee from before the sword, and his young men* (or *chosen warriors*) *shall become tributary* (literally, *tribute*). *No man's sword,* but that of God. The objection that the prophecy, as thus explained, was not fulfilled, proceeds upon the false assumption that it refers exclusively to the overthrow of Sennacherib's host, whereas it describes the decline and fall of the Assyrian power after that catastrophe.

9. *And his rock* (i. e. his strength) *from fear shall pass away, and his chiefs shall be afraid of a standard* (or signal, as denoting the presence of the enemy), *saith Jehovah, to whom there is a fire in Zion and a furnace in Jerusalem.* The true explanation of the last clause seems to be that which supposes an allusion both to the sacred fire on the altar and to the consuming fire of God's presence, whose altar flames in Zion and whose wrath shall thence flame to destroy his enemies. Compare the explanation of the mystical name *Ariel* in the note on ch. 29 : 1.

CHAPTER XXXII.

THIS chapter consists of two distinguishable parts. The first continues the promise of the foregoing context, vs. 1–8. The second predicts intervening judgments both to Israel and his enemies, vs. 9–20.

The first blessing promised in the former part is that of merciful and righteous government, vs. 1, 2. The next is that of spiritual illumination, vs. 3, 4. As the consequence of this, moral distinctions shall no longer be confounded, men shall be estimated at their real value; a general prediction, which is here applied to two specific cases, vs. 5–8.

The threatenings of the second part are specially addressed to the women of Judah, v. 9. They include the desolation of the country and the downfall of Jerusalem, vs. 10–14. The evils are to last until a total change is wrought by an effusion of the Holy Spirit, vs. 15–18. But fearful changes are to intervene, for which believers must prepare themselves by diligence in present duty, vs. 19, 20.

1. *Behold, for righteousness shall reign a king, and rulers for justice shall rule.* The usual translation is *in justice* and *in righteousness,* as descriptive epithets of the reign foretold. But the preposition here used may have been intended to suggest, that he would reign not only justly, but for the very purpose of doing justice. It is a question among interpreters whether the king here predicted is Hezekiah or the Messiah. The truth appears to be that the promise is a general one, as if he had said, the day is coming when power shall be exercised and government administered, not as at present (in the reign of Ahaz), but with a view to the faithful execution of the laws. Of such an im-

provement Hezekiah's reign was at least a beginning and a foretaste.

2. *And a man shall be as an hiding-place from the wind and a covert from the rain* (or *storm*), *as channels of water in a dry place* (or *in drought*), *as the shadow of a heavy rock in a weary land.* The meaning is, that there shall be a man upon the throne, or at the head of the government, who, instead of oppressing, will protect the helpless. This may either be indefinitely understood, or applied, in an individual and emphatic sense, to the Messiah. The figures for protection and relief are the same used above in ch. 4 : 6 and 25 : 4. The phrases *heavy rock* and *weary land* are idiomatic, but require no explanation.

3. *And the eyes of them that see shall not be dim, and the ears of them that hear shall hearken.* Some understand here *seers* or prophets, and their *hearers;* but most interpreters apply both words to the people generally, as those who had eyes but saw not, and had ears but heard not. Compare the threatening in ch. 6 : 9, and the promise in ch. 29 : 18.

4. *And the heart* (or *mind*) *of the rash* (heedless or reckless) *shall understand to know* (or *understand knowledge*), *and the tongue of stammerers shall hasten to speak clear things* (i. e. shall speak readily and plainly). The bodily defects here mentioned denote others of an intellectual and spiritual nature, neglect and ignorance of spiritual matters. The minds of men shall begin to be directed to religious truth, and delivered from ignorance and error in relation to it.

5. When men's eyes are thus opened, they will no longer confound the essential distinctions of moral character, because they will no longer be deceived by mere appearances. Things will then be called by their right names. *The fool* (in the

emphatic Scriptural sense, the wicked man) *will no longer be called noble* (men will no longer attach ideas of dignity and greatness to the name or person of presumptuous sinners), *and the churl* (or niggard) *will no more be spoken of* (or *to*) *as liberal.* The last clause, like the other, contains a specific illustration of the general truth that men shall be estimated at their real value.

6. The Prophet now defines his own expressions, or describes the characters which they denote. *The fool* (*is one who*) *will speak folly* (in the strongest and worst sense), *and his heart will do iniquity, to do wickedness and to speak error unto* (or *against*) *Jehovah* (while at the same time he is merciless and cruel towards his fellow-men), *to starve* (or *leave empty*) *the soul of the hungry, and the drink of the thirsty he will suffer to fail.* The futures in this verse express the idea of habitual action; he does and will do so. The infinitives convey the same idea in a different form, by making prominent the design and effect of their unlawful course. The common version, *work* and *practise* needlessly departs from the form of the original, in which the same verb is repeated.

7. Such is the fool: as for the churl, although his making money be not sinful in itself, his *arms* or *instruments*, the means which he employs, *are evil.* He that hastens to be rich can scarcely avoid the practice of dishonest arts and of unkindness to the poor. *He deviseth plots to destroy the oppressed* (or *afflicted*) *with words of falsehood, and* (i. e. *even*) *in the poor* (*man's*) *speaking right* (i. e. even when the poor man's claim is just, or in a more general sense, *when the poor man pleads his cause*).

8. As the wicked man's true character is betrayed by his habitual acts, so the noble or generous man (and according to

the Scriptures none is such but the truly good man) reveals his dispositions by his conduct. *He devises noble* (or *generous*) *things, and in noble* (or *generous things*) *he perseveres* (literally, on them he stands).

9. Here, as in many other cases, the Prophet reverts to the prospect of approaching danger, which was to arouse the careless Jews from their security. As in ch. 3 : 16, he addresses himself to the women of Jerusalem, because to them an invasion would be peculiarly disastrous, and also perhaps because their luxurious habits contributed, more or less directly, to existing evils. *Careless women, arise, hear my voice; confiding daughters, give ear unto my speech.* Women and daughters are equivalent expressions. Careless and confiding (or secure) i. e. indifferent because not apprehensive of the coming danger.

10. Having called their attention in v. 9, he now proceeds with the prediction which concerned them. *In a year and more* (literally, *days above a year*), *ye shall tremble, ye confiding ones, for the vintage fails, the gathering shall not come.* The English Version makes the time denoted to be that of the duration of the threatened evil.

11. He now speaks as if the event had already taken place, and calls upon them to express their sorrow and alarm by the usual signs of mourning. *Tremble ye careless* (*women*), *quake ye confiding* (*ones*), *strip you and make you bare, and gird* (sackcloth) *on your loins.*

12. *Mourning for the breasts* (or *beating on the breasts* as a sign of mourning), *for the pleasant fields, for the fruitful vine.* The same act is described in Nah. 2 : 8, but by a different verb.

13. *Upon the land of my people thorn* (and) *thistle shall come up, for* (they shall even come up) *upon all* (*thy*) *houses of pleasure, oh joyous city!* or, *upon all houses of pleasure* (*in*) *the joyous city.*

14. *For the palace is forsaken, the crowd of the city* (or *the crowded city*) *left, hill and watch-tower* (*are*) *for caves* (or *dens*) *forever, a joy* (or favourite resort) *of wild asses, a pasture of flocks.* The use of the word *palace*, and that in the singular number, clearly shows that the destruction of Jerusalem itself is here predicted. The Hebrew word in this verse originally meaning a hill is applied as a proper name (Ophel) to the southern extremity of Mount Moriah, overhanging the spot where the valleys of Jehoshaphat and Hinnom meet. "The top of the ridge is flat, descending rapidly towards the south, sometimes by offsets of rock; the ground is tilled and planted with olive and other fruit-trees." (Robinson's Palestine, I. p. 394.)

15. The desolation having been described in v. 14 as of indefinite duration, this verse states more explicitly how long it is to last. *Until the Spirit is poured out upon us from on high, and the wilderness becomes a fruitful field and the fruitful field is reckoned to the forest.* The general meaning evidently is, until by a special divine influence a total revolution shall take place in the character, and as a necessary consequence in the condition, of the people. The attempt to restrict it to the return from exile, or the day of Pentecost, or some great effusion of the Spirit on the Jews still future, perverts the passage by making that its whole meaning which at most is but a part. For the meaning of the figures, see the exposition of ch. 29 : 17. In this connection, they would seem to denote nothing more than total change, whereas in the other case the idea of an interchange appears to be made prominent.

16. *And justice shall abide in the wilderness, and righteousness in the fruitful field shall dwell.* This may either mean, that what is now a wilderness, and what is now a fruitful field, shall alike be the abode of righteousness i. e. of righteous men; or that both in the cultivation of the desert, and in the desolation of the field, the righteousness of God shall be displayed. In favour of the former is the use of the word *dwell*, which implies a permanent condition, rather than a transient or occasional manifestation. It also agrees better with the relation of this verse to that before it, as a part of the same sentence. If this be the meaning of the sixteenth verse, it seems to follow clearly, that the whole of the last clause of the fifteenth is a promise, since the same inhabitation of righteousness is here foretold in reference to the forest and the fruitful field. It is possible indeed that these may be put for the whole land, as being the two parts into which he had just before divided it.

17. As the foregoing verse describes the effect of the effusion of the Spirit to be universal righteousness, so this describes the natural and necessary consequence of righteousness itself. *And the work of righteousness shall be peace, and the effect of righteousness rest and assurance* (or *security*) *forever.*

18. *And my people shall abide in a home of peace, in sure dwellings, and in quiet resting-places.* There is something tranquillizing in the very sound of this delightful promise, which as usual is limited to God's own people, implying either that all should have become such, or that those who had not should be still perturbed and restless.

19. *And it shall hail in the downfall of the forest* (i. e. so as to overthrow it), *and the city shall be low in a low place* (or *humble with humiliation*) i. e. utterly brought down. If this be read as a direct continuation of the promise in v. 18, it must

be explained as a description of the downfall of some hostile power, and accordingly it has been referred by most interpreters to Nineveh. Others, thinking it more natural to assume one subject here and in v. 13, regard this as another instance of prophetic recurrence from remoter promises to nearer threats; as if he had said, before these things can come to pass, the city must be brought low. This construction is entirely in keeping with the Prophet's manner, as exemplified already in this very chapter. (See the note on v. 9 above.) However natural and probable certain applications of the passage may appear, the only sense which can with certainty be put upon it, is that some existing power must be humbled, either as a means or as a consequence of the moral revolution which had been predicted.

20. *Blessed are ye that sow beside all waters, that send forth the foot of the ox and the ass.* The allusion in this verse is supposed by some to be to pasturage, by others to tillage. There is still more diversity of judgment with respect to the application of the metaphor. Taking the whole connection into view, the meaning of this last verse seems to be, that as great revolutions are to be expected, arising wholly or in part from moral causes, they alone are safe, for the present and the future, who with patient assiduity perform what is required and provide, by the discharge of actual duty, for contingencies which can neither be escaped nor provided for in any other manner.

CHAPTER XXXIII.

THIS chapter contains a general threatening of retribution to the enemies of God's people, with particular reference to Sennacherib or the Assyrian power. The spoiler shall himself be spoiled in due time, through the divine interposition, and for the exaltation of Jehovah, vs. 1–6. The state of desolation and alarm is followed by sudden deliverance, vs. 7–13. The same vicissitudes are again described, but in another form, vs. 14–19. The peace and security of Zion are set forth under the figures of a stationary tent, and of a spot surrounded by broad rivers, yet impassable to hostile vessels, vs. 20–22. By a beautiful transition, the enemy is described as such a vessel, but dismantled and abandoned to its enemies, v. 23. The chapter closes with a general promise of deliverance from suffering, as a consequence of pardoned sin, v. 24.

1. *Woe to thee spoiling and thou wast not spoiled, deceiving and they did not deceive thee! When thou shalt cease to spoil thou shalt be spoiled, and when thou art done deceiving they shall deceive thee.* The two ideas meant to be expressed are those of violence and treachery, as the crying sins of arbitrary powers. In themselves the words are applicable to any oppressive and deceitful enemy, and may be naturally so explained at the beginning of the prophecy. This verse describes the enemy as acting without provocation, and also as having never yet experienced reverses.

2. *Jehovah, favour us; for thee we wait; be their arm in the mornings, also our salvation in time of trouble.* Isaiah here interposes his own feelings, and offers his own prayer that God

would be the strength of the nation, and then, with an immediate change of form, presents the prayer of the people. *Arm* is a common Hebrew metaphor for strength or support. *As to the mornings* is an indefinite expression, understood by some to mean *early* or *quickly*, by others *every morning*, with allusion to the daily attacks of the enemy, or to the daily morning sacrifice.

3. *At a noise of tumult* (or *tumultuous noise*) *the peoples flee; at thy rising the nations are scattered.* The *rising* meant is the act of rising from a state of seeming inaction, or as when one rouses himself to strike. These words are commonly applied to the divine interposition in the case of Sennacherib's attack upon Jerusalem.

4. *And your spoil shall be gathered* (*like*) *the gathering of the devourer; like the running of locusts running on it.* By another apostrophe, the Prophet here addresses the enemy collectively. The word translated *devourer* is a descriptive name of the locust. (See the verb in Deut. 28 : 38.) *As locusts gather*, i. e. greedily and thoroughly, not leaving a tree or a field till they have stripped it. The construction of the last clause is: like the running of locusts (shall one be) running on it (i. e. on the spoil). The verb denotes specifically the act of *running eagerly* or with a view to satisfy the appetite. It is sometimes used to denote desire itself.

5. *Exalted is Jehovah because dwelling on high* (or *inhabiting a high place*); *he fills* (or *has filled*) *Zion with judgment and righteousness.* The first word, being a passive participle, seems to denote not merely a condition but a change. *High place* denotes a lofty and commanding position.

6. *And he shall be the security of thy times, strength of salvations, wisdom and knowledge; the fear of Jehovah, that is his treas-*

ure. The simplest construction is the one which supplies the subject from the foregoing verse, *he* (i. e. Jehovah, or *it* i. e. his righteousness) *shall be etc.* The object of address is supposed by some to be Hezekiah, by others the Messiah, but is most probably the people or the believer as an individual. *His treasure* may refer to the same, or mean the treasure of Jehovah, that which he bestows.

7. *Behold, their valiant ones cry without; the ambassadors of peace weep bitterly. They fearful cry aloud.* Some here, as in ch. 29 : 1, give *Ariel* the sense of *altar*, but the latest investigations, although still unsatisfactory, tend strongly to confirm the version given in the English Bible. The messengers mentioned in the other clause are probably the three men sent by Hezekiah to Rabshakeh (2 Kings 18 : 18), or perhaps the bearers of the tribute, weeping on account of Sennacherib's refusal to fulfil his promise. Some suppose them to be called valiant, because they ventured into the enemy's camp; others because they were probably military chiefs. Their weeping is agreed by all interpreters to be in strict accordance with the ancient usage, as described for example by Homer.

8. *The highways are wasted, the wayfarer ceaseth; he breaks the covenant, despises cities, values no man.* These are the words of the Prophet himself. The scene presented is that of the actual condition of Judea during the Assyrian invasion. (Compare Judges 5 : 6.) The verbs of the last clause agree with Sennacherib or the Assyrian. The meaning is that he despised the defences of the conquered country, as unable to resist him. The last words may either mean that he has no regard to any man's interest or wishes, or that he does not value human life.

9. *The land mourneth, languisheth; Lebanon is ashamed, it pines away; Sharon is like a wilderness, and Bashan and Carmel*

cast (their leaves). The most fertile and flourishing parts of the country are described as desolate. That the language is figurative, may be inferred from the fact that none of the places mentioned were in Judah.

10. *Now will I arise, saith Jehovah, now will I be lifted up, now will I exalt myself.* The emphasis is upon the adverb *now*, which is twice repeated to imply that the time for the divine interposition is arrived, and that there shall be no more delay.

11. *Ye shall conceive chaff, ye shall bring forth stubble; your breath (as) fire shall devour you.* The first clause contains a common scriptural figure for failure and frustration. (See ch. 26 : 18.) Chaff and stubble are named as worthless and perishable substances.

12. *And nations shall be lime-kilns* (or *burnings of lime*); *thorns cut up, in the fire they shall burn.* By *nations* we are to understand all nations that incur the wrath of God. The same word *burnings* is applied to the aromatic fumigations used at ancient burials (Jer. 34 : 5), to which there may be some allusion here. The ideas expressed are those of quickness and intensity. The thorns are perhaps described as *cut up*, to suggest that they are dry and therefore more combustible.

13. *Hear, ye far, what I have done, and know, ye near, my might.* By *far* and *near* we may understand all without exception. This is an apostrophe, expressing the magnitude of the event predicted in the foregoing context.

14. *Afraid in Zion are the sinners.* Not *at* or *near Zion*, meaning the Assyrians, but *in Zion* i. e. in Jerusalem, referring to the impious Jews themselves. *Trembling has seized the impious*, a parallel expression to *sinners.* What follows might be

understood as the language of the Prophet himself, giving a reason for the terror of the wicked. It is more probably, however, the language of the wicked Jews themselves. Some refer it to the past, and understand the verse to mean that they are now in terror who once said thus and thus. But it is more probably the present language of the wicked Jews, when actually seized with terror. Not those *who once said*, but *who now say etc.* The interpretation commonly adopted supposes the words to be expressive of the feelings excited by the slaughter of Sennacherib's host. If this be a specimen of God's vindicatory justice, what may we expect? *Who of us can dwell with* (*this*) *devouring fire? Who of us can dwell with* (*these*) *perpetual burnings?* Many make the language still more emphatic, by supposing that the Prophet argues from the less to the greater. If these are God's temporal judgments, what must his eternal wrath be? If the momentary strokes of his hand are thus resistless, *who of us can dwell with the devouring fire, who of us can dwell with everlasting burnings?* The last words may then be taken in their strongest and most unrestricted sense.

15. This verse contains a description of the righteous man, not unlike that in the fifteenth and twenty-fourth Psalms. *Walking righteousnesses* i. e. leading a righteous life. *Walk* is a common Scriptural expression for the course of conduct. The plural form of the other word may either be used to mark it as an abstract term, or as an emphatic expression for fulness or completeness of rectitude. In order to retain the figure of walking, the preposition *in* may be supplied before the noun; but in the Hebrew it seems to be governed directly by the verb, or to qualify it as an adverb. *And speaking right things*, or (taking the plural merely as an abstract) *rectitude* or *righteousness.* The idea is not merely that of speaking truth as opposed to falsehood, but that of rectitude in speech as distinguished from rectitude of action. *Rejecting* or *despising* (or combining

both ideas, *rejecting with contempt*) *the gain of oppressions* or *extortions*. *Shaking his hands from taking hold of the bribe*, an expressive gesture of indignant refusal. *Stopping his ears from hearing bloods*, i. e. plans of murder. *Shutting his eyes from looking at evil* i. e. from conniving at it, or even beholding it as an indifferent spectator. According to the natural connection of the passage, this verse would seem to contain the answer to the question in v. 14, and is so understood by those who make the question mean, who can stand before this terrible Jehovah? But on the supposition of an allusion to eternal punishment, the answer is absurd, for it implies that the righteous man can or will endure it. This may either be regarded as a proof that there is no such allusion to eternal punishment in v. 14, or as a proof that this is not an answer to the question there recorded. Some separate this verse from the preceding context by a larger space than usual, making this the beginning, as it were, of a new paragraph. To this construction there is the less objection, as the sentence is evidently incomplete in this verse, the conclusion being added in the next.

16. *He* (the character described in v. 15) *high places shall inhabit*. This does not denote exalted station in society, but safety from enemies, in being above their reach, as appears from the other clause. *Fastnesses* (or *strongholds*) *of rocks* (*shall be*) *his lofty place*, i. e. his refuge or his place of safety, as in ch. 25 : 12. To the idea of security is added that of sustenance, without which the first would be of no avail. *His bread is given*, including the ideas of allotment or appointment and of actual supply. *His water sure*, or, retaining the strict sense of the participle, *secured*. At the same time there is evident allusion to the moral usage of the word as signifying faithful, true, the opposite of that which fails, deceives, or disappoints the expectation, in which sense the same word with a negative is applied by Jeremiah (15: 18) to *waters that fail*.

17. *A king in his beauty shall thine eyes behold.* Most writers suppose Hezekiah to be here referred to, either exclusively or as a type of Christ. To see the king *in his beauty* means in his royal state, with tacit reference to his previous state of mourning and dejection (ch. 37 : 1). *They* (i. e. thine eyes) *shall behold a land of distances* or *distant places.* The most natural explanation of this phrase would be *a distant land*, in which sense it is used by Jeremiah (8 : 19) and a part of it by Zechariah (10 : 9), and by both in reference to exile or captivity. The verse before us, taken by itself, might be understood as a threatening that the Jews should see the king of Babylon in his royal state and in a distant land. Interpreters seem to be agreed, however, that in this connection it can be taken only as a promise.

18. *Thy heart shall meditate terror.* This does not mean, it shall conceive or experience present terror, but reflect on that which is already past. What follows may be understood as the triumphant exclamation of the people when they found themselves so suddenly delivered from their enemies. *Where is he that counted? where is he that weighed? where is he that counted the towers?* The counting and weighing may be either that of tribute or of military wages. The *towers* are the fortifications of Jerusalem. By *counting* them some understand surveying them, either with a view to garrisoning or dismantling; others the act of reconnoitring them from without, which some ascribe particularly to Rabshakeh or Sennacherib himself. The general meaning of the verse is plain, as an expression of surprise and joy, that the oppressor or besieger had now vanished. The Apostle Paul, in 1 Cor. 1 : 20, has a sentence so much like this, in the threefold repetition of the question *where*, and in the use of the word *scribe*, that it cannot be regarded as a mere fortuitous coincidence. It is probable, that the structure of the one passage suggested the other. The expression *it is written*, in the preceding verse of the epistle, introduces

a quotation from ch. 29 : 14, but does not necessarily extend to the next verse, which may therefore be regarded as a mere imitation, as to form and diction, of the one before us.

19. *The fierce* (or *determined*) *people thou shalt not see.* Thou shalt see no more the Assyrians, whose disappearance was implied in the questions of the foregoing verse. The essential idea seems to be that of firmness and decision, perhaps with the accessory idea of aggressive boldness. *A people deep of lip from hearing* i. e. hard for thee to understand. *Deep* denotes obscure or unintelligible. The preposition before *hearing*, though not directly negative, is virtually so, as it denotes *away from*, which is really equivalent to *so as not to hear* or *be heard.* (See the note on ch. 5 : 6.) *Barbarous tongue* (or of a barbarous tongue), *without meaning* (literally, there is no meaning). The verb in its other forms, means to mock or scoff, an idea closely connected, in the Hebrew usage, with that of foreign language, either because the latter seems ridiculous to those who do not understand it, or because unmeaning jargon is often used in mockery.

20. *Behold Zion the city of our festivals.* Instead of the presence of foreign enemies, see Jerusalem once more the scene of stated solemnities. The address is to the people as an individual. *Thine eyes shall see Jerusalem a quiet home, a tent* (*that*) *shall not be removed* (or *taken down*). The whole of this description is drawn from the usages of nomadic life. *Its stakes shall not be pulled up forever, and all its cords shall not be broken,* or in our idiom, *none of its cords shall be broken.* The peculiar beauty of the imagery lies in ascribing permanence to a tent, which from its very nature must be moveable. This may either imply a previous state of agitation and instability, or that the church, though weak in herself, should be strengthened and established by the power of God.

21. *But there shall Jehovah be mighty for us* (or *in our behalf*). The connection of the verses is that Zion shall never be weakened or removed, but on the contrary Jehovah etc. *A place of rivers, streams, broad* (*on*) *both hands* (or *sides*), i. e. completely surrounding her. Most interpreters connect these words directly with *Jehovah.* The most obvious explanation seems to be that this clause is an amplification of the adverb *there. Jehovah will be mighty for us there.* What place is meant? A place of rivers and streams broad on both sides, i. e. spreading in every direction. The situation described is one which has all the advantages of mighty streams without their dangers. *There shall not go in it an oared vessel* (literally, *a ship of oar*), *and a gallant ship shall not pass through it.* The parallel expressions both refer, no doubt, to ships of war, which in ancient times were propelled by oars.

22. *For Jehovah our Judge, Jehovah our Lawgiver, Jehovah our King, he will save us.* This is a repetition of the same idea, but without the figures of the preceding verse.

23. *Thy ropes are cast loose; they do not hold upright their mast; they do not spread the sail; then is shared plunder of booty in plenty; the lame spoil the spoil.* There is, at the beginning of this verse, a sudden apostrophe to the enemy considered as a ship. This figure would be naturally suggested by those of v. 21. It was there said that no vessel should approach the holy city. But now the Prophet seems to remember that one had done so, the proud ship of Assyria. But what was its fate? He sees it dismantled and abandoned to its enemies. The eagerness of the pillage is expressed by making the lame join in it.

24. *And the inhabitant shall not say, I am sick* (or *have been sick*). This may either mean that none shall be sick, or that

those who have been so shall be recovered. *The people dwelling in it* (*is*) *forgiven* (*its*) *iniquity.* Some suppose this to be an explanation of the sickness mentioned in the first clause, as a spiritual malady. Others understand it as explaining bodily disease to be the consequence and punishment of sin. The words may be taken in a wider sense than either of these, namely, that suffering shall cease with sin which is its cause. Thus understood, the words are strictly applicable only to a state of things still future, either upon earth or in heaven.

CHAPTER XXXIV.

This chapter and the next appear to constitute one prophecy, the first part of which (ch. 34) is filled with threatenings against the enemies of the church, the latter part (ch. 35) with promises to the church itself. The threatenings of ch. 34 are directed, first, against the nations in general, vs. 1–4, and then against Edom in particular, vs. 5–15, with a closing affirmation of the truth and certainty of the prediction, vs. 16, 17. The destruction of the enemies of Zion and the desolation of their lands are represented by the figures of a great sacrifice or slaughter, the falling of the heavenly bodies, the conversion of the soil into brimstone, and the waters into pitch, and the inhabitation of animals peculiar to the desert. This is a general threatening of destruction to the enemies of Zion, Edom being particularly mentioned, as an enemy of ancient Israel peculiarly inveterate and malignant, and thence used to represent the whole class of such enemies. Thus understood, the prophecy extends both to the past and future, and may include many particular events, not excepting the destruction of Antichrist, as the greatest event of this kind which is foretold in prophecy. Compare the note on ch. 11 : 4.

1. *Come near, ye nations, to hear, and ye peoples, hearken. Let the earth hear and its fulness* (that which fills it, all that it contains), *the world and all its issues* (or productions, all that comes forth from it). This may either be explained as an appeal to inanimate nature, like the one at the beginning of the book (ch. 1 : 2), or as an appeal to men, poetically represented as the fruit of the earth, which is the sense given in the ancient versions. It announces, as about to be delivered, a prediction of great moment and deserving the attention of the whole world.

2. This verse assigns the reason for the invocation in the one before it. *For* (*there is*) *anger to Jehovah.* The English Version has, *the indignation of the Lord is*, an idea which would be otherwise expressed in Hebrew. The construction is the same as in ch. 2 : 12. *Jehovah has anger* (or *is angry*) *against all the nations. And wrath* (is to Jehovah) *against all their host.* Not *their armies* in particular, but their whole multitude, all that belong to them. (Compare the same expression in Gen. 2 : 1.)—*He has doomed them*, or devoted them irrevocably to destruction. For the peculiar usage of the Hebrew verb, see the note on ch. 11 : 15.—*He has given* (i. e. appointed and abandoned) *them to the slaughter.* The past tense describes the divine determination or decree as really and literally past.

3. *And their slain shall be cast out.* The Hebrew word strictly means *their wounded*, but usage gives it the specific sense of *wounded mortally*, and for the most part in battle. *Cast out* i. e. unburied. This suggests the several ideas of

contemptuous neglect, of a multitude too vast to be interred, and perhaps of survivors too few to perform the duty. (Compare ch. 14 : 18–20.) They shall not lie unburied merely for a time, but until they rot upon the ground. *And (as to) their corpses* (or *carcasses*), *their stench shall go up. And mountains shall be melted with* (or *by*) *their blood*, as they are sometimes washed away by rains or torrents.

4. *And all the host of heaven* (or heavenly bodies) *shall consume away.* This verb is commonly applied to the pining or consumption occasioned by disease. In Ps. 38 : 5 it means to *run* as a sore. The ideas of *sickly lights* and *dying lights* are not unknown to modern poetry. *And the heavens shall be rolled up* (or *together*) *like a scroll*, i. e. like an ancient *volume* (*volumen* from *volvo*) or a modern map. As God is elsewhere described as having stretched out the heavens like a curtain, their destruction or any total change in their appearance would be naturally represented as a rolling up of the expanse. *And all their host* (referring to *the heavens*) *shall fade* (or *fall away*) *like the fading of a leaf from a vine.* This beautiful comparison with the decay of plants makes it the more probable that the preceding clause alludes to that of animal life. *And like the fading* (*leaf*) or *a withered* (*fig*) *from a fig-tree.* The context clearly shows that the terms used are poetical, and that here, as in ch. 13 : 10, the idea which they are all intended to convey is that of revolution, sudden, total, and appalling change. The imagery of the passage has been partially adopted in Matt. 24 : 29 and Rev. 6 : 13, neither of which however is to be regarded either as a repetition or an explanation of the one before us.

5. All this shall certainly take place, *for my sword* (the speaker being God himself) *is steeped* (saturated, soaked) *in heaven.* The phrase *in heaven* probably refers to the divine determination and foreknowledge. In the sight of God the

sword, although not yet actually used, was already dripping blood. The sword is mentioned as a natural and common though poetical expression for any instrument of vengeance. *Behold, upon Edom it shall come down.* The name *Edom* is here applied to the inveterate enemies of the church at large, and not to any one of them exclusively. The fulfilment of those threatenings cannot be traced in the history of ancient Edom. They ceased to be a people not by extirpation but by incorporation with the Jews. The name *Idumea*, as employed by Josephus, includes a large part of Judea. The Herods, the last royal family of Judah, were of Idumean origin. *And upon the people of my curse* or doom i. e., the people whom I have doomed to destruction. (See v. 2.)

6. *A sword (is) to Jehovah* (or *Jehovah has a sword*) *; it is full of blood.* The genitive construction (*the sword of Jehovah*), although not ungrammatical, is not to be assumed without necessity. *It is smeared with fat.* The allusion is to fat and blood as the animal substances offered in sacrifice. *With the blood of lambs and goats*, mentioned as well-known sacrificial animals, *with the fat of the kidneys* (or the kidney-fat) *of rams*, mentioned either as remarkable for fatness or as a parallel expression to the foregoing clause. *For there is to Jehovah* (or *Jehovah has*) *a sacrifice in Bozrah and a great slaughter in the land of Edom.* Bozrah was an ancient city of Edom, perhaps the same with the modern *Busaireh*, a village and castle in Arabia Petraea south-east of the Dead Sea.

7. *And unicorns shall come down with them, and bullocks with bulls. And their land shall be soaked* (or *drenched*) *with blood, and their dust with fat shall be fattened.* The unicorn has been commonly regarded as fabulous in modern times; but of late some traces of it have been found in Thibet and other parts of Asia. But even supposing it to be a real animal, we have

no reason to believe that it was ever common in the Holy Land, as the one here named would seem to have been from the frequency with which it is mentioned. The modern writers are divided between a certain species of gazelle or antelope and the wild buffalo of Palestine and Egypt. The name may here be used either as a poetical description of the ox, or to suggest that wild as well as tame beasts should be included in the threatened slaughter. *Dust* here denotes *dry soil*, which is said to be enriched by the bodies of the slain. So Virgil says that Roman blood had twice enriched the soil of Macedonia, and similar statements have been made with respect to the field of Waterloo. To *come down* in the first clause is by some explained as meaning to come down to the slaughter (Jer. 50:27. 51:40); by others to fall or sink under the fatal stroke (Zech. 11:2).

8. *For* (*there is*) *a day of vengeance to Jehovah, a year of recompenses for the cause of Zion*, i. e. to maintain her cause. This verse connects the judgments threatened against Edom with the cause of Zion or the church of God. On the construction and meaning of the first words of the sentence, compare ch. 2:12.

9. *And her streams* (those of Idumea or the land of Edom) *shall be turned to pitch, and her dust to brimstone, and her land shall become burning pitch.* This verse announces nothing new, but repeats the same prediction under other figures, borrowed from the overthrow of Sodom and Gomorrah, which throughout the Bible *are set forth for an example, suffering the vengeance of eternal fire* (Jude 7). To the fire and brimstone there mentioned, pitch or bitumen is added, as some suppose, because the soil of Idumea, lying adjacent to the Dead Sea, is bituminous and abounds in veins or springs of naphtha. The first clause expresses in the strongest terms the idea of *utter and permanent*

destruction, as complete and terrible *as if* the streams were turned to pitch.

10. *Day and night it shall not be quenched; forever shall its smoke go up; from generation to generation shall it lie waste, forever and ever, there shall be no one passing through it.* The remarkable gradation and accumulation of terms denoting perpetuity can scarcely be expressed in a translation. This is especially the case with the last and highest of the series. A striking parallel to this verse is found in the statement (Gen. 19 : 28), that when Abraham looked toward Sodom and Gomorrah, *the smoke of the country went up as the smoke of a furnace.* These sublime and fearful images are copied in the book of Revelation. (14 : 10, 11.) Keith, in his Evidences of Prophecy, has collected some remarkable illustrations of this passage from the incidental statements of modern travellers with respect to what was once the land of Edom. Thus Volney speaks of thirty deserted towns within three days' journey; Seetzen, of a wide tract utterly without a place of habitation, and of his own route through it as one never before attempted; Burckhardt, of the passage as declared by the people of the nearest inhabited districts to be impossible, in accordance with which notion he was unable to procure guides at any price. These are striking coincidences, and as illustrations of the prophecy important, but are not to be insisted on as constituting its direct fulfilment, for in that case the passage of these very travellers through the country would falsify the prediction which they are cited to confirm. The truth of the prophecy in this clause is really no more suspended on such facts, than that of the first clause and of the preceding verse upon the actual existence of bituminous streams and a sulphureous soil throughout the ancient Idumea. The whole is a magnificent prophetic picture, the fidelity of which, so far as it relates to ancient Edom, is notoriously attested by its desolation for a course of ages.

11. *Then shall possess it* (as a heritage) *the pelican and porcupine, the crane and crow shall dwell in it. And he* (or *one*) *shall stretch upon it the line of confusion and the stones of emptiness.* Having declared that man should no longer pass through it, he now explains who shall be its inhabitants. These animals should not only occupy the land, but occupy it as the successors and to the exclusion of mankind. The essential idea is that of wild and solitary animals. (Compare ch. 13 : 21, 22. 14 : 23. Rev. 18 : 2.) Here again a remarkable coincidence is furnished by the statements of travellers with respect to the number of wild birds in Edom. Mangles, while at Petra, describes the screaming of the eagles, hawks, and owls, seemingly annoyed at any one approaching their lonely habitation. Burckhardt speaks of Tafyle as frequented by an immense number of crows and of the birds called *katta*, which fly in such large flocks that the boys often kill two or three at a time merely by throwing a stick among them. The apparent inconsistency between this clause and the description of the country in the verse before it only shows that neither can be strictly taken, but that both are metaphorical predictions of entire desolation. In the next clause the same idea is expressed by an entire change of figure. The *line* meant is a measuring line, mentioned elsewhere not only in connection with building (Zech. 1 : 16), but also with destroying (2 Kings 21 : 13). The *stones* are stones used for *weights* (Deut. 25 : 13. Prov. 16 : 11), and here for *plumb-line* or *plummet*. The same figure is employed by Amos (7 : 7–9) to denote a *moral* test or standard, but in this case as a symbol of destruction. The plummet is here mentioned as a parallel to *line*, both together expressing the idea of exact and careful measurement. The sense of the whole metaphor may then be either that God has laid this work out for himself and will perform it, or that in destroying Edom he will act with equity and justice, or that even in destroying he will proceed deliberately and by rule.

12. *Her caves and there is no one there* (i. e. her uninhabited or empty caves) *they will (still) call a kingdom, and all her chiefs will be cessation* (i. e. cease to be). The great variety of explanations which have been given of this verse, and the harshness of construction with which most of them are chargeable, may serve as an excuse for the suggestion of a new one, not as certainly correct, but as possibly entitled to consideration. All interpreters coincide in giving to the first noun, the sense of *nobles*, which it certainly has in several places. (See 1 Kings 21 : 8, 11. Neh. 2 : 16. 4 : 14.) But in several others, it no less certainly means *holes* or *caves*. (See 1 Sam. 14 : 11. Job 30 : 6. Nah. 2 : 12.) Now it is matter of history, not only that Edom was full of caverns, but that these were inhabited, and that the aboriginal inhabitants, expelled by Esau, were expressly called *Horites*, as being troglodytes or inhabitants of caverns (Gen. 14 : 6. 36 : 20. Deut. 2 : 12, 22). This being the case, the entire depopulation of the country, and especially the destruction of its princes, might be naturally and poetically expressed by saying that the kingdom of Edom should be thenceforth a kingdom of deserted caverns. How appropriate such a description would be to the actual condition of the country, and particularly to its ancient capital, may be seen from Robinson's account of Petra (Palestine, II. pp. 514–537).

13. *And her palaces* (or *in her palaces*) *shall come up thorns, nettles and brambles in her fortresses.* The natural consequence of her depopulation. The situation here described would of course be the resort of wild and solitary animals. *And she shall be a home of wolves, a court* (or *grass-plot*) *for ostriches.* The general sense is that of an enclosed and appropriated spot, a play-ground or dwelling-place.

14. *And wild* (or *desert*) *creatures shall* (there) *meet with howling creatures.* The verb sometimes means to meet or encoun-

ter in the sense of attacking (Ex. 4 : 24. Hos. 13 : 8); but here it seems to have the general sense of falling in with. These lonely creatures, as they traverse Idumea, shall encounter none but creatures like themselves. *And the shaggy monster shall call to his fellow.* For the true sense of *satyrs*, see the comment on the plural form as it occurs in ch. 13 : 21. The interpretation most consistent with itself and with the etymology is that given above, *shaggy monsters*, on the ground that it corresponds better with the general descriptive meaning which, as we have seen above, most probably belongs to the words in the preceding clause. If that clause speaks of wild and howling beasts, and not of any one class exclusively, it is more natural that this should speak of shaggy monsters generally than of goats. *Only there reposes the night-monster and finds for herself a resting-place.* If the terms used above represent the animals occupying Idumea, first as belonging to the wilderness, then as distinguished by their fierce or melancholy cries, and then as shaggy in appearance, nothing can be more natural than that the fourth epithet should also be expressive of their habits as a class, and no such epithet could well be more appropriate than that of *nocturnal* or belonging to the night.

15. *There shall the great owl make her nest, and lay, and hatch, and gather under her shadow: there shall the vultures also be gathered, every one with her mate.* As to the particular species of animals referred to in this whole passage, there is no need of troubling ourselves much about them. The general sense evidently is, that a human population should be succeeded by wild and lonely animals, who should not only live but breed there, implying total and continued desolation.

16. *Seek ye out of the book of Jehovah and read.* The most natural interpretation seems to be that which makes this an

exhortation to compare the prophecy with the event, and which is strongly recommended by the fact that all the verbs are in the past tense, implying that the Prophet here takes his stand at a point of time posterior to the event. *The book* may then be this particular prophecy, or the whole prophetic volume, or the entire scripture, without material change of sense. The persons addressed are the future witnesses of the event. *One of them has not failed.* This refers to the animals mentioned in the preceding verses, as signs of desolation. As if he had said, I predicted that Edom should be occupied by such and such creatures, and behold they are all here, not one of them is wanting. This is a lively and impressive mode of saying, the prediction is fulfilled. *One another they miss not.* The verb has here the sense of mustering or reviewing to discover who is absent, as in 1 Sam. 20 : 6. 25 : 15. *For my mouth, it has commanded; and his spirit, it has gathered them*, i. e. the animals aforesaid. The last phrase is a more specific explanation of the general expression *has commanded.* The sudden change of person from *my mouth* to *his spirit* has led to various explanations. The simplest course is either to suppose that Jehovah speaks in one clause and the Prophet in the next, or that the Prophet really refers the command to his own mouth instrumentally, but then immediately names the Divine Spirit as the efficient agent. This is the less improbable because the first clause of the verse, as we have seen, contains an appeal to his own written prediction. The Spirit of God is not merely his power but himself, with special reference to the Holy Ghost, as being both the author and fulfiller of the prophecies.

17. *He too has cast the lot for them, and his hand has divided it to them by line.* An evident allusion to the division of the land of Canaan, both by lot and measuring-line. (See Numb. 26 : 55, 56. Josh. 18 : 4–6.) As Canaan was allotted to

Israel, so Edom is allotted to these doleful creatures. Having referred to the allotment as already past, he now describes the occupation as future and perpetual. *Forever shall they hold it as a heritage, to all generations shall they dwell therein.*

CHAPTER XXXV.

A GREAT and glorious change is here described under the figure of a desert clothed with luxuriant vegetation, vs. 1, 2. The people are encouraged with the prospect of this change and with the promise of avenging judgments on their enemies, vs. 3, 4. The same change is then expressed, by a change of figure, as a healing of corporeal infirmities, vs. 5, 6. The former figure is again resumed, and the wilderness described as free from all its wonted inconveniences, particularly those of barrenness and thirst, disappointment and illusion, pathlessness and beasts of prey, vs. 7–9. The whole prediction winds up with a promise of redemption, restoration, and endless blessedness, v. 10.

The chapter is the description of a happy condition of the church after a period of suffering. Thus explained it may be considered as including various particulars, none of which can be regarded as its specific or exclusive subject. Without any change of its essential meaning, it may be applied to the restoration of the Jews from Babylon, to the vocation of the Gentiles, to the whole Christian dispensation, to the course of every individual believer, and to the blessedness of heaven. The ground of this manifold application is not that the language of the passage is unmeaning or indefinite, but that there is a real and designed analogy between the various changes mentioned, which brings them all within the natural scope of the same inspired description.

1. *Desert and waste shall rejoice (for) them, and the wilderness shall rejoice and blossom as the rose.* The construction of the pronoun in the first clause is obscure and doubtful. Some refer it to the animals mentioned at the close of ch. 34 ; some to the judgments there threatened against Edom ; some to the Jews returning from captivity. As the pronoun is not expressed in any of the ancient versions, some explain it as a mere appendage to the verbal form, and translate simply, *shall rejoice.* The last word in the verse has been variously explained to mean the *lily*, the *narcissus*, the *crocus*, etc. The common version (*rose*) is not only quite as probable, but more familiar, and suggests more clearly the essential idea of beauty.

2. *(It shall) blossom, it shall blossom and rejoice; yea, (with) joy and shouting;* or, *yea, joy and shouting (there shall be). The glory of Lebanon is given unto it* (the desert), *the beauty of Carmel and of Sharon. They* (who witness this great change) *shall see the glory of Jehovah, the beauty of our God.* The same idea of complete and joyful change is again expressed by the same figure, but with greater fulness, the desert being here described as putting on and wearing the appearance of the spots most noted for luxuriant vegetation.

3. *Strengthen hands* (now) *sinking, and knees* (now) *tottering make firm.* With the prospect of this glorious change the people are commanded to encourage themselves and one another. The hands and knees are here combined to express the powers of action and endurance. The participial forms represent the hands as actually hanging down, relaxed, or weakened, and the knees as actually giving way. The passage thus explained is far more expressive than if we make the participles adjectives, denoting a permanent quality or habitual condition. In itself, the language of this verse is applicable either to self-encouragement or to the consolation of others. There is no reason why

the words should not be taken in their widest sense, as meaning, let despondency be exchanged for hope. That self-encouragement is not excluded may be learned from Paul's use of the words in that sense (Heb. 12 : 12). That mutual encouragement is not excluded, is sufficiently apparent from the following verse.

4. *Say ye to the hasty of heart* (i. e. the impatient, those who cannot wait for the fulfilment of God's promise), *Be firm, fear not; behold your God* (as if already present or in sight); *vengeance is coming, the retribution of God; he (himself) is coming, and will save you.* The connecting link between his vengeance and their safety is the destruction of their enemies. (*Seeing it is a righteous thing with God to recompense tribulation to them that trouble you.* 2 Thess. 1 : 6.) This verse shows how the command in the one before it is to be obeyed, by suggesting, as topics of mutual encouragement, the vindicatory justice of God, and his certain interposition in behalf of his people. *Hasty*, i. e. impatient of delay in the execution of God's promises, includes the ideas of despondency and unbelieving fear. Compare the analogous expression in ch. 28 : 16, *he that believeth will not make haste* or be impatient. The words are really a promise of deliverance to God's people, and include, as the most important part of their contents, the *unspeakable gift* of Christ and his salvation.

5, 6. *Then* (when God has thus come) *shall the eyes of the blind be opened and the ears of the deaf shall be unstopped. Then shall the lame leap* (or *bound*) *as an hart and the tongue of the dumb shall shout* (*for joy*), *because waters have burst forth in the wilderness and streams in the desert.* The change in the condition of the people is now represented by another figure, the removal of corporeal infirmities. The reason assigned in this last clause for the joy to be expressed shows clearly that the miraculous removal of disease and the miraculous irrigation of the desert are intended to express one and the same thing. The essential idea in both cases is that of sudden and extraordinary change. The simple meaning of the passage is, that the divine interposition which had just been promised should produce as wonderful a change in the condition of mankind, as if the blind were to receive their sight, the dumb to speak, the deaf to hear, the lame to walk, and deserts to be fertilized and blossom as the rose. In the process of this mighty transmutation, miracles were really performed, both of a bodily and spiritual nature, but the great change which includes these includes vastly more. The original form of expression is not that they *shall* rejoice for waters *shall* burst forth, but that they *shall* rejoice because waters *have* burst forth already, the last event being spoken of as relatively past, i. e. as previous to the act of rejoicing which the future verb expresses.

7. *And the mirage shall become a pool* (or the sand lake a water lake, the seeming lake a real one), *and the thirsty land springs of water*, (*even*) *in the haunt of wolves, their lair, a court* (or *field*) *for reed and rush.* The idea of complete and joyful change is still expressed by the transformation of a desert and the consequent removal of its inconveniences, among which the Prophet here particularly mentions the tantalizing illusions to which travellers in the wilderness are subject. The first noun denotes the illusive appearance caused by unequal refraction in the lower strata of the atmosphere, and often witnessed both at sea and land, called in English *looming*, in Italian *fata morgana*, and in French *mirage.* In the deserts of Arabia and Africa, the appearance presented is precisely that of an extensive sheet of water, tending not only to mislead the traveller but to aggravate his thirst by disappointment. The phenomenon is well described by Quintius Curtius in his Life of Alexander the Great. It is also referred to in the Koran. More deceitful than the mirage (or *serab*) is an Arabian proverb. Its introduction here adds a beautiful stroke to the description, not only

by its local propriety, but by its strict agreement with the context.

8. *And there shall be there a highway and a way; and there shall not pass through* (or *over*) *it an unclean* (*thing* or *person*); *and it shall be for them* (*alone*). Job (12 : 24) speaks of *a wilderness in which there is no way*, and Jeremiah (18 : 15) of *a way not cast up*, to both which descriptions we have here a contrast. The comparison suggested is between a faint track in the sand and a solid artificial causeway. The desert shall cease not only to be barren but also to be pathless or impassable by reason of sand. The obvious meaning of the last clause is that the people of Jehovah shall themselves be holy. (Compare ch. 1 : 25. 4 : 3.) This is also the meaning of those scriptures which exclude from Zion (or the sanctuary) the Canaanite (Zech. 14 : 21), the uncircumcised (Ezek. 44 : 9), and the stranger. The pronoun *them* has no expressed antecedent in the sentence, and has been variously applied; but the precise import of the original expression seems to be, that the highway shall belong exclusively to them for whose sake it was made, for whose use it was intended.

9. *There shall not be there a lion, and a ravenous beast shall not ascend it, nor be found there; and* (*there*) *shall walk redeemed* (*ones*). The wilderness, though no longer barren or pathless, might still be the resort of beasts of prey. The promised highway might itself be exposed to their incursions. But immunity from this inconvenience is here promised. For a similar promise, in a still more figurative dress, see Hosea 2 : 18, and for a description of the desert as the home of deadly animals, Isaiah 30 : 6. The primary allusion is no doubt to the highway described in the foregoing verse. Hence the phrase *ascend it*, i. e. from the level of the sands, through which the road is supposed to be cast up. These terms are intended to complete the great prophetic picture of a total change in the condition of the desert,

under which general idea we may then include a great variety of suitable particulars, without however making any one of them the exclusive subject of the prophecy.

10. *And the ransomed of Jehovah shall return and come to Zion with shouting, and everlasting joy upon their head; gladness and joy shall overtake (them), and sorrow and sighing shall flee away.* The whole series of promises is here summed up in that of restoration and complete redemption. Zion is mentioned as the journey's end; they shall not only move towards it but attain it. The words *everlasting joy* may either be governed by the preposition (*with shouting and everlasting joy upon their head*), or construed with the substantive verb understood (*everlasting joy shall be upon their head*). The latter construction seems to agree best with the Masoretic accents. In the last clause, *joy and gladness* may be either the subject or the object of the verb. The latter construction is given in the English Bible (*they shall obtain joy and gladness*) after the example of the Targum, Peshito, and Vulgate. In favour of the other, which is given in the Septuagint (καταλήψεται αὐτούς), may be urged the analogy of Deut. 28:2 (*all these blessings shall come on thee and overtake thee*) and of the last clause of the verse, where *sorrow and sighing* are the subjects of the verb. "The highway before described not only leads to Zion the church below, but to the Zion above, to the heavenly glory; and all the redeemed, all that walk in this way, shall come thither; at death their souls return to God that gave them, and in the resurrection their bodies shall return from their dusty beds and appear before God in Zion." (Gill) The allusions to the Babylonian exile are correctly explained upon the principle that minor and temporal deliverances were not only emblems of the great salvation but preparatory to it.

END OF VOL. I.

www.ingramcontent.com/pod-product-compliance
Lightning Source LLC
LaVergne TN
LVHW020112110826
845151LV00001B/138

* 9 7 8 1 4 2 5 5 4 3 3 1 0 *